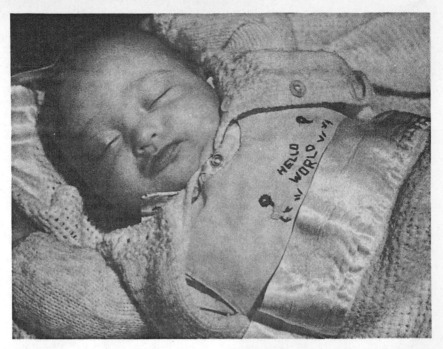

This revised and fully updated edition of the acclaimed TO LOVE AND LET GO contains more than 50% new material. Included are 10 years of follow-ups on the original stories plus important new information and stories.

Critical acclaim for *To Love and Let Go:*

"An astonishing work, in every way a first of its kind and another groundbreaker for Suzanne Arms, whose prose is sensitive, insightful, and at times even poetic."

—Patricia Holt, Book Review Editor
San Francisco Chronicle

"Powerful and moving! ... Worthy of the time and attention of anyone whose life has been touched—directly or indirectly—by adoption."

—*Los Angeles Times*

"A new way of thinking about a crucial part of the adoption process, one that allows the biological mother a significant part in the decision, gives her a measure of dignity during a highly emotional sequence, and helps her deal with the grief associated with its aftermath."

—*Kirkus Reviews*

"Deeply moving, personal accounts of the adoption experience from the viewpoint of biological mothers, adoptive parents and adopted children."

—*Library Journal*

"I find many books interesting or informative, but rarely am I deeply moved by a book. This one touches something very deep in the heart of women, some feeling that all women, on some level, must share. It is a groundbreaking book, and an important contribution to the literature that deals with what it means to be a woman."

—June Singer, Jungian therapist and author

"(*To Love and Let Go*) evoked so many powerful and painful feelings in me that have been blocked for nearly 30 years. Thank you for giving me back my past!"

—an adult adoptee

"This book gave me the courage to go ahead with our open adoption. It educated me and, most importantly, gave me insight and compassion for the birth mother's situation."

—an adoptive mother

"The most moving book I ever read. It brought me to tears and changed the way my wife and I did our adoption."

—an adoptive father

"Last summer I stopped in a bookstore, and the next thing I knew I was reading (*To Love and Let Go*) and had lost track of time. The myth of the irresponsible, abandoning mother is hard to break. Suzanne Arms has contributed an invaluable document."

—a birth mother

"This book inspired me to search for the son I fathered but never knew. I found him and reconnected with my past, and now he is an important part of my life, and my close friend."

—a birth father

ADOPTION
A Handful of Hope

Suzanne Arms

CELESTIAL ARTS
Berkeley, California

CELESTIAL ARTS
P.O. Box 7327
Berkeley, California 94707

This is an updated and greatly expanded edition of a book previously published in 1983 under the title *To Love and Let Go.*

Cover and text design by Nancy Austin
Cover photo by Suzanne Arms
Author photo by John Wimberley
Composition by Pamela Meyer
Set in Sabon

Library of Congress Cataloging-in-Publication Data
Arms, Suzanne.
Adoption: a handful of hope / Suzanne Arms.
    p.   cm.
Rev. ed. of: To love and let go. 1st ed. 1983
ISBN 0-89087-551-0
    1. Adoption—United States—case studies. I. Arms, Suzanne.
To love and let go. II. Title. III. Title: Adoption.
HV875.55.A76 1989
362.7'34'0973—dc19   88–13861
                                                                CIP

First printing, 1990

Manufactured in the United States of America

0 9 8 7 6 5 4 3 2 1

ACKNOWLEDGMENTS

I would like to thank my friends Susan Berthiaume, Bob Gordon, Mary Offerman, Lolly Font, and Katherine McCleary, and also my daughter, Molly Arms. Each of them gave me loving support and wise counsel during the many phases of writing, rewriting, and editing this book.

I would also like to thank Nancy Mills, Roxanne Potter, Kate Bowland, Mary Jackson, June Whitson, Harriet Palmer, Faye Gibson, and Candace Fields, who, in their midwifery, have been models of skillful support and compassionate service to mothers, babies, and families. They know how to stand "with woman" (*midwife*) and how to empower her and dignify her work in giving birth and mothering.

Thanks also to my editors, David Hinds and Paul Reed at Celestial Arts, for their openminded interest in this subject, and for enabling my work to get out into the world.

Finally, this book greatly benefited from the constant reassurance and constructive criticism of my husband, John Wimberley. To him I am continually grateful and want to give a special thank you.

CONTENTS

PART II: ADOPTION IN PROCESS:
The Challenge To Evolve

PHIL:
Half a Century of Change

The evolution of modern adoption from World War II to the present, as seen by an adoption attorney whose career spans those decades. How changing social attitudes toward women and children create the context for adoption practices.

PHIL:
Looking Back, Looking Forward

An examination of a decade marked by a growing grassroots movement to revolutionize how society thinks and acts about relinquishment and adoption.

PART III: STEPPING INTO THE FUTURE:
Journeys Into Open Adoption

PAT:
Too Soon a Mother

A sixteen-year-old girl becomes a woman through the process of coming to terms with an unplanned pregnancy, childbirth, and the relinquishment of her baby for adoption. Her journey into an open, private adoption.

PAUL AND VICKI:
Parents-in-Waiting

The story of a couple in their midthirties awaiting the birth of their second child. The difference between this somewhat unconventional adoption and the closed, private adoption of their first child.

The adoptive parents look back on seventeen years of parenting. Their growing appreciation of the significance of different kinds of relinquishment and adoption upon the children and the interplay between heredity and environment.

The perspectives of two sisters, ages eleven and sixteen, each adopted privately: one open, one closed adoption. Their early memories and current thoughts about their lives and on what adoption means to them.

The story of a young woman who, because of circumstances, must make all decisions regarding her unplanned pregnancy on her own. Her efforts to create an ideal adoption, guided solely by her vision of what is best for herself and her child.

The anxiety and reluctance that the chosen adoptive parents bring to open, private adoption. The birth of their son and the exchange and parting they share with his birth mother. The promises made.

WORDS TO THE WISE:
Creating Better Adoptions

A detailed list of suggestions to help anyone considering placing a baby for adoption, adopting a baby, or involved in an adoption. How to create both a positive experience for the birth mother and an optimal prenatal environment for the child.

CLOSING

The author's perspective.

ADOPTION RESOURCES

A listing of self-help services, organizations, and professional groups offering information, referral, support, counseling, and other assistance to anyone interested in or involved in adoption.

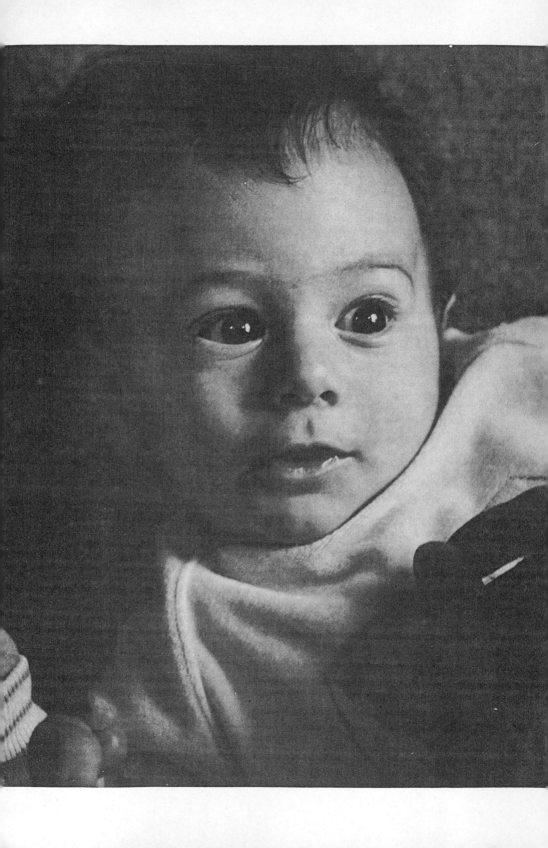

To every woman who
has given up a child to whom she gave birth,
especially those who suffered the grief
alone and in silence

To every adopted child
who has suffered from feeling unwanted or unworthy,
especially those who have been denied knowledge of
and contact with their birth parents

To every adoptive parent
who has experienced the fear, doubt,
and insecurity of not knowing how to help
an adopted child

and

To every person who recognizes
the needs and rights of adopted children
to have knowledge of and access to their heritage
and who have the courage to open their own adoption
and include the birth parents

INTRODUCTION

In THE SPRING of 1977, I began working on a book about adoption. It started out as the story of a young woman who, at the age of sixteen, made the decision to relinquish her child at birth. I hoped to show this woman's feelings and aspirations, and also show the courage it took for her to do this in the way she did—participating actively in each step of the process, rather than letting other, older individuals shape the events that would alter the course of her life.

I thought that if her story touched people's hearts and moved them to compassion, it might help change the stereotype of the "bad" woman who relinquished her child (the birth mother), and grant birth mothers the respect and compassion they deserved. I felt that this culture did not understand how hard it was for a mother to make an irrevocable decision about her child's life, especially in the midst of pregnancy—an emotion-charged time like no other—knowing that the decision she made would alter the course of two lives.

As an intimate observer of this young woman's journey, I could cast her story in the light of a dignity which she herself did not feel. I witnessed the critical importance that people's kindness and support played in a birth mother's experience of pregnancy, birth, and the inevitable loss which follows relinquishment. Beyond that, I saw how an individual's yearning for something out of the ordinary, and her courage to reach for it, set into motion an adoption that transcended expectations.

This would be a hopeful book, one that looked at adoption from the perspective of those two people who are particularly vulnerable: the birth mother and the child she relinquishes. I believed that showing how relinquishing a child and being a creative participant in the adoption could be an empowering, rather than a demoralizing, experience. It could give other women the courage to consider this alternative.

It takes courage for a person to choose a path that is considered to be unacceptable, and to make that choice with eyes open, realizing that, given the circumstances, and her yearning to do what is best for both herself and the child she carries, adoption can be the right choice. Freely chosen, this path need never be the cause of remorse or guilt.

I was unable to feel satisfied with writing one woman's story. I wanted to tell a number of stories from different perspectives, to show the impact closed adoption had on people's lives and then to show what open adoption could offer. I also wanted to show what happened when a woman felt powerless to shape her child's adoption and was excluded from her child's life, and the impact upon children of growing up disconnected from their roots.

And so I continued to gather stories. The finished book, which I titled *To Love and Let Go,* first appeared five years after I began, in 1983. The responses I received, in letters, phone calls, and conversations after I had made public appearances, showed me that I had touched a sensitive nerve. Birth mothers and adoptees confided that they felt understood in their innermost feelings and that for the first time they realized they were not alone.

From adoptive parents and those considering adoption,

and from people working in adoption, there were two distinct reactions. Some felt I was setting people up for inevitable hurt and failure by portraying an openness in adoption that would be impossible to achieve and would create vast complexities and problems. They felt I didn't understand that closed adoption—or at least their particular closed adoption—had been, or was being done, that way for everyone's best interests. They might admit that there could be circumstances in which other people might benefit from openness in adoption, but to imply the entire system needed changing was naive.

These people spoke passionately about the disastrous effects that opening up adoption would have on children, how it would confuse their senses of identity and make them insecure. Sometimes they admitted open adoption made *them* feel insecure and afraid that their lives could be invaded at any time by birth mothers.

What I sensed strongly as I read or listened to their words was their fear. The underlying fear of many adoption workers was that they might no longer be indispensable. From adoptive parents, and in particular from first-time adoptive parents, I felt their fear of being displaced by the birth mothers in their children's hearts, and an anger that they would not be considered the "real" parents. They would be the ones doing the full-time work of raising the children, but would get no credit. These fears were seldom mentioned directly; they were usually couched in terms of the *children* not being able to handle open adoption. Open adoption was seldom mentioned in terms of adopted children having the need and therefore the right to know their birth parents and other birth relatives.

I empathized with adoptive parents who were able to say that they were afraid to let their children's birth mothers into their lives. It is common in our society for first-time parents to be anxious and self-protective in their desire to be "perfect." Adoptive parents might be unusually insecure because of the emotional havoc created by infertility and the humiliation and vulnerability created by trying to get pregnant through medical science. I wished I could offer adoptive parents more examples of how open adoption could work that would dispel some of their fears, show them what benefits there were for them in open adoption.

I also found some adoption workers, a surprising number of adoptive parents, and many birth mothers were greatly inspired by the true stories in *To Love and Let Go*. For them it struck a deep chord: "There *must* be a better way than closed adoption!" It gave them the confidence to try an open adoption, which many of them had never heard of before. They used the stories of these women and men as guides in creating their own open adoptions and wrote or phoned to say enthusiastically that it had worked out well.

Birth mothers shared the book with potential adoptive parents, and by their reactions to the stories gauged their attitudes. Adoptive parents gave the book to their birth mothers so that they could have the reassurance of knowing that other women had been in their position and felt the way they felt. For birth mothers who were reluctant to form a relationship with the adoptive parents, the book made them feel more secure that this was a good thing for them and for their children.

Many who began reading the book with skepticism ended up feeling that open adoption simply made sense! Some realized for the first time that closed adoption was cruel, denying children an essential piece of their identities and denying birth mothers a say in the processes of both relinquishment and adoption.

In this book I have included the stories from *To Love and Let Go,* plus updates on every person. There are also a number of new stories, which I included to complete the picture of why closed adoption fails everyone and how open adoption works and what it offers everyone.

The stories were difficult to write. They required that I get sufficiently involved with each person to understand his or her story in depth, and then work with him or her in rewriting and editing to make sure that I told the story in a way that reflected his or her deepest sense of what was true and the issues that the story addressed. My commentary within each story takes each case out of the realm of the individual and places it in a larger context. I am indebted to the people who contributed. They generously shared personal material with me in the hope that others reading their stories might find their own experiences.

It is important to define some basic terms in adoption. The *birth mother* is the woman who carries and gives birth to a child whom she relinquishes for adoption. (The *birth father* is the biological father of that child.) *Relinquishment* is the formal and less emotionally charged term for a mother voluntarily giving up her parental rights and responsibilities to her child. I tend to use this term rather than *give up*, because the latter term tends to carry the connotation that the birth mother is uncaring.

Closed adoption refers to adoption in which the birth parents and adopting parents do not know each others' identities or addresses. It is possible in a closed adoption for birth parents and adoptive parents to know a lot of information about each other but not know each others' names or addresses. This is not open adoption, because the birth parents are denied any future participation in something that is of great importance to them—the well-being of their child. And it denies the child access to what belongs to him or her.

An *agency adoption* is one in which an agency or organization takes the relinquishment of the birth mother and legally holds the parental rights to the child until the child is placed with the adoptive parents and the final adoption papers have been signed by a judge. In *private adoption,* which is also known as *independent adoption,* no agency takes the relinquishment of the child. Instead the birth mother places the child directly with the adopting parents. For this reason it is sometimes known as *direct adoption,* even though the child might not be placed directly into the adopting parents' hands by the birth mother herself.

Both agency adoption and private adoption are legitimate forms of adoption; in some states, however, private adoption is not yet recognized by law or is specifically prohibited. This does not mean that individuals living in states where private adoption is not legal cannot have a private adoption. It simply requires more creativity, usually including going out of state to do the adoption and then bringing the baby home. Laws prohibiting private adoption will change only when there is sufficient political pressure.

In both agency and private adoptions, a *home study* of the adoptive parents is done by a state worker or designated agency. In either case the home study, as well as an interview with the birth mother (and, if possible, the birth father) is a required part of the adoption to make sure that the adoptive parents can provide an adequate home for the child and that the birth mother fully consents to the relinquishment and has made the decision for adoption without outside coercion. Private agencies and government agencies attempt to ensure that no adoption occurs without full consent and that the child's welfare is always given highest priority. This does not, however, guarantee that a child will be well cared for in his or her adoptive home.

There are also *gray market* or *black market adoptions*, that is, adoptions in which some person makes large amounts of money from finding babies for adults who want them. When adopting parents work through a legitimate agency or organization, or, in the case of private adoption, with a respected attorney, they greatly reduce their chances of being exploited in this way. Private adoption tends to be more costly for adopting parents than agency adoption. But it is easy for adopting parents to check around and make sure that the costs are reasonable before they pay any money to anyone.

Gray market or black market adoptions exist because the demand for adoptable babies far exceeds the supply and because adoptive parents may be in an economic position to pay whatever the going rate is to get children. The economic inequity that exists between women who relinquish their babies and people who adopt babies is a sad fact of life; no book on adoption can change that. My hope is that by showing how birth mothers (and birth fathers) and adopting parents can be sensitized to each others' needs and the future needs of the children, adoptions will thereby be created that empower everyone, including the children.

In *To Love and Let Go,* I made the mistake of assuming that private adoption was synonymous with open adoption. I have since discovered that this is not the case. It is quite possible to have, and many people do have, a privately handled adoption that is closed. Some adopting parents seek private adoption only because it is a way of getting a baby more quickly. They have no desire to know or to form a relationship with the birth mother and birth father, and they have no intention of keeping them informed of the child's well-being or of permitting them any communication with the child, even if the child asks for it. This is a cynical approach to private adoption, although the individuals involved seldom realize it.

In more than a decade of studying adoption and hearing of all manner of adoptions across North America and in other countries, I have come across few people who want to hurt or betray anyone. Most birth parents and adoptive parents are people of goodwill; they simply don't know what their options are and haven't had any help in thinking through the consequences of each option. But much suffering is caused by ignorance, and ignorance is not an excuse for doing harm to another human being, especially a child, who is by definition vulnerable and dependent upon the adult world for his or her very survival.

I am often asked about my personal relationship to adoption. Although I am not a mother who has relinquished a child, an adoptee, or an adoptive parent, the issues of relinquishment and adoption are of great importance to me.

What initially drew me to the subjects was my concern about what happened to women and babies in childbirth (including the prenatal and postpartum periods), and my awareness of the critical importance of creating strong, loving relationships between parents and children. I was aware that children had to be able to depend upon their parents to protect them from harm and to trust that their parents would not harm them;

those initial feelings of trust permitted them to venture out into the larger world with a sense that all would be well and without a need to put on a false face or to take a defensive or aggressive posture.

I knew how difficult it was to form and maintain such relationships between biological parents and their children, because so many forces placed great stress upon personal and family relationships. I realized that adoption had to create additional stress on both adoptive parents and adopted children, because the spontaneous biological bond was missing and had to develop through goodwill, high ideals, and prolonged intimate contact.

I discovered that the deeper reasons I felt compelled to explore the problems and possibilities of adoption were other issues that also were of great concern to me. Many adults carry deep within them a sense of having been abandoned or deeply wounded early in their lives. Many children grow up feeling inadequate and as if nothing they do will make them "good enough" to be loved. Keeping secrets from children and telling lies to children is destructive to their sense of trust. Each of these issues is often part of adoption, because adoption includes either being relinquished or being orphaned, and either one means abandonment to a child. Therefore, I realized, the potential for pain and loss and even abuse existed within most adoptive families.

Even as a child I was deeply upset by harm done to children by adults; whether purposeful or not, whether due to abuse or neglect. As a nursery school and day care teacher, I was shocked to see how many young children were tense, anxious, and distrustful of adults. They had learned very early to cope with difficulties in ways that hid their real needs—by aggressiveness, competitiveness, fearfulness, or passive compliance. Many seemingly normal families, including my own, I learned, were infused with lies, deceit and abuse.

At twenty-six I gave birth. I was so shocked by the experience of modern childbirth, with all of the medical intervention in a natural, spontaneous process, that I spent the next decade studying and writing about the subject and trying to effect major social changes so that other women would not have to repeat my experience. I began to relate to issues through a feminist perspective, but I was still foremost an advocate of children, and, like so many people in the helping professions, I was unaware that I carried my own wounded child inside as I fought to bring about change in the world.

It was humbling to experience myself as a mother unable to give my own daughter as much as I had given other people's children as a teacher. I adapted and she adapted, but neither of us thrived! And had it not been for the strength of the bond I felt for her no matter what she did, I could have abused her. I wondered what parenting was like for those who, for one reason or another, were not able to feel deep bonds of affection for their children.

I attribute the healing of the birth experience, traumatic to both me and my daughter, to the fact that I very much wanted to be a parent, had nine months of pregnancy to become acquainted with the life I carried, and had almost unbroken contact with her from birth through the first year of her life. I was also fortunate to have a child who was easy for me to love, who did not seem to resist or reject my efforts. Despite a difficult beginning we were able to breastfeed and have an easy physical closeness that naturally grew into a deep, loving bond. Despite our innate individual differences, we share a joy in each other that neither of us has ever had to question or fake. I wish all other parents and children were so fortunate.

Even with such a bond between us, it was incredibly difficult to parent. I was not fortunate when it came to other circumstances: Molly and I were on our own and without any economic or emotional support by the time she was eighteen months old. Parenting in adversity was a trial and it took every bit of will and restraint I had. Over time I lost the arrogance that said, I can do better than all those other parents I see around me who hurt or neglect their children! I gained tremendous respect for any parent who tried to be decent and kind in the face of inner and outer stresses and who managed somehow to control his or her impulses to harm his or her child when emotional storms arose.

Adoption as we have come to know it—with the child cut off from his or her biological parents and placed with adoptive parents who have little or no contact with the birth mother (and therefore with the child) before or during birth—poses difficulties for every adoptee, birth parent, and adoptive parent. Sometimes it is unavoidable that the birth parents are unknown: the child may be orphaned or come from another country, with all information about the birth mother lost.

I know a young woman from Asia who was adopted as a young child. She had been left in a basket as a baby, with no identification. This was a common practice in her country, because unidentified babies were taken into the foundling homes; there was no other way a woman who could not care for her child could be guaranteed that her child would be taken in. Not only does this young woman have little chance of finding out anything about her birth parents, she does not even have any way of knowing her true date of birth. When she was adopted she was given a date of birth, but there was no way to know anything more than her approximate age when she was found. The result was that she grew up with a sense of never really belonging anywhere and a deep mistrust of everyone, which she struggled to cover up with a mask of smiles and pretense.

In addition, this woman was adopted by a husband and wife in North America who were not able to form emotional bonds with her. She was rejected by her adoptive mother in every way; her mother apparently felt this child did not meet her expectations. The father permitted his wife to abandon her emotionally, leaving the girl feeling she had been abandoned for the second time. It has been a difficult road for her, but recently she said that she was learning to live each day as if it were the only day there was.

The difficulties some adoptive parents face come on top

of the normal stresses and difficulties parents and children experience in their relationships with each other. Adoptive parents who work long hours outside the home when their children are young, who have marital strain or abusive relationships with their partners, or who end up in divorce are like any other parents. They start out thinking they will parent in partnership and in love, and then find themselves unsupported or alone. Adoptive parents may use the same unhealthy coping tools that other parents do: alcohol or drug dependency or addiction, workaholism, abusiveness to each other or to their children.

In each adoption the biological bond between birth parent and child is unformed or has been broken, and the child grieves that loss. The biological bond between adoptive parent and adopted child is lacking, and a bond of affection and trust must be forged in a different way. Some adopted children, even as young babies, resist attempts at closeness on the part of their new parents.

Some adoptive parents feel so hurt over prior attempts to have children and over infertility work that they are overanxious and fearful as parents or have unrealistic expectations of what children are and what children bring them. Adoptive parents and adopted children usually come to adoption carrying their wounds; they may not find it easy to trust others. Some adults and some children are better at spontaneously grieving and letting go of hurts than others. These are facts that must be faced and worked with; it does not help to deny them.

Open adoption—adoption where the initial bond is not severed and where the child is not left to feel abandoned by a mother and father he or she does not know, and where the adoptive parents and birth parents create the adoption from a relationship they have created together—is a sane approach to adoption for everyone involved. I believe people need to know the hazards of assuming that they can find their way through the lifelong process of adoption on their own—without maps, skilled guidance, and a community of support.

Adoption is neither an easy solution to the problem of

having become pregnant in impossible circumstances nor necessarily the answer to infertility. And parenting a child—*any* child, but certainly any adopted child—is not easy for those still in some ways children themselves psychologically, still hurting from past experiences, or without financial or emotional resources.

Adoption can be a blessing! Relinquishment can also be a blessing, though few birth mothers feel this until the initial grief is over! But neither adoption nor relinquishment is a choice that is right for everyone. I hope this book clarifies which of the major dangers and stumbling blocks have been set up by the standard adoption process and which are intrinsic to adoption. It is important not to think adoption is the answer to all unwanted pregnancies or all infertility.

There is tragically little understanding of the importance of the biological mother–child bond, of the psychological devastation that results from breaking this bond and then acting as if it had no value, or of the ongoing importance of the birth parents in the adopted child's life. The transition from being with birth parents to being with adoptive parents is a critical one for adopted children. They will live with its effects, for better or for worse, for many years, perhaps for the rest of their lives.

I focus on the beginnings of adoptions, because that is where the greatest potential exists, the most opportunity for the healing of wounds that have occurred in the womb, at birth, or at relinquishment, and prevention of future problems. It is in the beginnings of life that the roots are established. Are not the roots that grow in the fertile soil of love and nurturing, and the shoots of strong, healthy relationships the best possible prevention of violence or despair?

Prologue

THE YOUNG WOMAN standing quietly off to one side of the auditorium waiting to ask a question hardly looks old enough to be expecting a baby, yet she is obviously about to become someone's mother. Her name is Martha and she has traveled a long way to hear this talk about birth. With teary eyes she tells a bit of her story, how she is a fire spotter for the forest service, how her boyfriend is a college student and they see each other only on weekends, how they hadn't meant to create this baby. When the young man declared himself unready and unwilling to be a parent, Martha saw no way she could be a mother alone and give her baby all she felt he or she deserved. She intends to relinquish this baby, but she wants a special beginning for her child, and parents whom she feels she can trust to raise and love him or her as she would.

I later introduce Martha to a close friend of mine, a midwife named Nancy, who I know will help her. Martha finds a friend in Nancy and spends the last weeks of her pregnancy at Nancy's home, helping care for her kids and finally laboring there before going off to a small community hospital for birthing. She has the natural birth she'd wished for. Through Nancy she has met a couple she has chosen to adopt her baby. Together they make the exchange and the parting gentle and loving. Martha's child enters her new home within hours of her birth. Martha hangs around town for a few weeks, living at Nancy's home, before she disappears back into her own life. She lets go reluctantly, as any caring person would, but she does let go, taking with her the name and address of the couple who are now the baby's parents. An attorney in the community has handled all the legal work. The state has sent its representative to visit Martha and make certain she does not feel in any way coerced, but has made her decision freely and wants to go through with the adoption. The potential adoptive parents also have been visited, in their home, and they have been granted approval to be adoptive parents. No other agency has been involved. The whole process—Martha's secure last month of pregnancy, her finding the kind of parents she wants for her baby, the exchange, her letting go, her beginning her grieving with the compassionate support of another woman, her being free to form a stable relationship before entering motherhood—is one of growth.

Until I met Martha adoption had always seemed a bit unsavory to me, and it had seemed to me that the parents who gave their children up for adoption were not quite real parents. Apart from one experience during college, I had known nothing of the pressures women had that led them to relinquish babies. In the 1950s, when I grew up, adoption wasn't talked about any more than divorce was. Parents were permanent fixtures in children's lives, and being adopted was tantamount to not being wanted. When kids felt like outsiders in their families, they would question whether they were adopted and wonder if that was the reason they felt so different. This was true for my sister. Our mother kept a full baby book for our older brother, from day one. She still managed to jot notes in my pink album and to collect my hair clippings and smiling black-and-white snapshots of me. But there were no baby pictures of my sister, and no envelopes of her hair clippings. By the time she arrived, enthusiasm and leisure for such recordkeeping had been swept away in the day-to-day business of being a mother of three young ones. Confronted with this lack of clear proof that she was one of us and her lack of resemblance to our immediate family, my sister concluded that she must be adopted. I associated adoption with my sister's sense of alienation and feeling of being unwanted.

In the early 1960s, when I was in college, adoption was almost as unacceptable a solution to unplanned pregnancy as abortion. But many women needed these solutions. As I was stumbling into adulthood and sexuality and becoming a woman, my friend Rosalie (who lived in my dorm) always struck me as being from another era, another culture: all modesty, circumspection, and gentleness. I was shocked when she whispered to me, head bowed, that she was three months pregnant. She asked me to help her get an abortion. The young man involved was a foreign student on campus, and he'd unceremoniously given Rosalie the boot as soon as she had told him the news. It had been her very first sexual encounter. Her father was a Presbyterian minister and she was sure he'd kill her if he ever found out. Abortion was still illegal in New York State in 1963, and I hadn't the vaguest idea how to find someone, let alone someone competent, who would perform one for my friend. So one weekend Rosalie faced the unthinkable, took the bus to her home, and confessed to her parents. She wasn't killed but she was beaten up by her father, called a slut by her mother, and thrown out of the house. I think she felt she deserved as much.

Rosalie dropped out of school and moved off campus to a converted studio apartment in an old house on the other side of the city. I used to visit her there each week. When she wasn't working at the menial job she'd taken to cover her expenses, she would read or walk or cook for herself; but she was always alone. It must have been a joyless pregnancy. A month before the baby was due, she gave up the apartment, left town, and checked herself into a home for unwed mothers in a rough part of a city fifty miles away. I think I was her only visitor. She looked whipped whenever I saw her, wearing a shapeless housedress and loafers, but she never complained about her treatment at the home. The food wasn't very good, she admitted, but the place was clean, cleaned by herself and the other women who lived there as part of the bargain of getting room and board; and she did have some time to herself to read. I could see that Rosalie was a prisoner and that the home smelled like a prison. They "let" me take her for a walk around the block once, but I never did get permission to see her room. For Rosalie this was just part of the punishment she accepted for having done a terrible wrong: she had become pregnant at the wrong time, with the wrong person.

I don't know whether Rosalie ever saw her baby before she relinquished the baby forever. She returned to school the next semester, and we never talked about what had happened. I still wonder what her experience did to Rosalie and to her child, both of whom had to live with the consequences of closed adoption, a system set up to protect both of them but that actually served neither.

This book is the stories of some of the women, men, and children I have known since Rosalie and Martha who have been involved in adoption. Some of the adoptions described were private, or independent, adoptions; some were agency adoptions. But I feel that they all have something to teach anyone interested in the adoption process. The stories are all true, and, to the best of my ability, and with much help from the people themselves, I have told them honestly. Each account is entered somewhere in the middle and left before it is over, because relinquishing or getting or being a child of adoption never really ends, any more than growing up ends.

Friends who read these stories as they were being written told me they were more than stories of adoption, they were stories of what it was like to let go of someone we loved. I had never realized how inescapable grief was for all of us who risked loving, especially when the ones we loved were our children and when true loving meant letting go. I had never understood how having the information and power to make personal choices freely didn't necessarily make the work of living less hard or painful. Rather it made the pain more sharply focused and more bearable. That which was chosen seems so much more easily understood and finally accepted.

I have been told these are women's stories. To be sure, they are about mothering; but I use that word in a genderless sense, in the sense of protecting, nourishing, nurturing life, the work of the mother. Relinquishing a child out of love and respect for his or her needs is one form of mothering. Raising a child as an act of resignation or in defiance of those considered to be authorities is also among the forms mothering can take, but neither is what we like to think of as good mothering. The women in these stories who chose adoption for their babies have reaffirmed my belief that mothering ought not to be an endurance contest or a battle waged to prove something. And they have taught me that there is more than one way to be a good mother. The children in these stories have reminded me that we really haven't the right to expect something in exchange for all we give a child. No child should have to barter for love and attention and the right to be well cared for until he or she can do that for himself or herself.

This book is a tribute to women who, for various and personal reasons, admit they cannot do justice to their children or to themselves by raising them. I chose to focus on women who relinquished their children at birth: they are a large, voiceless group and a misunderstood one. But I recall others too, especially one mother I met at a childbirth conference. When she heard that I was writing a book on women who relinquished children for adoption, she told me how—after she had been pressured into going through with an unplanned pregnancy and tried desperately to raise her baby alone—she had found herself two and a half years later on the verge of either committing suicide or going crazy. And so she had made the terrible decision to relinquish her child then, and the relinquishing and letting go had been all the more painful for the time she'd spent trying to be that good enough mother to the child she loved and seeing herself fall short of her own expectations. This woman is the product of a society that considers itself enlightened, yet still tells women what to do with their sexuality and their reproductive systems. This makes it all the more difficult for a thoughtful woman of any age or circumstance to choose either abortion or adoption. It is a myth in this society that in raising children parents have even the partial support of a community. Parenting done in isolation, without financial or emotional resources, can only be felt as a burden and seldom brings the joy that should be associated with the process.

It continues to amaze me that women such as Maria, Pat, Alexandra, and Diane show so much raw strength, because they are all young and, except for Diane, have little around them from which to draw strength and inspiration. Their maturity is exceptional. Even in the most difficult circumstances (where, for example, the young woman is barely a teenager herself and has no skills to earn a living and no support to help her raise a child), most women today who become pregnant and continue with the pregnancy then go on to raise the baby. They hardly ever consider adoption. It is simply not thought of as an expression of caring for a child to relinquish him or her for adoption, though there are many who would seek to adopt a child and can find none. The social pressures of our culture have much to do with this, as do the naive yearnings of many women to prove their womanhood by being mothers against all odds. Part of the reason must also lie in the form adoption takes, a system that often locks out the birth mother, takes away her sense of power, and treats her as an obstacle standing in the way of her baby and the "good" parents who will adopt him or her.

The women in this book do not consider themselves extraordinary or deserving of special praise for relinquishing their children for adoption. But they *are* exceptional in their honesty and willingness to admit that they were unready and unwilling to be mothers. That takes a very special kind of courage. In telling us about the path they took, with all its risks and pain, they show us what it is like to love *and* let go. And in the future perhaps others will find the road easier because of them. And we who observe and care about pregnant women, mothers, and children will be better able to offer support and love because of our increased understanding of their needs.

Parenting should not be a form of punishment for having sexual relations or a way of working out unconscious and unmet desires and needs on another vulnerable human being. Children deserve and need to be able to depend upon the adult world, and to ask much of their parents, without feeling guilty for existing. Children do not belong to their parents in the sense of being possessions. Nor are they capable of supplying their parents' missing parts. If children deserve to be treated as individuals with needs and rights, their mothers, and their fathers too, who face seemingly impossible personal decisions regarding their desire *and* their ability to parent, deserve compassion and support for the difficult and lonely choices they make for themselves and on behalf of their children.

Adoption is a woman's issue, and it needs to be both humanized and feminized. Women bring a unique perspective to adoption and to all that is involved in giving birth and caring for children, an understanding that arises from the fact of inhabiting a female body. Adoption must also be considered a feminist issue in all its many facets. Birth mothers are in an inferior position of power in this society; that position needs to change.

I hope these stories expand the reader's sense of what is possible and set the reader to dreaming, envisioning, and working toward a less violent and better world, where everyone feels valued as a part of life, and where human frailties, poor judgment, and inadequacies do not lead to guilt, shame, remorse, or punishment. It is sufficient that people must live with the lifelong consequences of their actions or failures to act.

PART I

LIVING WITH DECEPTION:

The Consequences of Closed Adoption

MARIA:

Somewhere a Woman Is Grieving

Maria is thirty-two, a mother watching her toddler at play. "Sometimes," she says, "I lose track of where the mother in me ends and I begin. My 'should' sense of what a good mother is seems so strong, I find myself giving and giving till there is nothing left. Maybe some of it is just overcompensation."

Fourteen years ago, when she was eighteen, Maria gave birth to a baby she relinquished for adoption. A bright young woman entering her second year at college, with all the benefits of a middle-class upbringing, she was as ignorant of her choices and as isolated as a fourteen-year-old girl bound by poverty. Largely because of the attitudes of her culture—midwestern America of the mid-1960s—Maria's reserve of self-esteem was quickly eroded during the months she waited for the birth of a baby she could only raise with shame or relinquish with guilt. When I met Maria the adoption was well behind her, yet she was still carrying around the pain and the guilt of it.

She had lived at home during the summer after her first year at college. She'd been dating a man five years older than she and had felt that she was madly in love. They had always used contraceptives when they made love—except for one time.

23

Maria thinks she may have been secretly hoping she would become pregnant so she could keep Bill's love; their relationship hadn't been very good during its last months. But when she realized she might actually be pregnant, she reacted with shame and fear and despair. Her situation was complicated by her ignorance and her isolation.

She started back to college the next month certain she was pregnant, not yet showing, and hoping for a miracle. "I called Bill to see about catching a ride back to school with him and told him then that I might be pregnant. He was very, very silent. I guess he refused to believe it." Maria had really known pregnancy was not the answer from the beginning, but the illusion of a future with Bill had kept her going. And unlike Bill, she then had nowhere to retreat. If she was pregnant it was happening to her body, an inescapable part of her. She finally made an appointment with an obstetrician near campus to find out the truth and asked Bill to drive her there. Well aware of his own responsibility, he agreed, but he waited outside in his car while she went through the humiliation of the examination alone. The diagnosis was rapid: Maria was three months pregnant. She went out to break the news to Bill.

"It was very cold that day and we didn't drive straight back to campus, but parked by the woods for a while. I can hardly remember our conversation, it was all so unbelievable, but we must have talked about what to do. My fantasy was to stay in town, to get a job and a place of my own, and to be close to him." Abortion was out of the question for Maria. It was still illegal then in Michigan, and she wouldn't have known where to begin if she had wanted to obtain an abortion outside the law.

Maria found that she no longer fit in on the campus; her anxiety about the pregnancy was incompatible with the life of a student. She drew inward and retreated from her friends and classmates. She was alone, despite her boyfriend's offer to help. She didn't feel he was really there for her. Instead she turned to the one person she felt she could trust, her older brother, Jay.

"He was working on his doctorate at another university,

and his wife was supporting them by teaching. They have a son who was then eighteen months old. I sat down and wrote Jay a long, intellectual-sounding letter telling him everything. He must have heard a cry for help, because he called me as soon as he got it and told me he was coming right down to get me. He drove all six hundred miles in one night." During the drive to his home they talked. "Jay said he'd stand behind me whatever I decided about the pregnancy. He said that Mom and Dad didn't have to know anything, and that he thought it would be good for me to live at his place. I could see what it was like to have a toddler and maybe I could make a better decision about whether to keep the baby. If I decided to keep the baby, Jay said he'd be a surrogate father, and I could go on living with them."

Maria had dreams about an education and a career, even though she didn't then know what she wanted to do. She was grateful for her brother's nonjudgmental support, but she felt like someone who had been exiled from her people for a misdeed, never able to return. Following her instinct to go where she would find support had meant leaving behind the man she loved, the father of this baby. As a result of her leaving college, her path and Bill's split permanently.

She and Jay arrived at his apartment on a Saturday, and that very night their father telephoned. The school had immediately noticed her absence and called her parents' home to find out if she was planning to return. He asked Kate, Jay's wife, if they knew where Maria was. Kate said she knew nothing about it, but she didn't make a very convincing liar. When she got off the phone, they talked about what to do. Finally Jay called his parents back and admitted that Maria was with them and that she was pregnant.

"My parents were outraged. They told him they wanted to have nothing more to do with me." It was something Maria would hold against them years later, but she didn't blame them at the time. She felt she'd brought it on herself.

By the following Monday Maria had pulled herself together sufficiently to go looking for a job. She found one as a clerk-typist at the university, giving a false name and the story that she was married to a man named Jay Ferris (her brother's name), who was getting a graduate degree. At her pre-employment physical the pregnancy was discovered by a perceptive nurse. Maria feigned shock and surprise. She then assured her supervisor that she would go to a doctor to make sure she was in good enough health to take the job, and promised to keep working right up until the birth and to return to work soon after. She got the job, her first. The pay was minimum wage.

People at work sometimes asked Maria about her husband and the baby, and her response was always the same. "I was the happy mother-to-be. I did a lot of sewing at my brother's and would come in every morning wearing something attractive. I would be told how talented or how pretty I was. All day long I kept a smile on my face. I went home exhausted and closed myself off in my room and cried, out of anger that I didn't get to tell the truth at work, and frustration that I couldn't express my feelings at home either. Crying helped a bit. Then I'd come out of my room and help take care of Jay's baby or make dinner."

Maria was withdrawing for self-protection, but the price was high. It meant more loneliness and self-pity at the very time when her thoughts ought to have been directed at taking care of herself and the growing life inside her. She had no energy left for positive feelings toward her own baby.

She was reluctant to see a doctor for prenatal care, but under pressure from Jay and Kate she made an appointment with someone recommended by a friend of theirs. On the first visit she couldn't bring herself to tell him that she was not married, but the next time she blurted out everything. Fortunately she had found a sensitive physician. Her appointment was the last of the afternoon, and he stayed for several hours talking with her. He asked if she was considering adoption—an idea Maria had already rejected without ever looking at it.

"I told him I wanted to keep the baby. He looked hard at me and said something that was a turning point in my life. He said, 'Maria, what would be easier for you? To keep the baby?

Or to give it up for adoption?' I answered that it would be easier to keep the baby. He looked me straight in the eyes and said, 'Well, what do you think would be good for your baby? To be raised by you alone, without a father, when you have no means of supporting the two of you? What will you be doing for this baby?' "

The mere thought of giving her baby up hurt too much for Maria to answer him. But that night at her brother's, she was so full of emotion she couldn't keep it to herself any more. For the first time she and Jay and Kate really talked, or rather Maria talked and they listened. Talking was a great relief. She saw that she needed help to face all the choices. Soon afterward Maria found the courage to take off early from work one day and go to see a social worker at the Children's Aid Society, an agency her doctor had told her about. She began to see the woman each week and continued right up until the birth. By making Maria feel that she cared and by helping her see all sides without judgment, the social worker helped Maria start thinking realistically about her future and her baby's.

Meanwhile Maria began to make friends with several couples who lived in her brother's apartment building and to babysit for their children too on her evenings and weekends. Becoming more involved with other people's children made her want this baby even more, yet she couldn't forget the doctor's question about what would be best for the baby. "I'd wonder, What am I doing to you, kid? What will life be like for you with me away at work all day, and just the two of us when I am home?"

Somewhere along the way, she doesn't really know when or how, she began seriously thinking about relinquishing the baby. Part of it was seeing the difficulties Jay and Kate had with their son, whose birth Maria knew had been unplanned. The parents were both gone all day, Kate working and Jay at school, and Jared was with a sitter from breakfast right up until dinner five days a week. "I would watch him cry as they left the house in the morning, and I'd watch Kate come home from work each day exhausted and unable to give him much of anything in the

evening except dinner. I wanted more than that for my child."
And given her lack of resources, Maria did not have much hope
that her life with her baby would be even that good.

It didn't occur to Maria to turn to the baby's father for
help in deciding what to do. Bill had withdrawn from her life
when Maria had left college, and her response had been to take
all responsibility upon herself. "It was *my* body. It was *my* trip."
Maria made no emotional demands on Bill and was unaware
of any anger she might have toward him, but she did find that
her love for him and even her memory of him faded as the
pregnancy went on. "It's funny, when I refer to him now,
it's as 'the father of my son,' not 'an old boyfriend of mine'
or 'my lover.' "

All Maria asked that Bill contribute was money for prenatal care and the birth, which he had agreed to do. "I had
pressure from Jay to go after Bill legally, to make sure he would
pay. I finally did but I didn't want to. I brought a paternity suit
against Bill, and he never tried to deny it. I think I did it so my
brother wouldn't reject me as our parents had. I was a guest
living in his house and I needed his love. But I felt very guilty.
I trusted Bill and I wished I'd followed my feelings and let him
do just what he felt comfortable doing, even if he didn't send
money." In the end Bill did pay all the medical bills and even
the cost of foster care until the child was placed for adoption.
But because the paternity suit forced the issue, it was never clear
whether he would have made this much of a financial contribution had he not been pressured into doing so. He was six
hundred miles away when his child was born, and apparently
never even knew when Maria made the decision to relinquish
the baby for adoption. Maria thinks he heard about the birth
from a mutual friend who came down to see the baby at
the hospital just afterward, but she never again intiated contact
with Bill and has not seen him since.

In the United States in the 1960s, giving birth was something
people didn't talk about much. A woman just went into a

hospital and came out five days later with a baby. Maria, like most women of her generation, was unprepared for giving birth, medicated heavily for labor, and left alone. With so much on her mind about herself and her baby's future, she had thought it would be a welcome relief to put herself totally into a fatherly physician's hands. Unfortunately, the loss of a major part of the experience to drugs and the suffering that came with laboring unprepared and alone left her with regret and longing she would carry all the way into her next birthing, twelve years later.

"Friday, April twenty-third, the baby was due, and I was still working full time. Saturday I had a show of mucus and a few light contractions. I thought I was going into labor. Sunday nothing much happened. I didn't go to work Monday, and I had a doctor's appointment on Tuesday. I'd been having light contractions but nothing much. He said my labor was beginning, and told me to go to the hospital when the contractions were coming every five minutes. I took a taxi from his office and by the time I arrived home, contractions were five minutes apart."

Nervousness in the face of the unknowns of labor may cause a woman's body to create frequent contractions even though the birth is many hours away. With the doctor having given her no real sense of what to expect in early labor, Maria began to panic.

"No one was home. I went to the neighbor's, and nobody was home there either. I had visions of calling another taxi and having the driver refuse to take me, because he didn't want to have a baby born in his taxi." Finally, Maria thought of calling a friend of their neighbor's, whom she had met a few times. She was babysitting for five children but drove right over in her station wagon, children and all, and took Maria with her packed bag to the hospital. Maria regained her confidence. "I felt I was ready. There were too many other things on my mind for me to be frightened of the birth."

Once in the hospital she was dressed in a hospital gown, was placed in bed, had her pubic hair shaved, was given an enema, was tagged with an identification band, and was left alone in the room. Her confidence quickly waned.

"I knew I was strong and I thought I'd be all right. But I was so uncomfortable lying on my back I sat up in the bed. I could hear a woman in another room screaming and screaming, and I thought to myself, Why can't she control herself! I also thought, Who am I to make any noise? I didn't want to be in anyone's way."

So she labored alone, kept herself quiet, and remained sitting up in bed. "Every couple of hours, a nurse would come into the room and tell me I had to lie down. As soon as the nurse left I would sit back up. It was the only way I could take the contractions. Finally it hurt so much I just got out of bed and sat in a chair. Then I paced around the room. I was *so* lonely."

Later that evening Maria's sister-in-law came to the hospital room. She brought along Maria's mother, whom Maria hadn't seen or heard from for seven months. Their awkward reunion did little to comfort Maria or help her labor. "I guess my brother thought she should be there with me and I was happy to see her, but the contractions hurt so much I had to ask them to leave after a few minutes."

They left. Maria had been unable to ask for the support and presence she so needed. She continued to labor in silent pain throughout that night. "Every few hours another nurse would come in, do an anal exam, a vaginal exam, check the baby's heart, and walk out. I began to allow myself to moan quietly during contractions, and that made me feel better. I could still hear screams from the other rooms, and there were men's and women's voices out in the hall; but whenever I pressed the button for help, a nurse would come in, do another anal exam, another vaginal exam, listen to the baby, and leave. Once, when she came in after I had pressed the button for help, I asked her couldn't she please stay. She just stood around. I didn't know what to say to her, nor she to me. Finally she left."

By then it was almost dawn, although Maria could not see

the sky because the room was windowless. There was only a clock. The contractions were very strong and close together, and Maria was afraid she couldn't go on this way. A different nurse came in and checked her and announced that she was ready to deliver.

In the delivery room Maria faced a different ordeal. There were people with her now, but she was strapped to a metal table with her legs spread apart, the subject of a lot of orders. "I was threatened a lot, told I had to push or that they would break the membranes. I didn't know what they meant. I didn't have any urge to push. But I pushed anyway, as hard as I could. They told me I had to push harder, that otherwise I'd be in labor the rest of the day! A man about my age came in. He put his fingers into my vagina, and suddenly water was spurting right in his face. Then the nurse gave me a shot, and they all told me to push again. Another man walked into the delivery room, my doctor—not the same nice doctor I'd seen in pregnancy. He didn't say one word to me, and nobody bothered to introduce us. My legs were up in stirrups and I was draped all over with sheets. I couldn't see the mirror to watch, because there was a screen in front of my face. I didn't ask any questions. I couldn't feel anything. Finally, somewhere in the room, I heard a baby cry. I couldn't see where he was. My doctor had told me in his office that I shouldn't look when the baby was born. I must have fallen asleep while they stitched me up, because the next thing I knew I was being wheeled down a hall. The day after the birth someone came into my room to ask me what I wanted put on the baby's birth certificate. I asked what sex the baby was and how much the baby weighed." Maria named her son William James, after her boyfriend and her brother.

Maria's childbirth experience did nothing but add weight to her already hefty bundle of guilt. Like many women who have had lonely, demoralizing births, Maria saw the experience as somehow merited. Childbirth, like pregnancy, was a punishment and there was no possibility of atonement or forgiveness.

"The baby was in the nursery and I was a nobody. I'd done

this terrible thing and I had no rights. I couldn't tolerate lying on my stomach in the bed, because I wanted the feeling of the baby still being there."

The next day Maria's mother came again to the hospital to visit. Maria told her of her decision to relinquish the baby for adoption, and that the social worker had said her mother would have to sign the papers before Maria or the baby left the hospital because she was underage. Her mother might have intended to comfort her daughter, but once there she could speak only of herself. Maria thinks she was trying to cover her own guilt, which she felt for not living up to something she expected of herself, that she should take and raise this grandchild.

"She'd already told me, when she came in to see me in labor, that she wouldn't raise my child for me. But when I told her I was giving the baby up, she didn't want to sign the paper. She said she didn't want me to hold it against her that I was giving the baby up. She didn't want to see the social worker either. She didn't know what I'd said to this stranger about her, and she said she didn't want to be judged by her."

The social worker was Maria's one comfort during that hospital stay. She visited several times, and always made Maria feel, as she had from the beginning, that she cared about her and wasn't judging her. Unlike Maria's mother, she had no emotional involvement in Maria's decision to have the baby adopted. She could offer nonjudgmental support more easily than Maria's family, because whatever Maria did was of no emotional threat to her own sense of security, as it so often is among family members.

Despite her refusal, Maria's mother did return the next day to sign the papers, and she came again five days later to take Maria home. Maria was still unable to assert herself, but before she walked out of the hospital she did one independent act: she stopped at the nursery window and asked to see her baby. "He was lying in a plastic cart way in the back of the room, behind a post, as if they knew I might want to look at him and had hidden him from me." When the nurse wheeled his cart to the window, Maria was surprised to feel no joy, no flutter of recognition at the sight of her son, only a sense of self-worthlessness.

"It was like going to a funeral home and looking at a dead person, just standing, looking, and turning away. I'd wanted so much to see some similarity to me and to Bill. I'd wanted him to be beautiful. I'd wanted to hold him. But I wasn't entitled to. He wasn't mine anymore."

Other women, feeling that same sense of having no rights once they have relinquished a baby for adoption, might go home to repeat the experience with another pregnancy and then insist on keeping that baby, out of defiance and to fill the bitter hole the first baby left. But Maria decided that she would never have another child.

"Obviously, because I had given a child up, I could never be a good mother." For the next ten years she carried the memory, confiding about his existence only to people she felt would give her support for what she'd done. She was finally able to say good-bye to her son after twelve years, when, pregnant for the second time, she began to work with a therapist. And despite the pain it brought her, Maria feels certain she did the right thing at the time for her baby and for herself.

"I guess it would have been possible for me to live on welfare with my child or to continue living at my brother's; but the baby's well-being was so much more important to me than my feelings. I feel a lot of sadness that I did give up such an important piece of myself, but I think under the same circumstances, I would do it again. I wanted my child to be a person in his own right. But I couldn't give him a sense of worth when I had none myself."

For Maria some sadness is still there, for the pain she endured and the loss. The guilt is gone at last, as she has at last been able to grieve and move beyond grief. But there is still the feeling of shame at how helpless she was throughout her pregnancy, her baby's birth, and the adoption.

Ten years after she gave up her son, Maria married and,

ready to start a family, became pregnant again. She lost the baby through a spontaneous abortion. At first she could not help feeling that the heavens were punishing her for her past sins. But she did not let it deter her from becoming pregnant again. This time she did not miscarry, and she was able to use what she had learned through pain so many years before to make sure that this pregnancy and birth was joyful. It was during this pregnancy that she felt compelled to write to the agency that had handled her son's adoption twelve years earlier.

"I had to know if he had gone to a loving and stable home, how long it had been after he was born before he had been given parents. Secretly I felt any bad news I heard would justify the last of the guilt I still carried. I still imagined terrible things." The woman who wrote her back said Maria's son was fine and well, that he had been adopted when he was three months old. He had made "a good adjustment" to his new home and was being "raised with the knowledge that he was adopted and that his biological mother's decision had been made for his best interests." That was all she learned. Of his current life and well-being, Maria heard nothing.

Even a small bit of news helps when someone is searching. "It hurts to know that my son had to wait three months before he was adopted, but at least I know he found a family who wanted him. I went to an adopt-search group meeting last year and heard a woman talk about finding and finally meeting her biological mother. She observed firsthand the way this woman lived. She could see the kind of person she was and imagine what her life might have been with this woman as her mother. She said she felt she wanted to thank her for having given her up. I think my son would thank me too. But I am still waiting for that knock on the door when he will come looking for me."

It was during the final weeks of her recent pregnancy that Maria met a young woman named Pat. She was at a gathering of pregnant women and their mates to learn more about her options for childbirth, because she was still searching for pieces missing from her first birth experience.

"Someone mentioned to me that there was a woman at the

meeting who was planning to give her baby up for adoption, and the adoptive parents-to-be were there too. When Pat introduced herself as we went around the circle, I felt a really strong connection with her. And a lot of envy too, like, Gee, I wish I could have done it all differently."

In Pat, Maria thought she saw all the strength she felt she had lacked and the support she wished she'd had. Private, or direct, adoption had never even been mentioned to Maria as a choice, yet she'd always wished her son could have been given a home and loving parents immediately. Pat's decisions to meet the parents who would raise her baby, to bring her baby into the world without drugs, to hold her baby, and to be able to part with her baby consciously all left Maria in awe.

"It's impossible to look back on the past and say for certain I would or would not have done this the same way, knowing all I do now. I think I'd probably still have given the baby up, although I might have thought seriously about abortion, now that that is possible. Most of all I would like to have taken more care to do what would nourish the child while I was carrying him in pregnancy. I wish I could have been glad to carry a life inside me and been happy in pregnancy. Today if I were to choose adoption for my baby, I would make sure the birth was a gentle birth, not a birthing like mine. And I would want some choice in the kind of people who would take the baby, to make sure I felt they would be able to give him the love and care he needed."

MARIA:

Time Heals

IT HAS BEEN NEARLY ten years since I last saw Maria. She is now forty-two and her daughter is eleven. She and her family moved to a large city in the Pacific Northwest several years after I wrote her story. They now have a small paper-making business they operate out of their home. Maria has remained involved in the field of childbirth all this time: first becoming a certified childbirth educator, and then, for the past eight years, teaching childbirth preparation classes to pregnant women and couples. I contacted her to ask if I could give readers an update on her story.

Her long-term interest, she told me, has been to help other women discover the options available today that were unavailable to her when she gave birth to the son she relinquished for adoption. "Partly it was his birth being so traumatic—not only the physical aspects, being strapped down and all—but *all of it*. Not knowing what my options were! I knew I wanted to help other women, let them know what was possible. If you don't know what your options are, then you don't have any!"

Teaching has been especially good for her, and sometimes women invite her to be a labor support at their births. The special feeling she gets from assisting another woman in bringing a new life into the world seems to more than make up for any painful memories it stimulates.

The son Maria relinquished through a closed, agency adoption recently turned twenty-two. As with every birth mother I have met, time means something special. Each passing year brings back painful memories and a measure of hope. For the past four years her birth son has legally been considered an adult, and for all that time Maria has been waiting. "I mark each birthday," she says; but she has not yet taken any action to find her son. "At some point, if I don't hear from him, I will contact him. I haven't yet felt the urgency to do so, but I think it would be fairly easy to find him because I'm motivated." She adds confidently, "I've learned how to make things happen for myself." For the present Maria will wait, with some impatience and with strong emotions. That is her nature. It is also a combination of traits she shares with most birth mothers.

"There has definitely been healing," she told me. "Partly, I think, it has been the natural effect of time. Partly it has been the work I have done helping other women in birth." Yet there is, for Maria and for most birth mothers—even those who remain involved with childbirth and adoption—still a wound. "It is still open to a degree," she said, "and I think it will always be open." It seems to be the old tenacious feelings of guilt that keep the wound open. Maria says, "Sometimes it's so easy to feel guilty, to hang onto the past instead of seeing what is ahead."

It was not easy for Maria to stop seeing herself as a victim of circumstances. "I was in that mode—'poor me'—for a long time, until I realized I *could* let go, I *could* go on!" She was finally able to do it. "I feel strong now. I know I wouldn't let anyone treat me now the way I let people treat me then! But I know I did the right thing then in relinquishing my son. My sorrow is that I was too young to understand or be ready for information or options."

Maria is proud of one part of her past, of having had the maturity to recognize her limits. "I did have the wisdom to know my immaturity would have made me a poor mother." That was always something that made living with the aftermath of relinquishment easier. Maria told me that another part of what helped her to let go and move on with her life was working on this book. "It helped to come out and talk about it." But there are still times when she falls back into the past, into old habits of self-abuse and self-pity.

"Occasionally I get into one of my funky moods, and one of the things that always pulls me out is thinking, He may knock on my door, and I certainly don't want him to see me this way! It's wonderful to know that he's out there, that he'll be here sometime."

When it feels appropriate to tell someone about it, she now does so with a measure of ease. She recently had a woman in her birthing class who was planning to relinquish her baby, and who had chosen the birth parents and with them was planning an open, private adoption. Maria told the woman that she too had made the decision to relinquish a baby and assured her she would find support—from Maria and from others—for what she was doing. At the final class, when couples who had already given birth came with their babies, this pregnant woman asked one of the couples if she could hold their baby. The class sat and watched her take the infant in her arms, and some of them cried openly along with her.

Those who must make and then live with painful and irrevocable decisions must allow themselves to feel the pain, not only for the path they have chosen but also for paths they could not take. The understanding and approval of others is essential to their healing.

The climate of approval of the various difficult decisions a woman may make regarding reproduction is fortunately changing. There is today less interest in hiding the truth from others, especially from those who are dying and from children. There is a growing recognition of the dark consequences of keeping people from the truth, of the harm created in the name of protecting others from what belongs to them. Times have changed and Maria is helping open the way for others to walk the path she walked with greater dignity than she was afforded.

For those who have not been able to experience the life they hoped for, there can be great joy, serenity, and healing through helping others reach their own visions. They cannot change the past, but they can transform the present. They can also see that they do not repeat their own mistakes. They can learn from the results of their ignorance how important it is to have knowledge and to be able to make choices consciously.

Maria realized she needed to tell her daughter that there was a part of her past of which she did not feel proud. She did not want her daughter to become a woman and feel that she was a victim of her life. As almost always happens, there was no "perfect" time to do this, just a moment when it seemed right. "I told my daughter when she was seven that she had a half-brother. I told her that at a time when she was sad that she had no siblings with whom to play. Although she still has no brother or sister to play with, she has some relief in knowing there is someone out there with whom she has a special connection." For her daughter there was no judgment of what her mother had done. "I was relieved to tell her," said Maria. "I want no skeletons in our family closet!"

JUDY:

Somewhere a Child Still Searches

STORIES ABOUT ADOPTED children who grow up and start on a search for their biological parents were rare a decade or so ago, but the evolution in adoption practices, which has been hastened by a demanding, vocal, and growing minority of adopted adults, is bringing out the natural desire of most people to know their roots. Judy is one of many adoptees searching for her hereditary past.

Judy has always known she was adopted, just as she has always known the love of two parents, her adoptive ones. She considers her childhood to have been a happy one and her family to be close, yet she feels she suffered from lack of knowledge about her roots and the void that lack of knowledge created in her sense of who she was.

"I was raised knowing I was a 'chosen' child, that there was something special about that, and that I was supposed to feel good about it. I remember lying awake at night thinking, Why did you choose me from all those babies? There was something uncertain about being chosen. If you were chosen you could be 'unchosen.' And I found out later it was not even true. As adoptive parents you can't choose a baby. You take what you get." Her "story" comforted her no longer.

"In my family there never was much room for negative feelings or for emotion. Whenever I wanted to say, I feel bad because I'm adopted, which I did at times, and whenever I felt rejected or unconnected, which I did, especially during my teenage years, I knew that to say so would seem ungrateful. Once, just before I went away to boarding school, my mom and I had an awful fight. I was shouting, 'You keep talking about me being chosen, but I sure never had a choice! And when I go out in the world, I'm going to choose someone I want, and it's not going to be you!' My mother, who always tried so hard never to let herself get angry at me, stopped me short with just two sentences. 'I do love you, Judy, and I wouldn't have adopted you if I hadn't wanted to! But you know, Judy, you can kill love; and you're doing a damn good job!' With that she turned and walked out."

That argument ended a long period of Judy testing her mother's love, but she didn't find the connection she was searching for until she met her other parents fifteen years later.

Judy had been told nothing about her birth parents. As her curiosity grew over the years, Judy satisfied her need for a past with a story she created from her imagination. She clung to this story because it was an answer to her question, "Where did I come from?"—and it also satisfied the curiosity of those who knew she was adopted and asked about her background. But it wasn't accurate.

"Two or three years ago Mom and I were talking late one night about my adoption, and I dropped something about my mother having been a 'red-haired floozie.'

"Mom said, 'Where'd you ever get such an idea?'

"I was floored. I really thought that was my story. For years I'd believed my natural mother was a red-haired floozie and a dancer. And that my father probably had been killed in the war. I though I knew what kind of a woman would give a baby up for adoption—a floozie, a prostitute, a whore. Well, Mom told me my mother was a beautiful, well-educated woman who was interested in music and dance, my grandfather was a superintendent of schools somewhere in the South, and they always thought my father must have been killed in the war.

"After that incident I needed to know the truth badly. I knew Mom had gotten me from a large agency in Texas, and that it was called Hope Cottage. My adoptive father used to tell me a story while I was growing up about how he was the one who carried me out of Hope Cottage and, as he was leaving, he turned to ask the woman who showed them out, 'Is that all?' She said, 'Well, just one thing—you haven't paid for her yet.' He was shocked and embarrassed that he'd forgotten that, and asked, 'Well, how much do I owe you?' 'That'll be one dollar,' the woman said, smiling. And my father, telling me the story, would always finish with, 'And I would've paid a million!' "

When Judy was sixteen she and her mother happened to pass through the city in Texas where Hope Cottage was located, and Judy decided on the spur of the moment she wanted to see it. Her mother didn't think it was a good idea. She warned Judy that the place was very institutional.

"We went, and boy was she right! I knew it was in a city, but my fantasy was still grass and trees all around. It was nothing like a cottage. Just a big, ugly, bare brick building. We walked up the stairs and inside, and I told the woman at the desk, 'I was adopted from Hope Cottage.' Well, she practically jumped up and down, she was so friendly.

"'Oh, you're a Hope Cottage baby! Well, come with me!' She took us into a large gray room with lots of steel equipment, and said, 'This is where the babies lived when you were here, Judy; at that time this room was filled with bassinets. And here was where you were bathed!' She pointed to one of the steel sinks along the wall. I felt stone cold and sick to my stomach. Then she took us into another room. That room was sunny and warm; and there were half a dozen kids playing at one end of it. All of them were disabled.

"'These children haven't found homes yet, Judy. You were lucky.'

"Oh, my God! I thought. I could have been one of them. Then we went out into the hallway and there, on the walls, were hundreds of pictures of babies. She said that I must send them a picture of myself.

"I said to myself, *Never*. I don't belong here. I don't want to be connected with this place in any way."

Judy and her mother left quickly, without so much as asking to see Judy's records. In spite of her mother's warning, the reality left her shaken to the core. It was years before she dared take the next step in her search.

Judy put her misgivings in terms of fear of her adoptive parents' rejection. "I didn't want to hurt my parents. What if I was betraying them by my search and they rejected me? Then I would have nothing! It was when I had a job teaching nursery school after I was married and we'd started thinking about having kids of our own that I began to think about searching. I joined a therapy group with my husband. The leader of the group, a man named Roy, turned out to have been married once before and had two kids from the first marriage. He told us all about it, how his son was now living with him, but how he and his new wife had felt it was too much for them to keep the little girl as well, so they'd left her with the mother. We heard that the mother, who lived in another part of the state, had a boyfriend who beat up the little girl. There was a lot of discussion in the group about what Roy should do.

"One session Roy dropped the news that one of the couples in our group would be leaving the group, because they were going to adopt his daughter and it would be too complicated for them to remain in the group. The couple, Michelle and George, were there that night and they all talked about their concerns. How was the little girl going to feel as she grew up, knowing her father and stepmother had chosen to keep her brother and to give her up?

"Everyone got into the discussion. Everyone, that is, but me. I sat speechless as everyone around me gave their opinions. I didn't realize that I felt myself as that little girl. All I could think about was that poor child. I hurt like I'd never hurt before. In another instant the whole room turned red for me. We'd been sitting around in the large circle, and suddenly I felt myself jump up and lunge at Roy. I threw my hands around his neck, and I heard myself screaming, 'I hate you! I hate you! I hate you!' Then everyone was pulling me off him, and I ran out to the car. I couldn't breathe easily for a long time. That was the first time I realized how much anger and hurt about my adoption I was carrying. That was a turning point in my life. I knew I had to work those feelings out; but I was terrified of flying out of control ever again." Judy knew she would have to search.

The subject of Judy's biological parents had been assiduously avoided among family and friends during her childhood, but the 1970s and her adulthood brought a new frankness into family discussions about such subjects as sexuality, birth, aging, death, and adoption. During a visit from her father when she was thirty, he told her that he'd seen a program on TV about adoption and that he wondered how she felt about being adopted. "He'd actually never asked me before. I told him about the anger and the resentment I sometimes felt, and that I was trying to think of my birth mother in a more positive light now that I knew she was not a red-haired floozie. I said I realized she must have gone through hell having me, coming as she had from the Deep South and being unmarried at the time.

"My father listened to everything I said, and then came back with, 'What do you mean, "unmarried"? Where'd you get that idea?'

"My insides felt like jelly. Once again I was about to find out I was not who I'd thought I was. Every small detail made a difference. Well, goddamnit, what excuse did my mother have for giving me up if she was married? My father told me he figured I must not have been her husband's child. So my mother had chosen her husband over me! The thought of that hurt tremendously."

A few months after this conversation, in the course of a routine physical, Judy found out that she had a rare inherited disease, Crohn's disease. Her condition is not serious yet, but it might become so. She was asked whether other relatives had ever been known to have symptoms of the disease. Of course, this was just one of the many pieces of Judy's puzzle that was missing—her genetic background.

The question was a spur to Judy to begin her search in earnest. "I had to find out who these birth parents of mine were. I believed you just couldn't have a baby and walk away thinking you had no more responsibility to it than giving birth."

She asked her doctor to write to Hope Cottage. Her adoptive father also contacted the home. A couple of months went by with no news. Then one day Judy's doctor called. She had heard from Hope Cottage. Did Judy want to know what she had found out?

"In the letter she read me over the phone, it said my mother was twenty years old when she had me. It gave her height, her weight, and said she'd had three years of college, was interested in music, and her father was, in fact, a superintendent of schools in some small town in the South. It also said my father was twenty-six years old at the time of my birth. The letter gave his height and weight too, but that was all. By law the agency was not permitted to hand out actual names, because birth parents could then come back and sue them for invasion of privacy. The agency also told my father I was wrong to try to contact my parents, that they were a prominent family in town, and that the maternal grandparents did not know their daughter had even been pregnant with me."

That information gave Judy material for many fantasies. Her husband and parents heard every detail of what she'd discovered and lived with the emotional turbulence that the news created in her. She remembered the home movies she had seen, and what her mother had told her of the day they brought her home from Hope Cottage. She was six months old, but so weak that she could not even hold her head up. It was a mild form of what is called failure to thrive in pediatric literature, a condition that results from emotional neglect. Babies need more than food and a clean environment. They need nurturing, something most easily given through a loving touch, carrying, and breastfeeding, but also through eye contact and the spoken word. Judy's first months seem, objectively, no more traumatic than those that thousands of children have experienced. But some essential nurturing was apparently missing, and she associates this start in life with some of the pain she has always felt about having been given up by her biological parents.

Judy joined an adopt-search group in her town, which offered support and the opportunity to share some experiences. There she heard of a woman in another state who, through the use of a computer terminal in her home, was successfully matching up people with their birth relatives and finding their biological roots. It was through her that Judy first heard about a judge in Texas who had, on occasion, been known to open closed adoption files to adoptees. Judy got the number of the courthouse from the information operator, and was astonished when the judge himself answered the phone. She was shocked when, after hearing her story, he said that he would contact the Bureau of Vital Statistics and have the information—her original birth certificate, with no names deleted—sent directly to her.

"Two weeks later my sealed adoption file arrived in the mail. The cover letter said, 'These are all the records that are contained in the sealed adoption file.' I flipped over the letter, and there staring out at me was my original birth certificate. Suddenly I was looking at my own mother's name—rather her four names, because it gave her maiden name and her married name too. My birth father was listed as her husband. The space for my name was blank. I couldn't believe how painful that was. But there was a name for me on my notice of adoption— Joyce Marie."

That night Judy phoned the information operator in the city where the birth certificate listed her father's address. She had slim hopes he would, thirty-one years later, still be living in the same town; but there was a listing for a man of that very name.

"I had to find out if it was the same man and if his wife, my mother, and he were still together."

Judy made the call the next day from her friend Maryann's

house, with Maryann standing by her for support. "A woman with a southern accent answered the phone. I asked, 'Is Francie there?' That was my mother's name according to my records. The voice answered straight out, 'Just a minute, I'll get her.' I froze on the spot. Maryann ran over and slammed down the receiver for me, just in time. I wanted to call her right back and say, 'Hello, I am your daughter.' But for her sake I wanted to give her some space to get adjusted before I got in touch with her myself. I knew it was going to be a real shock." After talking it over with her friend, Judy decided it might be better if she went through a third party. Maryann offered to be the intermediary and make the next call. Judy would listen on an extension phone.

"Maryann dialed the number. A woman with a thick southern accent answered. Yes, she said, she was Francie. Maryann very carefully began speaking. 'I am acting as an intermediary for a woman who believes she is your daughter,' she said first. Pause. 'She very much wants to make contact with you, but she does not want to put you in an awkward situation.' There were several moments of silence.

"'Well. This *has* come out of the blue! You know, this *is* quite a shock. I'm going to have to think about this and discuss it with my husband. I've got other people to consider here. I've got three children and three grandchildren.' She paused. I could hardly breathe. She asked for more information about me.

"Maryann read directly from my birth certificate. More silence.

"'I'll have to get back to you.' She spoke slowly after the long silence. 'And it might be a few weeks.' "

Maryann gave her name and phone number, instead of Judy's, because they had decided that Judy would that way be protected from any threatening phone calls that might come in the middle of the night telling her to lay off her search. "I was so excited I could have died. I decided to give her three weeks to call back; but more than that I would not wait. I would call them myself if I had to. That first call was on a Saturday. The following Wednesday a man with a southern accent called

Maryann; and it was obvious he was just scared to death. 'We want *nobody* in this family contacted! Do you understand? *Nobody.*'

"Maryann just managed to get in a few words, saying that I had an inherited disease and that I wanted and needed to know my roots, and that I wanted to meet my mother.

"'Well.' He paused a moment. 'She can certainly get a medical history. I can understand her wanting that.' Then, 'But what does she think she's going to get by a meeting? Let me speak to her! You give me her name and her number!'

"Maryann said she wasn't at liberty to give him that information without checking with me first." So they arranged that he would call Maryann back two weeks later to the day at the same time.

Judy went to Maryann's before the appointed time, and so did all her close friends. They all waited with their eyes on the telephone, but he didn't call—one hour, two hours, three hours passed. Finally they all gave up and went home. The next morning Maryann's phone rang. It was him and his voice was angry and hostile. He was defensive about not having called the night before, saying they'd had people over for dinner without notice. There was no apology. He wanted Judy's name and her telephone number, and he didn't want any phone calls from her. Maryann attempted to set another time for the following Thursday evening for him to call back to speak with Judy at her house. He kept on arguing. Judy remembers what Maryann told her of the conversation, word for word.

"'I want to call her when it's all right with *me* to call!' That's what he said. He was fighting for control and I could relate to that; but he wasn't going to get it! Maryann had a list of times when it was good for me and she read them to him. She says he turned his mouth away from the phone and spoke to someone, asking whether they'd be home on Thursday. It was Francie and she must have been standing there by the phone the whole time. So it was set. Next Thursday, eight P.M., their time."

Judy was compelled to press on, despite the resistance she had found. She was fortunate to have friends around her who would be there as she took each anxious step. They were all with her at Maryann's, waiting once again.

Five P.M. West Coast time came and went and he didn't call. After another hour Judy couldn't wait any more so she called him. He answered and their conversation began with a tussle about his failure to call at the appointed time. It turned out there was only two hours' time difference between the two states, not three. "There we were, battling across a couple thousand miles, and I was thinking, 'This is crazy!' Finally I suggested we get on with the reason I'd called.

"'Well, who's *this?* Is this the daughter?'

"'Yes. This is the daughter. Me. Judy.'

"'Judy? Judy who?'

"We danced some more. It was a regular battle of wills. I gave him my full name and all the information I had about him and my mother. I also told him it was his name listed on my original birth certificate as the birth father. He wouldn't say anything. When I began to tell him more about my disease, though, he listened really intently and began to ask me questions. I was more impressed with him than I had thought I'd be.

"'I *can* tell you this, Judy,' he began. 'You come from very good stock. On *both* sides!'

"I asked him if he knew my birth father.

"'Oh yes. I know him quite well; and I know he doesn't have any such disease, I can tell you that.'

"I said, well, he couldn't be certain of that, because I hadn't known I had it till recently myself. I explained all about the disease, how his wife could have it, their children, and it might not show up for years."

He assured Judy that she would have her medical history, but he added that any further contact, such as Judy's getting to know her siblings, was out of the question. Judy's birth had been a secret in the family for thirty-one years, and there were now other children to protect.

"I found out that they had a twenty-nine-year-old daughter and two sons, aged twenty-six and twenty-four. The older two were married, and the youngest son still lived at home. Francie had just been in the hospital for three months and she was still convalescing.

"'Well,' I asked, 'where *is* Francie? I thought I was going to get to talk with her.'

"'She's vacationing with one of her daughters.'

"'*One* of her daughters!' I was shocked. 'I thought there was only one!'

"'Well,' he said, 'apparently she has two daughters!'

"That was his first acknowledgment of me. I could tell he wanted me to promise I would never get in touch with my sister and brothers, and to say that all I wanted from them was the medical history, that when I got it they would never hear from me again. But I'm not a good liar, so I told him, 'My first goal is to meet my mother. Later we can discuss my meeting my sister and brothers and my father too.'

"He flipped out again when I mentioned that, and said that if I made any attempt to contact any of them I would lose *all* communication.

"'Look,' I told him, 'I'm not looking for parents, I've already got wonderful ones; everything's worked out the best for me.' I wanted him to know that. He talked a bit about the decision to give me up and said my mother had even considered abortion, because there was so much embarrassment for a woman pregnant out of wedlock back then. There had been curiosity about how I was, he said, but 'it's something you try to bury and put out of your mind.'

"I asked him straight out what my chances were of meeting my mother.

"'Well, I can tell you this, Judy,' he began. 'You've got a greater chance of meeting your birth father than you do of meeting your birth mother.'

"Suddenly I just had to tell him, 'Richard, I think *you're* my birth father, and I just wish you would tell me.'" The voice on the other end of the phone chuckled and refused to answer the question directly; but he promised to call her again soon, after talking to his wife. Before they hung up he told Judy that Hope Cottage had already written to them and suggested they hire a lawyer to protect themselves from her in case she found them. The director of the agency had actually told him she thought it was terrible, Judy's trying to locate them, and dangerous too. Under no circumstances, the director told him, should they ever tell their other children about Judy.

Judy put the pieces of the puzzle together and told herself that Richard must be her father, and that he and her mother must have married after she had become pregnant, but that they couldn't go back to their hometown with a baby born so soon.

In that first conversation Judy found an opportunity to share some of her beliefs about adoption with the man she believed to be her father. She talked about the damage that she felt ignorance, repression, and lies had done to everyone in the "adoption triangle." When the conversation ended she was left with a great deal more information than she'd started with and hope as well.

Judy's search must have had a profound effect on the two strangers who lived thousands of miles from her. A few weeks later, after Richard had had time to chew over the shock of Judy's arrival in their lives, there was a brief and hostile call from him.

It was after this call that Judy had her first bleeding episode from her disease, which, though minor, caused her a lot of fear. She sat down and wrote Francie a letter and included in it a medical questionnaire. She felt the need for communication of any kind. Another five weeks went by. Finally, beside herself with the need to hear, she phoned. Francie answered. She showed great reluctance to go any further in her relationship with Judy, but she was willing to talk, and they spoke for quite a while. One of the things she volunteered was that her own parents did know of her pregnancy with Judy, but they had been told the baby had died at birth.

Judy laid her hopes on the table when she asked Francie, "Do you want to meet me?" She was really saying, "Do you care?" Francie answered, "Oh, Judy, I don't know. I think so."

Her voice was soft and she added, "But I've had to start a whole new life." Judy heard her crying. "You have to let me do this my way," Francie said. Judy thought she understood what she must be going through. "But only once in our conversation did she reach out to me at all. She asked at one point, out of the blue, 'Judy, are you musical?' She said none of her other children was musical, and I guess that was a very important thing for her. I wished I could tell her I was a concert pianist, anything so she'd be proud of me and want to know me."

Judy felt that all her life she had been missing a sense of being glad to be alive—partly because of her knowledge that she grew in the womb of a woman who didn't want her. Her own mother hadn't been happy that she'd been born. She had to begin to accept that she and her biological mother were two separate human beings and to realize that she did not any longer need that mother's love in order to love herself.

Soon after this conversation with Francie depression hit. "I found myself one day in bed in the fetal position. For three hours I couldn't move at all. I felt so utterly rejected. I'd always felt powerless about having been adopted. Growing up, I felt my cousins weren't *really* my cousins, my grandparents weren't *really* my grandparents, my brother wasn't *really* my brother."

Judy's search also reawakened many feelings and memories on the part of Meg, her adoptive mother, feelings that had lain buried for years under the weight of social custom. Today she can readily admit to feeling she had missed a piece of the process by not knowing the parents who had relinquished Judy. This lack of information had always seemed significant to her and to her raising of Judy.

"While Judy and I were talking recently about her adoption, I realized that even in the thrilling excitement of getting her, I had felt there was something that could have made it more fulfilling. I remember wishing, even then, that there could be a way to meet her parents, at least her mother. What harm would there have been if we'd met, in some neutral place, perhaps without knowing each other's names? I felt a void when raising Judy, because I couldn't tell her more about her past. I think I would have been far more at ease if, when the 'terrible teens' had started at our house, I could have been able to say, 'Let me tell you some more about your birth mother. I know because I met her.'"

Some adoptive parents claim their bias in favor of keeping adoption files closed results from a desire to protect their children from the pain of knowledge. Meg feels her daughter's pain, yet she has no desire to protect Judy from living her own life. "Every parent who loves her child wants to see her settled and secure; but who is these days? I also had traumatized feelings when Judy first separated from her husband. But I understand Judy's feelings about her need to search."

Six months after I interviewed Meg, Judy finally met her birth parents; but it was not until her adoptive father, Sam, had stepped in on her behalf and written a blunt letter telling them that not knowing Judy would be their loss. In a way her search had become their search too. Judy continued to assure them that she was not rejecting them as her parents, and they never felt threatened by her searching. When the birth parents flew out to California, Meg and Sam were there with Judy to greet them in the lobby of a downtown hotel. Sam went out onto the street to watch for Francie and Richard. Judy and her mother, waiting nervously inside, could not take their eyes from the revolving door. Then suddenly there they were, walking toward her, and Judy found herself standing among four of the most important people in her life.

She felt like a child once more. No one spoke directly to her as the two sets of parents grabbed onto small talk to fill the space. The five of them sat down to lunch together. At first no one seemed able to swallow a bit, and then everyone began stuffing the food down as they continued to talk about the weather, vacations, where each of them had lived. From her place at the table Judy watched it all. She noticed immediately that Francie would not make eye contact with her, but that Richard periodically turned to give her a hard stare that felt like he was trying to peer inside her.

After lunch Francie invited everyone up to their hotel room. There she cast her shoes off and curled up on the double bed, which took up most of the space in the small room. Judy sat on the foot of the bed near Francie. Her father sat behind her and her mother leaned against a bureau, facing them. Into this circle Richard thrust a chair. "Well," he started, "*someone* needs to lead this discussion, and it might as well be me." He stared hard at Judy as he spoke, with the same combination of aggression and curiosity she had felt from him in their phone conversations. "Now that you've got us here, what is it you want? I want to hear it all!"

Judy had a hard time finding words to begin, but she stated her goals in a straightforward way. First, she said, she wanted to know her medical history. In addition to that, she wanted to meet her brothers and sister. And besides that, she wanted to know who her birth father was.

The discussion quickly turned into argument, and it went on for five straight hours. Voices rose to angry shouts and everyone wept. At the heart of the drama was the conflict over whether Judy had the right to do what she was doing, opening up her closed adoption. Francie, still tightly curled up on the bed, did everything she could to force her position on the others. She said Judy might be her daughter, but she still had no right to do this thing. It was allowing her no sleep, making her sick, and she would not tolerate her making contact with anyone else in the family. For her part, this meeting was to be both the beginning and the end of it. Judy's parents supported Judy's position on her right to search, first attempting to persuade, then trying to soothe the hurts. Suddenly Richard turned to Judy, and with tears in his eyes, blurted, "Judy, I have to tell you. I *am* your father!"

There was a momentary silence. Then Richard began to talk. He described their family and the children who were all her full siblings. Judy's pictures of her life swam before her.

She could not take in all of this new information. The hotel room meeting wound to an end with everyone thoroughly exhausted and shaken.

Three days later Francie and Richard pulled up in a rented automobile out in front of the small shop Judy owned that sold imported gifts and clothing. Judy had arranged everything carefully; her parents had had to return home, but her friends were there in the shop posing as browsing customers. Her birth parents were on *her* home territory now, and she felt the stronger for it. Francie and Richard stayed a few minutes and then drove with her the mile to where she lived at the edge of the university campus in a small, well-kept cottage. She invited them into her living room. In contrast with the other, this meeting was subdued. Judy was surprised and touched when Francie brought out photo albums she had carried with her on the plane, giving her a full accounting of her heritage, introducing her to the various aunts and uncles, showing her pictures of her sister's wedding, of her brother's children, whom Judy was never supposed to meet. At one point Judy had to ask them to close the book—she could not take in so much all in one sitting. She wanted to take a picture of them, but Francie would not permit her. But Richard asked for a picture of Judy. "*No!*" his wife shouted. "You can't do that! What will you tell people when they see it?" He answered that he would say it was a young woman they met in San Francisco during their vacation. "After all," he added, "there are lots of young women who like me."

They ate, and then while Francie sat on the couch in the living room and Richard wandered around the house looking at everything, Judy went to see if she could find a picture of herself to give him. She couldn't find anything but a proof of an ancient baby picture, of her at nine months sitting at a photographer's studio. "That's nice, Judy," was all her mother would say when she looked at it, "but we can't take it. We would have no place to put it." The double message might have been unintended, but it was all too clear. Meanwhile, Richard made a thorough search of the cottage, opening Judy's closed bedroom door, reading everything posted on her refrigerator, asking who the man was in the photographs in her room. (It was Judy's adoptive brother.) Then he came across a list of questions Judy had written after the last meeting, brought it into the living room, and said, "Well, Judy, you better ask all these questions now." But there were no satisfactory answers. Francie would give no details about her pregnancy or Judy's birth. When Judy asked why they chose the name they did for her, Francie insisted there had been no name—she had neither seen nor named Judy after the birth. Judy held back from asking a number of her questions.

She was relieved when they finally left her home and drove off for a weekend on the coast—and thoroughly surprised when Richard called her later the same night and said they were still in town. "Why aren't you at the conference?" he demanded. What conference? "The one posted on your refrigerator." She told him she had decided not to go after their visit. She wanted to rest and assimilate everything that had gone on. Why was he calling? "I've never been so upset in my life," he told her. "I can't sleep. I don't know what to do!" Judy recalled that Meg had told her that when she had called Richard to cancel a second meeting of all five of them, he had said he'd felt like putting his arms around Judy when they had said good-bye, but he hadn't felt he had the right. Judy acknowledged that the whole experience since their arrival had been very upsetting to her too, and that was why she had chosen not to go to her workshop. "If I'd only known that," Richard said, "I'd have invited you to go up to the country with us today." That was the very last thing Judy could have handled then. Their parting had been emotional enough, watching them leave in their rented car, seeing them both turn around to look at her one last time, with tears running down their faces. Richard told her he couldn't stand driving back through her town without stopping to call her. He couldn't bear thinking of her standing on the curb, a lonely little girl. Judy quickly assured him that she was in fact neither a little girl nor lonely. She was happy, she said, and next time he visited she would introduce him to her life and

friends. There would be a next time; he had assured her of that
at their most recent meeting. But now, standing in a phone
booth somewhere in the center of town, the man who was her
biological father could only repeat how this was the most
upsetting thing he'd ever been through. He seemed incapable of
breaking the phone connection, unable to shut Judy out of his
life, he who had for more than a year refused to admit he was
even her father.

Winter passed. The meeting in the fall had been so rich, though
exhausting, that Judy found no need to contact Richard and
Francie afterward. But when summer came, and she had still
had no word about when they might come to see her again, she
decided it was time to make contact with her siblings directly.
Through the information operator she found a phone number
and address for her brother Tim, who Francie and Richard had
said was going through a divorce, and she wrote him a letter.
A few days later he telephoned her. Unlike their parents he was
not in the least ambivalent in his feelings. He was surprised and
shocked, he said, but he was also delighted and curious.

   During the next few months, Judy established a good
relationship with Tim by phone. When Tim asked Richard
about Judy, Richard tried at first to deny her existence and then
refused to speak about her. Tim took it on himself to tell the
other children about Judy, and since then Judy has spoken once
to each of them on the phone, without sensing any great
warmth on their part. Her sister sounded less interested in Judy
than in the details of her search, as though this might give her
some clues about what it would be like one day with the
daughter she herself had recently adopted. She did open up to
Judy a bit about that.

   But the full welcome Judy had once hoped for from her
birth family has not been there. Richard has strictly forbidden
the children to mention Judy to their mother, or to have any
further communication with her. He feels that his wife's health
is too fragile. Judy's birth mother is convinced that her life has

been damaged not once but twice by Judy, because her relation-ship with her other three children will never be the same now that they know of Judy's existence. Judy, she feels, came back into her life just to torture her. Judy's father's loyalty is clear: it lies with his wife, and with his belief that the truth brings too much pain.

And Judy, now? The woman who conceived and bore her considers her a burden, a shame and a pain she wants only to forget. Judy cannot pretend this isn't so or that it doesn't hurt. But she is not sorry that she searched for and found her parents. She knew when she started her search that although the majority of adoptee searches resulted in happy reunions, some did not. And she was searching for the truth, for knowledge to fill the void inside her, not for simple happiness. Her overriding feeling today about her search is that it has given her life new meaning. It was always the process, not the end result, that motivated her. Nor is the process complete. Judy is still young. Her parents' attitude may still change; if not, she has at least gained a brother. She and Tim are making plans to meet. No longer does she say, "My life began when I was adopted. And I have never felt connected to anyone or anywhere." Who would deny her this search?

JUDY:

From Anger to Self-Acceptance

Eɪɢʜᴛ ʏᴇᴀʀs ʜᴀᴠᴇ ᴘᴀssᴇᴅ since I finished writing Judy's story. In that time little has changed in her relationship with her family of origin. She has still not met the two brothers and one sister who are her full siblings. One brother showed no interest in establishing contact with her. At the end of her only conversation with her sister, who had adopted a baby, that sister did acknowledge her: "My God!" she said, "you're my *sister!*" Judy told me what happened next. "Apparently at that very instant our mother arrived at the door and my sister had to hang up. All she said was, 'Mother's here! I've got to go!' And she hung up. I've never spoken to her since. She had my phone number and I just figured that if she could handle it she would contact me."

Judy recalls every detail of her attempt at establishing a relationship with the family she has never known. Regarding her sister she says, "It was all a complete surprise to her, a shock and everything else. She said she probably wouldn't do anything with our relationship, at least until our mother passed on, because she thought she would feel too guilty. But she said it explained an awful lot of my mother's behavior toward her

59

during her whole adoption process. And she told me she was very grateful for that."

For a time Judy had phone conversations with her brother Tim. He seemed receptive to having a relationship with her, even interested in a meeting. The problem was that his interest in Judy was causing him difficulties in the family; he couldn't talk to anyone else about her. Their father, who knew about the initial calls, continued to flatly insist that Tim cut off all contact with Judy. It seemed that everybody felt they had to protect Francie. Although Tim was a grown man (in his early thirties), he seemed unable to keep his budding relationship with Judy separate from his relationships with the rest of his family. Under the continued pressure and verbal threats of his father, he stopped calling Judy and refused to respond to her calls.

In the last conversation with her father that Judy initiated, "He said he wanted nothing more to do with me, ever again. I had been contacting my siblings against his demands that I not do so." Her mother had gotten on the phone too. "They were both totally abusive and it was really painful! They were furious with me, felt betrayed, and felt their other children would never be able to understand, never forgive them. My mother said to me, 'You have not only ruined my life once, you have ruined it twice!' Then they hung up."

Two years later, in the middle of the night, on Christmas Eve, Judy's father phoned her one more time. Judy says, "He was extremely emotional and told me that he had had to call. Everyone in the family had been over for Christmas Eve, including their adopted granddaughter. He started crying when he said, *Everyone except you!* He'd held his granddaughter in his arms and, he said, it had felt like I had come back to them. He missed me and felt horrible about it. He felt he had not only ruined their own lives, but mine as well. And he was sobbing, 'I love you. I love you. I don't know what else I can do.' He said, 'I feel like somehow I've got you back, through Amy. When I hold her in my arms, I think I'm holding you.'

"I told him I was sorry he was feeling so bad, but I wanted

him to know that *my* life was not ruined! I was sorry if he felt his was, but mine was not, and adoption had been the best thing for me. I had gotten the parents I had needed. And it had really been meant to be. I told him that, as for there being nothing else he could do, I didn't believe that. I felt he was making a choice to cut me out of his life and to continue to feel guilty and to hang on to all of that pain. I felt there was another option. That wasn't how it had to be. He said, 'I don't know how to do it any other way.' I told him I was there, I would always be there, and if he ever wanted to do it a different way, he should let me know."

Like a kind parent consoling a sobbing child, Judy told her father, "I don't want you to feel guilty anymore. I love you and care about you." She was telling the truth, for by then she had resolved much of her own pain and anger. Today she says, "The anger is gone. It gradually went away as I healed. To a large extent the pain is gone too. I don't think it ever will completely go away. And at times it comes up. But I think I have resolved it as much as I ever will. I do not regret *for one second* making the search and finding what I found! That's *my story.* That's what I set out to find!"

Judy still owns a small imported clothing and gift boutique. She and Juanita, her lover of ten years, have a new house and a new dachshund puppy. This past Christmas she sent her birth parents a card. "I wanted to let them know that I think of them, that I'm doing well, and that I have a new address and telephone number. I didn't expect a reply, though it would have been nice." The thought of her other family still brings up sadness. Perhaps it always will.

Her health, which was the reason she initially felt driven to search for her birth parents, she describes as "100 percent better now. I think my problem has at last been identified. I've finally gotten into the hands of someone who knows about food and environmental allergies. That's what I had felt the problem was for years. Others have called it Crohn's disease, but I think it's allergies. I think my search and the healing I've done around that has helped too. It's not the whole answer, but it is one stress that has been relieved."

"*Search!*" That's her advice to anyone who has been adopted. "It's worth it, no matter what! But you have to search with *no* expectations. You have to be willing to face whatever it is you are going to find. Because what you are searching for is *your story!* And if you search long enough you will find it! After all is said and done, I believe the process of searching promotes healing. Therefore even 'rejection,' every adoptee's worst fear, doesn't negate the experience!"

Judy is alluding here to the core issue for the person who has been adopted: the feeling that somehow he or she does not belong, has no roots, has no real connection to this Earth, does not really matter or even exist. This is the root of the person's suffering, and it often becomes apparent as the child enters puberty. The feelings of disconnection and isolation can exist no matter how loving the adoptive parents are, no matter how secure the childhood.

If Judy's observation is correct, then the process of searching may be crucial to the psychological development of most adoptees. But although the act of searching may empower someone who feels disempowered—and disembodied—as a result of having been relinquished by the biological mother, it is not a simple solution to a complex issue. Judy's story raises important questions about what can be done in adoption to prevent such deep wounding. Certainly we should think about the structure of adoption, how it might be changed to promote the adoptee's well-being. We need to see what will allow an easier transition for the adopted child from its natal environment to a new, unknown environment. A form of adoption in which the original bonds are not severed, but kept alive, may be one essential part of the answer.

TOM:

A Question of Ethics

THERE IS LITTLE WRITTEN about birth fathers. Their role in adoption and their importance in their children's lives has been largely ignored. Until they begin to participate in this process, as they have begun to participate in the care of the children they raise, we will not truly know how significant they are to the children of adoption.

In addition to the part birth fathers play, and could play, in the lives of adopted children, there is the question of what it means to a man that he has fathered a baby that has no part in his life. Although that child does not develop within his body, it is of his genes, his spirit. I recently heard a practical definition of the word *ethics*. Ethics involves personal decisions. It is the difference between "having a right to do something" and "doing what is right." In this story a man makes an ethical decision.

Tom is a birth father. He is turning fifty, and his story begins many years ago, at a time when the full responsibility for coping with unplanned and unwanted pregnancy rested upon women's shoulders, weighed down women's wombs. It was only in his midthirties that Tom discovered the importance of having fathered a child about whose existence he knew, yet for whom he had not taken responsibility, had never even known. There comes a time in your life to take stock of what has passed and to tally up your deeds. To turn and look back, to face the consequences of actions and inactions that have affected not only your own life, but other people's lives, takes courage. This is especially true when there is no outer pressure to do so, and no great inner pain—the sort of pain that women find inevitable from carrying and birthing a child that they then relinquish—that demands it.

Tom leans back comfortably in a chair, a small man in his middle years. His hair is still thick and wavy, but the brown is now sprinkled throughout with gray. Pale blue-gray eyes, with fine lines at the corners, gaze without focus across the room as he looks inward at scenes from the past.

"High school, Bloomington, Indiana, 1956. I was a junior and Anne was a senior," he begins. "She was taller than I was. I really felt like I was something to be going with an older woman and to be shorter than she was too! I loved her personality. She was very pretty, a willowy blond with a musical laugh, very graceful." They went together that entire school year. She was graduating but didn't want to go to college. "She just wanted to be around kids, wanted to be married and have a family." Tom was a traveler; he loved playing tennis in all the big tournaments in the Midwest. "I hitchhiked around to each place, had friends on the circuit." He worked hard for the privilege of being free each summer, earning the needed money by working an eight-hour shift in a pizza place three nights a week during the school year.

Not only were their aspirations different, but so were their backgrounds. Anne's father was a line worker for the telephone company; theirs was a large, orthodox Catholic family and Anne was the youngest. Tom was the only child of a divorced mother who was a regional representative for World Book Encyclopedia and, though she didn't have a degree, she'd been to college. Tom's mother expected college to be a part of his future, but at seventeen his vision of the future had yet to be formed.

Like other kids their age, Tom and Anne went to high school parties together, but also spent time alone when they could. "We'd park out by the quarries in the back hills. I had a curfew but she didn't. My mother found that very strange and somewhat puzzling." Often they would park the car Tom had borrowed from his mother in front of Anne's house and make out (in the vernacular of the day), sometimes until well after his curfew. "A few times, I recall, we'd be out there around two in the morning and hear the irritating rap of a nightstick on the window. The windows would be all steamed up and I'd roll my window down one inch. It would be a cop and he'd say, 'Is your name Tom?' I'd say yes, and he'd say, 'Well, you'd better get home. Your mother's worried about you.' "

It was sometime in the spring when Anne got pregnant. Tom recalls when it happened: "Well, it wasn't the first time we'd done it. Generally the car was our bedroom. I just figured it couldn't happen to us!" Like most teens, they didn't use birth control, but Tom did know something about a woman's fertility cycle. "I tried to figure out Anne's fertile times, kept account in my mind. I was pretty aware of the very night. It seemed to me a dangerous time. I was getting ready to take off for the summer of tennis, and she was about to graduate. We'd been talking about splitting up."

The passion was still there, but they were trying to be realistic about the future. At least Tom was. "I didn't want to go play tournaments feeling tied up to a relationship back home." He knew well that the next step expected of him, if he and Anne kept up their relationship, was to marry her. Like most young people his age, he wanted more adventure in his life before settling down and having kids. The possibility that Anne might get pregnant had never been discussed. "Once or twice Anne was a little late and I worried about that. I don't know that she worried. She was easygoing and accepted things as they happened. And she loved kids! She was a great babysitter."

He was playing in a tennis tournament in Louisville in

late July when he was called to the phone. "It was my mother. I sort of knew before I even touched the phone that there was something awful if Mother was calling at the tournament. She said that Anne and I had been very foolish, and she was coming down to pick me up." There was nothing more to say over the phone. "I was destroyed. I didn't know what to do!" His mother arrived grim faced. "Normally we were very close, but this was something she just couldn't accept. Yet," Tom recalls the paradox, "she had always been the one who'd encouraged my independence. I was hitchhiking out of town to play tennis when I was thirteen. She would take me to the city limits and let me out of the car and wait across the road, watching until I got a ride." Like many parents in the mid-1950s who encouraged independence in their children, Tom's mother didn't take independence to include premarital sexuality.

Back at home Anne and Tom never once talked together with all the parents. Anne would talk to Tom's mother when he wasn't around. He never talked to her parents. "I heard her father was incensed. But her mother was just the opposite: carefree. She said, 'Well, the kids will just get married!' I didn't know what her father would do to me! And I had dreams of her brother in the Marines coming back and ambushing me with a bayonet. I'd heard secondhand that he had said he would kill me. I also heard her dad had a warrant out for my arrest." There was an entire afternoon Tom spent hiding at the movies, just trying to keep a low profile, and another when he hitch-hiked out of town before daylight, "so I couldn't be nabbed by the sheriff and served papers."

Meanwhile, Anne and he talked a few times. "I'd pick her up in my mother's car. We'd drive to a lonely street—not the quarries!—and talk. I just couldn't see getting married. She wanted to, but she didn't want to force me. She was disappointed and hurt, but she really could understand, which only made me feel worse." There was some thought of abortion. "But we were so badly connected with those things. Abortion had a very dark, criminal image in those days. Rusty hangers, dark alleyways." He did locate a doctor who did abortions.

"My mother came by the information, but I made the appointment and I went alone." It was forty miles away. The man was apparently an authentic doctor, but practiced his secret trade out of his home. Tom remembers well the drive, sitting in the waiting room, feeling despondent. "He gave me some white pills, and I paid him for the visit—Mother had loaned me the money—and left." Anne took the pills but nothing happened. She remained pregnant.

"I don't know whether it was my idea or Mother's, but I presented to Anne the idea that if she wanted to have the child, why didn't she go live with her brother. He was married and had kids, and they could help her go through it. It seemed like a sort of solution. Of course, the darker side of me was happy that it would take Anne out of town." Anne wasn't showing yet but she wouldn't be able to hide it much longer. Anne went home to think about it and talk to her parents. Tom heard from her a few days later; her parents didn't oppose the idea. So just a few days after graduation, Anne left town for a visit with her brother. Tom's mother gave her a traveling case and a little money. Two girlfriends took her to the bus. "I wasn't there. I was gone, off playing tennis." That was the end, as far as Tom was concerned. He never saw Anne after that.

Tom's mother remarried at Christmas and then moved to Texas. Tom was sent to a military school in West Virginia for the last half of his senior year. After two months at school, a "stork-o-gram" arrived in the mail. "My God," says Tom, "that's really what it was called!" "Congratulations!" it said. The postmark showed it came from the base where Anne's brother was stationed. "As the old saying goes, I didn't know whether to shit or go blind. Whew! I thought they'd throw me out of school." The rules were very clear: you couldn't be married and go to military school. "Then I thought the posse would come and rap on my door and take me away in chains. I wondered who at school had seen it. The envelope said stork-o-gram right across the top. I burned it in my wastepaper basket." But none of Tom's worst fears came to pass. He never heard a word from Anne or her family.

Nineteen years later. Tom was living with the woman he has been with for fourteen years. He had a two-and-a-half-year-old stepson named Ben. Ellen, his partner, had always known there was another child in Tom's past. When Tom entered a period of reflection and self-doubt, she began to urge him to find his son. Tom was nervous and began to think of reasons why it wasn't a good idea. "I didn't know how my mother would feel. She wasn't the kind of person who liked to take risks, and she was of another generation."

"My other son would have been nineteen. I was in my midthirties, and I'd started asking myself questions: Am I the kind of person I want to be? Is there anything in my life I want to clean up?" There was. In his words, "I wanted to get myself on a firm moral footing. I had thought about it periodically every couple of years, like a recurring bad dream." He remembers vividly his feelings once he knew he was going to search for his son. "It was a fantastic mix of excitement and fear."

The search turned out to be surprisingly easy. "It took me all of six days by telephone! I started with one of Anne's best friends from high school. She was the chairperson of their class's high school reunion." Tom knew this fact because he had first called an old friend who had, as a teenager, been well informed about the politics of Bloomington. "I told him I wanted to find Anne. He told me to call this woman who was still living in town, married to an old buddy of mine. With one call I got within six years."

When he told her classmate he wanted to find Anne, she asked the inevitable question. Why? "I said that I just wanted to talk to her and see how her life was. She warned me in a mothering sort of way, treating me like I was still a junior and she a senior, but she gave me the last address and phone number she had." It was in the town where Anne's brother had been stationed when Anne went to live with him and have the baby. Tom tried the number. It was no longer in service. He called information to see if there was a different listing for the same last name. He ran into a dead end. But Tom was not discouraged.

His next attempt was to reach Anne's older sister. "She was still in Bloomington. I'd forgotten that. Then I remembered somehow and called her and asked for Anne's address." Once again he was asked why. The sister immediately recalled that Tom and her sister had gone together in high school. From the way she talked, he could tell she had never known their relationship had resulted in the baby Anne had given birth to the year after she graduated from high school. Apparently Anne's affection for Tom and her natural good nature had prompted her to keep the secret. The sister was helpful and gave Tom information about Anne, but she didn't have her sister's current address. Anne had been married and divorced several times. She'd moved around a lot recently and hadn't remained in close touch with most of the family.

She did give him the name of the town and the phone number where an older brother worked, saying he would probably have Anne's current address. Tom's stomach began to rise up in his throat. It was the same brother he'd heard had threatened to kill him that spring nineteen years ago. How would he feel hearing from Tom? The next day Tom took the risk and dialed the number, recalling another man from the past. "It was the same base where my father, whom I'd seen only twice when I was growing up, had once worked." Having grown up not knowing his father was another reason Tom felt his urge to search was so strong. "I wanted to stop this cycle, fathers not knowing their sons."

He didn't expect to get Anne's brother on the phone directly. It was a Navy base, and they wouldn't let just anyone be put through. He also knew the Navy would be helpful. "I told them I was trying to get a hold of this person, and I was told they couldn't give me any information about him but they could get a message to him." Tom left his name and phone number and the message for Anne's brother to please call him collect. Within a few hours the phone rang. It was Anne's sister-in-law. She had gotten the message from the base operator and hadn't even waited until her husband came home from work to make the call. Tom explained that he was an old friend of Anne's, trying to get in touch with her. The woman on the other end of the line sounded relieved. She said that Anne's mother was sick and when she had gotten the message to call, she had assumed it might be someone calling about that.

Tom hung up from their conversation with the information he wanted: Anne's new married name, her new address, and her current phone number. The goal was in sight. Anne and their son were living near San Diego, just an hour's plane ride away. He wanted to see them. What would Anne's reaction be? Tom never worried that she would try to prevent him from contacting his son, but how would his son react to a father who had abandoned him and his mother?

"I was scared the *whole* time during the six days I was searching! There was this whole gamut of emotions I'd go through each time I did anything: the guilt, the fear, the elation of possibly making progress. Every day was like that. It was a bit like raking your guts with a garden rake!" And yet it was also an adventure, and part of the excitement was not knowing what he would find. "I sort of expected Anne to be the same. I didn't think she would have changed." But everything else was an unknown.

It was in the middle of a work day when Tom got the information about Anne. He waited until early evening to dial the phone. She answered. "By that time she had heard I was going to call; her sister-in-law had called and told her." Tom describes Anne, as he had known her, before proceeding with his story. "You have probably seen few people who moved as slowly and gracefully as Anne did," Tom says. "She was like one of those African women walking with a big water pot on her head. I just knew that was the way she still was when she said hello. I said, 'It's Tom.' She said, 'Wellll, Tom.' Slow, very slow, just like that. 'I always wondered whatever happened to you,' she said. 'Well, you know, I tried to call you once or twice. A few years ago. I got sort of lonely and I wondered, Whatever happened to Tom?' We just chitchatted for a while. I said, 'I guess you know why I'm calling.' 'Yes,' she said, 'and the golden boy'—that's what she called him—'is right here.'"

Tom's mouth drops open in mock astonishment as he tells it. "She started describing him a bit. 'Jeff's six foot one, has golden curls down to his shoulders, and is going to be a rock 'n' roll star.'" Tom is five foot seven. "I could hardly hang onto the phone. I wanted to have this conversation! But I sort of wanted to hang up and go off and digest this stuff. It was coming too fast!"

Without pausing for Tom's response, Anne handed the phone to their son. Tom didn't have time to find the right words to begin. "I just asked him, 'Do you know the story?' He said, 'Yes, my mother told me.' He said, 'When I was twelve I had a feeling that my father wasn't my real father, and I asked Mom about it.'" Tom learned that Anne hadn't told Jeff because she'd thought he was too young, but in response to his question she'd sat him down and told him the unvarnished truth.

Tom and his son had a brief conversation. Tom found out that Jeff had two younger sisters also living at home. "I said I wanted to come down and visit, but I was concerned about his mom's new husband and wanted everything to be okay with him too." Jeff said he thought that would be good. His mother said it would be fine if Tom came. Everyone was curious to see each other, but there was awkwardness too.

"The strain was just under the surface. It never erupted but it was that way for a long time." It dissipated slowly, he said, with each visit and each phone call. The tension was only natural. What they were about to begin was an intimate relationship. Yet they were strangers, at least Tom and Jeff were. It would take time for everyone involved to feel fully at ease.

The next month Tom flew down to visit his son and his old high school sweetheart. He went by himself. "I just wanted to be alone. I wanted it to work!" The visit lasted ten days. Tom's partner, Ellen, began to wonder and worry after days had passed. Tom called her several times, but he didn't know when he'd be coming home. Ellen couldn't help but feel left out and a little jealous. By the end of a week, Tom felt things were going well in San Diego; he asked Ellen to fly down.

The first eye-to-eye meeting between Tom and his nineteen-year-old son, Jeff, was, in Tom's words, "awfully *awkward*." When Tom arrived in San Diego, he took a room in a motel not far from Anne's house. He rented a car and followed the directions Jeff had given him and pulled into the driveway. Anne greeted him at the door. "I felt numb," says Tom. They stood looking at each other until Anne invited him inside. Jeff was home, she said, in his room. She took Tom into the living room and pointed out Jeff's door. It was shut and there were sounds of voices behind it. Jeff had invited his entire rock band over to witness what was about to happen.

"They came out one by one, these nineteen-year-old boys. They didn't know if they were punk or new wave—it was the beginning of that movement. Jeff was the last one out, wearing blue jeans. He was like an odd stranger, and there was an edge in his voice when I asked him a couple of questions, like resentment." Tom realized Jeff might be uncomfortable in such a crowd and looked for a way to get him alone. At that moment one of Jeff's sisters came in the front door with her friends, one by one, staring at Tom. And a few minutes later the other sister arrived. "I was this lab specimen sitting there, trying to make conversation with Anne, she trying to make conversation with me."

Tom finally got Jeff to go to his motel room with him. Jeff seemed most interested in Tom's writing career; Tom wanted to know all sorts of things about Jeff's growing up. "It was nice. We loosened up a bit. We began to notice we had some strange things in common: the way we tilted our heads, the way we moved, the way we said certain things. Sometimes I'd be there with my hand on my head and he'd be the same way. It was a little freaky!" Tom also couldn't help but notice their facial similarities.

That first evening broke the ice. After that Tom saw Jeff

every day. "He was very good about taking me around to the places where he'd grown up, to his school, to see his friends. We went out to eat with some of his friends and I met others. We just hung out. I sat in his room with him, and we talked and he went through his Rolling Stone memorabilia. I was the generation of the first rock 'n' rollers: Bill Haley, Little Richard. Anne had gotten suspended from school her junior year, sent home for dirty dancing to a Ray Charles record!"

It's been twelve years now since Tom first met his son. Jeff has been living in San Francisco, not far from Tom, for the past five years, ever since giving up his rock 'n' roll career. He worked hard at that for many years and almost made a go of it. The band traveled around the country and did a few shows in Europe, but they never made the big time. Eventually Jeff gave up music. Then he moved to San Francisco with his girlfriend. After a few years they married and Jeff began college. Tom expresses delight that Jeff chose to live near him and go to the same state college from which Tom, and Tom's aunt before him, had graduated. Tom, Tom's aunt, and Ellen all attended Jeff's Phi Beta Kappa honor society party.

Jeff's marriage didn't work out, and he is single again, but now he has a degree in economics and works downtown in the financial district. He and Tom see each other almost every week. "He's one of my best friends," Tom says. "We're a family. Ellen and me and our kids, my aunt, and Jeff. He's part of *all* our family gatherings here *and* back in Bloomington!" Jeff currently lives in his father's old apartment. Because it had such a low rent, Tom had kept it as his place to write after he and Ellen had moved to a large loft closer to downtown. Tom couldn't help Jeff with college tuition on his and Ellen's slender income, but he offered the use of the studio to Jeff while Jeff was going to college. Jeff stayed on after graduating, and now it is his.

According to Tom's recollection, his son never once asked for or implied that he wanted an apology from him. Perhaps it was the way his mother had raised him, not expressing bitterness about Tom. "I apologized once to him, when he was nineteen. He said he thought I was taking the whole thing too seriously." Anne sometimes comes up to see Jeff. She usually stays with Tom and Ellen and their two children. For Tom, it has been an added bonus to have Anne back in his life as a friend. "Whenever we are in her area, she is a must-see."

Tom will be fifty next summer. Looking back at the years of not knowing, of worrying about the past, he can see there were effects on him. "I don't know, really, the extent to which I was affected by what had happened, by not resolving it. I always felt incomplete, that it was my dark side working that I let it go on and on. I felt better once I talked about it with Ellen. She was the first person with whom I ever talked about it in any depth. But there was still this unknown out there. It seemed like it was time to grow up."

In talking about his reunion with his son, Tom discovered that some of his men friends had been through similar experiences. One of them, inspired by Tom's search, initiated his own search and had a successful reunion with his long-lost daughter. Sometimes the two fathers talk about getting together with their grown kids, just to see what it is like. For Tom there is a feeling of completion now. "There are still parts of the story that are weird," he says, "because times were so different then." He adds quietly, "Then is not now. Who we are now is not who we were then. Sometimes it's hard to rationalize or justify my behavior back then."

As for all the energy spent in self-criticism during the years before he searched, Tom can see the toll it took on him. "I sure was hard on myself mentally. It was many years before I could go back to Bloomington. I always felt somebody there would want to put me in jail, that I was an outlaw, not welcome." Tom did return to his hometown for his twenty-fifth high school reunion. He took Jeff with him. He expected something special to happen there but nothing did. "We were just another man and his son, just another couple of guys. Probably nobody knew. And if they did, there were too many things in their lives for them to really care."

ANN:

Family Secrets

ANN IS TWENTY-THREE years old, the youngest of eight children, most adopted in infancy, and all adopted within an eleven-year period. Her parents recently celebrated their fortieth wedding anniversary, and today still live in the home they bought when Ann was three: a large, sprawling ranch-style house with seven bedrooms in a suburb of San Francisco.

Ann's other siblings have all moved out, but she continues to live at home so that she can afford to go to a nearby college. In two years, when she finishes school, she plans to get an apartment of her own. She looks forward to that day, for the family home is not the place where she feels either comfortable or safe.

I met Ann in a therapy group for women survivors of sexual abuse and incest. She spent many sessions hardly speaking, sitting with her knees tucked up under her chin, her eyes cast down, and when she did speak it was usually in a self-mocking tone of voice. What had happened to her as a child was, she assured us, all her fault. She was certain of that. How could it be otherwise: it had gone on for many years, it had involved more than two people, and she had not stopped it.

75

Prior to coming to the group she had confided in only one person, a woman named Kay, who was almost the same age as Ann's mother and whom Ann has known for twelve years, ever since Kay led Ann's Girl Scout troop. Kay was, in fact, the only person older than Ann whom Ann trusted, and it was Kay who had kept telling Ann that there was hope, kept telling her that she could heal, and kept encouraging her to seek help.

Like everyone else in the therapy group, Ann was struggling to break free from the internal bondage she felt and from the pervasive feeling that she was unlovable, sick, and broken inside. Ann was the youngest, the only one who still lived in the home in which the abuse had occurred, and the only adoptee in the therapy group. She was also the quietest, although each woman had difficulty talking about what had happened to her. Everyone, at various times during their first months, talked about feeling as if she were a pressure cooker about to explode. It was that internal pressure that kept everyone coming back and saying something each week.

Each of the women had begun having memories of her abuse only within recent months—a year, at most. For Ann, it had been nearly a year since she had first remembered anything. Usually memories of childhood sexual abuse return in fragments, as from a long-forgotten dream, with a sense of unsubstantiality, combined with horror, that make the person doubt the truth of the memory. In Ann's case the first memory had come crashing through her waking reality in full, a visual flashback that had shattered the silence her mind had imposed so that she could survive.

Each woman admitted her desperation, which had driven her to come to a group of strangers and a therapist she didn't know; each came with no belief that doing so could really help. All brought a longing for healing and the courage to try.

Slowly everyone shed some of their initial awkwardness and got to know each other. It was impossible not to begin to feel familiar with each other after spending every Tuesday evening for months seated in a circle in a small room with the woman therapist gently guiding the talk and drawing out each woman. A measure of trust in, fondness for, each other evolved from the common need for understanding and support.

After coming to group every week for about four months, Ann began to sit differently in her chair. Her legs were no longer tucked up under her chin and tightly encircled by her arms. Her head wasn't always tilted downward. She would sit with her legs crossed, and sometimes she would look at someone when she spoke. She no longer waited until last to say something and she used a self-mocking tone of voice less often, but when she spoke the foot of her crossed leg usually tapped up and down rapidly. We learned from what she told us that she was not ordinarily so diffident. The rest agreed that in other areas of their lives they were outgoing people, competent in work, and able to express their feelings; but in group they felt stifled by something no one could name.

Ann permitted me to write her story for this book. I have changed all the names in her story. As an adoptee abused within her family—a family whose interactions were marked by denial, secrecy, and a compulsion for perfectionism—she is a poignant example of the dark side of closed adoption.

As the victimized child she grew up unable to confide in her adoptive parents, because she felt compelled to maintain the family's facade of perfection. As an adopted child she grew up feeling she was not entitled to call her abuse incest, because the perpetrators were not blood relatives. Ann was caught in a terrible psychological bind. Telling anyone the truth would have meant betraying the family she felt she must protect at any cost. She felt she was fortunate to have been adopted; she couldn't jeopardize that. Speaking up would have meant either becoming the cause of other people's pain or being rejected again.

Like most abused children, Ann showed a peculiar loyalty to her family, the need to hold it together, whatever price that might exact from her. Like most children from dysfunctional families—a family that maintains a facade of perfection is certainly not functioning in a healthy way—Ann knew she was expected to keep up the facade and keep the family's secrets hidden. Like all offspring in such families, she could not possibly put her needs first or even think of herself, because she had no value except for the role she played within the family. She knew she was not loved simply for being herself; love, in her young eyes, came from doing what was expected of her. Finally, like most adoptees, Ann felt a tenuousness and impermanence about her existence that came from knowing nothing about the mother who had placed her for adoption or the circumstances that had caused her to be relinquished.

I believe we need to break the silence that exists about the abuse of adopted children, and the special danger posed for the adopted child when there is abuse.

Adoptive parents are not exempt from the kinds of internal and external stresses that lead birth parents to strike out at their children. They are as likely as anyone to come from dysfunctional families—families patterned around the addictions and denial of the parents. They, like any parents, can find themselves with a child who is not easy for them to understand or love. In addition, because the child does not come from their family's genetic pool, it is possible that the child can have traits that are frustrating and incomprehensible to the adoptive parents. They cannot say their child's stubbornness is just like Aunt Jane's, or their child's withdrawal is just like Grandfather Sidney's.

Adopted children come to their adoptive parents with a certain amount of psychological baggage because they were relinquished. That is something the adoptive parents have no control over and were not the cause of, and it can be exasperating if this baggage seems to be standing in the way of the child accepting the adoptive parents' love. Adoptive parents and adopted children do not have the benefit of the physiological bond that exists between other parents and their children (which comes in varying degrees, depending on how much the child was wanted, what kind of pregnancy and birth the mother and child had, and so forth).

The physiological bond between a parent and the child who is genetically his or who has come from her womb makes a parent feel protective toward the child. It creates a natural barrier that restrains a parent from abusing his or her child. Even the physiological bond, however, may not be strong enough to protect the child when the parent is enraged or in pain. But adoption poses an additional, complicating factor. And adopted children, I believe, are particularly vulnerable to any abuse because of the fact that they have all been relinquished by or lost their original parents.

Closed adoption, with its accompanying pattern of denial and secrecy, is a perfect setting for physical and sexual abuse. Adopted children from closed adoptions, in my observation, often feel an especially crippling lack that comes from being severed from their origins. That feeling of lack becomes a sense of worthlessness and a sense of not even being entitled to have one's own feelings. There is a growing body of wisdom, based on clinical observation and research, that a pervasive sense of shame—feeling I am bad, I am worthless—is at the root of most dysfunctional human behavior, from addictions to violence. I propose that there is a form of shame among children of closed adoption that is based on the way in which the relinquishment and adoption have been carried out. It is, I believe, a deep sense of having been abandoned because of inadequacy, and it produces a feeling of guilt for even being alive.

Is it not logical that, in order not to have to continually feel the pain of abandonment, a child would create a false image of himself or herself that is a "good" self? Is it not also logical that an adopted child might need to see his or her adoptive parents as either perfect or awful? And, either way, doesn't the child need to maintain a certain distance from the parents? This theme may be repeated by adoptive parents who do not feel they are good enough because they couldn't have children of their own, and who therefore end up seeing their adopted child as either perfect or awful.

When adopted children are the victims of any form of abuse within the family, rather than turn the blame outward, they, like children generally, tend to turn it in on themselves. This is what Ann was doing in assuming the abuse was her fault. It is terrifying for people to think of how vulnerable and dependent they were as infants. What if a person sensed as an infant that he or she could not depend upon the big person upon whom he or she needed to depend? The specter of being abandoned a second time may be locked inside every child who is adopted. This fear is given added force when the child has no knowledge of or contact with the mother who placed him or her for adoption.

I hope that Ann's story will give adoptees—particularly those who were abused in any way as children—permission to bring their secrets out into the open. They will then discover that their sense of guilt and shame and any self-abuse they have acted out is an understandable part of a pattern shared by many adoptees (and, interestingly enough, by most birth mothers who have not been able to resolve their guilt and shame). If adoptees only knew that what haunted them was common to people who were adopted, especially in closed adoptions, then they might not feel so alone and might be able to seek help and healing, as Ann has.

Ann let me tell her story because, as she said, "It may help someone who is struggling and hasn't talked to anybody."

Ann is not by nature either reserved or inarticulate. But when it comes to the subject of abuse, she speaks with great difficulty, and that made it difficult to interview her. It proved easiest for her to have a list of questions she could answer in her own time with her friend Kay at her side. She spoke her responses softly into a tape recorder at Kay's home, a home that is a haven for Ann, and Kay's low voice is on the tape repeatedly, gently reminding Ann of things she's forgotten or doesn't want to say, helping her find words to say out loud what she is holding back, and all the while giving loving support. Ann's words come out haltingly, and often with the same self-mocking or self-deprecating tone in which she spoke during the first months of group therapy.

"I was nearly the last one adopted. My mom and dad decided to adopt kids after my mom had had a number of pregnancies that had ended in miscarriage and had been warned that it would be very dangerous to her health to try again. When they first began looking into adoption, they wanted children so badly they told the agency they would take any child, healthy or disabled. Most of the babies who came to them were diagnosed as having some sort of physical impairment, but only a few of us turned out to have problems that couldn't be fixed with minimal treatment.

"All but one of us was adopted as a baby. The one who was not was taken in as a foster child at birth. My mom took her even though she was born addicted to drugs her mother had been taking in pregnancy. Mom saw her through her initial period of illness from withdrawal, cared for her as though she were her child, and eventually she and Dad were allowed to adopt her."

All the adoptions were done through the same religious social service agency. The couple won the hearts of the workers at the agency for their selflessness, and Ann's mother was once given an award from the agency declaring she was Woman of the Year.

Ann has always known she was adopted: "My parents began telling each of us when we were very young, so I never knew anything else. We never had to find it out from other people. I remember bragging about it at one time; all of us used to." Being adopted never emerged as an issue for Ann during her entire childhood. "It was just part of my reality." She didn't resent it or regret it or wish it were otherwise. "I didn't think about it at all."

She knows nothing about her birth parents. "I wish I did know now, but I don't want to ask. I don't want to make Mom upset, and I know that would, because it did when some of my other brothers and sisters asked her for information when they were trying to find their biological parents." As far back as Ann can recall, her mother has had a bad heart. "I remember her having an attack in her early forties, when she had to go on an oxygen tank. She's never been really well." Her mother's physical problems have deeply affected Ann, who feels responsible for her mother's well-being and for keeping the family together. Ann has not considered that being adopted might have had anything to do with the deep feeling of responsibility she has for her entire family.

Ann's earliest memory is of the day her family moved to the home in which they now live. She was three years old. "I don't know how we got there, but I remember seeing the yard at the side of the house. It had a garden and there were flowers. I also remember my room. It still looks the same today."

She has pleasant memories of being at her mother's side every week when her mother hosted the local Cub Scout troop. She loved being part of all the boys' activities. "They paid attention to me!" When she was four years old, she and her older brother Anthony were put in the hospital for minor eye surgery to correct congenital problems they both had. "I remember my brother having stitches in his eyes, but I don't remember mine."

She remembers the first day of school. She rode the school bus with her best friend, who lived on the same block, and Ann's mother waved good-bye from the bus stop. She liked school; she really liked her teachers those first few years, as they gave her personal attention. "I was part of a group of kids who sucked their thumbs!" Her friends could come to her home after school and sometimes Ann went to their houses. It was a happy time. She doesn't recall feeling like she lacked anything.

Ann began to play the drums when she was nine, and she has vivid memories of the night each week the entire family gathered in the living room to play music. "Each of us kids played some musical instrument. We'd have a recital and take turns playing. I *never* liked to perform."

The children—who ranged in age from Ann to her oldest brother, who was eleven years her senior—all had their own group activities, such as Scouts, that kept them busy after school as they got older. The family also did a lot of things together, going on trips to the lake and trips to the mountains to ski. And every Sunday, every religious day, there was always church. "We *had* to go to church, even if it meant rushing back from a camping trip and changing into our church clothes without time for a shower." For as long as Ann can remember there was always early morning religious instruction, taught in the family room by Ann's mother, who believed that the local religious school didn't teach it properly.

Theirs was, to all appearances, a model, happy family. "There was nothing wrong," Ann says derisively. "No divorces, no children born out of wedlock. At least not that anyone's supposed to know about!" In fact, there have been a number of early divorces among the older siblings, and even a child born to a sister who wasn't married at the time. But the outer world was supposed to believe it was an ideal family. And the family maintained its facade; that's the only way their parents would have it, "especially Mom." The parents' attitude has made it difficult in recent years, because on holidays none of the divorced siblings are permitted to bring their new sweethearts to the house. The older kids have begun to rebel against that and stay away on holidays. Ann has not been able to fix that.

However perfect the family might have seemed to the outside world, that's not the way it felt to Ann, especially once she got old enough to observe her mother. "My mother was always so preoccupied, always busy helping other people and doing projects to help people. She had pen pals around the world, with whom she corresponded regularly. She was a teacher's aide at my school, on the PTA, and always volunteering her time to some cause or other."

With all the outer-directed busyness, there was a distinct lack of attention toward the children at home. "My mother was always there," says Ann, "but she was never *there*. I don't ever remember there being any kind of affection, except when we kids left for school in the morning or went off on a trip of some kind. Then we always gave her a kiss on the cheek. It was like a command performance; there wasn't any feeling." Ann remembers she got the most positive attention when she was sick and stayed home from school. "Mom would bring a hot lemon drink and whatever I wanted to eat. Sometimes she would sit with me."

If her mother was preoccupied and always busy, she was at least usually at home. Ann's father, on the other hand, she seldom remembers being at home. "And when he was home, he was always involved in his projects." Ann recalls seeing few signs of affection between her parents. "Dad was always in the den, and Mom was usually in the kitchen. A kiss on the cheek, maybe, now and then. But I never saw them hug."

Behavior was judged by her mother, and her standards were strict. "You had to do things according to her rules, and if we didn't, Dad was gonna hear about it! Mom never sat still. And we were always expected to be doing something, to keep busy and to be doing something productive." It must have been a huge job for one adult, trying to take care of the house and all the children, in addition to carrying out so many other projects. At one time, Ann says, there were five children in diapers. Everyone beyond the diaper stage had chores to do each day, a schedule of which was taped to the refrigerator door.

Her mother regularly resorted to threatening the children with, "If you don't mind me, I'll tell your father!" Ann says, "She also spanked us until we did what she told us to do and were 'happy campers' again. Whenever she told Dad he would also punish us. We would get it doubly! But his wasn't so bad *most* of the time, except when he used the belt. Usually we just had to sit 'time out' or do push-ups. I was mostly afraid of Mom." When her mother reached her limits, she was known to grab the offending child (by the hair if the child was a girl) and throw the child against the wall or kick him or her. Usually, however, punishment was limited to yelling and spanking. As

Ann grew older she discovered ways to stay on her mother's good side.

But she never found any way to avoid the criticism that was meted out frequently to all the children. "There was *always* something you could do better! It's still that way." Just last week Ann cleaned up her room, which she has to do regularly, according to an agreement she has with her parents. "Dad came in and looked around and said it wasn't good enough. Then he told me exactly what I should have done, how I should have put things in boxes I should have gotten from the garage, how I should have organized everything differently."

Sometimes there were alliances among the children, and periodically a few of them would get together to talk about what a "jerk" Dad was or how "Mom and Dad are unfair!" They never dared present their case to their parents. Ann has a sister with whom she is close. They are only a few months apart in age, but as children, Ann always took care of her. There was also one brother who managed to be close to all of his younger brothers and sisters. "We could talk to him."

From as far back as she can remember, Ann was the good kid, careful to avoid getting in trouble. This eventually brought her special favors and trust from her parents, as, for example, when she was a teenager and was free to join whatever club she wanted and to do whatever she wanted after school. But what made life easier with her parents didn't help life with her siblings.

"I wasn't well liked among the girls, and all the kids thought I was spoiled, that I got away with everything. They teased me all the time about it, because I never did anything wrong." The others would get in trouble at school and even run away from home occasionally. Not Ann. She didn't dare. "When one of us got into trouble at school, Dad—he didn't believe in allowing other people to punish his kids physically—would come to school. He'd whip the kid himself in the principal's office. It had a large window, so everyone in the schoolyard could see who was being punished!"

Ann grew up trying to be the rescuer of the underdog. She can't stand dissension and has always tried to keep the family peace, ever since she was five. That was the year the sexual abuse started. At least that's as far back as the memories go. "I couldn't tell my parents, because I wanted to keep the family together. Dad already had hate in his eyes for one of my brothers, and I didn't want to be the cause of any more of that."

When it began she was in kindergarten. It began with her oldest brother, who was sixteen at the time and big for his age. To Ann, "He didn't seem sixteen, he seemed much older!" Ann didn't know this brother well; they were not close. He was not around the house much.

"It was always at night. He took me out to the garage. That was where things would happen." She can't go on, can't say anything more. Later on the tape, she does. It was mostly fondling, and her brother never said anything while he was doing it, at least not that she can presently recall. It wasn't simply him fondling her. Ann also had to fondle him. "When it was his turn, he always guided my hand. I hated it! Every time he decided to go out to the garage, I knew it was going to happen."

She thought it was a secret what she and her big brother did, a shameful, dirty secret. But in retrospect she realizes that her father, if not also her mother, must have known. She recalls once hearing her father threatening her brother: "If you *ever* touch her again! . . ." That's all she can remember.

The abuse by her brother continued, and she does not know precisely when it stopped, but it finally did. She never considered telling her parents. She was afraid of what they might do to her brother, "especially what Dad would do! He didn't have any respect for my brother, and I didn't want it to worsen due to me. So I kept it a secret. Dad tends to become really violent." There is a long pause on the tape after that admission. Kay carefully draws Ann out with more questions. "We were never allowed to get angry, not us kids!" Ann continues.

"*That* was disrespectful! Feeling sad was 'feeling sorry for yourself,' and we weren't supposed to do *that* either!"

She does recall an incident where a neighbor called the police and accused Ann's father of physically abusing one of her brothers in the back yard. That had made him very angry and he had later taken it out on her brother. "He gets angry a lot." At one point Ann admits she had been afraid her father might even kill her brother.

The abuse did not stop there; it had only begun. Three other brothers began to sexually molest her during the next few years. Recalling them all, she says, "There were two that don't bother me as much as the main one. It seemed like his went on forever!" The three other brothers used the family room couch, so the family room is forever marked in her imagination with being molested and being unable to protect herself from the repeated violations.

How could that have happened with Ann's mother usually home? Kay asks that question, knowing the answer but wanting Ann to say it. "It always happened after dinner," answers Ann. "Mom and Dad were always in the kitchen, because I could always hear them!" Theirs is a large house, all on one level, so it was not difficult for the children to do things without their parents' knowledge. But sexual abuse is something apart from the ordinary secrets children keep from their parents.

What the younger brothers continued they must have learned from somewhere. "I know now for sure that Leonard at least was sexually abused by the oldest." What drove the oldest to abuse his younger sister and younger brother no one yet knows. But it must be assumed he was only taking out his own rage on those smaller and less able to defend themselves. Something had to have produced the rage that fueled his assaults.

The brother whose abuse she says most disturbed her was Leonard. He began when Ann was in the sixth, or perhaps the fifth, grade and did not stop until Ann was in the tenth grade. "It seems much longer than five years," she says very quietly. When it began Ann had already developed breasts. She developed young. "He would always get me into the family room and start touching me after I had changed into my pajamas. On the couch, that's where everything with him happened."

That is what she thinks was the case when she first shares some of the details of her abuse. A week later she tells me that she had a sudden memory of more than one occasion where it had also happened in the back yard during the day. That both shocks and disturbs her, as new memories of this sort always do, because it leaves her wondering what else she doesn't remember. But this, I have found, and others have observed, is the way memories of sexual abuse often return, in bits and pieces, often beginning with less offensive memories. It is as if the unconscious mind, which has worked so hard to protect the person from the trauma of remembering, has to test whether the conscious mind can handle a small amount of the truth before it will disgorge more.

Ann hesitates again before continuing. Kay once more prompts her, this time asking if it had always started with kissing. "Yeah. And then we'd always wind up lying on the couch, with me on the bottom." He began with her breasts. "After he finished with his hands ... then he moved to the lower region, the usual things. . . . Then it was his turn to get satisfied." Her voice sounded full of the disgust she felt each time she remembered it. At first her brother had had to guide her hand. After a while he didn't have to; she did whatever she was expected to do.

Later I learn that this brother, for whatever reason, never entered her vagina with his penis, at least not as far as she can now remember. She can recall him ejaculating in her mouth a few times. She has yet to share any of these details with the group, as if saying it out loud in that situation would be too disgusting. Most, but not all, other women in the group have dared to talk about much of the details of their abuse. It is cleansing to do so. For some it has been particularly disturbing that they can recall no visual details, only bodily sensations of pain and invasion and feelings of trauma and terror.

Ann does not remember her brother Leonard ever talking to her while molesting her. Perhaps he imagined that by his being silent, his little sister would not remember what he was doing. It is often this way. Children are not supposed to remember. That is one of the cardinal beliefs of child rearing of the past several hundred years. It is what has allowed adults to do despicable things to children, especially very young children or infants, with the belief that there will be no reprisals. The child will never remember.

Ann felt sick, dirty, and guilty each time. "There was nothing I could say or do. I was scared." To make it worse, Leonard was her favorite brother. Again, she couldn't possibly tell her parents, because of her fear of her father's violent reaction. "Plus I was afraid of what Leonard would do to me if I said anything. I was afraid I would lose his love."

Ann survived by pretending to herself and the world that nothing was going on. "If I said anything, the family would be pulled apart." The molestations by her other two brothers did not continue for long, and occurred during the time Leonard was abusing her. With them there was collusion. "I know the two of them talked about it, because I can remember playing a fun game with the two of them!" Her voice is full of sarcasm.

The abuse from Leonard finally came to an end when he went into the Air Force. At that point Ann blotted all memories of sexual abuse from her mind. She dated a few times in high school. "I did it because it was expected." Mostly she kept busy with activities, among them sports, Glee Club, and Scouts.

The memories surfaced suddenly last year, when she was twenty-two, after six years of lying hidden. It may seem unbelievable to some that victims of childhood sexual abuse can totally block all of the incidents and every trace of the feelings from waking and dreaming consciousness, during the time of the abuse and for many years afterward. But the denial, for Ann and for others in the group, was so total that, even during the time the abuse was going on, she could not admit to herself that it was happening. So of course she also could not admit it to anyone else, even someone as close to her as Kay, who was close to Ann during most of those years.

At twenty-two Ann had a boyfriend, and they went to a nearby resort for the weekend. Ann says she went with a premeditated purpose in mind. "I wanted to see if I was still alive or not." She means sexually alive. "It was with somebody I cared about, and I thought that might make a difference." She suspected there was something wrong, because she had had no sexual response with anyone she had dated. "We were on the couch, and I should have had feelings of some kind, but there were no feelings there."

"I knew I had no sexual feelings before that weekend—I *never* did have any—but I just thought there was something wrong with me." Instead of her feeling sexual arousal with a young man she cared deeply about, there were *no* physical feelings whatsoever. Ann was too numb psychically to be able to stand outside of herself and say, "My feelings are shut down." From the inside it felt to her like she was sick. Instead of arousal, there suddenly came a flashback to her brother and herself on the couch in the same position. "I was really frustrated, mad, angry. This guy was someone I cared about, and I couldn't have any sexual feelings with him."

After that weekend when the memory surfaced, Ann began having nightmares. "They were really memories of what had happened." Sometimes she would wake herself up during the dream, and when that happened she would feel as if the abuse had just occurred. Other times she would wake with the clear memory and horrible pain in her vagina. The day after the nightmare, Ann would be moody and morose. But she didn't consider telling anyone about it until one day it became too much to contain, she was so afraid.

Kay first learned about what had happened during Ann's weekend with her boyfriend when Ann said, "I have something to tell you, and *don't* let me get out of it!" Kay sat her down on the couch and slowly drew out of Ann what was bothering her. Ann was adamant to Kay that her parents, especially her mother, must never find out. "Everyone thinks we are the perfect family! All my friends *love* my mom. People come over and she always is so friendly and takes care of them. But she forgets that when it comes to me."

Ann showed fine judgment in selecting Kay to be the one she told. Kay is a recovering alcoholic who works hard on her own healing, and so she easily has compassion for Ann's mistrust and fears and never judges the way Ann functioned to survive. She offers Ann the right balance between simply listening and supporting whatever Ann is feeling and pushing Ann to keep facing the issues that have been making her feel so crazy. In Kay's presence Ann paid her the highest compliment: "With her I can say whatever I want and know she'll never say I'm wrong. I've said a few things that I thought might change her opinion of me, and it didn't at all. If I said some of those things at home—not anything about the abuse, just personal things—it would change everything!"

Ann and Kay both describe Ann's parents as extremely critical people, especially Ann's father. Ann says, "They are *so* judgmental." Ann grew up feeling nothing she did was ever good enough; there was always something that should be improved. Ann says her mother still keeps everything bottled up inside and never confides her real feelings to anyone, even her closest friends. How could she when she has put so much energy into making the world believe hers is the perfect family? She may enjoy playing confidante when others have problems, but she herself must remain above it all.

Ann is not taken in by her mother's seeming compassion for the problems of others; being faced with the fact of abuse within her own family would be something different. She says, "My mother is so set in her beliefs, she would *never* accept it! Also, I didn't want *anyone* outside the family to know. I felt really bad for what I did. I thought it was all my fault!" She adds, "Of course, I don't think that now." Kay congratulates her, saying, "That's the first time I've ever heard you say that and sound like you meant it!"

Kay has had to remind Ann on numerous occasions that

a child is never to blame for the sexual experiences an adult or older child draws him or her into or forces upon him or her. Even if the child acts in a way that adults would say is provocative, the child is never asking for sex. The child is not in a position of power in the relationship and therefore cannot be held responsible in any way for what can only be termed sexual *abuse*. This is something many people do not understand, that there can be no real consent between a child and an older person when it comes to sex. The child is always a victim.

Once the dreams began coming, there was no controlling them. They came wherever Ann happened to be spending the night. "If I was at Kay's house overnight, she would sometimes wake me up because I was moving around in my sleep." Kay adds that when she got up in the night and checked on Ann, she would find her curled tightly in the fetal position, kicking out at some invisible thing and agitated by whatever she was dreaming. Sometimes she could soothe Ann by talking to her and stroking her head; at other times the only way to calm her was to wake her up. During the dreams, and sometimes afterward, there would be dreadful physical pain inside her vagina.

Kay kept her promise to Ann and did not reveal anything to Ann's parents, though she began to encourage Ann to seek help so she could heal. She knew that even her love for Ann would not be enough to heal such serious wounds. For a year Ann told no one else about the abuse.

"Everyone I thought of telling I figured would tell my parents. They'd say the reason they told was to help me. I didn't want that. *I* wanted to deal with it. I wanted to tell them when I was ready." The abuse had destroyed her trust in anyone older than her, with the exception of Kay. Even Kay hadn't learned about it for seven years. Ann was in a bind. To tell someone she first had to trust that person. "I didn't trust anybody. Inside or outside the family." Trust was probably the first thing the abuse had destroyed.

On the one hand it seems logical and ethical that Ann should have the right to control what information she lets others know about herself. But when it comes to abuse, victims of any age are seldom able to see the situation clearly. There is too much guilt and a misplaced feeling of responsibility. That's one of the symptoms of the terrible wounding caused by the abuse.

Because she was molested by four of her brothers, Ann felt that there was something about her that made them do it. That simply increased her sense of isolation, guilt, and despair. Ultimately it led to her feeling that she deserved to die. When Ann first came to the group she was having frequent thoughts of suicide.

Once she had finally broken the silence, it was only a matter of time before Ann would have to take action for her own healing. "I couldn't go to individual therapy," she said, "just because I'm scared of one-on-one situations with somebody I don't know. It took me months to talk very much in the group. It takes me a long time to talk with somebody about what's really going on inside me."

"What made me realize that I needed outside help, because I didn't think I did, was talking to my friend." When Kay first suggested Ann look for a group for women survivors of childhood sexual abuse, Ann resisted. "I flipped out! *No way!* I told her, 'I don't want *anybody* to know. What if somebody in that group knew my family!'" There was no way she would ever tell anybody else, she said adamantly. And she wasn't going to go through therapy! Today she can laugh about those pronouncements. Kay can also joke about it, because she no longer is in the difficult position of feeling like Ann's welfare is totally in her hands.

By the time Ann finally reached out for help, it had become a matter of life and death. The suicidal thoughts and feelings were coming often. She was at Kay's house one afternoon talking about the incest, and Kay once again said she should call and find out about therapy. It was a day Ann remembers clearly, for it was a turning point. "Kay put the suggestion in my head," says Ann, "but *I* made the call! She handed me the telephone book, and I opened to the yellow pages." Kay suggested she look up Community Services in the front section. There was a heading called Victim Assistance. From that she got the phone number of what turned out to be an agency that worked exclusively with sexual abuse and incest. That group had pioneered in the field of treatment and was known for keeping families intact while making it mandatory (if necessary, with the help of the courts) that *everyone* within the family participate both in individual counseling and group therapy.

The first call didn't produce instantaneous results. The one group specifically for women who had been sexually abused as children met during the daytime on a day when Ann had a class. Her phone number (she gave Kay's) was taken down, and she was told someone would call her to tell her about other available groups. "I just went to pieces afterward!" she recalls. "I started crying and everything." Kay was there to comfort Ann and congratulate her on the big step she had just taken. The next day there was a call from a therapist who ran a Tuesday evening women's group. She wanted to meet with Ann and talk about what that group would be like and what Ann wanted from a group, so the therapist and she could find out if it seemed right for her. Ann could not find time in her schedule of classes and a part-time job. So it was decided that she should go to the first session and see how she felt afterward. "I didn't say much on the phone, and when I did go I think she was really shocked to see me. She hadn't thought I would!"

It was essential, Ann felt, that her mother not find out that she was going to counseling. "If she found out I was going . . . ooohhh! I'd be in deep trouble!" It was her parents' code: "You *never* talked about family matters to anyone outside the family." This made it difficult during the first months of group therapy, because it meant Ann had to lie to her mother each week about where she was going Tuesday night. "And I *hate* having to lie!" Ann says emphatically. "I don't feel I should have to!" She continues to find proof that her mother is not a safe person in whom to confide. "Just today," she says, "Mom said one of my brothers tells everything about our family, especially the negative things! She said, 'It's not a proper thing to do!' "

Ann made a commitment with herself and with the group therapist that she would try out the group and give it eight sessions before giving herself permission to quit. The therapist asked for the same commitment from everyone in the group. Like everyone else in the group, Ann began going with reluctance and reservations.

Week after week when she did manage to speak, she would usually make a cryptic remark about what the previous week had been like and how she had either "felt like killing myself" or "gone crazy" at a friend's (Kay's) house. Suicide was on her mind. The pot was boiling and because the lid was still on, she was in danger of exploding. Once she said, "I picked up a kitchen knife in my friend's kitchen on Saturday, and I thought about killing myself with it. But I didn't want to mess up her house." Ann had company; most of the rest of the group had also at least thought about killing themselves as the solution to their anguish over the abuse.

For the first few months after the first memory had come, when the nightmares were also coming often, she thought about suicide several times a week. "I had thoughts, feelings, even plans. It always seemed the only solution." Whatever way she thought of doing it, in her mind it had to look like an accident. After several months of group therapy and frequent sessions talking with Kay about all the things she couldn't yet say within the group, the urges changed somewhat. She still continued to imagine killing herself, but whether it appeared to be a suicide no longer mattered; at least that constraint was off.

The evening Ann started group therapy, she mentioned killing herself, and the therapist asked her to promise to call her if she ever felt like she would act on her impulse. Another woman in the group gave Ann her phone number and also asked her to please call her if she ever thought she might do it; this woman's only brother had committed suicide, and it was a constant fear that she herself would do the same or that another around her would. Kay also extracted a promise from Ann that she would not do anything without calling or coming to see her first.

"That promise has stopped me on several occasions," Ann says. Today, six months after starting group therapy, the urge is still strong when it comes, but it comes much less frequently. But with Ann, as with most of the women in the group, there are still sweeping moods of self-hate and the impulse toward self-destruction.

One additional piece of information about Ann's background she had not permitted anyone, even Kay, to know until recently. It had made her too ashamed, even more ashamed than the abuse at the hands of her brothers. One of Ann's sisters had also made sexual overtures to her when Ann had just entered high school, during the time her brother Leonard was abusing her. "That's a hard thing to tell somebody," Ann says, "when you're not sure of your own sexuality."

It was her favorite sister, Frances, the person for whom Ann had covered on numerous occasions when Frances had done things that would have gotten her in trouble had her parents found out. On that occasion, as on many others, Ann felt she needed to protect someone else more than herself.

When Ann first started with the group she hated it. "I felt it was a waste of my time! I know I'm not comfortable speaking because it's speaking about me, but I have come a long way. In the beginning I had a hard time saying anything. But once recently I was the second one to speak!" (The group sometimes follows a ritual of everyone checking in, each woman saying how she is doing and how the intervening week has gone. Ann used to be the last one to check in, but no longer.)

It is hard for her to say precisely how much she has changed since she began attending the group. For a number of months, she never wanted to be there and would sit in the group wishing she could be at Kay's house. With Kay there was always the extra encouragement for Ann to keep talking, to say a little more, to look at something she didn't want to look at. Within the group there was no pressure to disclose more than she felt safe disclosing. Trust formed slowly. For each person the process of healing has its own innate rhythm and sense of timing.

Kay feels Ann has come a long way in her healing. She reminds Ann that she has come far enough to have recently told another friend about the abuse. Ann nods. "This girl was talking to me one day and she was very upset. She wouldn't tell me what the real reason was, and I thought I knew. She was acting exactly like I had. I felt like she needed to be held, just like I do." Ann realized that telling her friend that she had been abused might help her friend face her own abuse. She had never before told anyone but Kay. Kay had told her there would probably come a time when Ann would be able to tell another person about her abuse. "She said I would feel I needed to tell someone, just for me, or to help them."

So Ann took the risk and told her friend that she had been sexually abused, hoping that might make her friend feel safe enough to confide in her. "Initially she didn't respond. She went away without saying anything, and I thought that must mean I was wrong! I felt like I was going crazy. But then my friend came back and told me she *had* been abused." It turned out not to have been incest but a case of sexual assault that was haunting her, for it made her feel dirty and guilty as well as frightened.

It happened one more time that a woman confided in Ann. "This time it threw me totally off, because I hadn't expected it. I didn't even know this person well. She was training under me at the restaurant [Ann is a waitress during some lunch hours]. She came up to me and said she wanted to talk. Then she told me her neighbor had raped her a few weeks before. I talked to her, but I didn't tell her about myself. I couldn't!" On that occasion her friend Kay was out of town, and Ann ended up "wildly upset."

Recently Ann has begun thinking about what part being adopted might have played in the abuse. At first she seemed surprised when I suggested that being relinquished by her birth mother might have contributed to her feeling of worthlessness.

Ann says, "I may be wrong, but I think children who are adopted, if they don't know their own history and don't know why their parents gave them up for adoption, think about suicide more."

She has only recently begun to think of searching. "I had never thought of looking for my biological mother, because my adoptive parents were my parents." But when the subject of abuse started to come up in her life, so did the idea of searching for her biological mother. "I think it's because I have . . ." she hesitates, "that I don't feel like I'm getting what I need or want from my parents right now. And I have this little dream which a lot of adopted people have about their natural parents. . . ." She does not finish the thought. "And I need that." It is difficult for Ann to speak out loud about her needs and what she is not getting, perhaps has never gotten, from her parents.

She does feel the makeup of her particular family has had a significant impact upon her: the isolation and lack of intimacy within her family has made it difficult to express many feelings and has made it seem impossible to ask for help. "I think the size of our family makes it harder. Everything is harder, especially being close to your parents. I really don't know if this would have happened in a smaller family."

Child abuse, including sexual abuse, occurs in families of every size, composition, and complexion. The common thread is that at least one person does not control his or her impulses and directs anger and frustration at the least powerful person in the family, the child. Another element common in families where there is abuse is the existence of a family myth, created by the parent or parents, which the children learn they must follow. Often they do not need to be told; children are keen observers of adult behavior and mimic it, because it is all they know. Certainly Ann's parents could have kept closer watch on their children in the evenings. But sexual abuse is not something that happens only after dark. The problem is not how closely the children were observed, but what caused them to abuse each other.

Today Ann is clear about what advice she would offer children or adult adoptees in a situation similar to hers. "I would say that no matter what you think this would do to your parents or your brothers or sisters, go ahead and tell someone. And I would advise telling someone other than your family first. Because you can try it out and see what response you are going to get. Realize that the person is probably going to have to tell somebody about it, especially if you are underage."

Ann does not recommend telling someone who is required by law to tell the authorities. "But once you start remembering, I think you ought to tell someone. Then your healing process can start and it won't take so long and your life won't get so messed up. Your life will get back to normal once you begin, and you can begin trusting again."

Knowing what she now knows about the difference it has made in her life to be in the process of healing, she still feels she wouldn't have told her parents but she certainly would have told Kay earlier. Kay was there for her all along; Ann simply wasn't ready to reach out. She suggests that you begin by testing the person to see whether you can trust that person to keep confidential what you tell him or her. "Try telling them something that you think they might tell your parents. And *see* if they do!"

Ann no longer speaks in such black-and-white terms about how she will never, under any circumstances, tell her parents. "Now it's, 'When I'm *ready* to tell my parents.' That's not for a while yet. I don't think it will be until I move out." She remains living at home, because as long as she does her parents will pay her college tuition and fees and she feels there is no other way she can complete college.

Probably Ann's mother has some clue regarding the sexual abuse that occurred within her family. Denial runs strong in dysfunctional families. Current research suggests that family members do know the truth; they simply can't admit it. Ann's mother is an avid fan of television talk shows and particularly relishes ones where some emotionally charged subject is being aired. She has called Ann in to watch shows on several occasions when the subject has been child abuse. "If we're watching a show together, and usually it's the father they're talking about— it's never the brothers or sisters—my mother is always protective of the family, especially the girls. She'll say, 'Well, I *always* checked on you guys'—she's talking about at night, after we had gone to bed—'and there's no way this could have happened in our family!' " Her disclaimer makes no sense; she is comforting herself by saying it.

Ann says it is hard for her to hear her mother flatly insist that nothing could go wrong in their family. "Mom is so blind! She doesn't realize it could be my brothers."

Despite the fact that Ann may never feel it is in her own best interests to confront her mother with the truth, she has hope for her future these days. "I don't have to hide anymore. It's still really hard to trust any male right now. Mostly it is the fear of having the flashbacks and the nightmares reoccur if I am really attracted to someone." Yet she can see the strides she has made. In the beginning it was a nightmare all day long, with unwanted feelings and flashbacks coming at any time, and then insomnia at night for fear of what might come, and, when she did sleep, waking up to horrifying dreams. "When I am dreaming these days, I don't have as much physical pain as I used to." The dreams do not come so often now, sometimes not even once a week. She knows it will continue to get better.

As Christmas holiday approached, and with it the prospect of all her brothers coming home, Ann began to get anxious. She kept rehearsing over and over how she would greet each of her brothers, how she would avoid each of them while they were home. She stayed away from home as many hours as possible each day, mostly at Kay's house. She was especially afraid of seeing her brother Leonard. "I don't know what I will say or do!" she confided in the group. She couldn't imagine giving him a greeting hug, much less looking him in the eye. Yet she managed to survive it. "I wasn't my normal sweet self," she said with a half-smile. "And neither was he. I was nasty and he was standoffish. We managed not to talk at all."

When it was over and all the relatives had gone, she began to talk with Kay about something she'd been secretly considering: writing a letter to Leonard. They had discussed it before. Kay was a firm believer that putting things into words and writing them down helped. A month ago Ann began to work on the letter. It took three weeks to compose. She wrote it at Kay's house. One Tuesday evening she brought a draft of it to the group and, prompted by everyone's interest, read it aloud. The therapist asked if she would like to have any comments from people, and Ann said she would. Everyone congratulated her, not only for her courage to write it but for how beautifully written it was. It was a clear, calm, yet feeling, letter. Ann has permitted me to reprint portions of it here:

> Dear Leonard,
> ... Before I go on—*no one* in the family knows about this except you and me. I hope it will stay that way. I feel I need to tell you what an awful thing you did to me. By law we are legally brother and sister—therefore what you did to me is called incest. You asked me why I don't have a boyfriend! It's because my trust in those I loved was broken, and it's going to take a long time for me to learn to trust again. Thanks to a couple of friends and the support therapy group I attend (Mom and Dad don't know about the group), my trust is developing slowly. If you wonder why I didn't stop you, it was because I was afraid of you and I couldn't tell Mom and Dad for fear of what they would do to you. I responded to your wishes for fear of losing your love. There are times when I actually hate you. There are times when I experience terrible nightmares of those times on the family room couch, and I am so scared,

so angry, so alone, and just want to die to be rid of the pain. (You don't need to worry about me committing suicide or anything else stupid, because I'm getting the help I need in that department.) . . .

I'm writing this to let you know what an effect all of this has had on my life. If you want to respond to this (I hope you will) or if you have any questions, you can write me at this address, so Mom and Dad won't wonder what you are writing to me about. If you send it to home, it will only cause me more pain. . . .

She told the group she didn't know what her brother might do in response. She had come to a place in her own healing where she had to say something. She expected nothing in return. She got a reply from Leonard within three days, just a short letter saying he would call her. She talked to him from Kay's house, and it was a long conversation. Throughout, her brother kept apologizing over and over for what he had done. He ended by asking Ann to please call him or in some way let him know at any time when she was angry at him, and he promised to write her a long letter. After she got off the phone and for the next few days, Ann felt guilty for having written the letter. Once more she was causing someone else pain. But she talked to Kay about it and realized that her feeling of guilt was inappropriate.

Overall, the whole experience was positive. She thinks now that perhaps the reason for her initial feeling of guilt was that the abuse was out in the open for the first time. Kay feels perhaps Ann's reaction had to do with the fact that during the conversation Leonard mentioned that he had been sexually molested by the oldest brother too. It had happened before Leonard began to molest Ann.

The letter her brother promised to send never arrived. Ann waited almost a month and then called him on several occasions. Each time she called he was out. She left messages but he never returned her calls. She feels betrayed and hasn't decided what to do next. She realizes she cannot give him power over her healing; that is in *her* hands.

"The bad times are still bad," she says, "but I can talk about it more." She is not afraid to reach out. The process of healing is uneven and jerky. When the highs are there she feels so good, she even forgets for a time. But within a moment it can feel like the bottom has dropped out of her world and she has fallen into a dark abyss. It can happen so suddenly that she doesn't even have time to realize that it is related to the abuse. Those times are dark and frightening. The times between the difficult times, however, have a more solid, substantial feel about them.

Ann still has mental lapses, times when she cannot put words to the feelings, the memories, even when they involve memories that she has already talked about. "I'm always having to ask Kay, 'What happened?'" Ann is slowly uncovering the pieces and putting them together. It is all part of the healing process. It's a long, uphill journey. Sometimes it also seems like a desperate battle waged against unseen enemies in the dark of night; but morning is finally appearing on the horizon, and the forces of darkness are dissipating.

PART II

ADOPTION IN PROCESS:

The Challenge To Evolve

PHIL:

Half a Century of Change

WHEN HE TALKS Phil Adams seems to be playing to a crowd, although he works in a private office and seldom sees more than two people at a time. With his arching, bushy gray eyebrows, his twinkling eyes, and the large, unlit cigar in his broad mouth, he looks the rakish old gentleman. This man may know as much about adoption law as anyone in the United States. He has been arranging direct adoptions for more than forty-five years, is the author of the standard text on adoption in the state of California, and is regularly quoted on the subject. To date he has personally shepherded about three thousand petitions for adoptions through the court system, and has never had one denied.

When Phil Adams became an attorney in 1938, adoption was a minor phenomenon in America. In the state of California, for example, there were fewer than one thousand adoptions per year prior to World War II, of which half were direct, or private, adoptions. (California has always had a larger proportion of direct adoptions than most other states.) At that time there were only two adoption agencies in his state, and they were small.

Phil recalls the strict social restraints before World War II, the strongly disapproving attitudes with which society viewed premarital sex and in particular the young woman who had made the mistake of becoming pregnant outside of marriage. The personal tragedies experienced by unfortunate young women and felt by a few guilt-ridden young men are still, for the most part, well-kept family secrets. The best a young woman could hope for was to hide the truth as long as possible, and then skip town and give birth out of everyone's sight. She would relinquish the baby for adoption and then quietly return, acting as if nothing had happened. There were few social agencies to help a woman through her grieving for the lost child and the pain of the experience she had been through alone. But society's ignorance didn't prevent individual trauma.

Then World War II began. With wartime priorities families were broken up, and young women were no longer so carefully protected. Their fathers were in the war and their mothers were suddenly in the work force, often putting in six-day work weeks for the war effort, leaving babies in the nation's first day care centers and older children home alone after school. Young women dreamed of serving their country too, and as soon as they graduated from high school, many went off in search of the current romantic dream—to serve their country in some faraway battleground. First came the Bataan nurses, then the Corregidor nurses, then the WACs, the WAVEs, the Women Marines, and the young women who joined the Red Cross and the USO. Phil Adams remembers the innocence of those years and also the noncombat casualties of war—the many unmarried young women who became pregnant.

"It was unthinkable for the family doctor to take those sweet young things aside and warn them what it would be like to be on, say, Saipan—with just a handful of other gals and twelve thousand lonely guys. Unheard of to give them a quick course in sex education and offer to fit them all with diaphragms. All of a sudden, here in San Francisco, they were delivering thirty to forty girls a month at the local military hospital! They were just nice girls in uniform who'd gone across the ocean to take care of our boys, that's all. But they weren't married, they hadn't the vaguest idea of how to prevent pregnancy, they couldn't get abortions, and, though they came home to deliver them, they weren't keeping the babies. There was no way they could."

Abortion was illegal in those days, and although there were doctors who would perform the operation, their services were too expensive and too hard to find for most women. Adoption suddenly acquired a new importance.

"Take my wife's good friend, Sally, who stood up for us at our wedding. Sally asked if she could ride along with me one weekend when I was driving to Los Angeles on business. Said she was going to visit a cousin there. I dropped her off at a house and expected we'd hear from her when she returned. But we didn't hear a thing from her for the next couple of months. Next time I drove down to Los Angeles, I tried to find Sally, but she had disappeared and left no trace. I told my wife, and for some reason we thought we should both go down and check all the maternity homes. We finally found Sally at a place called St. Anne's. The interesting thing was that she'd had this baby five or six weeks earlier, but she was still there because in those days at these homes a mother usually had to agree to remain at least six weeks after the birth in order to nurse her baby."

It is likely that strong bonds formed between Sally and her baby by the end of the period of nursing, making it that much more difficult for her to relinquish her baby. But the practice at least assured the child of the benefits of close, one-to-one human contact through his or her first several weeks of life. Perhaps for Sally the benefit of knowing she was giving her baby something precious, that only she could give, outweighed the pain of becoming attached to someone she knew she would leave behind. In those days there was scant choice in the matter of infant feeding. The rejection of breastfeeding in favor of artificial formulas couldn't occur until the formulas themselves had been made safe and convenient. Today, with baby formulas the popular way to freedom in mothering and no obligations placed on a mother planning to relinquish her baby, it has become not only possible but usual for women choosing adoption to carry their babies for nine months, give birth under sedation and anesthesia with no participation or consciousness, and then be separated forever from their offspring without so much as a glimpse.

Phil's story of Sally shows how much adoption practices have changed since the 1940s. "We found Sally at St. Anne's, and Alice brought her and the baby back to San Francisco on the *Harvard,* a boat that sailed the coast between Los Angeles and San Francisco. I drove back from Los Angeles and met them, and we took Sally to St. Elizabeth's Infant Hospital, where Sally left the baby. A few weeks later she finally signed the papers and gave the child up for adoption, but in the meantime there was no veil of secrecy or partitioning babies off from their mothers. She could visit her baby as often as she wished. I've always wondered why recently many women haven't even asked to see their babies before giving them up."

Sally and the Adamses never were able to find out where the baby went after the baby's stay at St. Elizabeth's, but that experience gave the young Phil Adams a taste of the need for help a woman had in arranging a humane adoption for her baby, as well as the need for the baby to have his or her advocate.

In 1943 Phil Adams, young attorney-at-law, handled his first adoption case as a licensed professional. As is usually the case in direct adoptions, he was the only attorney involved and represented the interests of all parties. The young woman in this first case had been referred to him by a local physician and was already past four months of the pregnancy when Phil met her. She wanted an abortion and her physician, who couldn't by law perform one, thought an attorney might be able to find the woman help. She was fortunate to meet Phil, as it's not difficult to imagine what might have been her fate had she insisted on an illegal abortion done quite late in pregnancy. Figures for maternal deaths in the first forty years of this century were still alarmingly high, and a large percentage of maternal mortality was the result of complications of abortion, either attempted by the desperate women themselves or done by physicians or lay practitioners who practiced in back rooms.

Phil knew where to send his client for a late abortion under the best possible, though illegal, conditions. One surgeon in San Francisco had a reputation for competence, but because of the increased risk to himself and to the woman from a late abortion, there was an $800 price tag, which was well beyond his client's means. So Phil offered her an alternative.

"I asked her, 'Have you ever thought of dropping four months out of your life and having this baby? I could find a nice place for you to stay until after the birth, and a good home for your baby.' When she said she'd like that, I took her to meet the woman she would be staying with, someone I'd helped in a similar situation a few years back, and then I referred her to a good obstetrician."

It was also Phil who drove the woman to the hospital in labor, and, when the admitting clerk asked for her surname and she hesitated, he jumped once more to the rescue. And so she was registered as Mrs. Adams. He then left her standing in the lobby with her suitcase and drove off. No fathers were permitted with their wives during labor. Those who stayed at the hospital were relegated to a small waiting room down the hall.

Meanwhile, Phil and the woman's physician had put their heads together about finding a good home for the baby, and had come up with the name of mutual friends, a couple; the wife had had a succession of miscarriages and very much wanted to have a child. The couple was telephoned and said yes without pause. And they would be delighted to take the baby as soon as he or she could leave the hospital. They also agreed to pay all of the woman's hospital and physician costs, which, in those days, Phil remembers, was all of $95 for a fourteen-day stay in a two-bed room.

"That was how long a woman was expected to remain in the hospital after birth. The medical opinion of the day said that after a woman returned home she was not supposed to walk up or down a flight of stairs for two more weeks!" With wartime nursing shortages her hospital stay was half the usual, and when she was ready to leave, Phil and a friend came to pick her up. The new parents went to the hospital to collect their baby, and the adoption was simply and speedily accomplished to the apparent satisfaction of everyone.

The second time Phil Adams arranged an adoption, he and his wife drove to the hospital themselves, picked up the baby from the nursery, and drove to the home of friends in a nearby town who had agreed to take the baby. It was the beginning of a long career of "being a professional wet nurse," a role he admittedly enjoys.

Phil Adams's third adoption occurred within the year and his specialty in adoption cases began. "A friend called me up saying she needed my help. Her husband had been away in the war and had just returned. She was a normal, lusty young woman who suddenly had been made a temporary widow by the war, and after she had crawled into the percales with one of their mutual friends in her husband's absence, lo and behold, she found herself pregnant. Of course, the only 'honorable' thing to do would have been to get a divorce, so she could marry this baby's father. But unfortunately the situation was complicated by the fact that she and her husband already had a child eighteen months old at home. Besides, they were well suited to each other, and it seemed like a crazy idea to get a divorce just for one mistake." Having recently finished his second adoption, Phil was full of creative ideas; he suggested that his friend and her husband needn't possibly wreck their first child's youth or ruin their own lives by rushing into a divorce. Why not, he suggested, place this coming baby for adoption?

"The idea knocked her over. She was a married woman, and such a thought had never entered her head. It was just *never* done!" But the solution Phil offered was better than anything the couple could think of, and it was the choice they made.

To further complicate the tale, the woman's older sister soon moved in with them, and shortly before her due date the married friend called Phil to say, "Guess what?!" It turned out that her older sister, Suzie, had been seeing the manager of the War Production Board, whose wife was committed to a mental hospital in another state. The plot thickened. "In those days you couldn't get a divorce on the ground of insanity. So Suzie was seeing a married man and had gotten herself pregnant! But everything coordinated perfectly. Suzie simply stayed home from work and took care of her sister's toddler while her sister went into the hospital for two weeks. When Suzie herself went into the hospital three months later to give birth to her baby, her sister helped her. That baby too was given up for adoption.

"In those days I was busy playing God. By then I'd personally handled three adoptions, and heck, that was three more than anyone else in town. It is interesting, all three of my first cases were adult, Caucasian females, and one of them was even married. Don't let anybody tell you this is the problem of the poor or people of some other color!"

By the time World War II ended in 1945, there were about 4500 adoptions (excluding stepparent adoptions) in just one year in the state of California, or more than four times what had been the average a decade earlier. By 1948 the number had risen again considerably; nearly 80 percent of the adoptions were private, legal placements, and the two tiny adoption agencies in the state were inundated with babies. There was suddenly a surplus on the adoption market, and attorneys like Phil Adams were kept busy trying to find homes for children.

From the beginning of his work in adoption law, Phil Adams saw his work as including counseling the mother planning to relinquish her baby, and assisting in the logistics of the transfer of the child to the new parents. Because of the conscientiousness of people like Phil Adams, it became an unwritten rule that the attorney in a direct adoption would assist the pregnant woman in finding housing and paying her bills, a job that in agency adoptions was fulfilled by the homes for the unwed. Phil took his job seriously, and today, many years later, he still maintains an up-to-date file of people willing to take pregnant women into their homes while the women await birth. The file was stuffed with names from the mid-1940s right through the 1960s, and it was well used.

By the late 1960s society was no longer being so unpleasant to women who got pregnant without being married. In fact, in the 1960s and 1970s a number of well-known women in the United States, Great Britain, and Europe wore their out-of-wedlock pregnancies and bore their out-of-wedlock babies with pride, more often than not also choosing to keep the babies and raise them, alone or with unmarried partners. The trend of the 1970s and the 1980s for unmarried mothers of all ages, races, religions, and social standings has been to keep the babies they bear, rather than give them up for adoption, although this may not always be a wise thing for mother or baby.

The fragmentation of the family that is partly responsible for society's new tolerance of unmarried mothers also means that the single mother is often particularly alone. What might at other times have been supported by close family life is today occurring in a vacuum. This means additional hardship for the mother, as she usually must leave the baby in the hands of strangers while she goes out of the home to earn their living. For the baby it means being deprived not only of the father, but of his or her mother's presence as well. Mothers who choose to stay home and receive state aid must live below poverty level, finding it difficult to get housing and carrying a social stigma for collecting aid. The new trend of single women and teenagers keeping their babies against all odds also means hardship for infertile couples who want children and are vying for babies to adopt from an ever-decreasing supply.

When he wrote a book on adoption (which also appeared in a text on family law for California's attorneys, as a section entitled "Adoption Practice in California"*), Phil Adams tried to envision the varied situations that could arise in adoption. The philosophy he expressed there is still considered unconven-

---

*Family Law for California Lawyers (Berkeley: University of California Printing Department, 1956).

tional. One of the controversial subsections is "The Personal Meeting Between Adoptive and Natural Parents, Where the Child Is Not Yet Born." In it he tells why, in his view, such a meeting should occur.

> In the great majority of cases, real enthusiasm and happy acceptance will be mutual between the adoptive and natural parents. When the petitioners have explored the background of the child's parents, they will look forward to the day when the child comes into their home with increasing eagerness and a feeling of security born of full knowledge of the situation. The natural parent, in turn, will have progressed from the first moment of dismay and panic to relaxation and serenity, knowing she has selected an appropriate home for the child. What, then, will more securely and permanently cement this decision than for the petitioners and the parent or parents to meet each other and to prove by personal acquaintance the rightness of the decision?
>
> The adopting parent who is haunted by fears of future attempts by an irrational parent to contact the child in its new home or to disturb the serenity will have such fears rapidly dispelled by seeing that the parent is a normal individual, acting with intelligence in a time of stress and quite obviously incapable of taking any action that would be to the detriment of the child or its new home. The natural parent will be reassured on seeing the adopting parents as warm, flesh-and-blood people, who are eager to give the child the love and affection it needs. Occasionally, such a meeting will demonstrate to one or another of the participants that the plans which appeared on paper to be acceptable have a serious flaw. This, too, redounds to the ultimate benefit of the child and the parties involved and can only result in the making of other plans which are better calculated to promote the best interests of the child and the parties.

His view that knowledge is good and promotes more responsible decision making—and that ignorance breeds harm—is everywhere evident in his writing. He dispels common myths that have perpetuated a closed-file, agency-directed system of adoption for the past half-century. Most people still assume that the anonymity peculiar to agency adoption is necessary and normal to all adoption. This is not in the least true, according to Phil Adams. The fact that it developed in agency adoptions and was made into law in a number of states after a strong lobbying effort does not mean that it is right or necessary. Despite the common argument that only with anonymity can the best interests of the child and all parties involved be served, anonymity, Adams writes, is "not so much an end in itself as a necessary byproduct of the most fundamental rule of an adoption agency, that it must be free at all times to make the ultimate decision of where a child will be placed." He notes that in 1954, two years before his book on adoption was published and accepted as the standard reference on the subject in his state, there were four thousand private, or direct, adoptions in California. In a little less than half of those cases, the biological parent was acquainted with the adoptive parents. The practice of biological parent and adoptive parents meeting each other was one that arose spontaneously and naturally in the history of adoption, he argues, and reflects a genuine need for firsthand knowledge and trust between the parties. It is Adams's contention that the real reason the practice of anonymity in both agency and some private adoption has been encouraged is that it enhances the status of the person or agency who stands between the various parties.

"To 'play God' in acting as an intermediary is an intoxicating experience whether one be an old friend, a relative, a physician, a lawyer or social worker," he writes. "The moment the principals themselves get together and talk over the situation between them, the status of all other persons is reduced to that of mere bystanders and advisors." * And that, he feels, is precisely the way it should be, his own and others' egos notwithstanding.

He recommends that the meeting between biological and prospective adoptive parents should take place not in a professional's office or clinic, but in a place conducive to informality

---

* *Ibid.*

and relaxation. The best arrangement is for the prospective adoptive parents to meet the biological parent on her own territory, in her home or in a comfortable restaurant. In a case where the child has already been born and might even have been living for some time with a biological or foster parent, Phil Adams believes it is even *more* crucial that such meetings occur. It is essential that the adoptive parents be familiar with the pattern of living and environment in which the child has spent his or her life, and this can be ensured only by having the adoptive parents make numerous visits to the child in his or her current surroundings prior to taking the child to another home.*

Until very recently, most social workers have, as a group, taken the position that only they can properly assist the biological mother through the adoption and in getting back on her feet afterward, so that she is not likely to repeat the same scenario. In several states, notably Delaware, Massachusetts, and Connecticut, social worker organizations have successfully lobbied to pass laws declaring that no one may file a petition for adoption without the express formal approval of that state's department of social welfare. Phil Adams sees this as Big Brother politics, taking away the right of individuals to make their own decisions. Most social workers and many other adoption professionals disagree; they have seen too many instances of private adoption where the rights and needs of the birth mother and the child have not been met, and where attorneys have been motivated by financial gain. It is still customary in both agency and private adoption for birth mothers to be neglected during the long period of grieving that follows relinquishing a baby.

Apart from ideological objections to the dominance of social workers in adoption, there is the practical reality that

---

*In state-arranged adoptions in Greece, it has long been the practice for the adoptive mother to go on several occasions to the maternity home where the baby is living, observe the baby with his or her professional caretaker, and listen as she describes the infant's temperament, preferences, and habits. Only after several weeks, when the adoptive mother is familiar with this particular baby, is she permitted to take the baby home and adopt him or her.

social workers often are overworked and unable to properly handle the number of cases for which they are responsible. It is not uncommon for an individual woman to see half a dozen different professionals in the course of her pregnancy. In the state of Massachusetts, in a well-publicized case of a mother who was clearly incompetent to raise children, it came to light that her history was full of documented statements about the danger she represented to her children. A product of a battered childhood and a ward of the courts herself, she was with no fewer than thirteen different social workers in a fifteen-year period, and not one had the authority to see that her children were protected. The children were neglected and badly beaten, and one was finally killed by the mother's boyfriend. The profession known for its heart utterly failed a family in need because of bureaucratic confusion, which permitted no individual professional the power to do anything.

The hold that social workers and adoption agencies have over state legislatures often makes things difficult for would-be adoptive parents, especially as most agencies today, for convenience, impose arbitrary rules regarding prospective parents' eligibility according to age, economic status, marital status, and sexual preference. Many a person who adds his or her name to an agency list finds himself or herself waiting six or eight years and then suddenly being classified as too old to be considered any longer. When a married woman in a midwestern state found herself unable to make any headway with local adoption agencies and turned to placing personal ads in newspapers, the local agencies attempted to frighten her into stopping her ads by implying publicly that she was stepping into the black market. She received several responses to her simply worded ads from young women who were pregnant and planning to relinquish their babies for adoption; but in each case, after an initial positive phone conversation, the pregnant woman was dissuaded from going any further by local adoption agencies. In that state recent additions to the civil code have made it virtually impossible for a person to adopt a baby except through an established agency, which this woman had already tried unsuccessfully to do.

In recent decades a number of court decisions have complicated the legal issues surrounding adoption. For example, in the case where a biological mother was not married at the time of conception, she was until recently regarded as the only person whose consent was necessary in an adoption. This was the result of a tradition, disparaging of women and children, that defined a child whose mother was not married at the time of pregnancy or at least of a child's birth as illegitimate. A child wasn't by nature considered legitimate or real—he or she gained legitimacy only through the mother's being married. This meant that a child whose father was unknown or whose mother was unmarried was a "bastard," a curse not only on the mother but on the child for his or her entire life. It meant too that the mother was solely responsible for her child's custody, and, until the state began to offer women financial support and services for the care of a young "illegitimate" child, she either carried the burden alone, or, as was common in the early part of the twentieth century, could have the child taken from her and placed in a workhouse or orphanage because of her status. The concept of illegitimacy at least gave a mother whose children were not taken away because of poverty or moral mandates the chance to choose adoption for her child and thus assure the child's survival. For many years adoptions were speedily accomplished with only her permission and the allowance of some legally defined waiting period, after which an adoption could become final.

Then, as of January 1, 1976, in California, and following that in many other states across the country, all of this changed. Under the Uniform Parentage Act, which was drafted by a concerned group of advocates and which, after many rounds of heated argument, is now being adopted by one state after another, *every* child is considered legitimate. *Every* child also has two parents. The father is placed in one of three categories. He is either the mother's husband (and, as such, is presumed to be the father); or he is that man who has been identified by the mother or others as the father, in which case he is the alleged father; or, where there is no person identified, he is the unidentified father. And a number of court cases have begun to assert the father's rights with regard to his children. One major case that made it all the way to the Supreme Court of the United States on appeal was that of *Stanley v. The State of Illinois*.

Phil Adams recalls this case in particular because of the impact it has had on subsequent adoption cases where the biological parents have not been married. He is glad he wasn't the attorney involved in all of the convolutions and appeals of the original case, and isn't at all sure that the decision on behalf of the father ever did any good for a certain Mr. Stanley, the plaintiff.

There were three children, ages about ten, twelve, and fifteen, all living with both their biological parents, a man and a woman who had never married. When the mother died, the state took the children and placed them in other homes. The father tried unsuccessfully to fight the state, declaring it had given him no standing or consideration, either as a foster parent or a custodian, much less a stepparent, despite the well-known fact that he had lived with, raised, and financially supported all three of the children, and all the children were commonly acknowledged to be his. The United States Supreme Court finally agreed to hear the case and reversed the Illinois high court decision, commenting rather obscurely that the natural father of a child was at least entitled to a notice of adoption proceedings.

The legal confusion over the rights and privileges of the biological father has grown recently as it has become more common for men to express concern and responsibility when they father children outside of marriage. They want a say in what happens to their children. Cases may now be brought to court where a man identifying himself as the father attempts to prevent the woman with whom he claims to have had intercourse from obtaining an abortion. In one such case the unmarried couple had separated after she had become pregnant. She chose to keep the pregnancy but give the baby up for adoption, and the father tried legally to prevent her from doing this. He got a restraining order in the state where they both lived. But all his efforts were to no avail, because she merely went to another state for the birth and prepared for the adoption in that state, placing the new baby with a couple who lived in a third state all the way across the country. Apparently the father's rights were terminated during the adoption proceedings when the mother insisted the identity of the father was unknown. But the man claiming to be the baby's rightful father did not stop there. He tracked down the whereabouts of the baby to the baby's adoptive parents' home. By the time he had done this, the child and the child's new parents were living in yet another state. Nevertheless the father filed for custody and won a judgment in his favor. A judge saw this man's rights as superior to those of the adoptive parents and ordered that the child be given to him. A higher court went on to affirm this judgment, and the state supreme court, as well as the United States Supreme Court, refused to grant a hearing or change the original decision. When the adoptive parents finally gave the child to his biological father, the child was then more than two years old, an innocent pawn in a system of legal delays and unclear laws. The adoptive parents were also victims. Today the biological father continues to raise his son. Whether the biological mother knows what happened and, if so, what she feels about all this, is unknown.

What has this meant for an attorney seeking to honor a mother's wishes and conclude a petition for her child to be adopted? Today both private adoption attorneys and adoption agencies must bring a legal action to terminate the relationship of an alleged father before any adoption can proceed. The father must be served papers and given an opportunity to declare his desires with regard to who should raise the child. Any man who has been alleged to be the father of a child is entitled to such notice if his whereabouts are known.

Phil Adams trusts the biological mother, no matter what her age or circumstance, to be the one to make the best decision for her child's future. Of all the individuals Phil has assisted in his long career, it is the mothers who relinquished their babies who have made the most lasting impressions on him. A number have become longtime friends and some have later even adopted children. It is the birth mothers, those who have made the difficult choice of giving up a child, upon whom he focuses primary attention. Whether the mother is a thirteen-year-old unmarried girl or a forty-six-year-old married mother of five, his attitude toward her has been the same.

"I regard every client as an adult, making up her own mind about things. Once a young woman is pregnant, she must be treated as a responsible adult. All I do is try to keep an eye out for practicalities."

He is purposely brusque and to the point with prospective clients, in order to catch people off guard so that they will reveal their true desires. And he does feel a responsibility for seeing that everyone—the birth mother *and* the prospective adoptive parents—is certain in his or her decisions.

"Mainly I want to know, 'How do you really feel about this?' and 'How are you going to live with it over the years?' If a woman comes in and she's made up her mind and I can see that she's certain, I leave it at that. Sometimes a woman feels incapable of making any decision. A child's future is at stake, as well as her own, and at these times a bit of prodding may be called for." To Phil, giving up a child is as pragmatic a decision as a person can make. Whenever a woman places her child for adoption through him, he assigns her priority to receive a child, should she ever want to adopt one herself. All life, for him, is a cycle. Those who give unselfishly should receive.

From his vantage point, nearly eight decades of living, surviving two world wars, a social/sexual revolution followed by a swing of the pendulum to the right, he has had his share of surprises. It was surprising to everyone when, in about 1960, there were suddenly more children to adopt than there were people to take them. Then this was followed, just a decade later, by a period when almost no children were available to adopt, but the numbers of adults wishing to adopt had increased. Changes in sexual mores, changes in the law as regards abortion, and changes in religious attitudes have altered both the number of unplanned babies born and what happens to them after birth. Today, fewer than 3 percent of unmarried minors who give birth currently choose adoption. The very pressures from peers and parents that led young women twenty years ago to leave town and give birth in secrecy now offer many teenagers a special status for being pregnant. And for many, when looking ahead to the complexities of being an emancipated woman with a career, having a baby seems far simpler and preferable. "Have your children while you're young enough to enjoy them and grow up with them" is the new adage among many teens. In addition to social pressures, impersonal factors such as fluctuations in the stock market have been found to have great impact upon the bearing of children and also on the desire of people to adopt. As for the future, at least in Western industrial nations, many people anticipate a further scarcity of infants of all races to adopt, in combination with increasing infertility among men and women of reproductive age.

What will happen in a world where children are at a premium is yet to be seen. Perhaps scarcity will cause societies to value children more highly and guarantee them greater rights, more care, and more attention. There also may be more children left homeless in other countries who are taken to other countries, such as the United States, for adoption. The ethical and political issues as well as the long-term consequences of transracial and transcultural adoption are hotly debated today. But for those who seek to become parents through adoption, and for those who choose or are forced to relinquish their children, adoption will continue to be a solution. And wherever it is an option, some individuals will see private adoption as preferable to agency adoption. At its best, private adoption offers simplicity and empowers both the birth mother and the adoptive parents. Today it is often birth mothers who are leading the way into more open adoptions. Many social workers now agree that adoption is best when the individuals themselves design the process and make decisions, using professionals for information, guidance, and support.

PHIL:

Looking Back, Looking Forward

TODAY PHIL ADAMS continues his busy adoption practice. His distinctive personality, caring yet blunt and unsentimental—with a good sprinkle of wisecracks—puts some prospective clients off and makes others love him.

At a time when the average American family moves so often most people have trouble keeping their address books current, Phil Adams is a stable figure. He has held onto the same telephone number—except for phone company changes in the prefix—and the same office in downtown San Francisco throughout his career. After handling more than two thousand adoptions, he has a broad perspective on the subject and continues to claim that he loves every minute of his work.

Phil looks ahead to the time when he will no longer be working, and has made plans to ensure that adoptees, birth parents, and adoptive parents will still have access to the information that is in their files. He recognizes his responsibility to all of those directly involved. Phil can guarantee this continuity for former clients, because his son is now a partner in the firm, and the files will remain at the same address even after Phil is no longer there to answer calls himself.

Each adoption has its own file, which is added to whenever any new information comes to the office. When a birth mother sends him a change of address or a letter she wants the child to read one day, it is placed in the appropriate file. The vast majority of files are surprisingly slender, with the most current piece of information usually being the copy of the formal decree of adoption. Some contain greeting cards sent to Phil years later by birth mothers who want to thank him for his caring and let him know how things are going in their lives.

It has been his experience that, after a few years at most, birth mothers cut off contact with the adoptive parents and stop informing them even of their current addresses. Each birth mother he has counseled over the years knows he maintains a file for her case. His observation is that women who have relinquished babies for adoption simply become involved in their current lives and let the past drop. "This adoption," he says with his typical touch of dramatic exaggeration, "doesn't stand out as Mt. Everest. No woman places her child for adoption today who wants to keep it. A woman is no longer overwhelmed or pressured into adoption by society. After the adoption she just wants to go on with her life."

Whether his reasoning is accurate, whether birth mothers still feel some guilt or shame that makes them think they have no right to stay in contact with their children, or whether they simply feel too much pain about maintaining contact, the result is the same. In his experience, adoptive parents' primary fear about open adoption—that the birth mother will stay around and haunt their lives—simply is not the case.

Phil often hears from adult adoptees who wish to search for their biological roots. The person they primarily want to find is the birth mother. Even with long-outdated addresses to work from, their searches will most likely be successful.

Much of the success adoptees and birth parents are having in locating each other is due to the growing number of grass-roots organizations that have sprung up. There are many of them in North America, and they are now appearing around the world, often in places where the revolution of attitudes about opening up the closed world of adoption has not yet permeated society at large. People are often amazed that those for whom they are searching can be found even after numerous changes of address and changes of surname. Responsible adoption attorneys like Phil Adams will have an important part to play for some time to come.

Phil Adams's attitude toward adoption and related issues, based on his observations and long experience, continues to be liberal in the true sense of that word: not bound by the orthodox, the traditional, the established customs. It would be ideal, he admits, if there were ways to screen out people who will turn out to be bad parents. But that is probably not any more feasible with adoptive parents than it is with biological parents. Except in extreme cases no one can know in advance which parents will abuse a child or what the actual child rearing will be like for a particular child.

Despite his strong stand as advocate for the interests of the birth mother, when it comes to a choice between the interests of either a birth parent or an adoptive parent and the needs of a child, he stands on the side of the child. For that reason he would like to see the decision to relinquish be made early in pregnancy and remain firm. "My general approach is that it is in the best interests of the child that there be some certainty about its future as early as possible."

There was a time, within many of our memories, when society's attitude toward women relinquishing babies for adoption was so hostile that it was necessary for the government to step in to protect their rights, especially their right to privacy. Today, Phil Adams observes, women of all ages—and he would argue that a thirteen-year-old having a baby *must* be treated as a woman—have more control over their lives. He points out as added proof that times have changed the fact that the overwhelming majority of single mothers—even very young ones— are now choosing to keep and raise their babies. He notes that women have claimed more of their own power, and that birth mothers no longer need paternalistic protection.

I would, for the most part, agree with him. Paternalistic protection no longer serves any purpose in adoption; instead it keeps people from assuming responsibility for their lives and actions, and victimizes birth mothers instead of supporting them. I too feel that, in general, women of all ages are taking more power over their lives, especially their reproduction. Recently I spoke with a midwife about a birth and adoption in which she had participated. Her client was a thirteen-year-old, herself adopted, who had come to the conclusion, without outside pressure, that she could not raise a child competently at her age, and on her own had made the decision to relinquish her baby.

This young woman had an older sister who, six months earlier, had had a cesarean birth. She decided that was not the kind of birth she desired for herself or her baby. She wanted to know what other kinds of birthings were possible, and her adoptive parents encouraged and supported her in her autonomy.

After gathering information she elected to give birth at home, because she felt that home was the place in which she was most likely to have a normal birth and where the baby could receive the most gentle passage. Her choice was courageous because it ruled out any possibility of taking pain medication during labor. She selected a nurse-midwife and prepared for a natural birth. With help from adults around her, she got legal counsel and picked the adoptive parents from a number of applicants.

An interesting side note is that she had been placed for adoption by her birth father in early childhood, after her mother had died from cancer and he had found he could not raise her by himself. Her adoptive parents raised her to think for herself and encouraged her to make her own decisions regarding this pregnancy. At this young woman's side during her long, hard labor and natural birth were both her birth father *and* her adoptive mother. This was an example of a teenager being given the chance to act as an adult and rising to the occasion. She showed a maturity of judgment and a clearsightedness that some women twice her age do not exhibit. Hers is not a typical story, but it is a hopeful one.

It can be argued that most women today seldom make their own conscious choices when it comes to reproduction and childbearing. This is because they do not have access to full information about all of the possibilities and the risks and benefits of every option. Also, they usually do not have the full support of others in choosing whatever option they wish.

The overwhelming majority of young women simply do not see adoption as a positive choice; they see it as a sign of weakness and a lack of caring. Because they rule adoption out without even considering it, how can we say that they have real choice in their decision to keep their baby?

There are a number of reasons for this, including the psychological mindset of many teens that says, I can do *anything* I want! This mindset drives them to take grave risks and to make decisions about their lives that are both self-destructive and irresponsible. Another reason so few teens consider adoption is that there is much negative peer and societal pressure for them to prove how mature they are by keeping their babies against all odds. Yet a further reason is the fact that the educational system does not fully address the issues of sexuality, birth, or parenting. And most teenagers who become pregnant haven't yet made plans for their lives and see a baby as someone to love *them*, rather than as someone who demands and needs skillful parenting.

I do not believe that people can make the best decisions for themselves and their children unless they have an informed vision of what is possible, a knowledge of all the options, risks, benefits, and their long-term consequences. Most people also need a large measure of social support to be able to make choices that are not common or popular. But this teen's story demonstrates the ideal situation in which a woman, however young, feels sufficiently self-confident to make important decisions. Women in many cultures have not felt this self-confident for many centuries.

Phil Adams and I agree that a woman has the capability of making clearheaded decisions during pregnancy and should always be encouraged to do so. She must have access to relevant information about all the possible choices she can make, and she needs support for making decisions regarding her child as early as possible. She should be encouraged in forming decisions and taking responsibility for living with them. This does not preclude the birth mother having a change of mind and heart immediately following the birth, prior to the baby going to his or her new parents. It simply puts the emphasis on early and firm decision making, keeping in mind that the baby cannot speak out with his or her desires and needs to be kept in mind at all times. Whatever safeguards are built into an adoption system should ensure that a baby is not to be fought over like a football.

Very few changes in societal attitudes have made their way into law. One that has regards the rights of biological fathers. Following the *Stanley* decision of the United States Supreme Court in the early 1970s (which I wrote about in my original chapter on Phil Adams), there has been a general trend toward recognizing the rights of the father.

The Uniform Parentage Act—the statute designed and proposed for enactment in every state—which made every child legitimate in the eyes of the law, was passed into law in many states during the past decade. California did it in 1976, and since then most states have taken some steps to recognize the attitude of the Supreme Court in the *Stanley* case. Some have passed a similar Uniform Parentage Act. A few—such as New York, Utah, and Nebraska—have taken a different approach. In those states if a man believes he is the father of a child about to be born and is concerned that the child might be placed for adoption by the mother, he may register with a specific state social service bureau. His estimate of the date of birth is recorded, along with the mother's name and address. Then if a petition for adoption is placed by this mother, the man is automatically notified. If he wishes he can try to prevent the adoption by asking that he be granted custody of the child.

So far, if the father of the child was not married to the mother or acting as the child's father, many states do not require his express permission for adoption to take place, but the father is entitled to notice if he can be located. If the parents were married to each other when the child was born, then the consent of both mother and father is usually required before the adoption can be finalized.

A major development in the past decade, which illustrates how societal attitudes are shaping practices even before laws are changed, regards the pressure to open closed adoption records and the growing acceptability of searches. Perhaps a majority of adoptees and birth parents have wished they could find and reconnect with their biological kin. But when adult adoptees request their birth certificates, they are sent copies on which the names and other information about the biological parents has been obliterated. If adoptees or birth parents made attempts to search, which usually meant contacting the agencies through which the adoptions were handled, they got no cooperation and often lectures about the harm they would cause innocent people if they persevered in their searches. This is beginning to change.

Also the past decade has seen a great deal of talk and much agitation by birth parents and adoptees alike about opening sealed records. Virtually nothing has changed in adoption law. But there has been a profound change in attitude about the right and need of adopted children and birth parents to search if they so choose. Many social workers and some agencies are reexamining their policies and doing what they can to enable people to create their own reunions.

It is now almost taken for granted that people have a right to search. This change in attitude has occurred along with a decrease in secrecy in current agency adoptions. Today some agency adoptions include prebirth meetings between the adoptive and biological parents. The individuals can privately exchange addresses and make verbal agreements when they meet. There is growing acceptance of the principles of open adoption, and eventually the laws will change to reflect this change in society.

A further change is the continued decline of newborn infants available through adoption agencies. That has come about as a result of yet another change: the growing self-confidence of birth mothers, who now usually want to play active roles in the adoption of their children. The percentage of private adoptions continues to rise in every state where private adoption is legal, because more and more birth mothers wish to be directly involved in all aspects of adoption—especially the selection of parents and the transfer of the baby to the new parents—and adoption agencies still usually do not permit this to happen.

This desire of birth mothers to make their own decisions and be active in the adoption process, in combination with the greatly reduced number of babies available for adoption today, has resulted in many agencies moving away from adoption as a primary focus and into providing other, related services for children in need (such as temporary placement and care of children who have been taken from their families by courts). For the most part agencies today are handling more cases involving older children than they are babies, and the babies they do see are not the ones most commonly sought in adoption—healthy white babies—but instead babies who are harder to place.

Still another change has been that more and more infants are being placed directly after birth. It was only fifty years ago that a birth mother was required to keep her baby with her for a number of weeks in order that it could be breastfed. Letting adoptive parents take a baby home shortly after birth was either strongly discouraged or prevented. With artificial milk providing an alternative to breastfeeding, it is no longer necessary that a baby remain with the birth mother to breastfeed.

In addition, birth mothers increasingly want their babies to go directly to the adopting parents as soon as possible, so that the babies suffer less trauma. It is now understood that strong bonds arise between mothers and children from birth and that babies are conscious of what happens to them at birth. Women choosing adoption for their babies wish to prevent themselves from forming attachments to their babies that will be difficult to break, *and* they want to help their babies form strong bonds with the adoptive parents. Making the transfer immediately after birth is, for many women, the ideal solution. This fits with the desires of adopting parents and the needs of babies as well.

One more change has been in the growing number of lay facilitators, especially in private adoption, people who act as intermediaries between birth parents and adoptive parents, helping make the transition for the babies smoother. These people often start out with some personal stake in the adoption process, being adoptees, birth parents, or adoptive parents. They find the adoption process so engrossing and empowering that they end up helping friends and eventually making a career of assisting others. Some have professional training in counseling; others do not. They perform a function similar to what the traditional marriage matchmaker did in societies where marriages were arranged by families.

A final change is the growing recognition that adoption does not end when the papers are signed and the court decrees it is final. The process continues to affect everyone involved throughout their lives.

Many organizations have sprung up in the past decade to assist and to fill the need for continuing services. They are staffed by laypeople and charge little or nothing for what they do. Their aim is to help people help themselves. They are part of the general trend toward the liberalization of adoption within postindustrial societies. They use computers, telephones, and the mail to get their work done, providing person-to-person links all around the world.

A new concept in adoption is taking hold in California and is quickly spreading across the country. This is the concept of Cooperative Adoption℠.* Cooperative Adoption is a form of adoption in which *all* the parents (birth parents and adoptive parents) agree to remain in contact until the child legally becomes an adult, which is at eighteen in the United States. Cooperative Adoption is predicated on the assumption that an adopted child has the innate need and therefore the right to have contact with both sets of parents. Even though this right is not mandated by law, the adoptive parents and birth parents (or, at least, the birth mother) agree to take responsibility for enabling the child to have contact with his or her birth parents while growing up, rather than only after he or she reaches adulthood.

In a closed agency adoption in which the birth parents and adoptive parents manage to exchange names and addresses before the adoption is final, they create the opportunity to remain in contact after the adoption is final and have a Cooperative Adoption. Some are planned to be cooperative from the outset, but many evolve from open adoption (where, at the least, names and addresses are exchanged). In these cases they become cooperative somewhere along the way, usually because the adoptive parents realize their children need to have contact with their biological parents.

Usually adoptive parents end up wanting a Cooperative Adoption after they have established a connection with the birth parents (or just the birth mother) that feels warm and trusting. Faced with the prospect of losing that connection and closeness that ends after the adoption, they opt to stay in

---

* Cooperative Adoption℠ is an internationally trademarked term developed by Sharon Kaplan and Mary Jo Rillera to promote the concept and to prevent false advertising claims by adoption attorneys, organizations, or agencies who might otherwise exploit the term.

contact with the birth mother or both of the birth parents. It may begin with a regular exchange of letters or phone calls, but it usually evolves into visits, with the child never feeling the need to search, because the link to the birth parents has not been severed. Cooperative Adoption is a natural evolution of open adoption, but a growing number of adoptive parents and birth parents are learning about Cooperative Adoption and choosing it from the start. Many adoptive parents feel it is their moral obligation to their children to give them as full a sense of family as possible.

Cooperative Adoption is both new and old. Traditionally, children who were orphaned or whose biological parents could not, for whatever reason, raise them, were adopted by other relatives or members of the community. Adoptions such as these were not necessarily legal entities, except in societies where there were specific codes of law relating to adoption. They were the simplest solution to an urgent need. Cooperative Adoption today is really new only in the sense that it occurs primarily between people who were strangers before the children were conceived.

Phil Adams saw what he termed hand-in-hand adoptions from the start of his practice. This occurred when the birth mother was someone the adoptive parents already knew. When she became pregnant and was not in a position to raise the child, the adoptive parents were already standing ready in the wings. They helped her through her pregnancy and perhaps even took her into their home to live until the birth. Often Phil first met the birth mother when she walked into his office hand in hand or arm in arm with the adoptive mother. That is how he got the name and that is how he learned that there was nothing to fear from the birth mother and adoptive parents knowing each other. It worked and he observed it working. "There was nothing for me to do but the paperwork!" These were not Cooperative Adoptions, however, because contact was not maintained as the child grew.

For those who feel queasy about the prospect of parenting an adopted child while the birth parents remain in the picture, it is important to understand that Cooperative Adoption does not imply communal parenting or that the adoptive parents are simply babysitters. Once an adoption is final, the adoptive parents legally have the full parental rights and control over what part the birth parents, biological siblings, or other biological relatives of the child have in that child's life. They set the rules until the child is an adult in the eyes of the law and is autonomous. They have the same rights and responsibilities regarding their adopted child that any parent has.

I recently met a nine-year-old girl, the child of a Cooperative Adoption. Her birth mother lives in Wisconsin, whereas she and her adoptive parents live in Northern California. Dara remains in close contact with her birth mother through letters and phone calls. She and her adoptive parents have visited her birth mother a number of times, and she has also visited her birth father (who has not been in a relationship with Dara's birth mother for many years). Dara's birth mother married a few years ago and with her husband has a baby, Dara's half-sister. Dara was a member of the wedding and takes a proprietary interest in her younger sister. There have been joint family visits over the years and a joint agreement to remain in contact for Dara's sake.

It was Dara's adoptive parents who consistently reached out to her birth mother in the first months and years, to maintain the close relationship that began when Dara's birth mother came to live with them toward the end of her pregnancy and stayed through Dara's birth. This is only one example of a working Cooperative Adoption where everyone seems to have benefited.

Adoptive parents and birth mothers (and a growing number of birth fathers) are cooperating prior to the birth, setting their own rules and writing their own postadoption agreements. When people get to know and trust each other prior to adoption (and usually prior to the birth), this is not a difficult process, but it works best if several skilled outside facilitators (counselors, advocates, lawyers) are brought in to make sure there is not an imbalance of power or an abuse of power by any person.

The primary responsibility of each facilitator is to see that the spirit of cooperation and the needs of the child are kept paramount. When there are two facilitators involved (and some people feel there should always be two), each one acts as advocate for one set of parents.

It may be some time before the spirit behind Cooperative Adoption is reflected in changes in laws, which would enable Cooperative Adoptions to be the norm. Then they will seem no more problematic than no-fault divorce and joint custody parenting, which are now viewed as the standard in divorce. Some people are worried that Cooperative Adoptions might create confusion in identity for the children involved. It will be up to them to prove that Cooperative Adoption does not serve the best interests of children, because there is every indication that it does. And, in fact, the issues in Cooperative Adoption may be easier to resolve than the issues in divorce. In both cases each parent would like to continue playing an active and responsible role in the child's life. In divorce, however, there is usually hurt and bitterness to be healed at the same time as the two parents must learn to make joint decisions on behalf of the child. In both divorce and adoption, families benefit from skilled outside support and guidance—and in both the process does not end when the papers are signed.

PART III

STEPPING INTO THE FUTURE:

Journeys Into Open Adoption

PAT:

Too Soon a Mother

IT WAS CHRISTMASTIME when I first received a phone call from Claudia. She said she had been given my number by a mutual friend with an interest in childbirth and children, and she wanted to apologize for taking my time. She had, she said, something private to talk about and hoped I might help. I could sense her discomfort about airing her family's intimate problems to a stranger over the telephone, but she had to talk to someone who might be able to give her some advice. Her younger sister back in Florida had gotten herself pregnant at the beginning of the summer. She had told this to her family only around Halloween. Claudia, who was the older sister and living three thousand miles across the country, had not been told the news until just now. The baby was due at the end of March, and Pat needed help. Claudia told me that the siblings in her family had always hung together in crisis, particularly the three youngest—she, Eddie, and Pat. I gathered it was not their style to ask for anything from anyone outside the family, but this was a situation beyond their combined resources.

Claudia sketchily described her sister as a capable, bright, and intensely private sixteen-year-old. Their family was traditionally Catholic, their mother originally from South America, and neither mother nor father was given to any outward show of affection toward the children. Pat's disclosure of her pregnancy had evoked outrage and shame in her parents. It had been proof of illicit sexuality and, it seemed, their mother especially had taken it as a personal insult and a matter for private anguish. She had made it known that after the baby came, Pat was to raise it at home but keep to her room and out of sight of the neighborhood. Pat was not only obviously pregnant and single, but isolated and alone, not a pleasant way to face childbirth and motherhood.

What Claudia wanted from me, I sensed, was some support for a conclusion she had already reached by herself. If Pat's parents were unable to provide the emotional support she needed, then Pat should be removed from them and brought to a place where she could live out the remainder of her pregnancy in peace and consider her options clearly. Claudia wanted badly to do something for her sister. I felt that if she could have, she would happily have taken the entire experience out of Pat's hands and gone through any amount of pain to save Pat from it. She was her big sister and felt helpless living all the way across the continent. Although she was almost the last in their family to know the story, it turned out that Claudia was probably the only one who had the resources and contacts to be able to offer Pat some real support. She sounded most anxious that Pat, out of fear or a desire to protect her parents, might refuse her help. She was thinking not only of her sister but of the baby and the needs he or she had that were not being met.

During that first phone conversation, we roughed out some possible plans, concrete support Claudia could offer Pat to entice her to leave Florida and come to California, where Claudia lived, as well as reasons to give their parents that would be acceptable. I remember asking her what kind of person Pat was. Was she the sort who, given a bit of a hand, would take off on her own? Or might outside offers of help just embarrass or embitter her and drive her into passivity? Previous experiments at being a "helper" had taught me it doesn't always work out as planned. Pat was not only a stranger with feelings I couldn't possibly know, but she was also a teenager. I gathered from Claudia that she had a lot of determination and stubbornness, and I didn't know if the physicians, midwives, birth educators, and the like whom I knew would be well received by her. I remembered how unpredictable and sullen I must have appeared some of the time as a teenager. The world I inhabited was bounded by home, school, friends, and my own painfully sensitive feelings. The family home might not be supportive, but it *was* home base. Anything else existed as a shadowy form, outside, distant, and something to which I could hardly relate. How difficult it would have been for me at sixteen to express what was going on inside me to some adult, especially when I often could not put it into words or make sense of it for myself. I did recall, however, that strangers could sometimes be easier to talk with than friends or family. They have no past shared experiences and therefore fewer preconceptions and judgments.

We ended our first conversation with Claudia determined to find some way to get Pat out to California and with me fairly sure Pat had a strong instinct for survival and would do well transplanted to a new environment if given enough support. I told Claudia I would start looking for services and people for Pat to contact. The use she made of them would be up to Pat. I would be there too. She would need a place to live, money on which to survive. I imagined she had given little thought to the baby and to the birth itself and would need a lot of preparation in a short time. I hoped she had given some thought to the health of the child she was carrying, to her diet and everything she took into and did to her body, for that would partially determine the health of this baby. She had some serious thinking to do about her options for keeping or relinquishing her baby and creating a support system for herself in parenting if she chose to raise the baby herself. She was young and might feel alone, but, as I could have told her, approximately one out of every five nineteen-year-old women in America today is a mother. This is in addition to those who become pregnant, face the prospect of having a child, and instead choose abortion. Pat's situation repeats itself daily around the country.

The next time I heard from Claudia, barely a week later, Pat was arriving on a plane; and two days later Claudia brought her to my house. Standing on my front door stoop with her summer blouse bulging over a pair of poorly fitting faded blue maternity pants, she might have been any pregnant young woman. Her olive-colored skin was unlined and perfectly smooth. Her mouth was a small bow. Her brown, straight hair was clean and pulled carelessly back by a clip. Her arms were lean and brown and her fingers long. As we walked inside I noticed the diffident stoop of her shoulders, which didn't match the firm set of her mouth. She was taller than I had expected and walked with her long feet turned out a bit. She was instantly likable, although she hadn't said more than hi. I led the way up to my room at the top of the stairs, so we might have a bit of privacy. I asked Pat to sit with me on the edge of the big bed. Claudia sat on the floor in front of us. Where to begin?

There was little time in Pat's life these days to spend on social niceties. Anyway, I already knew far more about her and her family than a stranger ordinarily would. So I started right in talking about what she'd need, where she might live, and how she was feeling, physically. Claudia's housing situation, tiny quarters in a friend's apartment under the prying eye of the landlady, didn't offer much hope. They'd need to go apartment hunting, but with what for money? Better go to social services and find out about Aid to Dependent Children first, because Pat's being pregnant qualified her immediately in this state for some support and for Women, Infant, and Children food supplements. I could taste the bitterness that suggestion left with both of them. Their familial reluctance to taking any handouts obviously ran deep, although they knew as well as I that it was the best we could do. Pat did not need to spend what little time she had before the birth job hunting. Once they had found a place to live and she had money to contribute for food, she would have to turn her attention to the difficult decisions about the birth and the future of her baby. I had seen the craziness that moving around late in pregnancy or changing homes just after birth could create in a woman of any age. Clearly Pat needed to be physically settled. She had apparently just spent a month living with one divorced sister and her child in Miami, feeling she was taking up too much of their cramped apartment space and intruding on their need for privacy. The next two or three months would barely give her time to get her life together.

California may have a decent welfare system, but it is *not* known for its public transportation. Pat would have to get around during the day by limited bus service, because Claudia needed her car to get to school, so they felt she should find a place to live that was on a main road near one of the downtown areas. There were many thrift and secondhand shops in which to find clothes. From the outset I filled Pat's head with the various possibilities of which I was aware. I wanted her to know she was in a different place now, and that there were real choices here and people who would support her in her decisions, not try to take the control or responsibility away from her. The conversation was supposedly between Pat and me, but it was Claudia and I who did all the talking. Pat's reserve unnerved me then, as it would continue to do. She listened with a look of polite, mild interest. Everything, even good news, must have sounded implausible and foreign to her ears. I rattled on about birth preparation classes, different kinds of approaches to labor, places they would be likely to find the best rents for apartments in reasonably safe neighborhoods. I would have taken her into our house that very afternoon, but not because she looked lost or needy. She didn't. She was graceful and eerily composed. Only her silence and that stoop of her shoulders beneath her deeply tanned, round face could have been interpreted as need. But what she seemed to want most was privacy and the familiar company of her sister and brother. Together, I sensed, they felt they could survive anything.

I sent Pat and her sister away with a heavy box of my favorite books on pregnancy and childbirth. With everything else that had filled Pat's mind for the past months, I felt it would be a relief for her to turn her attention to the health of her baby and the birth ahead. I lent them a few dollars to do something pleasurable: a meal out, perhaps, a movie, a new maternity shirt. I knew I'd get it back and I did, within the month. It wouldn't hurt to have a few hours of play time before facing the state bureaucracy at the welfare office, the rejection of apartment managers who hate children and single mothers, and the shock of leaving her familiar, if unsupportive, home.

Early in December Claudia had received a letter from her younger sister, postmarked Miami. In it there had been no mention of what Pat was doing in Miami—their family home was far from there, and Claudia had not heard that Pat had moved away. What she had read had puzzled her. Pat had talked about leaving Florida and joining the Air Force, about having to get out and see the world before it was "too late." Too late for what? Pat was only sixteen and barely out of high school, having graduated early.

One week later, while she was making Christmas candy for the children at her school, Claudia impulsively picked up the phone and called home. She casually mentioned the letter from Pat and asked her mother what was going on and why Pat had sounded so strange. Her mother said she had no idea. Everything was fine at home, just fine. Then she mumbled something Claudia couldn't quite catch, but Claudia thought she heard the words "something terrible," and suddenly feeling panicked that something terrible had happened to her baby sister, she pressed for details. She insisted that her mother tell her what was going on. The truth came out at last: Pat was six months pregnant. Claudia was furious to think she might never have found out at all if it were not for her own detective work. Everyone knew the special love she had for Pat. Why, hadn't she practically raised her? If only she'd known at the beginning, there was so much she could have done, Claudia kept telling herself after she put the phone down. But her mother had said they had found out about it only a month ago and that before they could discuss what to do, Pat had packed her bag, stormed out of the house, and gone to live with another sister. They were planning to bring her back home to live after Christmas, when all the relatives had gone. But what would their neighbors say? All her mother could talk about was her own bitterness and humiliation. The hurt had apparently driven both parents so deep into isolation they couldn't share it with anyone, even their grown children.

Claudia knew she would have to come up with a solution. And she had no interest in participating in a coverup of the truth just to protect her parents' feelings. Her mother's final request over the phone had been that if she spoke to Pat she must not, under *any* circumstances, let it slip how she'd found out. What was she supposed to say to Pat? She sat down feeling sick. Flashing through her mind were pictures from the past, memories of the unwed mothers she'd seen when she had been a high school student working in Mercy Hospital as a candy striper volunteer. The unmarried pregnant girls had always entered the hospital through the side entrance, from an un-marked building where they lived, next door to the hospital. They had always come carrying a few belongings for their stay. And they had always left the same way—through the side door. Alone. She'd seen them lying on recovery beds all alone after their birthings, when she was cleaning up in the delivery suite. She had never known what happened to their babies, and she'd wondered at the time what life was like for the girls when they left the hospital. Then a picture of Pat came to mind, the way she'd looked when Claudia had last seen her. Tall and tanned and sassy, with long, slender legs and a childish awkwardness to her walk. Why, she was just a kid, hardly old enough to be interested in sex. She'd never really dated. Their mother was strict with all the girls about dating. How could she be preg-nant? It was a question Claudia never would directly put to her sister. But she tried to imagine Pat as she must look. She could see Pat taking buses around Miami. Walking along the street. Alone. The same girl growing to a woman's body but wearing an unironed maternity shirt over blue jeans. What she imagined made her cry. And what could she do, three thousand miles away, barely able to support herself alone on the meager teacher-training salary at the Montessori school? Somehow she had to get Pat out. And that one thought kept coming through.

That was when Claudia called me. The next evening she telephoned New Orleans, where her younger brother, Eddie, had been living for six months. It was his eighteenth birthday. She'd forgotten. Eddie sounded depressed over the phone—his three roommates had moved out of their apartment on short notice and left him stuck for the entire month's rent. His first attempt at independent living was already losing its luster. When Claudia asked him directly whether he knew about Pat, he didn't know what she was talking about. So she told him briefly all she knew. His immediate response was, "The three of us should be together!" So she'd found one ally in the family.

Now Claudia was ready to speak to Pat herself. She was surprised when the voice that answered the phone in Miami was Pat's, and she tried to sound casual. She said she'd heard Pat was there for a visit and how were things? From Pat she received the same noncommittal answer she'd gotten from their mother. "Oh, nothing special. Everything's fine." Pat had always said that when there was something bothering her that she didn't want to talk about. In fact, the more she didn't want to divulge her feelings, the "finer" things would be. Claudia knew her sister. When she wanted to remain silent, Claudia was sure that even beating it out of her wouldn't work. She had told friends that Pat could survive a concentration camp. No one would ever get anything out of her she didn't want known; she was an expert at appearing not to care just when she cared the most. She couldn't help admiring her sister's strength of will and she respected her privacy; but this time she felt she had to pry. Pat needed help and from the sound of her flat, unresponsive voice, Claudia thought she must be feeling very low. And so the bare truth was slowly dragged out. She was pregnant. Six months pregnant. And she would admit to having made no plans at all for her future, for the birth, for the baby, or for herself. From the sound of it, she had no energy to do anything but get through the days, one at a time.

Claudia hesitated before trying out the solution she and

Eddie had come up with. Because Pat never did respond to pressure, Claudia suggested first that maybe she might like a change of scene. She told her how beautiful the weather was in California. This year it was particularly bright and warm. To Claudia's surprise, Pat offered no immediate resistance to the idea—but she had no enthusiasm for it either. Claudia knew if she were to get Pat out of Florida, she and Eddie would have to lay all the groundwork by themselves. Pat would be no more able to participate than if she were in a coma. She sounded half-dead. Claudia told her sister not to worry, that she would discuss the idea with their parents. "I love you," she told Pat. When she hung up she cried.

It took several lengthy cross-country conversations before Claudia's plan was accepted by their parents. They had to agree that it would solve one huge problem: what to say to everyone if Pat did come home to live. They wouldn't offer any financial help, but Claudia felt she'd gained a victory.

Despite Pat's current frame of mind, it was Claudia's hope that the remainder of her pregnancy and birth might become a positive experience from which Pat could grow and which she could even look back on with some pride. She began to seek advice on getting the best kind of care for Pat and the baby. Pat's problem energized her and gave an added purpose to her own work with young children.

When Eddie heard from his sister that his parents had offered no help at all, he sputtered a few choice remarks and went into action. The next day he took his meager savings out of the bank and wired all of the money to their older brother in Florida. He had called and explained Pat's situation and the need for her leaving Florida for the time being, and asked him to buy a ticket and get Pat onto the first available plane. Claudia would meet her at the airport.

Eddie was only two years older than Pat, and he found it easy to put himself in her position. In his eyes her very survival was at stake, and her pride, just as his was, during this first year out on his own. Helping her out gave him a reason to get out of his own depression.

When Pat flew into San Francisco International Airport on

New Year's Eve, a familiar face was waiting at the gate. And Eddie was already packing up to join them.

As a child Pat had periodically been given messages about what it was like to grow up. "I knew there was a certain time, maybe between sixteen and twenty-five, when you knew from then on your opinions and decisions counted, when you would be worth something." She might not count for much at home, but in her imagination it would come one day in a flash. "I wondered about it a lot, about whether I was ever going to make it to that day." And so she'd spent many hours observing the adults around her, looking at the things they did and the preoccupied, serious way in which they seemed to go about their lives. Pat never checked any of her perceptions to see if they might be true. Her life at home had made her very quiet and self-protective, and there was little intimacy or communication between her and her parents.

She had entered her teens with a sense of urgency, a need to test her parents' iron rule and her mother's old-fashioned attitudes, a need to see for herself what life was all about. Pregnancy at sixteen had put a heavy lid on further exploration for now. She had withdrawn deep inside herself and built tall walls to protect her feelings from all outsiders. She had used this time to explore the world within herself in a way she'd never done before; but it was a lonely, isolated world and not very connected to outside reality or to what was going on inside her body.

It was her brother Bobby who drove her now to the airport, just as three months earlier he had driven her to the clinic where she'd made the appointment for an abortion she could not go through with. And in just the same fashion he dropped her off outside the airport, leaving her to find her own way and avoiding his embarrassment at an emotional scene. It was an abrupt good-bye to childhood, to family, and to home, and a lonely walk into a new future. And Pat couldn't help but feel sorry for herself.

"I stared out the huge window at the planes and said

good-bye. I could never come back." She carried with her a small dark blue canvas bag, her book bag from the eighth grade. In it she'd packed one sweater and several full shirts. She'd also put in one faded denim skirt. It would fit after she had the baby. She was wearing the only pair of maternity pants she owned, a faded blue cotton. They were a bit baggy in the seat and knees and a touch short for current fashion, but at least they didn't bind across the waist. It had been a relief to give up at last the elastic girdle she'd been wearing to hide the truth.

Her father worked for an airline, and Pat had always pictured him out in some distant blue sky, a free spirit, different from what he was at home. She'd idealized the freedom of his flying. But her flight was different. Whether it was a banishment or an act of independence was debatable. At first all she felt was relief, from the pit of her stomach all the way up to her throat. The tension that had always been there, ever since she had discovered she was pregnant, was suddenly gone.

No one seemed to pay any attention to the round-shouldered, brown-skinned young woman with the blue book bag and the protruding belly. But her condition was obvious, even though she was too preoccupied to think about it for the time being. Then suddenly a stranger's remark brought it home. "As I was going through baggage check, the man there said something like, 'There you go, Mama!' At first I figured he was talking to someone in back of me in line. Then he said it again. When I turned around, he added, 'You better get used to it, Mama.'"

The plane was full and Pat found herself sitting next to a middle-aged woman. When the stewardess came by with drinks, Pat asked for milk, and, as though this gave her an opening, the woman started talking. "I guess it was because I'd ordered milk, instead of alcohol or coffee or tea. She said, 'I see you're pregnant.' She began telling me about her pregnancies, how she wished things had been different with her births. She asked me about my husband. I told her I was going to meet him in California."

The five-hour flight marked a rite of passage for Pat. From

now on both she and the people around her would openly acknowledge that she was going to be a mother, even though she might be just a teenager and wore no ring on her finger. There was pleasant anonymity in being known to no one on the plane. She could create a new past to her liking and take any identity she wished.

Yet leaving home, however positive her reasons, would be difficult. Pat couldn't simply wipe out all the training of her family and church as if it had never existed. She was bringing along herself, all the baggage of brooding and self-doubt she had carried with her ever since she could remember. It would take time to trust that things were in fact different now and even more time to feel comfortable with those differences. Her family had spent a year living in California when Pat was very young, and she had some vague memories of those times. But she had forgotten how different the air would smell and feel, the different look of the trees, and the sight of rolling hills where she was used to flat land. A sense of home and security is built of such recognition of the familiar. And so Pat arrived. She hardly dared dream of how it might be, this new life. All she knew was she was opening another door.

She stepped from the plane, walked up the tunneled ramp to the lobby and the crowd of people at the gate. There among the faces of strangers she spotted one face she would know anywhere. She had to smile a bit, seeing the anxious look and furrowed forehead of Claudia, who swept her eyes searchingly over Pat's face and body. Claudia always had been concerned about her. Sometimes that had felt like a heavy cloak Pat wanted to shrug off. But today it felt fine and welcoming. Claudia asked how much luggage Pat had brought with her. She raised the crumpled canvas bag and shrugged and laughed. Hardly anyone noticed the two women who bore a strong resemblance to each other and who left the building with their arms around each other, smiling.

Claudia had not gotten very far in making living arrangements. She was going to try to limit the number of people who knew about Pat to those whom she could really trust and who might be of help. Her landlady, a prying woman who lived in the front of the home where Claudia had her tiny apartment, didn't fall into either category. There was an immediate touch of intrigue to Pat's arrival. She would have to stay at Claudia's place until they found something more suitable, and Claudia waited until dark to bring Pat home. They sneaked in, bedded down for the night in Claudia's single bed, and got up early to leave before the landlady was up. They would not have enough money to find another place until Eddie arrived and could get a job.

Before the week was over, one of Claudia's classmates told her she was going out of town for two weeks. She asked if Claudia and Pat would stay at her place, keep an eye on things, and feed her cat. The apartment was roomy and made a good temporary home for the two sisters. Using it as a base, they made trips to the welfare office and the store. Claudia took Pat with her to class.

Just a week after Pat had arrived, Eddie came by bus, carrying his plastic waterbed mattress folded flat under his arm and a handful of clothes. The three of them bedded down in the borrowed apartment, and Eddie found a job as a shipping clerk at Sears. He was able to get part of a paycheck at the end of his first week. They went looking for apartments and found a cramped and rather unattractive place whose main advantage was that the landlady took no apparent notice of Pat's bulging figure and obvious youth. The neighborhood was racially mixed, a blend of working-class young people and a few families. Unemployed and out-of-school teenage boys worked on their cars and motorcycles and revved them up and down the street for the benefit of one another and any girls who were around.

The apartment had three tiny square rooms, a kitchen with a window whose light was partly blocked by a tall bush, and a bathroom. It was on the first floor of the building and faced the noisy street. Eddie took the larger bedroom and put up his waterbed; Claudia took the other bedroom. Pat said she preferred the living room, though it contained nothing but an uncomfortable old couch. She would take the cushions off at night and use them for a sleeping pad on the floor. They settled in and divided the shopping, cooking, and cleaning-up chores. Pat was left on her own during the days. Claudia was busy studying for exams, and within a couple of weeks Eddie had a girlfriend in the building. Life began to fill up and take on a comforting steadiness.

Claudia had taken Pat to the county social services department the day after she'd arrived in California. The social worker who had interviewed Pat had been brusque. Claudia had been uncomfortable and protective, Pat uncommunicative. The interview had quickly turned into a grilling. The social worker had wanted the identity of the baby's father. Pat had refused to give any name or to talk about the man. The woman's belligerent remark, "You know, we have ways of finding out. We'll get the district attorney to interrogate you!" hadn't budged her. But then the woman had begun to ask why Pat had not had an abortion. "We have enough unwanted children in the world...." "Without people like you giving birth to more" had been the unspoken end of the sentence. Pat's hands had clenched in her lap, but she would not be moved. Claudia had barely kept control. She had been raging inside; but this social worker had stood between them and Pat's eating for the next months. She had said nothing.

Claudia knew nothing of Pat's inner thoughts about the father, or who he might be; she continued to be unwilling to broach the subject of the conception with her sister. It must have been a bad experience, which Pat would like to forget, for her to have kept so silent about it. The social worker's prying and verbal attacks had been, in Claudia's eyes, a clear-cut case of harassment, and she had been angry enough to take the matter to the social worker's supervisor the next day, something her natural timidity would never have allowed her to do on her own behalf. She had received an apology and a promise that the worker would be reprimanded, and within three days Pat had her first check from the state. It was little more than enough for her share of the rent and utilities and bus fares. But in addition there were food stamps. It would be enough for her to get by on.

Claudia mentioned in passing the unnerving interview at the welfare office to her landlady. Feeling distaste at the woman's overly solicitous comments, Claudia knew she'd made a mistake to mention it. But it was too late. The next day the woman cornered her as she was leaving the apartment. She told her she'd set up an appointment for Pat with someone from her church, the Mormon church, so Pat could make arrangements for the baby to be adopted into a "good" home. At the same time the worker at social services was busy on the phone setting up a similar appointment with the state adoption agency. In Claudia's protective eyes it seemed as if everyone was willing to take the baby, but no one was interested in her sister. After all, it was Pat's baby and it was up to her to decide with whom she wanted to place the child, or if she wanted to place the child for adoption at all. Pat and she had only begun to talk about Pat's desires.

Though Claudia intellectually supported Pat's right to make her own decision about the baby, it was beyond her understanding how Pat, or anyone else for that matter, could consider giving up her own flesh and blood. On the bus ride back from the state adoption agency interview, Claudia hesitantly broached what had been going around in her head for some time. She offered to help Pat raise the baby if she chose to keep him or her. Pat didn't say much, so she went on. She'd even take the baby herself if Pat would find it a help. She knew it sounded preposterous, her being single, still in teacher training, and with no prospect of a decent salary for a year or more, but she had to offer. What she was really acknowledging was her aching to be a mother. She couldn't bear the thought that Pat's baby might go to a stranger. When Pat made no response, Claudia didn't press further. She gave her sister credit for being wise enough to know what was best for herself.

Pat seemed to have made up her mind to place the baby for adoption, so Claudia made an appointment with the Catholic adoption agency and took Pat for an interview. She assumed their church would have a better alternative than the state agency, where things had seemed so impersonal and cold. The woman there told Pat that the baby would live in a foster home for several weeks until they placed the baby with a family. Pat asked if she could see the baby at all during that time. No, it was their policy that the biological mothers not see their babies once they had made their decision. Pat asked if she might be able to see the home into which the baby went. The woman said firmly that this was *never* done. Both the state and church agencies apparently took the same line. They would gladly accept her baby, but they wanted as little as possible to do with Pat's needs. Claudia firmly told her landlady that Pat was not interested in meeting with anyone from the Mormon adoption agency, but she wondered what alternatives were left. Pat didn't offer any help. She hardly spoke about her plans for the baby, and Claudia waited for something to surface in her sister that would give her some idea of what they should do next.

Meanwhile, Pat was finding things to her liking around the apartment. "The people all around us in the building were what my parents would call 'lower class.' They crowded into their apartments, and it was always noisy through the walls." But she felt safe living amidst such a mass of people in a complex of apartments. Because she was pregnant she felt she had nothing to fear from strange men, and Pat always had liked to strike up conversations with strangers. Her brother and sister quickly assumed parental roles toward her and worried about her casual friendliness. As they went to work and school each day, they left Pat at home with admonishments about what not to do. "Eddie would always scream at me if he caught me talking to people. He told me that's how I got into these messes." But Pat was enjoying most of the hours she spent out of everyone's way. At the first opportunity each day, she fled the dreary interior of their bare, undecorated, and poorly lit apartment for the light and fresh warm air of the outside. Although it was midwinter the weather was mild, and there were several big city parks within walking distance. She had always loved to walk.

"I would go to the park every day and sit in the same spot with my book." The books changed and her belly grew larger, but her favorite spot was the same, a grassy knoll near a few trees alongside the tennis courts.

"People would come up and talk to me between their tennis games." Most of those who came and stood or sat and struck up conversations were men. They must have been fascinated by the young woman, always alone and wearing the same outfit, sometimes with an old brown sweater thrown over her shoulders, always with some book. She was getting browner-skinned by the day and seemed to be enjoying her aloneness. "The guys would ask me what it was like to be pregnant and what I was going to do after the baby came." With no one there to contradict whatever story she chose to make up about the pregnancy, Pat found it easier to say that she had been raped. This would inevitably bring a murmur of sympathy and usually silenced further questions, but once in a while the listener's curiosity got the best of him or her.

"Once a lady came over to me and started asking questions. After I'd told her the story, she told me how her daughter wanted children so much and how she couldn't have any of her own. She acted really interested when I told her I was giving up the baby for adoption. She was nice enough but I felt like she wanted to grab the baby inside me and run off with it for her daughter." Pat was to find that adoption was an emotion-packed subject and that once hearing she wasn't planning to keep the baby, people would usually launch right into a story about this or that relative or acquaintance who couldn't have a baby of her own but who would love to adopt one.

Claudia gave her the name of the physician, Dr. Creevy, who was most highly recommended by her friends as being someone who really cared about women and birth, who listened and did things the way you wanted. She went with her to the first visit and was surprised to hear her sister open up so quickly to this man. His manner was gentle without being paternalistic, and he seemed truly interested in Pat, not in prying at all into her privacy. Claudia heard Pat tell this stranger more in that visit than she had heard in weeks of living under the same roof with her. Pat talked about wanting to have the baby adopted into a loving home and about her disappointing visits to the adoption agencies. She told him her thoughts about the adoption. She might like to be able to meet the parents, so she could feel sure about letting the baby go.

The doctor pricked up his ears at that remark. He had attended several thousand births in his fifteen-year practice and had had few experiences with women planning to give up their babies for adoption. But in each case he had offered to help find suitable parents from among a number of his own patients or acquaintances who were unable to conceive and wanted to be parents. And he had been involved already in three cases of private adoption, where the baby had not gone to a foster home, where no agency had been involved, and an adoption attorney—Phil Adams—had handled all the arrangements.

At their next meeting, after the long history had been taken and the physical exam had been done, the physician, Pat, and Claudia sat in his office and talked for almost an hour. He wanted to know if Pat had thought of having natural childbirth and to recommend it if she hadn't. He wasn't the first to mention the phrase. I had broached the subject to her at our first meeting. Claudia had been resistant to the idea from the first. She had told Pat of her fear that having an unmedicated birth would be very painful, both physically and emotionally, especially because Pat would be giving birth to a baby she'd never see again. A friend of hers had relinquished a baby years ago, and her opinion had been that it would be impossible to see your baby and hold your baby and still stick with a decision to relinquish him or her for adoption. Claudia couldn't resist interjecting her anxieties. Wouldn't it leave too deep and vivid impressions, permanent emotional scars on Pat if she were to go through the birth awake, seeing and feeling everything? The physician did his best to reassure her. No, he said, her sister would not necessarily find the experience more traumatic if she had natural childbirth. First of all, natural childbirth was definitely better for the baby, because the baby would have no drugs in his or her body in the first hours and days of life, the time when the baby had the job of adjusting to a new world without the food and oxygen from his or her mother's body. And the women he saw, almost without exception, felt natural childbirth had been one of the finest experiences of their lives. If Pat was going to make a life for herself without the baby, then her memories of a good birth experience might be especially helpful, he felt. Whatever she chose, and it was her choice completely, he did insist that she go to childbirth classes and prepare for the labor as if she were planning an unmedicated, spontaneous delivery. That way, no matter what she finally chose to do, she would know as much as possible about the process and about her body. So in the end it was Claudia who accompanied Pat to the series of eight childbirth classes and Claudia who diligently practiced all the many ways she could support Pat during labor to make Pat's work easier. And it was Claudia who would accompany Pat right into labor, be at Pat's side throughout, with warm cloths and pressure against her spine.

Some women never experience the euphoria that is one of the many delights pregnancy can bring to those who are ready for it. Those who do talk about a heightened sense of smell and taste, a magical quality to the light, a greater appreciation for the beauty in life, and a feeling of the preciousness of the fleeting moments until birth, all triggered by the growing lives inside them. Emotions during pregnancy run a deep and shifting course, and there are wistful times, memories of girlhood past, which seem all the more sweet for having now been left behind. For the woman who chooses pregnancy and looks forward to parenthood, all the emotional ups and downs that wash over her are taken as they come. For the woman who backs into parenthood, who faces birth with fear, who never has felt comfortable with her body and its changes, or with the feeling of being swept away in pure sensation and emotion, pregnancy can be a particularly traumatic time—a constant struggle against the feeling she is losing control. In a very young woman, who has experienced little of her own potential, pregnancy can seem like the beginning of a life sentence without reprieve, or a fantasy of playing dolls with a real-life baby who will always love you. Pity any woman who finds herself pregnant and not wanting to be so, who cannot make the shift of mind into becoming a parent, a *source* of love rather than the *object* of affection. Pity her all the more if she is without a mate, without the love of another adult to share the adventure with her, or without the support of other loving people around her willing to help her care for this child and respect this child's needs as a separate human being.

The time for relishing the sensations, changes, and blooming of pregnancy came late for Pat. It had been thwarted in her home by shame and guilt, and there was a void where there should have been someone else eager to share the adventure on which she was embarking. Any pleasure she might have felt had been diminished by the manner in which she had become pregnant. Yet in the end the pregnancy and the baby growing inside her won out. Not long after arriving in California and settling into her life there, she found herself experiencing that giddy elatedness at last. She described it as excitement, a feeling of being fully alive. The baby had been moving and dancing inside her for months, but with no one to share in the magic of it, Pat had never paid much attention. Considering her age and the sorts of substances teenagers in modern society fill their bodies up with, Pat ate comparatively well and kept herself free of drugs. She didn't skimp or try to diet in a desperate attempt to keep her own shape. The exercise she gave herself in walking every day was a benefit to her body and a rhythmic pattern for the baby. It was soothing to her mind, which was also linked to the baby by their shared chemistry. Her body had been pregnant a long time, but now her mind and spirit were filling out too.

She sometimes found herself alone in the apartment, naked in front of a mirror and liking what she saw. It was at such moments that she began to feel a relationship forming with the one inside. "I would do lots of things with the baby when nobody was around. I'd dance. I would put on a record of Eddie's and dance in front of the mirror." Pregnancy is a sensual time. Pat became more and more comfortable looking at herself, rubbing her skin all over with almond oil. "I liked to take off all my clothes when I was home alone. I even took a mirror sometimes and looked between my legs." She'd never dared to look before. And so she made peace with her own body at the same time that she began to acknowledge the bond with the little body inside her. One day she began talking to the baby, and that began a game of conversation and playfulness many expectant mothers delight in. "At first the baby was just an idea in my head. I had felt for a long time, ever since I dreamed about a little girl baby trying to swim to the surface as I was drowning, that this baby wanted to be born. But it took a while to feel in tune with it." The "in tune" feeling could come only when Pat felt free to enjoy the pregnancy. "When I took baths I would think about how good it felt, and I would tell that out loud to the baby, like I was talking to a friend in the room. Pretty soon we'd have conversations every day." The baby held up his or her end of the conversations by kicking in response to pressure from a hand on the belly, or by suddenly increasing activity after some movement of Pat's.

"I would say, 'You know that I love you, don't you? I'm doing what is good for you with this adoption. You'll be better off for it, I know.' I'd tell her that, just like we were old friends. I never told anyone about my conversations with her, because I didn't think they would understand." But by the last weeks of her pregnancy, Pat spent more and more time in the apartment talking and playing with the baby. She would tell the baby all about her activities at the end of each day. "I had no one else. And she would listen. When she moved or jerked her elbow, I'd say, 'Oh, so you think what I'm saying is funny, do you?'"

Pat dared to tell the baby her uncensored thoughts, not just what she thought the baby would like to hear. "I'd tell her I was looking forward to having my own belly back. 'It's nothing personal, you know, but you've got to come out. You can't live in here forever!' "

There was laughter once more in Pat's solitary life, especially when she was alone with the baby. Eddie, Claudia, and Pat shared their moments of lightness too. Teasing one another began, and laughter bubbled up as regularly as did the arguments so familiar to families sharing tight quarters. Claudia noticed in particular how much pleasure Pat got from her walks and the kind of protection pregnancy did seem to bring her. She began to call her sister Duck when Pat's splay-footed gait became more pronounced at the end of pregnancy, as her pelvic bones shifted and she walked with a bounce. On their walks together the two women would invariably run into the same people. The neighborhood young men would always stop what they were doing, bow or nod, and offer a familiar, "How're you doin' today, Mama!" One of them, who was usually seen underneath the hood of his car, brought flowers to the apartment on several occasions. The nuns at the local church where Pat went every day smiled and often asked how she was doing. In their rough, sprawling neighborhood with streetwise young men, everyone made Pat feel welcome and showed an interest in the baby.

Visits to the church, like her walks to the park, played an important part in her feeling of well-being during the last weeks. "It didn't matter what particular faith it was, I think it was just the ritual of going there and thinking about the spiritual for a few minutes every day." She had gone to church every day too when she was a little girl in uniform attending Catholic school. The ritual was one of the things she'd missed in public high school. The neighborhood Catholic church had an informal feeling. "The priest would see me there each day and after a while he'd say something like, 'Good for you!' as if he were sort of glad to see me pregnant."

Although the ritual of going to church gave her strength and support, church doctrines were another matter. Pat began seriously to question the principles of her faith in the time she was waiting for the baby to come. She could not forget what kind of adoption her church had wanted to give her. She now knew a great deal about herself and what she wanted for her baby and was disappointed that her own church didn't offer her any solutions that fit her desires.

She returned for a weekly visit with the doctor and, as she had on many of the other visits, sat quietly as he did much of the talking, answering his questions with monosyllables until she had something she wanted to say. It was a surprise to her that the physician and nurse practitioner both wanted to listen to her, because she found it as difficult as ever to talk about herself. Often she wasted precious time pulling away from their questions, making them have to figure out just what kind of birth and adoption she wanted. In the curious mental construct only a teenager could make, Pat felt she didn't need to talk because anyone you needed to explain things to couldn't possibly see your point anyway. It was an excuse for continuing her pattern of being disappointed in authority figures. Fortunately for her she had picked several strangers in this drama who wouldn't join her game, who were determined to help her achieve the very best.

At one of the first visits, her physician had given Pat and Claudia the names of several childbirth educators in town and recommended that they call the one he had found best for preparing women for natural childbirth. Claudia had called and signed the two of them up for the next series of weekly classes. There were eight classes and the baby was then due in seven weeks. Pat went initially because she had the sense to realize that what she had learned about birth from women such as her mother wasn't useful or accurate. For her mother and her aunts, birth meant horrible pain, and you needed to be unconscious or numbed with drugs to survive it. For some reason she never had believed them. "It didn't make any sense the way people were telling me you should give birth. Everyone always pushed the pain of it and the need to stop all the feelings. And I knew in the back of my mind what I wanted to do for the baby but I didn't say anything." She went to the classes and there had her eyes opened to the possibilities. Soon she even found herself talking more easily with the doctor about what she was learning and what some of her hopes were.

Claudia had been the logical partner for Pat in the classes, but her role there and at the birth was never really discussed between the sisters. She was shy about pushing or intruding on Pat's privacy in any way, but it was maddeningly difficult to work with Pat in class because she seemed to pull away during every practice session. One of the major goals of the teacher was to facilitate communication between partners so that they could work smoothly together in the unpredictable course of labor—when a laboring woman often finds it impossible to talk, and she is so engulfed by sensation that she is driven out of all her rational faculties and into body language. Instead of accepting Claudia as a surrogate mate for the purposes of the classes, Pat spent a great deal of her time looking critically at her sister. She did feel they had a good relationship and were a team as they practiced the breathing and did massage for relaxation with the other six couples in the class. But, as Pat once confided to Claudia after class, they weren't a *real* couple, merely a pretend one. What she was thinking, but couldn't say to Claudia, was, "You aren't the father or my husband, but I think you really want to be the mother of this baby!"

As Pat went through the last weeks, with the strange blend of awkwardness and grace so peculiar and common to women late in pregnancy, she found her belly was the drawing card for many unwanted conversations. The mere sight of her walking, usually alone, with no ring on her finger and obviously young, was enough to attract the attention of many women who had carried their own stories of pregnancy and birth around for years, unfinished and needing to be retold. They would come up to her on the street or on the ground where she was sitting reading and would pour out their own stories. Stories of pregnancies unplanned, of months and months of nausea and backaches and babies coming too soon and too close together, husbands too insensitive or too busy, and births that had been traumatic encounters with fear and suffering, loneliness and remorse. They would give her unasked-for advice all mixed up with their own vivid memories, and they would leave Pat depressed.

At the classes she saw a wholly different side of childbirth, not the ordeal she'd heard so much about but the personal satisfaction and the adventure of working to your fullest capacity and learning to be in harmony with the natural process, even with pain. Claudia's presence helped, although the two of them never did break down the barriers and awkwardness they felt. The sisters struggled with unspoken communication, and touching, which was so important to Pat's relaxation during birth, didn't come easily. Claudia occasionally voiced her hurt. "What is it?" she'd say. "I know you can't stand me to touch you, but can't you just say you love me?" And Pat would sullenly reply, "I can't talk now. I don't feel anything." Even though Claudia was older and had some sense of what Pat was struggling with—and that it had nothing to do with Claudia—it was difficult not to perceive Pat's coldness as rejection. Pat was essentially alone and in need of the very kind of support she couldn't ask for or tolerate. That was the hardest thing for both sisters, knowing that not only was Pat going through labor on her own with the baby, but that she would be alone after the birth and on into the future. Even the love and affection of a sister couldn't soften this truth.

As Pat grew into a feeling of kinship with the baby, her concern for the baby's well-being carried over into her dream life. During those last weeks she had two dreams, which she remembered clearly on waking. The first was full of anxiety and feelings of helplessness, but ended triumphantly.

"It was daytime and I was in town driving my first car around, a goldish gray 1963 Fairlane. Way out in Port St. Lucie, there is flat land with streets but very few houses and nothing else. That's where I was. I knew I was about to have this baby, and at the same time the car was running out of gas. I didn't know what to do. Should I keep going or should I try to get back to civilization and find help? Then I thought, How will I feed the baby? Next thing I knew the baby was there, lying on the front seat next to me. At first I didn't know what to do with it and didn't pick it up. I felt stranded. Finally I picked it up and started caring for it. It was a girl." The dream ended there.

The second dream was a more refined version of an earlier dream, which had recurred throughout the pregnancy. In the first version, as she told it, she was walking, striding rather, out into the hills. She was alone. In the next version, she was bringing the baby back over those same hills, carrying the baby in her arms. In its final version, dreamed just before the birth, Pat saw the same hills and once more she was striding out into the distance. It was daytime again, morning perhaps, and the sun was out and the hills were green and round and empty. Over the crest of one hill and down below, she spotted a small, still, blue pond. At the edge of the pond, she made a bed for herself to lie in. There she must have given birth, for in the next sequence the baby was lying between her legs on the grass. She scooped the baby up in her arms and took off, striding back up across the hills she'd come from, as the sun warmed the two of them.

The idea of being alone, of accomplishing this thing all by herself, seemed important to Pat. Nowhere in any of her dreams did she imagine the birth as it would be, taking place in a cramped and sterile room filled with people. Always in her imaginings she was alone, with the baby and a benevolent nature. And always the birth itself was missing. But she did see herself taking responsibility for the baby, after initial confusion and anxiety. Pat had come of age and was now thinking consciously of the well-being of this baby. She felt the responsibility for the baby's welfare keenly, another life for which she was sole caretaker.

Thus it was that by the time her prenatal visits with her physician had begun to focus on concrete options for the adoption, Pat was herself ready to voice her desires and concerns, to make decisions consciously, and to picture the probable consequences of her actions.

At first there had been a question whether her labor would

wait for the finish of the childbirth classes. She had a due date of late March, and the series didn't finish until the first week of April. But when the last class ended, the baby still showed no sign of coming. Pat's days were now filled. Her appointments with the physician were now twice a week. There was still more preparation to be made for the adoption. Her physician had encouraged her to participate in the selection of the parents. He had spoken most warmly of one couple to whom he had lived next door for several years. They were already raising a little girl they had adopted from birth and had, he recalled, been eager for a second child. Pat thought they sounded interesting. He offered to call them and find out whether they might like this baby. Then he gave her a brief description of private adoption, a legal process in California and many other states, which avoided foster homes and allowed the baby to be given directly to the new parents. She would have to work with an attorney if this option interested her, and he told her again of the attorney in the city who had arranged several adoptions for patients of his. Pat liked the idea that in private adoption the baby could go directly from her to the new parents, and she wondered why no one in Florida or at the agencies had ever mentioned this possibility to her. The attorney, the doctor said, would insist on meeting her before he would agree to work with her, in order to discuss all of her rights and the legal details. He also liked to be able to confirm for himself that the woman was not being railroaded into anything that she would later regret, that she understood what she was getting into, relinquishing her baby and doing it without the anonymity of going through an agency. In just one office visit Pat found herself moving much closer to her unspoken goal—to be able to see for herself that the parents were good, kind people, and to be able to keep the baby from spending any time in foster care after birth. Her doctor said he would call the attorney and set up an appointment for them to meet with him as soon as possible.

The visit to Phil Adams in San Francisco went well. Her physician accompanied her and brought along his eight-year-old daughter, whom Pat had met before. Pat talked freely with the attorney. He seemed to have just the right blend of solicitousness, sternness, and teasing to draw out a reticent teenager. By the end of an hour, she announced that she was ready to meet the couple, as he suggested she should. Afterward the physician took Pat and his daughter to a park, to dinner at a Japanese restaurant, and to a concert. Things were falling into place quickly, and Pat could not help showing the relief it brought her. She was playful and talkative.

Meanwhile the couple her physician had called were quite interested. The news that there might be a baby for them had come when they had least expected it and had put all hope for another child behind them. They too called Phil Adams, who had handled their first adoption, five years earlier. He told them Pat was certainly a healthy young woman who should have a healthy child. They could hardly have been more surprised when later that evening Pat's physician called to ask if they would like the chance to meet Pat. They would indeed. The date was set for the following Friday. The baby was already due—overdue even—so the baby could arrive any day.

And so Pat found herself late Friday afternoon dressing with a bit of extra care in anticipation of seeing her physician, myself, and two strangers who were to play key roles in her life. The young woman who stepped out of the doorway, quickly crossed the street, and slipped into the car seemed very different from the one who had stepped off the airplane just a few months earlier. Her shoulders were hardly stooped at all, her skin glowed with color, and her blouse was freshly ironed. She hadn't even considered asking her brother or sister to accompany her this evening. She felt comfortable going without a chaperone. I was there only as her advocate, in case she should need one. If the evening went well and she felt good about the couple, she told herself, she would look no further for parents for her baby.

How little needs to be said or done on momentous occasions. The simple preparations had been laid well, and in spite of the short notice the evening was a resounding success. Pat talked little but was perfectly at ease. It was as if the trials and strains of the months preceding had all been leading her to this. She had found a happy solution to the biggest unknown—what would become of her baby.

An hour and a half slipped by quickly. Pat's physician suggested everyone might like to come to his home to sit in on an informal meeting for couples in his practice who were contemplating home birth. It would give them more time to be together with no agenda or pressure.

At the house fifteen people sat in a large circle around the living room, and they all introduced themselves to the group by stating briefly what their interests were in home birth. Halfway around the room a woman named Maria briefly told about her first birthing and what a chilling experience it had been. She said she'd relinquished that baby for adoption. She'd been eighteen at the time and living in the Midwest, and ever since then hospitals in her mind were associated with very negative feelings. She was trying to make this coming birthing a positive experience. As she talked her face tightened, and she didn't try to hold back the tears. Though her first birthing had been almost thirteen years earlier, the memory and its pain were fresh. Hers was not the only story of an unpleasant birth experience among the group. Nor was she the only one determined to do it differently this time. But it was she who caught the pregnant teenager's attention.

After the meeting Pat walked over to Maria. It was the first time in her pregnancy that she had met anyone she felt might understand exactly what she was going through. Maria's first birthing also had meant loss instead of an exciting adventure into parenthood. The two women felt an immediate connection, and Maria offered to drive her home so they could talk some more. Pat smiled broadly as she said goodnight to everyone.

The prospective parents returned to their home elated at the events of the evening. They had liked Pat right off and felt her concern for the baby and her strength and gentleness. She had even mentioned to them during the evening that she would be happy to have them at the actual birth if they would like to be there. That they would have to think about. They'd never imagined such a thing. As it turned out, there was no need to rush anything, for her due date came and went and there seemed to be no birth in sight. Her physician, having long before made plans for a weekend away with his family, was faced with having to cancel his few days of play or possibly miss Pat's birth. He was uncomfortable with not being there, as he felt he could not guarantee things would go as Pat wished unless he was there to act as a buffer between her and the regimentation of the hospital. And so Pat was invited along on the weekend with his family, and they stayed in a suite at a motel on the coast. She played with the little girl, and they all took long walks on the windy expanse of beach. Pat was quiet. Her mind was full of the curious preoccupations that make a birth both an imminent reality and a fantasy to a mother-in-waiting. In addition there must have been the memory of the brief encounter that had left her pregnant. Now she would soon be face to face with the child that was the result. The arrival of her baby would be a meeting up with the past, a past she'd tried to erase from her mind.

There is a belief among physicians and midwives that a woman's going much beyond two weeks past due date is cause for concern. Very late, very large babies, like very early, very small ones, may have more difficulty in labor. Impatience and pressure in the field of obstetrics and newborn care pushes many physicians into artificially ending pregnancy and stimulating labor with drugs when a woman is hardly a week "overdue." Pat's physician, without real cause to act and being cautious and not one to hurry when nature takes its time, felt it best to let the labor begin when it would. He did a test to see whether the baby was still getting enough nourishment from the placenta. The baby was. So he waited. But when Pat had gone two and a half weeks past due date, he began to make noises about the possibility of inducing her labor. Pat didn't like this at all, although she wouldn't tell him so. She felt sure that the baby was going to come in the baby's own right time and that there was no cause for concern, but she left his office on a warm spring day in mid-April with the news that, if the baby had not started labor by the coming Saturday, her physician wanted to hospitalize her for induction of labor. Three days more. That was all the pregnancy she had left.

I stopped by the apartment unannounced that afternoon to see how she was doing. Pat was at home in the living room, deep in thought. She told me of the deadline. I asked if she thought there was any reason she herself might be holding up the labor. I knew it was possible for women, like the females of other species, to postpone the onset of labor and inhibit its progress from fear and anxiety. There is ample record of mammal mothers-to-be suddenly stopping labor when under stress, particularly stress caused by a sudden change of environment or the unwanted presence of a human observer. Many a family after waking the children to come and see Spot have her puppies has found Mama simply won't perform to a crowd. Pat thought about it. She said she could think of nothing in particular that was bothering her. So I approached it in a different way and asked whether there might be any reason Pat could think of why she would not want the birth to happen now. She was quiet for some minutes, thinking, and said finally that she didn't think so. Only, she added vaguely, she guessed she hadn't really made any plans for herself for after the birth. It was, she said, as if everything would end with the birth and giving up the baby. I suggested perhaps it would be a good time to begin visualizing what kind of a life she wanted for herself after the birth. Perhaps her mind was holding up release of the hormones that started labor in order to hang on to the pregnancy, which had become the most familiar, most stable part of her life. Of the women I've met who were without mates, or whose partners were unsupportive, or who planned to relinquish their babies for adoption at birth, many did seem to start into labor several weeks after they were due or had difficulty making normal progress when they did go into labor. I never underestimate the power of the unconscious to influence what goes on in the body.

Pat spent the rest of the day in the apartment, alone. She told me later she did a great deal of turning over in her mind what we had discussed. Perhaps she did have some control over when this baby came, although she couldn't imagine just how. But she had to admit to herself that it was odd that she hadn't given a thought to making plans for her own future. Friday night passed and still labor did not begin. When Saturday came Pat telephoned me, sounding greatly disappointed; she had not yet had even a twinge of a contraction. She was resigned to her physician's decision, but she didn't like it one bit. It didn't seem right, she said, that one minute she could be wandering around leading her life, and the next minute some chemical injected into her vein could force her body to give birth. But she had to admit she was twenty-one days late. She was adamant that there could not be any error about when she had gotten pregnant. And I was not about to press her about the past.

Four months in a new environment had done a lot for Pat. It had boosted her self-confidence, given her the feeling her opinions might be worth something. But it was not enough to overcome years of training in obedience to adults. No, she could not refuse a doctor's insistence. And so, after a phone call from him, she once more packed a few things in her blue school bag. She didn't forget the green hand-knit baby sweater that she'd been given at class. The teacher's mother enjoyed knitting, and had sent enough baby sweaters for everyone in the group. This would be her parting gift to the baby. Eddie and Claudia got ready too. I went to her apartment and found Pat washing her feet in the bathtub. She had put on one of her well-worn maternity shirts over her stretched-out blue pants. Eddie drove Pat and Claudia to the hospital. I followed in my car. Fifteen minutes later the four of us trooped into the lobby of the large medical center and up to the admitting desk.

PAUL AND VICKI:

Parents-in-Waiting

WHEN PAUL AND VICKI first decided to look into adoption, it was early in the 1970s and they had been married for five years. Abortion was by then legal in the United States, following the Supreme Court's ruling. Partly as a result of that decision, infants available for adoption were rapidly becoming a scarce commodity, as many more women chose to abort an unwanted pregnancy rather than face giving birth to a child they could not raise. By the time Paul and Vicki began searching for a second baby, three years after getting Amanda, children to adopt in infancy and in good health were virtually nonexistent.

Vicki had entered married life without any great eagerness to have children. She had had a career as a biologist that was as promising as Paul's, and their life together had seemed complete. But after a few years they had begun to feel pressure, especially from Paul's mother, to start a family. She belonged to a club of women in their sixties who had gone to high school together in a small midwestern town and who had met monthly ever since graduation. At their meetings they played cards, ate, and talked about grandchildren. For years, Paul says, his mother had been the only one of the group who had no grandchildren to brag about and not even one on the way.

"We were told about that on occasion," says Vicki. "Paul's mother would manage to drop into a phone conversation, 'Suzie has a new grandchild! Mary has a new grandson! Kate has six grandchildren, would you believe that! And you know, it's really interesting: I'm the only one who has none!' "

It was subtle pressure, but pressure nevertheless. Paul was expected to continue the family line.

Decisions about having children and the timing of conception, even in a day of supposed contraceptive freedom and legalized abortion, are often made whimsically, as if real choice is too difficult to face when it comes to having children, too awesome to approach consciously and with planning. So, like many others around them, as their twenties began to slip by and their careers prospered, Paul and Vicki gave up using any contraception without ever making a conscious, shared decision to become parents. But when after several years Vicki was still not pregnant, their decision became painfully conscious. In a matter-of-fact way that hints at the emotional energy beneath, Vicki describes their dilemma.

"I was twenty-nine and unable to get pregnant after trying and trying. Pretty soon we thought about adopting, and it wasn't very long before our families knew we were looking for a baby." They were teased a bit. "Paul's middle sister was then dating a guy, and she once suggested to us that she had the perfect solution to our problem. 'You know, if you two paid me enough. . . .' " Surrogate motherhood was unheard of then, and it caused quite a laugh in their family. But when Vicki's gynecologist, Don, called her into his office after one more visit to determine the cause of their infertility, it was suddenly no laughing matter. He knew Vicki well and felt he could put it bluntly. "Look, Vicki. I can't find anything physically wrong with you or Paul. There are some people who just don't get pregnant with a given person." Vicki asked what that meant and he explained. "I was told I had four options. I could give up on having kids. I could get divorced and marry someone else, because I'd probably get pregnant with different sperm. I could have artificial insemination with a donor. Or we could adopt."

As Vicki saw it, her choices were more limited than that. She had no intention of ending her marriage, and found it difficult to consider artificial insemination as a possibility. "I didn't want to carry somebody else's child!" She found Paul shared her distaste for artificial insemination, and separating just because they couldn't have children together was as unthinkable to him as it was to her. That didn't leave much choice.

"We thought about our options for a long time," Paul reflects. "It really didn't bother me that we weren't having children, but the idea of adoption did at first. I guess I had the typical response of many men in my culture, that it's not *my* blood." But by now Vicki wasn't willing to accept being childless permanently.

First, as Paul recognized, there had to be some coming to terms with the fact of their apparent infertility. The process of accepting an unwanted truth is an internal one and must have been a particularly lonely one for Vicki. Paul knows this. "We talked about it, sure. And then, after a while, we didn't talk about it anymore. There were times, I know, when I wasn't home, when Vicki did a lot of crying."

Then Vicki began to press Paul about adopting a child. After a while he agreed that it would be all right to adopt, but as young a baby as possible. Among the middle class and the wealthy, for those who were considered neither too young nor too old and who offered the kinds of homes that pleased adoption agency workers, adoption had always been an easy matter. That is, it had been as long as adoptable infants were in rich supply. Vicki and Paul found they lived in a neighborhood that was a virtual sea of adoption—with the people next door, the couple across the street, the couple behind them all adoptive parents. They assumed that finding a child would be easy. But they were several years too late. Finding a baby proved no easy matter for them.

Their need for help in finding a child necessitated exposing the privacy of their well-ordered life and themselves to the scrutiny of strangers. Vicki began with the county adoption agency, that established agent in the adoption business, which sets standards and rules on suitability and matches potential parents with available children. She was quickly rebuffed—at twenty-nine she was considered too old. Her local agency had made an arbitrary cut-off age, because they were receiving so many more applications from people seeking healthy infants than there were babies available. Next she tried the Children's Home Society, an established and respected large private agency and the only other agency in their area. They weren't even interested enough to take Vicki's initial application. Shocked and discouraged, she returned to her gynecologist's office. He might not be an adoption agency but he might have some suggestions, because he had delivered so many babies. He told Vicki he'd been involved in surprisingly few adoptions in the fifteen years he'd been in practice. But he did know of an attorney who specialized in adoption, whom he'd used on two occasions. He was reputed to be rather an institution himself, because he'd handled so many legal private adoptions.

Vicki didn't know the difference between an agency adoption and a private adoption before she met Phil Adams. But she got a quick education after she went to his office for an appointment. Paul went with her, and what they heard from their attorney was not encouraging.

"At something like $75 an hour, he went into great detail discouraging us, saying it would be years, if ever, before we would ever find a baby. He sat there with a vile cigar, teasing us and telling us stories about adoptions he'd handled. He wanted to know which one of us was going to take care of this imagined child, because I had a good job and Paul was also working full time at his. I said I was, that I was going to give up my job, at least for the first few years, to stay home with the child. 'What do you mean!' He practically leaped out of his seat, he was so excited. 'My wife is a teacher, and she wouldn't dream of giving up *her* job for any kids.' I gathered from that remark that they didn't have any children, at least not together; then he said he'd raised four in his first marriage."

Along with the story-telling, Phil gave Paul and Vicki some

serious practical information about the philosophy of private adoption. Vicki carefully remembered everything he had told them. "Assuming we could find someone wanting to give up a child for adoption, we should get as much information as possible about both parents, and we should in turn give as much information as possible about ourselves to the mother. He strongly recommended that we meet each other in advance if at all feasible. Above all, he felt we should do it all as adults, out in the open, not hiding behind doors and sneaking around." It was this matter-of-fact, commonsensical approach that attracted Vicki to Phil Adams, despite the cigars and offputting remarks. She returned home with Paul, determined to be the squeaky wheel who made enough of a nuisance of herself with the attorney to keep their cause in front of him. She chuckles today, recalling her frequent phone calls to his office to inquire whether he had any news for them yet.

Although they would have the choice of whether to accept a particular infant that became available, even in private adoption Paul and Vicki would still be taking the luck of the draw with regard to which child came to their attention. Private adoption has its own screening process, which is an unwritten one. Only the most persistent get references in the first place, and these references usually come from friends or physicians who come across a pregnant woman planning to relinquish her child, and they pass along the news. Most obstetricians regularly get form letters from people they don't know who are searching for a child and are writing to every physician in the phone book, sending out pictures of themselves and résumés of their lives. Each person searching for a child must find his or her own best way. For some it is a form letter. For some it is prayer. For some it is telling everyone they know and everyone they meet. The process may be agonizingly slow, full of detours, sudden hopes, and shattered expectations. A child you hear is available one week goes to another couple the next week, and you are always one step away from being there at the right time. Vicki's persistence, however, paid off surprisingly quickly.

"I think Phil just couldn't stand getting any more of my phone calls, so he found us a child." They had first gone to his office in December, and their daughter, Amanda, was born the following May. Phil called once in March to tell them about a woman who would be giving birth to a mixed-race child. She and Paul talked a lot about taking this baby. Then they went to see Phil, hemming and hawing and indecisive. "He took one look at our faces and said, 'Forget it! If you're not comfortable with it, forget it!' " That was that. Raising this child in the area where they lived, where there wasn't a Latino, black, or Asian person for miles, Paul and Vicki felt, would bring too many problems upon the child. Another consideration for Vicki was the grandparents. "They come from a different generation, and I couldn't see them playing grandparents to a child of a different race. I believe a child needs a full, extended family, and our parents' attitudes do make a difference."

Another set of parents was found for that baby, and a month later Phil telephoned, saying he might have a baby for them. He had just received a letter from a woman due to give birth in six or eight weeks. She was married and living out of state and had heard of Phil from a friend. She was asking him to help her find parents for her baby—people who would take the baby home directly from the hospital, so the baby wouldn't have to be placed in a foster home. In her letter she expressed a preference that this be a Christian home, but, more important, she wanted to be sure that the parents were healthy and financially able to raise a child. Phil told Paul and Vicki the couple didn't have enough money to pay the medical bills for the birth, and that they would therefore be expected to pay them—this practice being a longstanding tradition in private adoption. They must agree to put the estimated total needed for the hospital and physician in a separate bank account, to which only the attorney and they had access. The hospital where the woman planned to give birth would then be sent a record of the deposit. Without that guarantee that the bill would be paid, the hospital would not admit the woman when her labor started. He had to warn them that there was always the possibility that once this baby was born, the birth parents might choose to keep the baby themselves. In properly handled private adoption, the greatest power initially lies with the biological parents, and every attempt is made to protect the woman giving birth so that she does not feel any pressure to guarantee her child will be placed for adoption prior to her signing final consent papers. But at least with no agency standing between the participants, the baby would be assured of a home with them right from birth. There would be no limbo time for the infant to spend in foster care. Paul and Vicki would have to take the risk in exchange for a speedy, humane adoption. They were thrilled at the chance.

On Monday Paul made the necessary transfer at their bank, and he and Vicki went in to work as usual. Vicki's employer was busy in meetings all day, and she didn't have a chance to talk with him about her plans to give up work soon. Tuesday morning she again went in to work, intending to talk with him about the baby and her leaving the job, at least while the baby was young. But there was no time for discussion or negotiation. Immediately upon arriving at his office, Paul received a call from the attorney. He hung up the phone, stunned and jubilant, and called Vicki. Vicki could hardly believe the news.

"Our daughter was born at seven this morning!" The birth had occurred four weeks earlier than expected, but the baby was not premature. They hadn't even had a chance to tell anybody they were adopting a baby, much less to get ready. This was Tuesday. They had only made the decision to get involved on Saturday. Vicki walked into her employer's office at ten that morning and announced, "My child was born this morning, and I have to fly to Nevada to get her."

Vicki was in a state of shock. She'd had no time to prepare for this leap into new motherhood. Physical and hormonal changes had not slowed her down and made her ready for the tremendous energy involved in caring for a tiny human being whose needs at first would seem unceasing. She could rely only on her intellect and her dreams to prepare her for the moment when she would carry a strange baby out of a hospital a thousand miles away and into her own home.

Wednesday and Thursday mornings Vicki went to work and tried to be a biologist. Then she went home and frantically went around to their friends' houses collecting things they would need for the baby: crib, diapers, clothes, receiving blankets. She made a plane reservation for herself and several calls to Phil Adams. Thursday afternoon after work she and Paul drove to San Francisco once more and had a telephone conversation with the baby's father and Phil at Phil's office, to set final arrangements. Friday morning, early, Paul drove Vicki to the airport and went on to work while she flew off to Nevada, carrying an armload of borrowed baby things.

They had decided that only Vicki should go to get the baby because they thought it would be harder for the father to meet Paul or both of them together than it would be to meet Vicki alone. Vicki carried with her all the necessary legal documents prepared by Phil so that they could accomplish a private interstate adoption. There had been no time for the prebirth meeting Phil encouraged people to have. The meeting with the father at the obstetrician's office ended up being awkward and strained. They took a taxi to the hospital together, and the one thing Vicki remembers him saying was that he had nearly called the whole thing off the previous night, because the baby was a girl and he had three boys. He was crying.

At the hospital Vicki was introduced as the woman who would be helping to care for the baby at home. A nurse brought the baby to them in the hallway and began to change her diapers on a gurney. She asked the father if he'd brought clothes to take the baby home in. He was at a loss and turned to Vicki, who gave the nurse the clothes she'd brought. When they were ready to leave, the father asked the nurse if she would please carry the baby to the taxi. At the taxi's door the nurse turned and gave the baby to the father before he had time to refuse. Vicki recalls his reaction was that of someone handed a hot frying pan. He passed her to Vicki immediately. When the taxi stopped he jumped out and took off, leaving Vicki with the baby. By the time she arrived at the doctor's office, he had already signed the papers and left by another door. Vicki never saw him again, and neither has his daughter. Vicki named the little girl Amanda, and she held her new daughter all the way to the airport, onto the plane, and home.

Certainly not the best closure to such an emotional event, even this brief, awkward encounter had given Vicki information she could pass on to Amanda as she grew up—about her birth father and the events of the day Amanda went home from the hospital, just three days after she was born. The process of absorbing and working through the experience of the transfer of Amanda was not helped by the rigidity of the law. Even without knowing any alternatives to what she had experienced in their first private adoption, Vicki sensed there had to be a better way.

When Amanda was two months old and colicky, crying inconsolably for several hours each evening, Vicki's gynecologist offered her another baby. She declined without asking Paul. Their hands were full. But when Amanda was two years old, they started looking for a second child to complete their family. Babies to adopt were by then scarce. Again, neither the county nor the private agencies would consider them unless they would agree to take a hard-to-place older, handicapped, or mixed-race child. And they did not see themselves as exceptional parents, able to take on the additional responsibilities required for a child with special needs. Phil Adams told them he had a file of several hundred names of people looking for children to adopt. In the previous year he'd been able to place only twenty-five babies, and he told Vicki bluntly, "Go find your own. I'll be glad to do the legal work."

Vicki's gynecologist was called upon once more. After several months he called one day to say he'd found another prospective mother who was planning to relinquish her baby at birth. It turned out that the woman had taken heroin early in her pregnancy, and Paul and Vicki turned down the offer. (That baby at birth appeared to be healthy and normal and was placed for adoption through the county.) No more babies came to their attention. Three years of looking passed, and they began to give up their dream of ever finding a brother or sister for Amanda. As resignation set in, they turned their attention to the benefits of having their only child now of school age.

"Amanda was pretty grown up by then," says Vicki. "She was in nursery school, and able to spend long weekends with her grandparents. Paul and I were back to making love in the morning, a luxury we hadn't had in many years. We weren't all that sure we really wanted to start all over with another child. We told ourselves we were fortunate to have one." They began giving away all the baby things Vicki had stored in the garage.

Then one Friday afternoon the phone rang. It was Don Creevy. He said, "Hi, Vicki. Do you want a baby?" That was all. She thought he was being flip, so she said, "Sure!" Then he said, "I'll call you later" and hung up. The offer was casual but not offhand. Vicki figured it must be a busy day and that her doctor was probably calling in between seeing patients. It suddenly dawned on her that it probably wasn't a joke, and so she called Paul at work.

Don called again that evening when he had time to give them more information. He told her the young woman in question had just turned seventeen. She'd only a few weeks earlier come across the country from Florida. She was living with her older brother and sister and felt she could not, under the circumstances, give this child what the child deserved. Like Amanda's young mother, she didn't want the baby to spend any time in foster care, and none of the agencies she'd been to would offer that guarantee. Vicki was intrigued. She felt ready to jump in once more, willing to take the risk, knowing that this mother also might ultimately choose to keep her baby and that she and Paul would be the losers. She decided not to say anything about the possibility to Amanda.

The next morning she called Phil Adams. In his typical mock offhand way he said, "Fine, sounds good! When can I meet this young woman?" Vicki called Don back and told him what the attorney had said. He said he would take it from there and bring the young woman to meet with Phil. It was up to Paul and Vicki to keep their hopes in proportion.

"We didn't have high expectations for getting this baby. There must be a great deal of desire for the companionship of a baby if you're a young, single mother. We knew it would be especially difficult for someone like her to give up her baby."

A week passed. Don called again; he wanted to know whether she and Paul wanted to meet the young woman. They did. He made reservations for dinner at a Japanese restaurant. Vicki remembers the evening with a great deal of pleasure.

"We drove to Don's home and then all went in his car to pick her up at the apartment she was sharing with her brother and sister. Paul and I waited in the back seat, and soon an attractive, dark-haired, olive-skinned, very pregnant young woman came across the street. She opened the door, looked in at us, and said, 'Hi!' She sat down next to me. We chatted on the way to the restaurant. She certainly was poised for her age, and friendly too."

Inside the restaurant they were seated along one side of a long cooking table, where they could watch the Japanese waiter preparing the vegetables and shrimp on a hot griddle right in front of them. Vicki, seated next to the young woman she'd just met, found it easy to broach the subject of child rearing.

"Paul and I are reasonably strict with kids by today's standards. I thought she should know that. That seemed fine with her. We talked about the religious question. Don had told me she was Catholic, and that she'd gone first to see Catholic Social Services about giving them the baby. I told her Paul and I were brought up in Protestant churches and that we believed a religious background of some kind was important for children."

The seating arrangement at dinner placed Paul farthest from the young woman. He stayed in the background, as he would at their next meeting too, listening and observing. He felt protective already of her feelings and sensed she might be more at ease with Vicki than with him. That didn't prevent him from forming some immediate and strong impressions of the young woman he watched.

"I didn't think of her as a child, not from the first. After all, she'd already crossed over that threshold, she'd done something that had made her an adult. It was probably a painful experience, but whether for better or worse, her childhood was over, and was before I met her—just freshly over. I could see she was still learning about being an adult, but she was no child, not with the kinds of decisions she was making."

For Vicki the evening felt particularly fruitful. Although she would dearly like to have this baby, she too felt protective of this young woman who was struggling with a crucial decision. She was torn between personal desire and feelings of admiration and support for the other woman. All she could do was stand by and wish her clarity in her thinking.

"We went home and for the first time since Don had called me, I began to feel settled about things. Up until then this young woman had been just a faceless seventeen-year-old who was thinking about giving up her unplanned child for adoption. But she seemed to know what she wanted. She told us outright at dinner that she couldn't promise anything, because she didn't know exactly what she'd be able to do once she had given birth and held the baby in her arms. She felt sure that adoption was the best thing she could do for the baby and for herself, but she couldn't make any guarantees. I thought that was one of the finest things she could have said—that she couldn't promise us—because it meant she was thinking carefully about what she was doing and not blindly trying to convince herself."

By the time the woman went into labor, Paul and Vicki were feeling there was much less risk of not getting this child than they'd felt with Amanda. They knew this mother was not being pressured by the father of the baby (who was not even in the picture), by her parents, by her physician or attorney, or by them. She was making her own decisions and had people around her who would support her in any decision she made.

Paul and Vicki had never considered being asked to attend the birth of their child. They'd never heard of it and never dreamed it was possible. When the idea was mentioned, first by Vicki's doctor and then by the woman herself, both Paul and Vicki were stunned and delighted. For Vicki in particular, being present could be a profound experience. With all but a very few women in North America giving birth in hospitals, few women are now privileged to participate in another woman's birthing.

The next time Vicki and Paul met with the dark-haired young woman, she was well into her labor. The setting was a cramped, windowless room on the third floor of the teaching hospital in the same medical center where Vicki had once worked. Despite the sterility of the physical environment, the experience was to become the fulfillment of this couple's dream and a profoundly emotional time for Vicki. The woman about to give birth to their second child was named Pat.

PAT:

Invitation to a Birth

THE DAY OF Paul and Vicki's second meeting with Pat proved to be further in the future than anyone had imagined, as Pat's pregnancy dragged on long past her end-of-March due date. Paul and Vicki went about their daily lives with five-year-old Amanda, going to bed each night with the uncertainty of when Pat's baby would be born and what Pat's ultimate decision regarding her baby's future would be. It was a waiting period for them that paralleled Pat's. Each expectant mother feels anticipation, uncertainty, and some anxiety about the birth ahead. For some the apprehension lies in what the labor will be like and how they will behave under its pressure. For others it is concern about whether their husbands or whomever they are depending upon for emotional support will be there when they go into labor. In addition, there is always the question, even if it is not voiced: Will this unseen child I am growing inside me be healthy and perfectly formed? For the sensitive birth mother, this last anxiety has an additional hook: Will this creation of my body be marred in any way by my imperfections, my thoughts and moods, my actions while I have carried him or her? Pat must have felt somewhat like the prize goose expected to lay the golden egg. Only after the birth was she able to express her feelings of embarrassment at having been the recipient of so much attention from the time she arrived in California. But she had chosen this path and felt that it was right.

Don called Paul and Vicki one Friday night with the news that if Pat had not begun labor spontaneously by the next morning, he planned to induce her labor artificially. They were ready.

They could now plan on the probability that they would be parents again within the next day or two. They found a neighbor to be on call for Amanda, and we sat near the phone all day Saturday. It was dinnertime before Don finally rang to say he was at the hospital with Pat and had just begun inducing her labor. He told them they might just as well get a bit of rest, because as this was Pat's first labor, even with the stimulation of artificial hormones, it would certainly take many hours.

"So we took Amanda to our next-door neighbors, in case we had to leave for the hospital in the middle of the night, and then we went to bed early. Just as we were falling off to sleep the phone rang. It was Don again, saying we'd better come quickly, because Pat's labor was moving very quickly and she would soon be pushing! Already! We threw on our clothes, jumped in the car, and went careening down to the hospital. It was 10:30. We went straight upstairs to the labor and delivery suite, walked in the door, and asked for Dr. Creevy at the nursing station. Don came out of one of the rooms and told us that Pat was doing very well. Then he took me right in to see her."

Although this was the same building where Vicki had worked for eight years, she'd never been inside the labor and delivery unit, and it was as strange to her as to a first-time mother. Propped up on a high metal bed, Pat was already quite far along in labor, and her appearance stunned Vicki. "She looked so exhausted!" Between contractions Pat looked over at Vicki and said hello. Then her attention was quickly absorbed by the next rush of contraction, and she could give no more thought to the awestruck woman watching her so intently from across the room. Vicki politely excused herself at the end of the next contraction, and said she would go sit out in the lobby with Paul.

It wasn't very long before a nurse came out to the lobby to get them. Paul and Vicki followed her into Pat's room and stood off to one side at the foot of the bed. She was working very, very hard, and the contractions seemed to give her no rest. Vicki was quickly absorbed into the fast-moving drama in front of her. It was the end of Pat's labor, and an emotionally fraught time for everyone.

"I'll never forget, during one particularly hard contraction, Pat cried out. After it was over, she sat there panting, leaning on one arm, her legs dangling over the edge of the bed. Then she suddenly looked right up at me with a mischievous grin on her face, and asked, 'Aren't you glad I'm doing this for you?' I will remember that face and those words till my dying day."

Vicki had slowly moved from the foot of the bed around its side until she was standing near Pat's shoulder. Paul felt awkward entering the privacy of the scene and stood watching from his semidarkened corner and made no attempt to participate. He admired the strength of will and physical stamina he saw.

"I tend to do things more as an observer than taking an active part, and I was sure impressed with Pat. When I heard the wisecracks she would make between some of those rough contractions just before pushing, I knew she was tough. Not tough-hard. Pat doesn't seem a particularly forceful person. But tough-strong. Whenever she could catch her breath, she was still funning everybody in the room. Then suddenly Don was saying, 'Wait a minute! That's the head showing! We're going to have this baby here!'

"Pat had been saying that she felt the urge to push and Don had been saying, 'Let's wait just a minute; I don't think you're fully dilated yet.' Then she was grunting, 'I've *got* to!' And he quickly checked her to see how far dilated she was and announced that the baby was down very low; not only could she push but she was practically ready to deliver. The room suddenly felt hot and exciting."

The labor room was only the size of a small bedroom, and it was by then filled to capacity with people. There were Vicki and Paul, a young physician in training, Don, two nurses, Heather, who was Pat's childbirth teacher, Eddie and Claudia, myself, Pat, and the baby about to be born. The group was suddenly silent and the air hot with breathing and with Pat's urgent effort. The sweetish smell of amniotic fluid began to fill the air. The membranes surrounding the baby, in which the baby had lived all those months, had spontaneously broken, dropping the baby even lower down the birth canal. Everyone sensed birth was imminent. Vicki was amazed at how the group functioned, as if it were a single organism.

"I've heard so often about how hospitals have rigid rules for how many people a woman can bring to her birth. They say it's because any extra would get in the way if an emergency arose. I never felt I was in the way. And there was one point, just before the baby's head came out, when Don, after listening to the baby's heart, wanted to give Pat some extra oxygen. All he did was say, once, 'I want some oxygen' in a serious tone of voice, and everyone stepped out of the way while the nurse reached over to hand it to him, as if we all had one mind."

Vicki's view of the actual moment the rest of the baby's body slipped out of Pat's was temporarily blocked by the physician's back as he bent over the foot of the labor bed. But as he stepped back she could then see a wet baby lying between Pat's outstretched legs, the baby's bluish cord still attached and extending up inside Pat's body, still pulsing with her life blood. The sight of that physical connection between Pat and her baby was a vivid reminder of the unnaturalness of what was to follow. No matter how gently the cord was severed, how gracefully the exchange was made, the baby was of Pat's body. Yet Vicki was already feeling connected to the little girl lying there on the bed with her arms outstretched as if startled at being born so quickly. It was only a moment before her little body was gathered up and lifted into Pat's outstretched arms, just long enough for everyone to see that this baby was fine and healthy. Meanwhile Paul's view of the birth had been complete. Ghost pale and stunned, he had absorbed everything from his place in the shadows at the foot of the bed. He'd never before even seen a film of birth.

"I wasn't shocked by all the blood. It was just that I was so keyed up! So I squatted for a while just before she was born. I remember when she gave her first cry, when she was only halfway out. She didn't make another sound after that, just lay there quietly breathing. I've read that some people feel babies are affected by all the noise, bright lights, and hurry of hospital delivery rooms. That makes sense to me now. To hear her give that one brief outcry and then to breathe without any encouragement! I was so very touched. It was intense and tense—different from anything I'd ever seen before. You could feel the energy in the room, especially as she was coming through and everyone grew quiet. Such a good feeling."

About the crowd in the room, Paul was clear that it was a support for Pat. "I think you could have put those same people together in a tent in the desert and the birth would have turned out just as well, because there weren't any negative personalities there. Well, Pat's sister did seem to have a lot of tension. I think I know how she must have been feeling about Pat's giving up the baby; but even she seemed positive about the birth itself. At the end nobody was focused on anyone but Pat, who was working to her limit. Then on the baby, resting after her journey."

After the few seconds it took for the physician to feel sure that the baby was breathing well on her own, in one smooth motion he slipped both hands under her wet body and brought her up onto Pat's soft abdomen, which was warm and glistening with sweat. Then he turned to Vicki and asked, "Would you like to cut the cord?" Vicki took the blunt-tipped scissors that were held out to her and cut through the spiraling, sinewy cord. There was utter silence in the room as everyone listened to the baby take her first breath independent of her mother. Don quietly asked Paul and Vicki what name they'd chosen for her.

"Abigail," Vicki said softly as she looked directly at Pat as if for approval. Pat looked into Vicki's eyes and nodded. She held Abigail closely and one of the nurses covered the two of them with a warmed blanket. More silence in the room as Abigail's eyes tentatively began to open for the first time since the birth. And as they opened she began to turn her head slowly until she was gazing directly up into her mother's face. For one brief moment Pat looked down at her and smiled. Then she reached out her free arm and grasped Vicki's hand. No one else moved as the two women shared a private smile of satisfaction. Paul hung back.

"I felt it would have been out of place if I did anything. It might have caused Pat's family pain if I had come too close then. But Vicki being there with Pat seemed to be okay."

During the entire time Pat held Abigail, stroked Abigail, and spoke to her, Vicki stood by Pat's shoulder, first clasping her hands at her breasts and then with her hands outstretched as if in waiting. No one in the room knew how the next minutes would pass and what Pat would do. It was all her decision and only hers. The medical resident and the nurses, the only strangers at this scene, seemed to understand and stood still, delaying their own rituals: the weighing, measuring, footprinting, tagging.

Then suddenly Pat passed a large clot of blood from her vagina, followed by a heavy gush of blood. Her placenta, the baby's blood and food supply, was beginning to detach itself from the wall of her uterus, as her uterus contracted with the stimulation of the baby's body lying so near to Pat's breast. Time to birth the placenta. The nurse said, to no one in particular, "Take the baby." Don said, "Give the baby to Vicki." What followed happened so swiftly it seemed a mirage. Vicki took the baby from Pat's arms, wrapped the blanket tightly around her body, and in one movement slipped around the foot of the bed and over to a straight-backed chair, which had all this time been sitting empty in a darkened corner of the room. There she sat rapt with little Abigail in her arms, hidden from everyone else's view. The baby had begun to cry the minute she was taken from Pat's arms; but soon she stopped. Of what happened next Vicki remembers little. She was unable to notice Pat or anyone else, except Abigail, for the next half hour.

From across the room Pat and her sister watched Vicki immersed in discovering this baby. Eddie was still hanging back near the other bed in the room. Pat, Claudia, Eddie, each of the faces told a different story of the mixed emotions felt; but Pat's face remained calm and curious and open. And so the first moment everyone had dreaded passed without ceremony or awkwardness. But this was not the end. Pat had granted permission, without words, for Vicki to be with Abigail and for Paul and Vicki to name her. It was still for Pat to make her conscious decision about the future of Abigail, and she would need some privacy in which to reflect upon all that had happened in the past brief dozen hours of her life.

Paul thought he knew what lay ahead: parting, grieving, and pain for a young woman he barely knew and so admired. He didn't like to think of it. "I was so glad I could be there; but I knew hard times were coming. Giving up Abigail for good, that was going to hurt. It hurt everyone."

It was then the middle of the night, though in the windowless room you could easily lose track of night and day. Everyone could use some rest. Nighttime was no time for making life decisions. Pat's doctor thought she looked tired. A nurse suggested that Abigail remain in the hospital overnight and be watched the few hours until morning, to be sure she didn't develop any problems. There was brief conversation among Pat, Don, Paul, and Vicki about what to do. Vicki suggested she and Paul go home and come back in the morning. Then Amanda could be with them. Pat, it was decided, should spend the night in the hospital along with Abigail. There was no mention of how the parting would take place. Pat merely asked Paul and Vicki to come for Abigail early. In her mind the decision was firm.

The knot of people began to dissolve. Heather, Pat's childbirth teacher, who had been so helpful to her in labor, bent over and hugged Pat before she left, whispering congratulations and words of praise for how beautifully Pat had labored. She promised to return in the morning if she could be of any help, and Pat said she would like that. One of the nurses and the resident left. The remaining nurse asked Paul if she might take the baby for a few minutes, to weigh and measure her and put medication in her eyes. Abigail did not make any fuss as she was moved this time, but, eyes wide open, continued to look out at the world around her. I too gave Pat a big hug and congratulations, and offered to return early in the morning in case she needed an advocate. I forgot to ask Pat whether she would prefer to have Abigail remain with her through the night, an omission I later regretted. Soon after I left, Don also said goodnight. It would be a short night's sleep before he had to return to check Pat in the morning, discharge her from the hospital, and see that arrangements for Abigail went just as Pat wished. He could get a call to attend another birth at any time, and in his haste to get some sleep, he failed to leave written orders that this baby should remain with her mother and that nurses should visit Pat's room to check on them so she never needed to leave her mother's side. Without this the staff assumed the baby should spend the night in the nursery along with the rest of the babies.

It was 2:00 A.M. Only Pat, Abigail, Claudia, Eddie, and one nurse remained. Once she had finished with her duties, the nurse gave the baby back to Pat. Eddie then said good-bye to his sister. He had no words to describe how he felt about what he had just witnessed, how proud and amazed he'd been, how moved, as the expressions on his face throughout the birth had shown. He merely told his sister he'd be seeing her back at the apartment. Then he picked up his guitar and left. That left only Claudia, who had no intention of leaving her sister alone in a hospital, even for a few hours. She offered to stay the night with Pat in her room, and Pat accepted the offer. The nurse began to get her ready for the move down the hall, through the swinging doors, across the lobby, and into the postpartum unit, where new mothers and babies stayed until they left the hospital. Claudia helped the nurse push the bed, with Pat and the baby in it. The room they gave Pat was semiprivate, with two beds, but she had no roommate. Claudia spotted the second bed as a place for herself to sleep, but the nurse saw immediately what she must be thinking and informed her that no one was permitted to use, or even sit on, the second bed. Hospital policy, she said. It was clear that she considered Claudia's presence a nuisance, and felt that if she insisted on staying the night she should make do in a chair. So Abigail was whisked off to the nursery across the hall in the arms of a stranger. Pat's sanitary napkin was changed, she was shown the button to press if she needed anything, and the nurse left, shutting the door behind her. The two sisters were alone.

Pat seemed to want to be left to sleep, so Claudia made no attempt at conversation. With the lights off she too tried to sleep, sitting up in the straight-backed chair next to the window. But when her head began to nod she jerked awake, feeling stiff all over. Finally she got up and placed her coat on the linoleum floor and lay down at the foot of Pat's bed. Thus she passed the remaining hours of the night. With no one else there to act as advocate on their behalf, the two sisters and little Abigail had been quickly absorbed into the hospital routine. The intimacy of the evening had dissolved once all the friends had gone home. There was a different set of nurses in maternity and in the nursery during the night, and the shift would change again at dawn.

PAT:

How Do You Say Good-bye?

It was a fine, warm, hazy spring day that began as food and medicine carts clanged in the hallway and people rushed to and fro. Pat and Claudia awoke as the noise seeped under their door. Pat waited patiently for someone to come in so she could ask to have Abigail brought to her. Meanwhile, outside the hospital, day came all too soon for her exhausted physician and for Paul and Vicki, who knew many nights of lost sleep lay ahead with a new baby in the home to care for. For Abigail there was no marking of a new day. She lay wrapped in a blanket in a plastic cot in a brightly lit, noisy nursery full of babies. The room had never darkened for the night, and it faced away from the morning sun.

As the sunlight slipped over the windowsill into Pat's room with the spare bed still unmussed, a new nurse came in to check on Pat. Whether she was surprised to see another person there too and wondered where she could have slept, she didn't say. Pat asked for her baby. Had she and Abigail lain together in Pat's bed during the night, Pat might have gazed for hours in quiet ecstasy on the face of her child, as so many mothers before have done when left undisturbed with their new babies.

That might have been one of her most precious memories. Instead Abigail was brought in to her at 8:00 A.M. by a stranger in uniform who knew nothing of Pat's circumstances or of the special time this was meant to be. There was little time to be together before Paul and Vicki would arrive.

Bright and early Paul and Vicki picked up Amanda from the neighbors. Feeling certain now of Pat's decision to give them Abigail, they told Amanda for the first time that she had a baby sister, and they took her with them to the hospital. Amanda was simply delighted. Vicki carried with her a tiny stretch-knit suit in which to dress Abigail for the short car ride home. They all three rode the elevator to the third floor and sat in the lobby just outside the maternity ward to wait until they heard what Pat's wishes were.

Meanwhile Pat was sitting up in bed holding Abigail, just finishing giving her a bottle of formula, a final maternal offering. Claudia sat on the edge of the bed, enchanted with the tiny person in Pat's arms, amazed at the alert gaze on the broad little face that looked so much like one of their family. The two sisters explored the tiny hands and feet, and unwrapped Abigail's little body so they could see and touch her.

Outside, the pediatrician on duty that morning, who was to discharge Abigail after examining her, heard that the new parents were waiting in the lobby and went out to speak with them. This was the first private adoption he'd encountered. Abigail was not even ten hours old and about to leave the hospital without her biological mother. In an attempt to reassure the new parents, whom he assumed must naturally be anxious, he began to recite a detailed list of instructions for the feeding and care of a new baby. He felt it was his responsibility as a professional to look out for Abigail's well-being, and he had no idea to what kind of people he was releasing this brand new baby. To Vicki, his instructions made it seem that her competence and judgment as an adult and a mother were being questioned, especially because her five-year-old daughter was sitting right next to her as visible proof of her qualifications.

Vicki was preparing to cut the pediatrician's monologue

off midsentence when a familiar face appeared at the door. Don came out into the lobby, and said that Pat was ready to see them. Paul quickly offered to stay out in the lobby with Amanda. Paul and Vicki had already signed innumerable documents, so they didn't have to deal with any of that now. It was the emotional material Paul was wishing to avoid. He said later, "I'm sure glad Amanda was there to give me an excuse for staying in the lobby, because I was really chicken. I knew it was going to be heavy in that room, and I don't like heavy scenes. I just couldn't take Abigail and feel totally happy, knowing Pat would be left back there crying."

When Vicki went into Pat's room with Don, she carried the outfit and receiving blanket she'd brought for Abigail. The papers Pat signed giving Vicki and Paul the right to take Abigail out of the hospital were attached to Pat's chart. Don had already spoken with Pat alone about Abigail and her right to change her mind. He would give her postpartum instructions later that afternoon. With nothing more to do and feeling he was more in the way than needed, he quickly withdrew from the room, leaving the women to talk and to orchestrate the exchange for themselves. Heather and I were there in the room with Claudia, Pat, Vicki, and Abigail. Abigail's beauty was everyone's immediate topic for discussion. Pat did not seem to wish to talk about herself and enjoyed the focus being on the baby. She appeared relaxed and centered, in much better shape than Vicki or anyone else had expected.

Sensing that Pat was ready, Vicki asked if she might change Abigail's clothes from the hospital outfit to the one she'd brought. Pat said that was a good idea and laid her daughter on the bed. If she was braced inside for what was coming, she didn't give any appearance of being so, or of feeling either remorse or confusion over her decision. She watched Vicki dress her baby. Vicki felt the difference between last night and now. "In the labor room we'd all felt like one family. It was so warm and soft and loving. But in this room. . . . This was a final parting."

Remembering those moments today, Vicki's face looks

pained. Tears fill her eyes and emotion softens her features. "I was thinking about the leaving," she says quietly. "We dressed Abigail together. Then because there was nothing more to do, I picked her up and put her over my shoulder. Pat said something very simple. I think it was, 'Can I kiss her good-bye?' I said, 'Sure.' And I held Abigail out to her. Then she kissed her and said good-bye and handed her back to me. Abigail was very quiet but Pat was already starting to cry."

Vicki's voice is thick. But suddenly she shifts and her words take on their usual quick, clipped rhythm.

"I don't think it would have helped Pat for me to cry too," she says. And so instead of stopping to comfort Pat, Vicki quickly turned away from her and carried the still quiet little Abigail out of the room, down the hall, into the lobby to the eager faces and waiting arms of Amanda and Paul. Once outside, Amanda and Paul's excitement quickly submerged all thoughts of Pat back in the room. Vicki was too busy watching the way her older daughter responded to her new baby sister to think of anything else. And she was pleased with Amanda, her older daughter, with how she greeted Abigail with a quiet seriousness and insisted on holding her at once. Outside in the sunlight Amanda asked her mother to stop for a moment and show her her baby sister once more. In the back seat of their car, Vicki carefully placed Abigail in Mandy's arms.

In Pat's room the morning sunlight was spreading an indirect glow over the hospital bed. I went back in to see Pat after I had seen Paul, Vicki, Amanda, and Abigail off. Pat was sitting on the edge of the bed, where I'd left her, leaning against her sister and sobbing quietly, her face covered with her hands. She had known that this would come, that she would grieve and the sooner the better, so she did nothing to attempt to stop the tears. But it wasn't more than a few minutes before she suddenly lifted up her head, wiped her eyes, displayed that same small grin she'd shown everyone in labor and I'd seen so many times before, and said quietly, "What could I say to her? How could I ask her to be good to Abigail?" Her voice cracked a bit as she added softly, "I *knew* she would be."

With those words said she lifted up her nightgown and began to examine her deflated abdomen, which had for nine months contained another life. She said nothing more for a long while. Then, as the bustle of the maternity floor went on outside the door, the two sisters began to whisper, heads together, arms entwined.

A reception party of one waited in the driveway as the family drove up—the little neighbor girl from next door. Vicki briefly recalled the pediatrian's anxious warnings, and, quickly dismissing them, she invited Sarah to come and peek at Amanda's new baby sister. It was the beginning of Abigail's second social whirl. Vicki couldn't believe what a stir they'd created. By lunchtime they had been visited by the entire school-age population of the neighborhood.

And so they settled into the turbulence of a household with a new baby. Rituals began to order their lives. Paul recalls, "Since I do the night feedings around here, after two the next morning Abigail already felt like mine. I damn near missed the very first feeding, though, she made so little noise. We had her bed in the den across from our bedroom. I woke up and heard cooing in the dark. When I walked into her room, she was lying on her back in the Port-A-Crib with her eyes wide open, looking very content." Abigail seemed at ease in her new home from the first.

One week later the newborn pictures that had been taken at the hospital nursery arrived in the mail. They were a lovely surprise. Because Abigail had spent only half a dozen nighttime hours in the nursery, the photographer must have worked quickly. The baby in the pictures looked indistinguishable from a million other babies except for the round cheeks that were unmistakably her mother's. The five miniature pictures were a reminder of the brief, intense time they'd shared with Pat at Abigail's birth. Vicki was surprised to discover that the pictures had been sent by Pat herself, who had carefully filled in the accompanying card with the time of birth and Abigail's weight and length. In the space marked Baby's Name, she had written simply Abigail. Where blanks were left marked Parents, she'd written her own name. There was one print missing from the group. Pat had kept that for herself, one tiny remembrance of the dark-eyed, round-cheeked little baby who looked so much like her but who now brightened the lives of three other people.

PAUL AND VICKI:

Adoptive Parenting

Paul and vicki have never seen themselves as different from any other parents, adoptive or biological. Paul found that any initial reluctance he felt about raising another man's offspring quickly evaporated in the day-to-day business of diapering, carrying, soothing, and caring for Amanda. "I think I was bamboozled when I was told how different it would be raising a child who wasn't part of me genetically. I don't know how long it takes and how difficult it is to bond with a child who enters your life after infancy; but I *certainly* know there is a bond this way. Amanda and Abby are mine and have been since almost the first week we had them. Cleaning up vomit in the middle of the night, you soon make no distinction about whose genes that baby has."

Vicki agrees. "Even with Amanda, and we didn't have her until she was three days old, I feel she is *my* child. The thing that matters, when one of them is being a brat and doing something I find totally unacceptable, is that she is *my* brat! What's genetic is genetic and I accept that. But the rest, whatever external circumstances have made her the way she is, that's *us,* Paul and me. I think it *must* be easier raising a child from infancy. I can't sit back and complain, 'Somebody must have traumatized her before she came to us, and that's why she is the way she is.' I think we are fortunate they were both so healthy from birth. I'm egocentric enough to look at each of them and think, 'That's *my* child and she is perfect.' "

Vicki is not talking about ownership, but about a deep sense her daughters are part of her. This is what is meant by the term *bonding,* and it is the strength of this parent–child love that holds families together through traumatic times and protects the lives of small children while they are dependent upon their parents for providing for all their needs. Society could do a lot more than it now does to support the bonds of affection between parents and their children. But nature provides its own special bonding between parent and newborn infant, and Paul and Vicki benefited from their early intimate contacts with Amanda and Abigail.

In retrospect, both Paul and Vicki feel that they also benefited from the long, anxious process of Vicki's trying to become pregnant, their lengthy agency search, and the wait until their attorney and Vicki's doctor found babies for them. The waiting, searching process gave them time to grow and adjust to change. Paul is sure it helped them to feel so attached to their children so soon and so easily.

"I think if we'd gotten a child right away, when we first went to the agencies, it would actually have been more difficult for us to adjust to becoming parents. It seems important to take the time to get emotionally ready for the disruptions in your life that come with a child, rather than having to do it afterward. One thing is for sure, when Vicki walked off the plane carrying Amanda in her arms, even though I had never seen her before, she was ours, and I didn't feel any strangeness toward her at all."

It remains to be seen just how their two daughters will feel when they are older—about having been adopted, about the manner in which they came to Paul and Vicki. Those feelings are likely to be mixed and to bubble up to the surface as they grow. At least Paul and Vicki are comfortable with that fact.

They have never felt they had to apologize to Amanda and Abigail or to protect them from even painful truth.

In answer to Amanda's question, when she was four years old, "Mom, did I grow in your tummy?" Vicki remembers answering, "No, dear, you didn't. You grew in another woman's tummy; but she couldn't take care of you and she gave you to us, because we couldn't make a baby and wanted to very much." Children absorb and process information like this at very individual rates. At the dinner table when she was seven, Amanda asked another question out of the blue. "How old was my mother when I was born?" Vicki again answered with only the briefest hesitation, "Your mother was twenty-one." Amanda then asked, "Why didn't our mothers keep us?" A dinner table discussion followed, first about Amanda's mother and father and their circumstances, and then about Pat, her having had no partner and no money and being just seventeen. In each case Vicki emphasized that "your mothers weren't ready." That was really all Amanda needed to hear. Her next question was, "What's for dessert, Mom?" She may turn the new information over for a while before more questions surface. She is a child. That is her style.

For Abby it might be different. Such conversation might go unnoticed by her for a time more, but the words are familiar and out in the open. There are many children in her neighborhood, including her big sister, who found a family the same way she did, through adoption. To her this is a normal way to begin life. She likes to have her parents read the little books about children who are adopted. These books have been around the house since Amanda came. One is even about a little girl named Abby. "Let's read about Abby," Abigail will say; sometimes she adds, "She's adopted, just like me!"

Abigail, at age six, has a distinctive and a passionate temperament. She is both enchanting and trying for her parents. Her short, sturdy legs and big, blue, luminous eyes have carried her into many kinds of mischief. She is hardly ever still and is fearless in the face of each new adventure. She has had an explosive temper since she was just a few weeks old, and, although it isn't triggered easily, it is impossible to ignore once it is unleashed. Paul was its victim on a number of occasions when she was young.

"Abigail was a hellion! If she didn't get her way she screamed, she kicked, she hollered. One morning, when she was two, she wouldn't put the caps back on the marking pens she was using. I said, 'Abigail, if you won't put the caps back on the pens, you don't get to use them. I'll take them away from you.' She lay right down on the floor and started screaming and beating the floor with her fists. When she got that way she was utterly helpless. So I just picked her up and laid her down on the couch in the living room as she continued to scream. She lay there screaming for a full twenty minutes more before suddenly it stopped. Then she just got up and went back to playing."

Paul and Vicki have worked consciously at helping Abigail gain control over her violent outbursts. They have sometimes wondered whether she inherited this trait. But Abigail is theirs now and they accept the angry part of her along with the rest. Like the proverbial little girl with the little curl right in the middle of her forehead, Abigail has been a child of extremes. But most often she is a generous, outgoing, affectionate child, whose little body, right from birth, has softly melted against anyone who has held her. Paul is understanding of her extreme swings in mood. She has a lot in common with his own temperament.

"When bedtime comes, for example, there is never a fight if I've gauged her right and she's ready to sleep. From when she was just an infant in her crib, she has always loved to sleep surrounded by her stuffed animals. She used to sit up in bed and play for maybe an hour or more, until she finally would fall asleep, and all the while she would be talking nonstop to her animals, singing and having a wonderful time. I used to stand outside her door and listen to her babble. It was so beautiful I could have listened all night." And there are other traits he loves. "Abigail has always had such gentle hands. She has always picked things up just so, right from when she was a baby. She has never broken anything; yet she has been so curious."

Such is the patchwork pattern of being a parent. For Paul and Vicki, especially for Vicki, being parents has both altered and enriched their lives. They hardly ever think about the mother and father each of the girls left behind at birth. They are well aware of the pain that giving up a child can create. At some point paths have to separate, and that is always a time for pain and loss for those left behind. For them and the girls' birth parents, separation came right at birth. There was no discussion of a future relationship. The possibility was left open. Paul and Vicki are reassured by the thought that each of the women was very young and had time to start again. One day, perhaps, there will be a phone call or a knock on the door, and then their paths will cross again. And it will be right.

Some people claim that the detailed information Paul and Vicki hold about their daughters' biological parents will only cause hurt if it is given out to adoptees, at any age. It is a moot question whether open files create a desire in adoptees to know their roots, or whether a system where knowledge is denied actually ensures an insatiable thirst for knowing more. Vicki's views on that question are based on her own experiences in adoption.

"I think if you *can* know something, then your need to know is not so great. A woman came from the county agency to visit us just after we got Abigail, to see whether, according to law, we were considered 'suitable' to be parents. She seemed very interested in our experience in open adoption and wanted to know whether we thought that meeting the birth parents and keeping the records open was a good idea. She told me our county adoption agency was just beginning to get the first crop of grown-up adoptees coming in and asking for their birth files. She said it was *incredible*, the need to know that these people had."

Paul and Vicki know much more than the average adoptive parent today about their children's heritage and the decision making the biological parents went through in choosing to place them for adoption. They have memories to share with each other and with their daughters when they choose, and the files for Amanda and Abigail are accessible to them and, more important, to the girls as they grow. All information in them is considered theirs and they own it.

There is still much they do not know. For example, though there is a letter from Amanda's mother in her file, a letter that shows her caring, they know almost nothing about her. Both Paul and Vicki find it disturbing that the woman who carried and nourished Amanda through gestation and labored to give birth to her may not have relinquished her with full consent. They have reason to believe that the mother only gave her written consent under pressure from her husband, that he was the decision maker in the family. Does she know that the baby she carried so long was in perfect health? Whether she was even told the sex of her baby, they don't know. "We only know she was twenty-one years old, that this was his second marriage, and they'd been married just ten months when Amanda was born. We also know that the father had three boys from his first marriage who were living then with his ex-wife and that he was committed to paying monthly child support plus a large alimony." Paul and Vicki were told she tried to get an abortion but it was illegal then to have one in their home state, and by the time they went to a neighboring state where it was legal, they discovered they had waited too long.

For all Vicki knows, that mother still has regret and longing. With Pat, she feels differently. She is certain that Pat made her own decisions. She could and did look Pat in the eyes, and she could see for herself that there was a bond of trust between them. To be sure, there are blanks in Abigail's history, especially with regard to her biological father and his medical history. According to Pat he had no reason to suspect there was a child in the world because of him. Pat has yet to search for him and let him know of Abby's existence. Paul and Vicki were cautious about pushing Pat in locating the father, because they were sensitive to her feelings and the painful memories she probably carried of her very first sexual encounter, but Abigail, they felt, had a right to know who her father was and a need to have a complete medical history. The father too may have a legal as well as an ethical right to know about the existence of Abigail. Paul and Vicki can be patient for the time being. Their girls are still young. They have heard from a mutual friend that even before Pat left California, she had already considered trying to track down the father. Given her nature, which is thoughtful and responsible, they have every reason to believe she will one day do this for Abigail and place the information in Abigail's file or send it directly to them.

Every parent hopes for a child who is healthy, and there is no better way to guarantee a healthy baby than to know the mother was in good health, had a positive attitude toward pregnancy, and gave birth without taking medication or anesthesia. Paul and Vicki were witnesses to Pat's state of health at the end of the pregnancy. Beyond that, all they could hope for was that she had cared for herself adequately during the emotionally traumatic early months. They do know that Abigail came into the world conscious and alert. She was birthed by a mother who had prepared for natural childbirth, who did not inhibit her labor and the supply of oxygen to the baby through fear and tension. Paul and Vicki were there. That is how they know.

They know their daughter was probably not traumatized by anything done to her while she was in the hospital. She could feel safe and loved from her very first experiences with people outside the womb. The room was full of friends, and she was welcomed by Pat as well as everyone else there, stroked and held and marveled at from the first moment. She was not left to lie for days in the hospital nursery in a plastic bed under the glare of lights with her care shared by dozens of strangers, which is the fate of many babies prior to placement. She was not passed out to a foster home to be cared for by a surrogate, and then taken away to yet another home with still different faces and unfamiliar odors and sounds. Indeed, there is much Paul and Vicki can look back upon and be proud of.

There will be more for them to know, more for both girls to discover. Paul and Vicki do not plan to throw everything open to them at once. Although they will support any search either of the girls initiates, at this time they feel that they will set the structure and guidelines when that day comes. Vicki plans to insist that the girls go through a third person, such as Phil Adams, for the initial contact with their biological parents. She expresses this in terms of protecting the parents' right to privacy, even to remain hidden if they choose to do so. Perhaps when they are actually confronted by a tearful daughter of, say, sixteen, who has searched and come up against a wall, their loyalty to the biological parents might change, but not now.

Has Pat's knowing their address and did her having lived so near them for such a time following the birth—more than a year, off and on—create a threat to their own security? No, they say, nor have they any worry about trouble from that quarter in the future. They trust Pat not to change from the person they knew before, during, and after the birth: honest and considerate. They expect she might contact them periodically, perhaps may even want to see Abigail from time to time, although they have not seen or heard directly from her since she sent them the newborn pictures of Abigail.

They feel that planning ahead for various possibilities helps. Vicki has even imagined a scene where Pat, unannounced, arrives at her door one day and asks whether she might see Abigail. Paul has doubts whether he would give in to such a request, but Vicki suspects she might just invite Pat into the house, welcome her as a friend, and tell Abigail who she was. Such a scenario would frighten and outrage many adoptive parents today, and might have sent waves of mistrust and fear through Paul and Vicki several years ago. But they have grown to trust in their capacity to face whatever comes to them.

Private adoption fostered a realistic attitude in Paul and Vicki toward their daughters. They were never able to pretend the biological parents did not exist or that there would be no future encounters with them. They were never offered a guarantee of protection in the way state and private agencies in the past have made promises to adoptive parents and biological parents alike that files would remain closed and identities hidden. Without an agency acting as an umbrella over them, shielding them from knowledge and the possible future consequences, they were able to grow into each new step, first meeting Pat, and then being present at Abigail's birth, and then taking their child directly from Pat's hands, and finally preparing for possible meetings or relationships in the future. Their attorney might have acted as a protective shield in the same way the agency system is set up to do. They could have asked for that and found an attorney who would have behaved like a guardian. But what is important is that there is nothing in the legal structure of private adoption to make secrecy or paternalism a requirement. Flexibility is in the nature of private adoption, and it is up to everyone involved to determine how loosely or tightly they wish to construct an arrangement. Private adoption assumes a respect for the parents, biological *and* adoptive, that *they* know what is best for themselves and for the child.

Those who support the standard adoption claim it protects everyone involved by always keeping files closed and sometimes by placing the child in foster care until the birth parents have relinquished all legal rights. Because Paul and Vicki not only met Pat before the birth but actually had Abigail in their custody for the entire six-month period before the decree of adoption was granted by the court, they had to live with a measure of risk every day. At any time in those six months, Pat had the legal right to change her mind and ask for Abigail back. If that had happened, short of legally proving her total unfitness to be a mother, there would have been nothing they could have done. Only by accepting this risk as part of the ground rules were they able to participate in the birth and start life with Abigail from the beginning. And they feel strongly that they saved her from unnecessary trauma by taking her directly from

Pat's arms. This is what made the risk worth it. It has already been shown that promises made in the past cannot guarantee laws will not change to erase those promises. Adoption is full of risks and uncertainties. But Paul and Vicki are at least prepared to expect change, which adoptive parents in standard closed-file, agency-directed adoptions may not be prepared for.

PAT:

Letting Go, Moving On

Wʜᴇɴ ᴀʙɪɢᴀɪʟ ᴡᴀѕ ᴄᴀʀʀɪᴇᴅ from Pat's room at the hospital, Pat's entire life shifted once more. She was no longer the young woman with the protruding abdomen of whom everyone felt protective. She was just Pat, a girl grown up too quickly, facing an uncertain future and a new beginning out on her own in the world.

Most women in modern societies do some mourning after giving birth. Some mourn the loss of their pregnant status and the attention it brought them. Some mourn the loss of being pregnant, particularly those for whom pregnancy was a heightened feeling of well-being, a special robustness. Some mourn the attention and kindness they received from those who cared for them at the birthing but that disappeared once birth was over. Some mourn their loss of dignity in giving birth and suffer from feelings of humiliation that traditional childbirth practices too often bring today, the loss of the dream that birth could be a miraculous experience. Some mourn the loss of independence, in having to be responsible now for another's life. There is usually something to grieve for amidst the headiness of new motherhood.

Pat had many things to mourn, above all the loss of Abigail. Only a mother who has lost a child can know this sort of sorrow. But it had been Pat's choosing, and the bitterness of her loss was eased by the knowledge that she had done what she felt was best, and had done it out of love for her child and understanding of a child's needs and her own lacks.

She did not have to grieve over the birth. It was simple, uncomplicated, and spontaneous; she had been surrounded by loving people. But now life moved back to its normal pace. It was all over so suddenly, that which had taken most of a year to build to climax.

All the people who had been so solicitous of Pat's welfare and on behalf of the life she carried were now busy with others. She couldn't expect to take the same place in their lives now that she had given birth. Her birth educator had new classes of pregnant couples to think about, her physician other pregnant women to absorb his attention. Even her sister and brother had other things to return to. Much as they loved and were concerned about their sister, they could no longer set aside their own needs.

Pat left the hospital with Claudia and Eddie only a few hours after Abigail did. It was in the apartment she did her grieving during its most acute phase, alone and in private. Those first weeks were a particularly solitary and dark time in Pat's life. She never had been one to talk very much about herself; it had always been nearly impossible to draw anything from her that she didn't want to share. So Claudia and Eddie could only watch the unenviable process of grieving and healing that her body and mind had to go through. She seldom left the apartment and spent most of her waking hours in her nightgown.

Milk filled her breasts right on schedule, despite the medication to suppress the flow, and then was slowly reabsorbed as her body realized that there was no need for it. But this took time—and swollen, tender, hard breasts were for several days painful reminders of the loss of Abigail. The bloody lochia, discharged remains of the placenta, still had to flow from her body. Her uterus had to remain firm in order to grow steadily smaller. Without a baby in arms and at the breast to stimulate the release of hormones to do this shrinking naturally, Pat had been told that she would have to massage her abdomen frequently every day until she could no longer feel the hard, round mass underneath her navel.

There was no longer that living, moving being inside her with whom Pat could converse. She could only talk to herself now and have conversations in her head. She belonged to no group of women like her with whom she might have shared feelings. There was in her case no loving parent to turn to, no chance to place her head on a comforting lap and sob and be held for as long and as often as it took. Claudia would gladly have filled this role, but, except for the few hours immediately after Abigail had left the hospital, Pat would not unburden herself to her sister.

She lived some miles from all the people to whom she had grown close in the past weeks. She had no car to get around in and made no effort to reach out for companionship. There was so much to go over in her mind. The sensations inside her body heralded its drawing inward, shifting the balance of weight on her spine back to its prepregnant state. Pat had to regain her balance in more ways than physically. Everyone gave her a lot of space in those weeks—perhaps too much, but she would never be the one to say so. She'd never been one to criticize, any more than she had been one to ask for help. Perhaps that was why she found herself daydreaming about going back to Florida, although it was only a few weeks after the birth and she was barely beginning to heal. Life without pregnancy, without Abigail, didn't hold much for her in her new home, and the void loomed large inside her.

When I visited Pat late one morning about a week after the birth, I found her in her nightgown, sitting slackly on the edge of the couch. Her shoulders were hunched and her hair was uncombed. There wasn't much I could say. Pat herself had said that life after birthing would be difficult, especially because she'd made no plans. But that realization had come such a short time before the onset of labor, there had been no time to begin to dream and make plans for herself. All that had waited until she had come back home to the dingy, empty apartment, from where Claudia and Eddie left for work each morning, leaving her alone with nothing but her thoughts. She made no apologies for her appearance, her lack of animation or conversation, and I asked nothing of her. I merely wanted to see how she was getting along, to let her know others and I were thinking of her, to sit with her.

Pat may have been hoping to hear how Abigail was doing, to hear that Paul and Vicki were taking fine care of her. Her arms may have ached to hold Abigail, to hold anyone. She never said so. All she did say was that there were days when it hurt a lot. She knew she could have phoned Paul and Vicki or written them. She had their address. They lived only a few miles away; but when she sent baby pictures to them, she chose not to include a note. When I said good-bye, hugging her gently and reminding her I would love to hear from her at any time, she thanked me for coming and said she was fine, really. Those were the same words she had told her physician when he had phoned each day during the first week after the birth.

When she returned to his office for her scheduled postpartum visit six weeks after birth, well-dressed and looking slim and a bit tanned, she smiled and told everyone there she was fine. She also said she was leaving. Abigail had come and gone only six weeks before, yet Pat had made the decision to go home at once. Everyone to whom she told this news begged her to wait at least a little longer, to give herself more time in peace before moving back into her parents' home. There was no rush. She needed very little money to live on. Why not get a part-time job nearby, spend time walking in the sun, visit museums, go to the beach, have dinner with friends? But it was as if she couldn't bear the quiet of her days and the calm of her life now. So used as she had become to being in the center of a storm, to years of fighting the authority of parents and school, and recently to the mounting excitement of the final months before the birth, that the time after Abigail was too quiet. She did not take our suggestion that it might be better first to spend some time in counseling, to resolve some of her feelings about her home life and the birth and Abigail's adoption, before going home. Instead she waited only until several of us had left town for summer vacation. Then she packed up her few belongings and slipped from sight. She left behind on my answering machine a short message. She was going home. She was sorry she couldn't say good-bye to anyone in person, but she hated good-byes and she just had to go.

It was nearly six months before she wrote to anyone but Claudia and Eddie. Her letter to me was brief. She said things were difficult back at home, but didn't explain. She was working at an office job and still living with her parents. Her letter had a wistful tone but no self-pity. Life, it seemed, was what it had always been for Pat, a continual struggle to feel good about herself in the face of constant criticism and her own guilt. She did say that the people who had been around her during the last months of her pregnancy and for her birthing still meant a great deal to her. She said also that it had been very hard to endure the kind attention she had gotten from everyone. Why had she been the recipient of so much kindness? Surely, she implied, she hadn't deserved it. How could she ever repay everyone for all they'd given her? She didn't know but she hoped there would be a way. Perhaps, she wrote, she might become a childbirth educator and work with other young pregnant women and pass along the help she'd received from others and some newfound insight. It wasn't until I got her telephone number from Claudia and phoned her that Pat mentioned Abigail to anyone. She said she would like to know how Abigail was doing and how Paul and Vicki and Amanda were. I was able to tell her, because I'd seen them recently, that they were all doing well.

In the spring Pat wrote once more. She was thinking, she said, of coming back. Claudia was no longer at the old apartment—she'd taken a job in a Montessori school in the Virgin Islands, where Pat had just visited her for a month. But Eddie was still around, and she supposed they could get an apartment together.

She didn't call me or anyone until she'd been in town nearly a month, and had found work and a place to live with Eddie. When she did call we made a date to meet at her physician's office downtown on her lunch hour. I arrived a few minutes late, opened the door into the waiting room, and looked around. Across the room someone rose from a chair. I hardly recognized her. She was wearing heels and a sleeveless printed cotton dress that was open at the neck. Her bare legs and arms were smooth-skinned, just as I'd remembered, but a richer, more nutlike brown than I'd ever seen them. I'd never imagined how exotic Pat could look when she was tanned and feeling good. I'd never seen her glowing, supple, and slim. I couldn't take my eyes off her. We hadn't seen each other in nearly a year. I was looking at a lovely, poised young woman, but in my mind I was seeing Pat the way she'd looked when she'd first arrived at my door, the way she'd looked at birth, the grace and dignity with which she'd relinquished Abigail, and the way she'd looked in her grief.

She was dressed for job interviews. She had taken work with a temporary help agency to get quick money. She had her own car now, Claudia's old blue one. She wanted me to know from the outset that she hadn't come back to try to connect with Abigail or Paul and Vicki. She didn't even ask how Abigail was, although she must have known I would still be in touch with Paul and Vicki and could have told her anything she wanted to know. It was clear that she didn't intend to live around the edges of Abigail's life. She'd returned simply because she'd missed the ease she'd felt when she'd lived here.

The one bright spot during the year had been the month she'd spent away, with Claudia in the Virgin Islands. That, she said, had been the most peaceful period of her life, the first time she had felt whole and right with the world from when she woke up in the morning until she fell asleep at night.

The warm sun, the friendliness of the islanders, the bubbling laughter and play of the children at the Montessori school, it all added up to a taste of paradise. Her experience on the island had left her changed and wanting more: more peace, more time, and a chance to explore life and express herself without pressure. But there were few jobs to be had and Pat had few skills, so when her visit had come to an end she'd decided to return to school. And so she had returned to California, because it was a place she had felt accepted for who she *wanted* to be, as well as for who she was. She said she hoped to learn some job skills to prepare herself for going back to Florida in the future, where she thought she would like to teach young children.

Pat found work soon, in the billing department of a small company, and within a month had charmed the office with her wry wit and her ability to do her job while being able to laugh off annoyances. After several months she was promoted to head of the payroll department. She was nineteen years old.

At the end of the summer Pat enrolled in a course. An institute in San Francisco offered a one-year program in childbirth education. She thought she would like to help other pregnant young women have good experiences in birth. The school brought her in touch with a small group of women from all around the country, many of whom hoped to become midwives. They were mostly young, but Pat was the youngest—though by no means the youngest in experience. This group of women and their instructors formed a kind of family for each other during the next year. Pat had to drive an hour each way to get to class, while most of the other students had found housing and jobs near the institute. Her full-time job, the long commute, living apart from everyone else, didn't offer her much chance to socialize; but the education proved nurturing. She was there to learn how to support and counsel a woman during an important time in a woman's life. It was considered essential that the students do introspective work in order to be sensitive to other people. Several of the classes were run as seminars whose purposes were interaction as a group and self-discovery.

Pat found herself in an environment like none she'd ever known, a place where it was not only safe to explore feelings but where such exploration was encouraged and supported by everyone. During the next six months she found herself going back to her experience of pregnancy, looking at things she'd never faced herself or told anyone, and also going back to her lonely childhood and her confined life under her parents' strict control.

After months in this environment where there was no competition, Pat slowly found herself able to trust what was happening. At first she found it difficult to find any strong emotions inside, so used was she to using her mind to shield herself from her feelings. In class whenever things became confrontational or conversation turned to her, she would retreat into a familiar spaciness, watch herself as from a distance, and listen to what words came out of her mouth as if they didn't belong to her but to a stranger. But she stuck with it, attending every seminar and class despite the frustration of often being the only one in the room who could find nothing inside of which to speak. Somewhere she'd found the inner strength to get through life thus far. Now she could take some time to examine how her defenses had helped and how they now inhibited her.

Pat liked to credit everyone but herself with her gains. She wanted the group to know it hadn't been she, Pat, who had found the strength to give up her child out of love for her. She attributed a special power to Abigail, and called her the source of the strength, saying it had been Abigail who'd kept her from harming herself during the early months of pregnancy. She had felt Abigail's presence all along. "If Abby could survive all my doubts about wanting her and my smoking early in pregnancy, even the circumstances of her conception, then she must be a special spirit." She described feeling as if her life in pregnancy had been a cresting wave, rushing headlong to crash on the shore—until she'd found supports: friends, parents for her baby, a physician for herself and her baby, and an attorney who helped her create the kind of adoption she'd dreamed of. It was others who had given her the necessary strength to balance on the crest of the wave and ride it through without crashing.

She talked on many occasions about how strange and embarrassing it had been to be the recipient of so much kindness and attention. Yet that had been what had made it possible for her to do what was right for her. What she had been striving for above all else had been to do what was right, what Jesus might have done in the same circumstances. Feeling certain she was doing the best for Abigail was what had sustained her through the end of the pregnancy, made the last weeks a happy time, and carried her through labor and birth and through her grief. Only once or twice was she able to put her head on the lap of a classmate and cry. But the friends she made in school made her feel so welcome and comfortable that she found she could go to them with her pain. She still missed Abigail deeply. But giving her up to Paul and Vicki was something she had no regrets about, just an aching in her most private places inside. And time, she found, was softening the memory of what she had given up, blurring the edges, soothing the aching.

I talked to Pat often and could see the growth she was making. There was one thing I felt I wanted to offer her. Although she had given birth herself, had been fully awake and conscious through it, she had never had the chance to see what birth *could* be—when the joy is not mixed with sadness. I asked her if she might like to come to a birth with me sometime, as an extra support for the family, not just an onlooker. Because she was planning to work with women who were going to give birth, it would provide valuable experience for that as well. She was excited at the idea.

The next birth I was asked to photograph seemed appropriate for Pat to attend. The woman was having her second baby at home with midwives. She had invited her parents and her sister to be present and hoped her two-year-old daughter could be there too. She appreciated the offer of another woman to help with the little girl, and said she also could use a little extra support herself in labor. Labor began late one evening. I called Pat and she was at home. We drove the hour to the house together and talked about what she was going to witness, how she might be of help. I hadn't needed to prepare her at all. Once inside the home, Pat went and sat on the couch next to the woman, who was resting. As I took out my cameras and talked to the midwives and the little girl and her father, I watched Pat slip unself-consciously into the role of support person. Soon she was stroking the woman's forehead during contractions, breathing with her, giving her a back rub.

Labor went on slowly all night. At dawn the grandparents arrived with their younger daughter. Pat moved from supporting the laboring woman, who now had two midwives and her husband to be with her, to supporting the grandmother, who was nervous and anxious for her daughter's well-being.

When the baby was finally born, the two-year-old was sitting curled in her grandfather's lap, the woman was sitting against her husband, and the grandmother had her hands clasped tightly together and Pat's arm protectively around her. Everyone shed tears of relief and delight. Pat was ecstatic. She bubbled about the birth all the way home, and she knew her presence there had made a difference for that family. It must have rekindled memories of her own experience and all the love and support she had had around her through labor and afterward. She said she couldn't wait to go to another birth, to be at another woman's side during labor.

At the end of the winter semester, Pat made the decision to return to Florida once again. This time she was sure things would be different. Her parents had left for an extended vacation, so Pat could stay in the empty house until she found a job and a place of her own. She enrolled in a week-long childbirth educator workshop in Atlanta as a stop on her journey. When she returned to Florida this time, it would be as a woman with a marketable skill she could use to help other women.

Abigail was almost two when Pat left. Before leaving, Pat remarked that had she been pregnant at that point, she thought she would have made a different decision about Abigail. She felt ready to be a parent.

Pat's life is very different today from what it would have been if she had chosen to keep Abby. She has had the time to experiment a bit, to learn more about trusting men, to learn about herself as a woman, in her strength and her vulnerability. She has learned to view herself with compassion. She has learned about herself as a sexual person as well. And she has done all of this without subjecting a young child to the difficult process of her own growing up. True, she could have grown too through the raising of Abby, although it would have been a forced maturity and hard on both of them. Abby would have borne the brunt of Pat's inexperience and youth. That may be the way many of us have been raised and have gone on to raise our own children, especially a first child. But who among us would say it is the best or the only way?

Today Pat is a woman, a woman who still carries an old picture of a new baby in her wallet. The pregnancy, the birth, holding Abigail in her arms, those were momentous events in her life; but they were not the end. They were, in fact, a beginning. It was a strange and difficult initiation into adulthood, but nevertheless a way in which Pat discovered herself while doing her best not to hurt a child in the process. And because her decision brightened the lives of two other people who were in the position to be good parents, who would call what she did a mistake?

Pat could be your daughter. She could even be you or me. You would, I think, be proud of her. Pat chose not to use having a baby as an answer to her own personal problems, and she has chosen not to try to fill the hole Abby left by having another baby before growing up herself. She has a past she can be proud of and a future to look forward to. She is on her way.

PAT:

A Life of Her Own

PAT LEFT CALIFORNIA WITHOUT ever having made contact with Paul and Vicki, without ever having heard how Abigail was doing or having seen her. After four months in Florida she moved to the island of St. Croix, in the Virgin Islands. Her sister Claudia had gotten a job for her. She would be an assistant teacher at one of the island's small Montessori preschools. Claudia had left the island by the time Pat arrived, but she felt secure going there on her own. St. Croix was a small island, and from her prior visit she had learned that everyone was friendly on the island and knew everyone else. She would not be lonely. The islands and the sea had always called to her.

In the first note I got from Pat, written in her large, full handwriting, I learned that she was living right on the beach, that school was going well, and that she'd met a guy she liked. She said the seminar she'd taken at the childbirth institute, the purpose of which had been for people to go deeply into their feelings, had "helped tremendously." "I feel pretty well cleaned out," she said.

At Christmas there was a card with Santa windsurfing and a note that ended, "Give Paul and Vicki and Abigail a hug for me. She must be a beauty." Pat later told me she had never felt the need to tell Paul and Vicki or the attorney of her changes in address. Because she kept in contact with her obstetrician and also with me, she knew Paul and Vicki would always be able to find her if they needed to.

Teaching, being around little children, was a joy for Pat. "I love their boundless energy and curiosity," she wrote. But within a short time, living on a seventeen-by-eleven-mile island began to feel constrictive, like life in a small town. "Everybody knows everybody's business," she wrote. Privacy was something Pat had always craved. When she first arrived she'd rented a room in someone's house, but that hadn't worked out, so she'd moved to another rented room. Then there was an accident, the car was totaled, and Pat landed in the hospital. Never one to dramatize or ask for sympathy, all she wrote was, "A few stitches in the knee, but I'm okay. I had one more car payment. Oh well, that's life in the big city!" She turned to walking everywhere, joined a tai chi class, bought a small rubber raft, and took up rowing. She said she'd done some sleuthing to discover what was going on in childbirth on the island, but found awareness in natural birth was lacking and the hospital a "zoo."

By summertime Pat had had enough of island living and, despite her fondness for the kids, decided to go back to Florida. Once more she moved back into the family home while she got on her feet. "Parent base station" was how she described it in her letter. She quickly found a full-time office job and began to earn money for her own expenses, paying rent to her parents. She was trying to save the $2700 it cost to train as a Montessori teacher. In the meantime she enrolled in junior college and started taking evening courses, sometimes dropping one after it had begun because she lacked interest and was tired after a full day's work. Her intention was to get an associate degree in early childhood education. Her mother was visiting family in South America. Eddie and Claudia had each made a trip back to Florida for a visit. "It was nice to have a reunion of 'us three' again," she wrote. All was going well.

Late in October of the first year back in Florida, she went to a Halloween party at a friend's place. Everyone was in costume. She got into conversation with a guy and spent the evening talking with him. "I liked him, from the look of his eyes through his mask, and the sound of his voice." They dated for the next few months. The relationship was slow to evolve. Pat was in no hurry and there was little time left after work and school. He was in the rock music business, like Abby's father had been, and did sound engineering for a reggae band. His name was Scott.

One night Pat stayed over at Scott's room. In the morning he insisted on driving her home and going up to the front door. "He wanted to talk to my mom, let her know he wasn't taking advantage of me, that he was serious. I kept telling him this was not a wise thing to do, meeting my mom like that." The meeting at the front door went well enough. Scott told Pat's mother just what he had said he would. Pat's mother seemed shocked at his bold candor but was polite. That evening she told Pat that she was not running a boardinghouse, there were decent hours that she would have to keep. By then Pat, aged twenty-two, had been independent too long to pay attention to a mother's ideas about a curfew. It was time to move on.

She found a room to rent and moved her few belongings. Most of the next year she and Scott lived in one room or the other, but they weren't ready to move in together. One of the things this relationship offered Pat that was essential to her was a lack of pressure, freedom to grow and feel her own separateness. Scott seemed to understand her need for privacy and respected it. Their lives included many interests they did not share, but the bond continued to deepen. "We gave each other a lot of space," said Pat. "It was a slow process of coming together, where you almost don't notice you're getting closer and closer. I got to work through a lot of things I'd never gotten to work through in a relationship." The letters slowed down. I learned that she was continuing to study tai chi, and that Claudia was pregnant and her brother planning to get married.

Pat didn't mention marriage in her infrequent letters. She

was taking her time. She had told Scott about Abby on their first date. "I said that I was a little nervous about being close with someone, that I was going through a healing process." She told him the story briefly. His reaction to hearing that she already had a child and that she'd relinquished her for adoption was like many other people. "How could you give up a child?" But from him, she said, it was different. There was no judgment. "He didn't act any different or treat me any different. I just felt I could open up to him." During the next months her boyfriend began to share more of himself with Pat, and the relationship continued to deepen.

During the next four years, Pat and Scott spent most of the free time they had together. They kept their separate rented rooms. Finally Pat graduated from junior college. She laughs as she recalls, "It took me four years to do it, but I was struggling, remember!" The last two years she switched from her office job to being an assistant teacher at a local Montessori school, which she continued for five years. Scott continued to work in sound engineering and play with a band on the side. They began to talk about marriage and children. "We both felt it was not time and there was no hurry."

Perhaps it was the inner work she had done at the child-birth institute—keeping a personal journal, getting in touch with her feelings, and sharing her feelings with others in a safe setting—that helped Pat feel complete about her relinquishment of Abby. Maybe it had helped to attend a birth, to give the kind of support that she had felt so embarrassed about receiving. Working with children, experiencing their needs, learning about their stages of growth had given her a chance to see why parenting was so difficult at any age, but especially if you were young and single. Abigail had opened her heart and taught her the pain of love. Pat did not repeat the past by getting pregnant quickly to fill the void or by rushing into a relationship. It is seldom easy to find your direction in life. But Pat realized that hooking her life to another person, having responsibility for someone else wasn't the answer. The issues of self-esteem that are faced by all teenagers and made more difficult by pregnancy have to be lived through. Pat understood the importance of giving herself time and space to grow up, to find out who she was and what she wanted in life.

When Pat was twenty-seven she discovered she was pregnant. "I suspected I was pregnant after about six weeks. There were physical, slight changes I felt. I knew the symptoms right away this time!" There was no question what to do. She would have the baby. "I was upset because I didn't feel quite ready to be a mother." But this time, ten years after Abigail, Pat knew she could handle it. She talked it over with Scott and they decided to get married. Pat's pregnancy went well. Naturally it brought back memories of pregnancy with Abby. "I wasn't as anxious as I had been with Abby and didn't worry too much this time." This time Pat knew what she wanted from a care provider and what sort of birth she was looking for. She shopped around and decided to use the birth center at a nearby hospital, partly because they employed midwives. Scott went to childbirth classes with her.

The birth was quick. She went into labor just before midnight. About 9:30 the next morning Scott drove her to the hospital birth center and stayed with her throughout the birth. The midwife was informed and supportive. The baby was born just past noon, shortly after Pat's bag of water broke, drenching the surprised father. The entire experience was positive, in Pat's view, especially having Scott so involved and supportive. "It was such a moving experience for him, something he'll never forget."

There were memories of the other birth and of the way Abigail had first looked. This baby had a lot of hair at birth, just as Abby had had, but it was a lighter color. "It did remind me of that other birth. But this birth felt great, because I was taking her home! There was no fear in me during labor, from anticipating what I would have to do afterward, like I had had with Abby." She had, she said, felt very confident in herself this time. Scott's mother, stepfather, and brother visited immediately afterward.

The new family went home twelve hours after the birth. They named her Melanie. "We went through tons of names, and we never liked the same one. Then I thought of his music and the name Melody. He didn't like that, but I then said, 'What about Melanie!'" Pat breastfed her daughter for the first two months. Then she went back to teaching. It was either that or lose her job; she wasn't permitted to bring the baby. She didn't want to put Melanie in day care. So Scott worked nights and stayed home days to parent. It was hard on their marriage, but good for Melanie and Scott. Pat credits his strong, close bond with Melanie to his presence and help at the birth and his full participation as father. "He's been a good mom to her, as well as a good dad, because he has been there from the beginning and has had to take care of her from when she was eight weeks old."

When Melanie turned two last year, her parents and she moved across the country, back to California, where they felt Scott would have an easier time finding work in music. Pat's parents had moved to San Jose the year before, and during that year her father had died, so they settled in temporarily with Pat's mother. It was only thirty miles from where Pat had lived at the end of her pregnancy and where she'd given birth to Abigail. She and Scott each found jobs and after a few months had saved enough to move to their own apartment. Their new apartment is halfway between Pat's office job and Scott's work in the audiovisual division of an electronics firm. Eventually Pat will go back to teaching. In the meantime her days are full, getting up early in the morning to get Melanie up and fed and dressed, taking Melanie to a nearby day care center, dropping Scott off at his job, and then driving on to her work. All before eight in the morning.

Their apartment is also just a few miles from where Abby and her family still live. Abby is now eleven. Pat never has gotten in touch with Paul and Vicki, although when I see her she frequently asks how Abigail is doing and sometimes asks me to say hello to Paul and Vicki.

Recently I asked her why she had not contacted them; Paul and Vicki had always expressed a willingness to hear from her and a genuine interest in how she was doing. "I didn't feel a need to. I felt by meeting them and talking with them and getting a sense of where I was going to leave Abby so that I could feel good about it, I was content. And," she added, "I felt it wasn't my place to interfere with that process, the process of Abigail and her adoptive parents developing their relationship. I always knew how to reach them, and I felt if something happened that Paul and Vicki needed to know about, I could reach them." Likewise, she knew they could always find her if they needed to.

One day soon there may be a reunion. Pat now says she is looking forward to seeing Paul and Vicki and Abigail again and to introducing them to her new family. She would like Abby and Melanie to know each other. But she is concerned about how Abby's older sister, Amanda, might feel, because Amanda is also adopted but has no contact with her biological mother. I told her I had recently seen and spoken with Paul, Vicki, Abigail, and Amanda, and that Abby had expressed in private an interest in seeing her. Pat seemed pleased to hear that. Perhaps knowing of Abby's interest, she will reach out to her.

I recently queried Pat as to whether she has ever made an attempt to find Abby's father. He does not even know about his daughter's existence, and he could provide Paul and Vicki and Abby with information regarding Abby's family history (and an important piece of her health history). She said, "I just don't feel I need to. I guess if I put the energy out there to find him, I probably would. But I haven't felt strongly enough about it to do it." She had, she said, hardly thought of Abby's birth father these past years. "I don't have any bad feelings about him. I just didn't know him well enough." She smiled a bit ruefully as she said that. It was, after all, she said, only one night in her life. One night a long time ago.

I saw Pat last week. She came to a celebration honoring the man who had been her physician for Abby's birth and who had arranged Abby's adoption. Pat came with her husband, Scott, and, although she arrived knowing no one except her doctor and me, she soon became acquainted with a number of people and made herself at home in the group. After a potluck dinner the time arrived to thank this man who had done so much in our community for natural childbirth and childbearing women. Pat was among the first to step up to the microphone.

She began by telling a little about herself. She said that she had first met Don Creevy at the age of seventeen, when she had been well along in pregnancy and planning to relinquish her baby for adoption but feeling insecure. That meeting, she said, had been an important occasion for her. She had hardly dared believe the kindness and special attention he showed her, making her feel as if she were almost a part of his family. It had made a dramatic shift in how she felt about herself and had given her the self-confidence to make the birth of her second child a dream come true.

I'd never seen Pat looking so radiant. Wearing a floral print dress, with her tall, slender body leaning slightly forward into the mike, she spoke with such ease and self-assurance that the roomful of people was moved. Her voice had the same wry humor and heartfelt warmth I'd come to appreciate over the years, but none of the self-deprecation it had once had. Her smooth brown arms, her long legs, and her wavy dark hair brought back memories of the anxious, withdrawn young woman I had first met more than eleven years before. Since that time Pat has achieved a sense of peace and calm; she has emerged an extraordinary woman.

PAUL AND VICKI:

Nature and Nurture

Pᴀᴜʟ ᴀɴᴅ ᴠɪᴄᴋɪ have not had any direct contact with either of their daughters' birth mothers in the past decade. Neither Vicki nor Paul met or spoke with Amanda's birth mother prior to the birth. As is common in private adoptions, a prebirth meeting between the adoptive parents and the birth parents had been discussed, but because Amanda arrived a month ahead of her due date, this meeting did not take place.

Amanda's birth mother and birth father were in a difficult position, psychologically as well as financially, which is typical of married couples who place a child for adoption. As with most adoptions, the decision wasn't simply a decision of the heart; pressures pushed them over the edge and into adoption. Amanda's birth father was already supporting himself, his new wife, his former wife, and the three school-age children from his first marriage. He was the sole wage earner in both families; this second marriage was less than a year old when Amanda was born, and although his new wife had been working prior to pregnancy, she had stopped midpregnancy and had been given no paid maternity benefits. They had both been working for a company that had gone bankrupt, and neither of them had been paid for the last six months they had worked at their jobs.

Amanda's birth mother discovered she was pregnant nearly three months after conception. She and her husband investigated an abortion; it was illegal in their state but legal during the first trimester in a neighboring state. But by the time she met with a physician in that state, she had gone past the legal deadline and was told she could not have an abortion under any circumstances. There was no choice but to carry through with the pregnancy and give birth to the child.

The decision not to raise their child was not easy to make, and, in keeping with the times and the place where they lived, the father had more say than he might in a similar situation today. This was the early 1970s in the rural United States, where husbands had the final say in marital decisions, and he was almost twenty years his second wife's senior. They made the final decision for adoption well into the last trimester of pregnancy. They were opposed to their baby having to spend any time in foster care, which was all that was offered to them by the local adoption agencies they contacted.

By the time they heard about private adoption and contacted the attorney, Phil Adams, it was the middle of the eighth month of pregnancy. Right up until Vicki arrived to claim Amanda, they were still considering reversing their decision. Vicki knows this because the birth father told her, during the brief time they were together at the hospital, that the previous night he and his wife had sat up late by the phone discussing whether they should call the attorney to tell him it was off.

A postbirth meeting would theoretically have been possible for the two couples or for Vicki and either or both of the birth parents, because this was a private adoption and did not have to follow agency rules. But the birth parents' way of coping with the emotional stress of relinquishment was to turn away from the pain. They had no counseling or support for doing otherwise and did not understand that there might be benefits in meeting the adoptive parents. Just as it used to be most common, and understood to be best for everyone, for the parents of a stillborn baby not to see the baby at all, it was also once the cultural norm in adoption for the birth parents never to see their baby.

By the time Abby was born the cultural attitudes had changed somewhat, particularly in many urban areas. Abby's adoption was definitely open; both Paul and Vicki met and spent time alone with Abby's birth mother, Pat, several times prior to the birth and were invited by Pat to be present for the birth. Vicki received Abigail directly from Pat's hands in a moment of shared intimacy. There is every reason for them to feel that Pat freely made both her decision to relinquish and her decision to have them as her baby's parents, as Pat did have emotional support from her sister and brother and outside support from her physician, her attorney, and me.

Pat benefited from knowing what all her options were and what some of the long-term implications might be. Pat did communicate with Paul and Vicki once after the birth, in the form of photographs she sent of Abby that had been taken in the hospital a few hours after Abby's birth. Pat was able to send the photographs directly to them because she had their names and address. The photographs are now in a box with all the rest of Abigail's baby pictures, pictures taken by Paul, other relatives, and me over the past eleven years.

Although there has been no further direct communication, Pat, Paul, and Vicki each understood they could contact each other at any time they felt it necessary. Pat has moved a number of times in the intervening years, but Paul and Vicki have always known they could reach her easily, because she has continued to stay in contact with both her obstetrician and with me.

Abby's adoption held the possibility of becoming a Cooperative Adoption, which is to say, an adoption where birth parents, adoptive parents, and the adopted child remain in contact and have an ongoing relationship of some kind. It has not become a Cooperative Adoption, but trust, communication, and willingness to keep possibilities open have been there from the start.

Amanda's birth father had not planned to be present during the morning when Vicki came to get Amanda, but he had to be; it was the only way they could do the exchange, given the circumstances and having had no warning. He had not been aware of a state law prohibiting anyone except a "natural parent" or state-licensed professional from taking a baby from a hospital. He had discovered that only on the morning Vicki was to arrive. He called the attorney as soon as he learned and told him that he didn't feel emotionally able to carry the baby out of the hospital and then relinquish her.

His plan had been that Vicki would take the baby from the hospital nursery, so that neither he nor his wife would have to face seeing their baby, much less seeing her in the arms of the new mother. He would simply go to the obstetrician's office, sign the requisite relinquishment papers, and leave. Unable to do that, he kept himself as distanced as possible.

"They didn't even want to know our names," says Vicki. "The nurse at the doctor's office told me that when the father signed the relinquishment papers, he had the doctor cover the top half, where our names and address were printed. Clearly he didn't want to know anything about where their baby was going." The birth mother had insisted on being put to sleep for the delivery, so that she could not feel the birth or see the baby afterward. This was one of the points that made the nurse feel the birth mother had perhaps not really wanted to place the baby for adoption. All of this information points to how this couple coped with loss, which was by trying to shut it out of consciousness.

In the case of Amanda's adoption, there were no family members or other people (except the attorney, who was out of state and never met them face to face) to help them through the process and inform them of all their options. They had decided on private adoption—and on this particular attorney, Phil Adams, whom they had heard of through a family friend—precisely because he had said he would guarantee that their baby would not spend any time in foster care, but go directly into his or her new home. This was important to them. Because of the geographical distance from both the attorney and the adoptive parents, there was little possibility of the adoption naturally evolving into an open one. Given the way the birth parents coped with the relinquishment, it may not even have been possible for them to participate in an open adoption, at least not without considerable counseling and support, and perhaps some passage of time. Thus the adoption of Amanda began and has remained closed.

There has been regular indirect communication between Paul and Vicki and Abby's birth mother over the years. Pat's obstetrician phoned Vicki twice within the first few years after they had brought Abigail into their lives to pass along a request he'd gotten from Pat for a recent photograph of Abby. On each occasion a photograph taken by Paul was promptly printed and mailed to him to send to her. Vicki says she and Paul would have been happy to do more than that, but that was all Pat asked for, and they have never wished to intrude upon Pat's privacy (or Amanda's birth parents' privacy, for that matter).

Whenever Paul or Vicki see Pat's physician now, which they occasionally do, because even though he has moved they still live only a few miles from each other, they ask if he knows how Pat is doing. Each time they hear a bit of current news that Pat has included in her yearly Christmas card and are reassured that she is doing well and continuing to develop and pursue her interests. Several years ago they heard Pat had married and had a child; they were pleased for her. Paul says, "We've always been interested in Pat's welfare. She's a nice lady, and our interest stems from that." "On the other hand," Vicki adds, "Pat clearly wanted to get on with her life, and we respect that."

Thus far there have been no medical problems in Abby's

life that might have benefited from information about both biological parents. It's been different with her older sister, Amanda, now age sixteen. Amanda has had severe asthma since she was a small child. "It sure would have been nice to have some information about that," says Vicki. "Amanda also has some learning disability connected with reading, and it would have been helpful to know whether anyone else in the family had it and what treatments had been tried."

It would take some effort for them to find Amanda's parents, because there has been no communication, even through the attorney, since that day when the birth father hurriedly handed his baby to Vicki outside the hospital. Probably the birth parents have moved at least once in the past sixteen years and would have to be traced to be found. Such searches have been made easier with the help of computers and various national registries for adoption, but the need hasn't been sufficient for Paul or Vicki to search. Also, they continue to want to respect the desire of Amanda's birth parents for privacy, which they have no reason to believe has changed in the intervening years.

Phil Adams, the attorney for both Amanda's and Abigail's adoption, has kept their files for the girls to have when they become eighteen, or sooner if Paul and Vicki ask for them. Vicki has never checked to see if there was a letter or an address from Amanda's birth mother. "I assume Amanda's file contains nothing beyond the adoption decree, because Phil would certainly have told us if he had received anything at all."

In the early years of parenting Amanda and Abby, there was an occasional question to answer about their adoptions. These were raised by other parents and friends. As Amanda and Abigail grew from toddlers to preschoolers, they each asked their parents the questions most children ask: "Where did I come from?" "Did I grow in Mommy's tummy?" Though they have never been told a story of their beginnings, they have always known they were adopted. This was Paul and Vicki's plan. Paul says, "We never told them things they didn't ask about, but we never made it a big issue and we never hid anything from them." They tried to make adoption a nonissue by answering every question as it arose in a simple, matter-of-fact, rational way. That is both Paul and Vicki's style, to be honest and direct, not sentimental.

From the beginning each girl showed her distinct personality, and they were as different from each other as one would expect two genetic strangers would be. Both Vicki, being a biologist, and Paul were well aware of genetic differences among people. But they, like most people at that time, assumed that a child could be greatly influenced in both personality and life direction by environmental factors. It was generally accepted during the early 1970s that children were born with varying potentials, but that environment played a more crucial role than genetics.

As Vicki can now see in retrospect, "The critical thing for us, coming into adoption—and perhaps this is true for most adoptive parents—wasn't that we wanted to be able to control our child, but that we wanted to be 'super parents.' When you have a child who does not fit within society's norms, society comes back at you, the parents, and says, 'What's wrong with you? You're not raising this child correctly!'" That is what happened in raising Amanda, and Paul and Vicki were not prepared for it, both because the teachings of the day placed greater emphasis on the importance of environment in shaping the individual, and because as an infant and preschooler, Amanda appeared to be exceptionally bright and creative.

Today, almost seventeen years after Amanda came into their lives, Paul and Vicki know a lot more about what is and is not possible in parenting. The pendulum of thought regarding how human beings develop has swung far in the opposite direction, with most researchers today placing tremendous importance on genetic factors that determine personality, attitudes, aptitudes, interests, and coping mechanisms. How this all affects adoptive parenting is just beginning to be understood. And despite the findings of research, this society still sees parents as the sole responsible agents in their children's development. There is as yet little public interest in the part genetic and prenatal factors play in human development.

Vicki was the primary caretaker of Amanda from the beginning, as Paul was working full-time as an engineer. During the first six months of Amanda's life, Vicki worked four hours each weekday outside the home to complete an unfinished research project. "It was a nice transition from being a full-time researcher to being a full-time mother." Once Vicki was home every day, she turned her full attention to satisfying Amanda's needs.

"I took her to the park a lot. We took walks. As she got older she helped me do everything in the house: laundry, cooking, everything." Vicki did not return to work in biochemical research. "I had chosen to be a mother, and I thought it was a full-time job. We lived very frugally so I could stay home. We didn't go out to dinner or to the movies or use babysitters much at all." This was the early 1970s; none of Vicki's college graduate friends who were mothers of young children worked in those days.

Today Vicki looks at Amanda's infancy and childhood from a different perspective than when she first entered parenting. "I had really never failed at anything that mattered to me. I thought that I could do anything. It wasn't that things were always easy for me; I always had to work very hard to succeed. But I felt I had infinite energy and drive and could do well in whatever I chose, including being a mother."

Like many who enter parenthood in their thirties and in midcareer, Vicki had learned that she could have a great deal of control over her life. She naturally saw parenting as one more potential accomplishment. "We live in an area of high achievers; everyone around here has expectations that are exceedingly high and very narrow. Everyone is expected to be tops and to be competitive. We expect to raise children who do exceptionally well in school and society. The schools around here expect the same of children." Vicki says problems can arise for children who do not fit into this mold. And, interestingly enough, it is upper middle-class, Caucasian neighborhoods like the one Vicki and Paul live in where a high proportion of adoptions occur.

"I didn't have any role models or physical help in caring for an infant, but I did have a lot of neighbors with small children. And in a sense that was part of the problem, because we reinforced these high expectations in each other."

Amanda came into their lives, at three days of age, as a tense baby who suffered from severe episodes of pain and crying, diagnosed as colic, during which nothing would console her. "At that point in time, it was commonly believed that nervous mothers caused colic. I knew I wasn't nervous. To me having a baby at home was wonderful, but it was no more difficult than doing a lab experiment. There were rules to follow, things to do, and as long as you did everything correctly, everything would come out fine! I felt comfortable being a mother."

"I couldn't understand how I could be causing Amanda's unhappiness, yet I felt guilty." At the time Vicki gave no thought to what impact Amanda's prenatal environment might have had on her after birth. Today she feels differently. "Now I believe a lot of it may have been caused by the fact that she spent the first months of her life in a uterus awash with the chemicals produced by tension and strain." Amanda's pain, for it was clearly physical pain, was hard for Vicki to handle. "I felt impotent."

"It was very consistent. Every day, from about three in the afternoon until about nine or ten at night, she would scream. It didn't matter if we rocked her in the baby carriage, held her close to our chests, walked with her, put her in the car and took a drive, placed her flat on the clothes dryer and turned it on. Nothing mattered. I felt inadequate. I thought that as a mother I should be able to console her, and I couldn't."

"My response for the first month or so was to hold her and cuddle her and walk with her the whole time she cried." When Amanda was a month old, however, Vicki took her to the pediatrician for her regular checkup and told him about the crying episodes. "He pointed out that it didn't seem to matter whether I was physically close to her, and that I would go crazy if I didn't get some space away from her crying. He suggested making sure she was in a situation where she couldn't possibly hurt herself—like in her crib—and that I then close the door and go into another room."

He also told Vicki that at about three months of age the colic would go away. "Literally at three months it stopped. Her birthday is the second of May, and on the third of August it stopped like a light had been switched off!" From the day the colic ended until she entered kindergarten, Amanda was considered by both Paul and Vicki to be a "lovely child." "I don't mean to imply she isn't lovely now," says Vicki, "or that she was passive as a baby. She certainly wasn't passive! She was constantly moving. But Paul and I had never been around kids before Amanda. Other people would say to us, 'How can you put up with that child; she never sits still!' But to us it seemed normal and wonderful."

From three months of age until she began school, Amanda exhibited no signs of being a person who was suffering from the long-term effects of either prenatal environment or relinquishment. There was, in fact, nothing to make Paul or Vicki feel that parenting an adopted child was different from parenting any child.

Abby, on the other hand, entered life as a calm and even-tempered person. She had no feeding or sleeping problems. Her sleep pattern was different from her sister's. Amanda would go nonstop all day, and ask to be put to bed. She would fall asleep in an instant. "There were times," says Vicki, "when I would kiss her good night and she'd be asleep before I got to the door." Abby, on the other hand, moved more slowly during the day and didn't need as much sleep at night.

She, like her sister, had her own room. She would go to bed willingly each evening, but then play in her crib as much as four or five hours. "We could put her to bed at eight, and at midnight or one she was still up there playing in her crib, singing or talking. When she got to the age when she could climb out of her crib, she would climb out, get a toy, and climb back in to play with it. Sometimes she would even wake up in the middle of the night and play for an hour or two. But she would never cry or, when she could walk, come and get us."

To this day Abby still needs a great deal of private time. She is popular with other children and is often invited to play with them, but it is not uncommon for her to decline simply because she would rather spend the afternoon alone, reading or climbing or riding her bike. Amanda, on the other hand, needs people around her and action all the time, just the way she did when she was very young.

There are other differences. "If Abby wants or needs something, she is able to make it happen for herself. She always has," says Vicki. "As a little girl, if she was playing a game that required a number of dolls, she would think it through, figure out how many she needed, and make one trip upstairs to her room to get them. If she couldn't get something herself or if she needed help with anything, she would ask for it." Abby is both goal directed and self-motivated.

Amanda is different in both respects. "Amanda doesn't seem to be able to make things happen for herself; either she doesn't know how or doesn't feel able. I don't know which it is," says Vicki. But she has been like that for as long as they can remember. Amanda flits from one activity to another, without any sense of completion before moving on. Also, Vicki notes, she lives in a dream world, visualizing clearly but not translating her visions into actions that will bring about what she wants.

From the time Amanda was very young, she has never shown any assertiveness on her own behalf. But she has always been eager and has had a difficult time remembering that there might be others around with needs too. "I can remember her at about the age of two, for example; there was a whole group of kids her own age who frequently went to the park in the car. Amanda always made sure she was the first to get into the car and then always sat right by the door, blocking everyone else's entry. Each time I asked her to move over, she would refuse, saying, 'But I want to be the first out!' It's not that she was mean or intentionally rude; she simply lived in her own world. And she still does."

Amanda also has difficulty competing or striving within a group. From age two or three, in a situation where she would have to compete with someone of equal or better skill, she would refuse to enter the fray and instead turn away and leave. "It was, If I can't win, I won't play!" says Vicki. This attitude, combined with learning disabilities that would become apparent only when she began school, would hinder her later in school.

Prior to entering school the only difficulty Paul or Vicki had with Amanda was her energy level. "When she was a small child I could never let her out of my sight. She was nine months old when I found her playing on top of the six-foot-high refrigerator and barely two when I found her thirty feet up in a redwood tree," recalls her mother. Being able to *do* things, to be in movement was an endless source of delight to Amanda. Vicki recalls Amanda at the dinner table each evening squatting on her chair so she could leap up from the table as soon as there was anything she wanted to go do. "She must have been ten years old before she could ever sit through a whole meal. Paul and I would say, 'You *have* to sit down. Sit down, please.'" But it was just parental frustration, nothing more. And they never related it to her not being their biological child.

With Abby, the only remarkable aspect of her personality that was difficult for her parents was her having occasional monumental temper tantrums. "The first one was when she was walking, which she didn't do until she was fifteen months old. They lasted until she was about three. It happened only when she was frustrated. The one I remember most clearly was when she was trying to do something with her wooden rocking horse. It must have weighed twenty-five pounds! I don't know what Abby wanted to do, but whatever it was, she couldn't. She got so angry that she burst into tears. Her crying got louder and louder, until finally she picked up this horse that weighed as much as she did and heaved it across the room. She was just a little over two years old at the time!"

"Whenever she had a tantrum, she would cry until she was exhausted, and that would be the end of it. Paul and I would just keep an eye on her, without letting her know it, to make sure she wouldn't injure herself." Paul and Vicki's responses to her tantrums were always to let her have them but appear to ignore them. Soon the tantrums ended, and Abby returned to being a generally happy child who found life endlessly interesting.

It was only when Amanda entered the local elementary school that things grew difficult for her and therefore difficult for Paul and Vicki as parents. From the beginning there were repeated incidents that pointed to Amanda's having low self-esteem. Though they did not stop to analyze what was happening at the time, by now Paul and Vicki have had ample time to look back on Amanda's life and put together a picture.

"I think three things were interacting," says Vicki. "One was Amanda's lack of ability to risk and attempt things." This trait was no longer true only in a group play setting; it occurred daily, both in the classroom and on the playground. "She had problems tackling anything new or hard."

The second had to do with how bright Amanda obviously was in comparison with how poorly she did in school. "Everyone who listened to her complex speech or observed her add and subtract figures in her head would say, 'She's so smart! Why doesn't she do her work!'" Amanda, it gradually became clear, had a learning disability, which showed itself early in an inability to learn to read but proved to be larger than that: a limited ability to take in information through either the written or the spoken word. She had no problem learning tactilely, through action, or through movement. Unfortunately, despite the urgings of research educators, little in public school was taught in these ways.

Amanda's third difficulty was her incredible energy. In

school she was unable to sit still, to listen, to concentrate, to focus on what was asked of her. She was constantly in motion, and the teachers found it a problem; it disturbed what they were trying to do with thirty children. Vicki began to receive phone calls from school. "From first grade on I would hear, 'Amanda can't be made to sit still!' The teachers would always reassure me that it wasn't that she was a discipline problem, just that she was disruptive." The expectation was that she and Paul should be able to make Amanda change. It was their expectation too.

For both Paul and Vicki, Amanda's inability to do what adults asked of her in school was troublesome. The problem had never arisen at home, because she was not being asked to sit still or focus for long periods. Being both cerebral people who since childhood had conformed easily to societal standards, it was difficult for them to understand why their daughter couldn't do as she was asked, especially because she was a loving, willing child.

"After we'd get a phone call, we'd talk to Amanda. We would always verbalize what we wanted, and what the teachers wanted. We would feel that Amanda understood this and also wanted to do what the adults wanted of her. We would always be dumbfounded when her behavior didn't change." It's difficult for one person to comprehend what goes on inside another person, especially when the other person is very different.

Amanda didn't have any particular problems relating to her peers. Both in the neighborhood and at school, she was popular and had close friends. As a two- and three-year-old she sometimes told people, "I'm 'dopted." It was like a badge of honor, being special because she had something a little different. Adoption didn't come up at school until she entered junior high school. Paul and Vicki did not belong to any support groups for adoptive parents. "We didn't feel adoption was an issue."

Abby came when Amanda was almost five. Amanda was the last of her peers to have a sibling. Having a new baby sister was exciting; it made her like everyone else she knew. "She was very good with Abby," says Vicki. "She always has been very good with Abby. They played together as small children and long after many siblings who are five years apart ordinarily have stopped playing together. Even now, if Amanda is around when Abby is getting dressed for something special, Amanda will do her hair or her nails." But over time, as Amanda did more and more poorly at school and showed low self-esteem, especially in relation to Abby, their relationship became strained. It is hard for a girl to have her younger sister be good at everything she tries and constantly receive attention for all that she achieves!

As Abby got more and more praise and compliments from teachers and other adults, problems at school became more and more of an issue in Amanda's life. She progressed through grammar school, every year falling further and further behind other kids her age. The problems weren't separate or isolated. Rather they interacted with and compounded each other, and the result was that Amanda soon developed a poor self-image. Both Paul and Vicki were aware that she wasn't doing well, but they had no sense of what the problem was. "I think we still assumed that she could do what was asked of her if she wanted to, and that if she did, things would get better." The fact that she was adopted did not, to them, enter into it. At this age Amanda never mentioned the subject.

At the end of second grade she was still unable to read well, and her parents began to investigate local private schools where class size was small and Amanda could get lots of special attention. They found a school close by their house known for good academics, structure, and good teaching in a nurturing environment.

"We knew Amanda was bright. We just thought she needed a better environment, and we thought in a small but structured setting she could focus more easily." Private schools cost money, and it was a great strain on their family budget. Third grade was a transition year; Amanda spent most of the year making new friends and learning to fit in. Nobody worried too much that she wasn't doing well academically, because it was assumed that she just needed a period of adjustment.

In the fourth grade things turned around a bit, and Paul and Vicki began to see some results of everyone's efforts on behalf of Amanda. "Amanda was working very hard, and she had a superior teacher who enjoyed teaching Amanda. It didn't bother her that Amanda didn't sit still." At last she had a teacher who liked her just for who she was and didn't try to change her. Amanda worked very hard and she did very well. She even made honor roll the first three quarters. Then in the spring two things happened: first, she was given a book to read by her remedial reading teacher. The book was difficult and overwhelmed her. "She quit. But she didn't just quit reading, she quit everything: history, math, everything!" notes Vicki. The second crisis was the onset of puberty, which was tumultuous and probably why her failure at reading hit her so hard.

Amanda was ten years old and just entering the throes of prepuberty, when the mood swings that are so indicative of that phenomenal change in a child's life began to appear. Vicki recalls, "Paul and I noticed that she was up and down in her moods but didn't realize it was puberty until the autumn." She had not yet begun to menstruate but was getting pubic hair. When she entered fifth grade she truly fell apart. It was almost instantaneous with the start of school.

The school year began with Amanda showing great determination to do well for about a week. Then she abruptly quit trying again. And when she quit trying academically but continued to disrupt the class—by falling off her chair or dropping things to get a laugh, all the behaviors that had previously drawn attention—she suddenly found herself ostracized by the other children. Amanda's fifth grade teacher remarked that this was the age at which most children tuned into learning and became active participants in the learning process. "Amanda was doing just the opposite."

At home Paul and Vicki found themselves yelling at her all the time. The school suggested someone sit with her while she did her homework. Vicki, being a perfectionist, would sit with Amanda for as much as four hours every evening trying to help. Abby, a kindergartner, was left on her own.

Outwardly Abby didn't seem affected, but Vicki is sure she felt left out. "She has told me that I used to spend all my time with Amanda. And I did! Amanda *always* seemed to need help, and Abby *never* seemed to need any. From nursery school on Abby did extremely well in all aspects of school." At the time Vicki felt the extra attention she was giving Amanda was working. But now she feels it only made Amanda hate school all the more.

In the middle of fifth grade, Paul and Vicki sought professional help. Vicki says, "She was failing at school, she was crying about everything, she had very few friends and was being left out of everything. She was truly unhappy."

They took Amanda to a local agency that had a reputation for helping children with learning disabilities. They met with a counselor, and in the course of the interview mentioned that Amanda had been adopted at birth. That fact was not looked at in her assessment; apparently it was not considered significant. The outside facts that were looked at and given great weight were the comments Amanda made to the test administrator about Abby.

Amanda talked at length to the counselor about her sister, and it became clear that she felt both threatened and overwhelmed by Abby. "She really isn't jealous of her. She loves her!" says Vicki. "But from the time Abby was a few weeks old up until today, people have often gushed about Abby and ignored Amanda." (Today, at eleven, Abby is on the swim team, works to earn spending money, and is beginning to do modeling; she organizes her days like a woman three times her age, is on the go from morning until night, never missing a beat or failing to perform superbly in any task. Amanda simply doesn't try to compete with her younger sister, but it is impossible for her not to compare herself; this has driven a wedge between the two girls.)

Amanda was given a battery of tests, and Paul and Vicki were given the results. "We were told that she was very bright and that she was probably mildly dyslexic. They felt she needed more help in school. It was recommended that she be taken out of private school, where there was high academic pressure, and put back in public school, but be given a private reading tutor to help her catch up."

Paul and Vicki agreed with the diagnosis, but not the recommendation. Public schools in their area had high academic pressure, because of the affluent and highly educated population they served, but in addition they had large class sizes. Vicki says, "We asked for recommendations for therapists, because we felt we were at the end of our rope and didn't know what else to do!" They selected a local child psychiatrist who was on the list and also known by a friend of theirs. He agreed to see Amanda on an individual basis.

Amanda went to therapy for almost four years, at first two or three times a week and then once a week. Private school tuition plus private counseling left the family financially strapped, with virtually no money for entertainment, family vacations, and so on. Amanda resented the fact that her family never went anywhere or bought anything. Paul and Vicki resented it too. "We couldn't help but have the feeling, 'If you'd just shape up, then we'd have all this money to play with.'"

Amanda began counseling at age eleven and ended at fifteen. In the beginning it was primarily a form of child therapy that involved nonverbal activities, known as play therapy. In Amanda's case she worked a lot with puppets. By the end it was essentially verbal. Periodically Paul and Vicki went to the therapist on their own. "Some of the sessions were simply feedback, in the sense that he would say in general what he and Amanda were working on. Some of them were guidance sessions, where he would ask us to try a particular tack at home with Amanda." He was the first person ever to suggest that adoption was a factor contributing to Amanda's unhappiness.

As is customary in therapy, the therapist kept everything that Amanda said confidential. Thus all that Paul and Vicki knew were some of the general issues, which included her being adopted. At the end of the four years the therapist felt the only issue Amanda had not confronted was having been relinquished. He told Paul and Vicki that the issue would not go away; she would simply have to deal with it later, when she was ready. This did not really surprise either Paul or Vicki. It also did not really mean much. Vicki says, "It wasn't an issue for us, so why would it have been an issue for her? We still didn't really attribute any of Amanda's behavior to her relinquishment."

As is also customary in therapy, especially child therapy, Amanda didn't talk about her sessions at home. Occasionally, however, she would tell her parents she hated it and would refuse to go to a particular appointment. "I always guessed," Vicki notes, "that when she didn't want to go it was because she was working on something that was particularly difficult or painful."

None of them saw any really tangible results over the years, but for Paul and Vicki it was essential that Amanda do this. "We felt that we had tried everything else: seeing school counselors, having her in private schools with very small classes and lots of personal attention, hiring outside tutors, talking to her, talking to our pediatrician, having friends and neighbors and relatives talk to her. And nothing had worked. This was the last thing we could think of to do!"

All the time Amanda went to the therapist, she continued to have problems both in school and at home. Amanda would not do whatever was asked of her. At home if she was asked to pick things up in the living room, she would disappear. Vicki says, "It didn't matter if we didn't make it immediate. We could say, 'Could you please do this by dinner or by the weekend.' Whatever we said, she wouldn't do it."

"It was the same at school. The minute you said, 'Please do this,' it was as if she said, 'No, I won't. You can't make me!'" Amanda never was hostile. She always smiled and folded her hands as she listened. Afterward, when confronted with what she hadn't done, she always had an excuse. In those days Vicki and Paul felt she was being defiant. Today, Vicki feels, it was not that. "Today I really feel she just couldn't do what was asked of her. I *still* don't know why!"

At the end of sixth grade, she was so far behind academically, socially, and emotionally, there seemed nothing else to do but hold her back in school for a year. Amanda was not brought into the decision, but seemed relieved when she was told. Because the school she was in was so small and socially inbred and because Paul and Vicki did not want Amanda to suffer any stigma from staying back a year, they moved her to another small private school. In retrospect, they are not sure if this was a good place for her. It was a very small school, with no more than six children to a class, and Amanda was becoming very social and needed a wider range of friends. On the other hand, she did very well academically at the new school. But her self-esteem did not rise.

"I think," says Vicki, "Amanda was already so convinced that she couldn't do anything that it didn't mean anything to her!" The next year she entered seventh grade in a public junior high school. Making every attempt to do what was best for Amanda, given the information they had about her needs, Paul and Vicki selected one where Amanda didn't know any of the kids, because she was a year behind her classmates. Amanda's academic story continued to be troublesome, and her parents continued to try to find solutions in the schools, moving from public school back to private school. But nothing really helped. Today, at the end of Amanda's sophomore year, with Amanda about to turn seventeen, Vicki is frustrated and sad. When we speak about her feelings, tears well up in her eyes. She and Paul, for all their efforts, realize that what they have done on Amanda's behalf has not been enough.

Paul and Vicki did not begin to put together a picture of Amanda until very recently. The psychiatrist's remark about adoption being an issue Amanda still had to confront started them thinking. Slowly Paul and Vicki began to notice signs that, for Amanda, being relinquished in the way she was by her birth parents had indeed produced some lasting negative effects. Amanda had, in fact, given strong hints about how much it disturbed her that she had not been kept by her birth parents.

On several occasions when she was really feeling upset,

she said to Paul and Vicki, "Why did my mom and dad throw me away?" Being "thrown away" is a theme Amanda's talked about once in a while since she was perhaps ten years old. Paul and Vicki have always attempted to reassure Amanda that it wasn't that she was thrown away: adoption was chosen for her as something that would be better for her than what her birth parents could provide. "We've always tried to help her see that it was a very difficult decision for them. We wanted her to know that this wasn't the *easy* way out for them. It was the hard way!" Vicki notes. "But I don't think Amanda has ever heard that!"

"Being adopted *has* caused Amanda problems, in the sense of her feeling some lack of identity, of knowing who she is," Paul agrees. "It might even be more of a problem for her than it would be for other adopted kids, because Amanda's a very complex and sensitive human being." "And fragile," Vicki adds. "I think other people may not realize this, because she's always been big, active, and unintentionally aggressive."

In addition to worrying that she was unwanted, Amanda occasionally expressed to her parents a sense of deep inadequacy. "She would tell me," says Vicki, "'I feel there is a piece of me missing.' She would also say, 'I feel there are three or four Amandas. Which one is the *real* me?'" This self-doubt did not disappear after puberty came on; it continues up until today.

Now both Paul and Vicki wonder, Might there be some physiological connection between Amanda's low self-esteem and her having been adopted. Vicki says, "Maybe it's biological, in the sense that some people right from birth tend to look at the world very positively and others very negatively." Abby, age eleven, is there during this particular conversation between her parents and me, and, hearing her mother's words, suddenly has something to add. "You mean like a glass on the table that has water up to the middle? Positive people would say it was half full, and negative ones would say it was half empty?" "Yes, Abby," Vicki says. "Just like that."

With almost seventeen years of experience in adoptive parenting behind them now, Paul and Vicki today are certain that each person is born with a basic attitude toward life as well as specific traits and predispositions. They also now wonder what they could have done different if they had had the information necessary to understand their oldest daughter. They were never blind to the girls' differences; they simply did what most well-meaning parents do: they tried to accept them as part of the package. And the differences were obvious from birth.

As Paul remarks, "These two girls came into our home differently! It became obvious with each of them that first night at 2:00 A.M. The first night Amanda was home, we put her in the crib in our room because we were afraid we wouldn't hear her when she woke up. The instant she woke up, she began to scream bloody murder! We put her in the next room and closed both doors between us from then on." They still could hear her when she woke and needed to feed, but they didn't awaken to deafening screams.

"When Abby came home," Paul recalls, "we also put her in the room next to ours and closed the doors, as we'd learned to do with Amanda. And I woke up in the middle of the night—I did the night feedings, and an alarm would go off inside me to tell me when it was time—and I walked in and Abby was awake and cooing. She was just twenty-six hours old, in a new home, yet everything was fine!"

"Some things are genetic, I think," Vicki says. "It's not to say Amanda's angry all the time, and Abigail's always happy. There's just a basic difference." They have had a lot of time to reflect on this observation and look at their two daughters' differing needs and responses to everyday situations. Vicki has ideas about what it all might mean. "I think possibly there are two reasons why Amanda has more trouble in dealing with the adoption than Abby. One is the genetic predisposition." "Of spirit," Paul interjects. "Of biology!" Vicki exclaims. "The second is a lack of identity. Amanda doesn't seem to have a sense of who she is and where she came from. It's roots!"

Roots. That term became widely discussed in the late 1970s, after the book and television miniseries called *Roots* appeared. Since then many people speak of their "roots" as being something vital in their lives. Vicki uses the term carefully. She is a biologist by training and doesn't like to throw ideas around casually that have no basis in scientific fact.

Paul and Vicki realize now that Amanda probably has been suffering for years from negative, long-term effects of relinquishment in her closed adoption. Amanda has given them clues in the statements she has made about being relinquished and how it has made her feel. She's never said she would like to find her birth parents, although Paul and Vicki have initiated the subject a few times. "We've told Amanda it's a real possibility and given her the rules she'd have to abide by: waiting until she was eighteen and then going through a middleperson." That, they say, is to respect the privacy of the birth parents.

The idea of a reunion with Amanda's mother or with Pat has not been a high priority for Paul or Vicki. But the possibility that one of their daughters might need to make contact with her birth mother before age eighteen has made them begin to question their earlier certainty that a person needs to be an adult before searching. "Having a reunion is not an issue for us," says Vicki. "It's not been a part of our lives."

Paul agrees. "I'd like to know how both birth mothers were doing. I would like to know that much. There's a connection there. They're sort of like distant relatives. They are their flesh and that is a connection we'll always have! We have a physical part of them. It's just there." They've always expected the girls might want to search and have said that would be all right with them, that they would support them in doing it, once they turned eighteen.

Meanwhile, Amanda is becoming more and more independent; she now has a driver's license and a used car of her own. In a little more than two years, she will graduate from high school and begin to live independent of her parents. Everyone thinks she will probably wait until she is of legal age before searching. Vicki says, "If Amanda came marching in one day and said, 'I can't wait any longer,' we'd certainly listen!" What they would do, Paul and Vicki say, would depend on their best sense of what sort of guidance and support Amanda needed from them. But at the very least, they would hear her feelings and respond. Still, Vicki wonders, what *is* in store for Amanda when she does search? Will she encounter rejection? That is something she would never wish on her child, but something from which she and Paul could not protect her.

Paul and Vicki do not live in a climate where people talk freely about how difficult it can be to parent certain adopted children. Our culture in general has difficulty acknowledging the fact that some parents are better at the job than others: more willing, more capable, and in better life circumstances. The culture also does not find it easy to acknowledge that some children are harder to parent than others: that from birth they exhibit distinct personalities and responses to life that cause difficulties for themselves and their parents.

The general American idealization of family and children often makes it difficult for parents to get the information, support, and help they need to give their children what their children need. Relinquishing a child, whether to adoption or to the child's other parent, has not been considered acceptable. Nor has it been okay for parents to talk openly about how hard it is to be a parent, whether the child is adopted or biologically theirs. How uncertain Americans often are about what they are doing with, to, and on behalf of their children!

Today people are beginning to talk a little more openly about what the experience of parenting adopted children is like. Some who raised both adopted and birth children claim there was no difference. Some admit they formed a special bond with one child but not another but don't relate it to whether the child they feel closer to is adopted. Few are willing to speak out about negative feelings they have for a child whom they adopted. That would not reflect well, they feel, on themselves. It is much easier to label the child difficult.

For Paul, as far as parenting his adopted daughters is concerned, he doesn't feel their being adopted has been a source of the difficulties he has experienced in being a father. "I don't think adoption has meant any difference for us, for Vicki or for me. When you're raising kids, you deal with emotional issues anyway. Amanda's feelings about having been thrown away by her birth parents, that's certainly an emotional issue. But it's just a different one." Vicki agrees with that. "Both Paul and I have felt very strongly that, from the day we got each of them, they were *our* kids! Right from the first night." Paul and Vicki are fortunate that they had no difficulty forming a strong bond of affection with each daughter. Nor has either of them felt the impulse to reject Amanda because of any feeling that she didn't meet their standards for what a child should be.

Paul is right that parents inevitably have difficult issues with which to deal. Some of these are emotionally provocative, and that makes them more difficult to handle. When a parent is emotionally overwrought, it is harder for him or her to see clearly, to be distanced enough from what is going on to respond appropriately and act with understanding, rather than simply reacting. Parenting an adopted child is complicated when the intensity of the child's emotions is exacerbated by traumatic events early in the life of the child.

Adoption itself may be enough of a traumatic event for some children that they are from infancy both especially vulnerable and either armored for self-protection or take the stance of the passive victim. One day there might be a way to measure scientifically any individual baby's resiliency. There are so many variables in even an infant's life that it is difficult to isolate the impact of the prenatal environment, the birth, the relinquishment, and the change of parents. Is adoption itself a crucial variable?

This question, of course, must be raised before it can be studied and answered, before predictions can be made and appropriate support given or intervention carried out. In the meantime parents today must take the responsibility on their own to observe, evaluate, and respond in the best way they can.

Paul and Vicki still live at the same address where they were when Amanda came into their lives. Many neighbors have adopted children over the years. For almost everyone in their circle of friends and neighbors who has adopted, adoption has meant getting a baby within days of the baby's birth. In response to my question about how these various parents and kids she knows are doing, Vicki ticks them off.

"One family has a child adopted at birth with whom they get along *better* than their two natural-born kids! Another family has two adopted kids: one does not really fit into the family; the other does, has always done very well, and is now in college. The daughter, whom they have a hard time with, never finished high school and is now pumping gas. Another family, who adopted an infant from Mexico, moved away four years ago. That girl was having some difficulties. But perhaps no more than any thirteen-year-old!" Down the street are two other families, each with two children, one adopted and one not. "They are all fine and they are teenagers now."

"Kids are pains!" Paul interjects suddenly and with emphasis in the midst of a recent conversation, as he winks at Abby, who is snuggled up next to her mother. "It isn't ever easy being a parent, and some kids are harder for some adults than others are." The three of us adults heartily agree upon that. I want to know what kind of advice Paul and Vicki would give people who were thinking about adoption, what might help them. Paul gives this some serious thought.

"First," he says, "you have to realize that the issue of adoption is going to come up with your children. You should think about that ahead of time, preferably before entering into it, because it will come up one way or another. Perhaps the sooner the better. I really think it shouldn't be forced, but questions shouldn't be suppressed once they start coming. They should be answered honestly." He doesn't say "comfortably," although he and Vicki have attempted to make adoption a comfortable topic of discussion in their home.

"Another issue is the question of bonding," Paul adds. That is a big one and one that is emotionally charged for many parents, whether their children are birth children or adoptive children. No parent wants to think that he or she is not properly emotionally connected to his or her child. It is tantamount to saying he or she doesn't love that child!

Bonding is a term no parent would have coined. It has the connotation of glue. To some it sounds artificial and cold. Yet to me it is a useful term, an accurate term. It originated in scientific literature as a word to describe the specific and special relationship between a parent and his or her baby, and then became generalized to refer to a special intimate connection between an individual and a baby.

Bonding refers to a depth of affection and feeling of responsibility that turns an ordinary person into someone willing to go to almost any length to protect a child from harm: with his or her life if necessary. Bonding also prevents a parent from taking frustration and anger out on the child. Bonding creates a framework of support, on all levels, upon which the child can rely and within which the child feels totally safe. It also forms emotional boundaries within which an adult will behave appropriately toward the child, who, because of size and age, does not hold the same power as the adult.

A child also bonds with his or her parents. For the child it creates a loyalty and connection to the parent that remains no matter what the parent does.

Many people find that it takes some time to fall in love with, feel that special connection with their children. For others it seems to begin in pregnancy and arise full-blown at the first sight of the child. Adoptive parents are not alone in having a concern with bonding. This concern affects birth parents and stepparents as well.

If the special bond doesn't happen easily, it doesn't mean a parent can't take care of the baby or child in the interim, while those feelings develop. That is a matter of will and attitude rather than emotion. Love grows from practicing loving behavior, from acting as if you loved the person, from loving intention as much as from natural feeling.

The question of bonding within adoption seems to be more a matter of individual human differences than an issue specific to adoption: these differences relate to how quickly a person lets someone into his or her heart. It is also affected by the parent's and the child's temperaments, and by how easily the two learn to interact.

An important goal in parenting is for the parent to achieve unconditional love for the child. Few people raised without unconditional love (what used to be called acceptance) find it possible to give this to anyone else until they have discovered what it feels like to accept *themselves* fully. This requires healing from, and letting go of, feelings of inadequacy and being unlovable. How many people have done this kind of growth prior to having children? Precious few, I think, from observation. For the rest it is a matter of being pushed to grow at the outermost edges, pushed by their children, who wrench love out of them and tap depths of feeling they didn't know they had.

Depending on the person, adoption may make more difficult the effort to bond with a child. This certainly must have an effect on the child, who has already come through a process in which he or she was left, not by just anyone, but by Mother, in the primal and archetypal sense of the word. Feelings of loss or rejection are much more powerful when they are felt at the very beginning of life.

Many variables can add to initial feelings of being unwanted or not good enough to have been kept. It never helps if the adoptive parent is unwittingly looking to the adopted child to fill a hole in his or her heart. A baby thrives on love, but a baby lives for his or her own purpose, not the purpose of the parent, and that purpose is his or her own growth.

Paul tries to think of other advice to offer those considering adoption. "For the good of the child, you should think carefully and honestly about, Do I need to have a child of my own flesh? Do I feel it is so important to preserve my own genes? If so," he says, "adoption is *not* the answer! If you are going to adopt a kid, you have to step away from the need to have *your own* child." Vicki agrees, "You have to give that one up." "And you have to give it up right then," Paul adds. Although Paul initially had some reluctance regarding adoption because of this issue, both Paul and Vicki affirm that the issue of whether the child was of their flesh and genes was not something they had ever felt strongly about.

Paul, Vicki, and I discuss the question of how well kids adjust to being adopted and what difficulties they might have that would set them apart as a group. We have all heard the statistics that indicate that the percentage of adopted children who end up with troubled lives is large. Much anecdotal evidence and some research indicates this.

Although they did not give it a great deal of thought at the time, Paul and Vicki are now interested in the effect the uterine environment has on a baby, particularly the effect it has on a baby who goes on to be adopted. They are aware that Pat went through a lot of stress in her early pregnancy; they also know, of course, that she ended the pregnancy with a great deal of support and in good spirits. She did not go through her entire pregnancy in a state of ambivalence about whether she would keep her baby. She was clear in her mind and felt she would relinquish her baby for her baby's well-being.

In Amanda's situation the birth parents tried to get an abortion and couldn't, and then elected to relinquish their baby for adoption. The mother, it must be assumed, lived in a state of emotional turmoil. A biologist, psychologist, or philosopher might ask, By what mechanism does a fetus know his or her mother's feelings and thoughts? We know now that a newborn baby has the same range of emotions as an adult, and that the baby is sensitive to pleasure, pain, deprivation, all the things to which adults are sensitive. What does it mean when a birth mother spends much of her pregnancy feeling ambivalent or hopeless? What does it mean to the baby when she is not clear about her decision to relinquish her baby?

Although the questions are now in their minds, Paul and Vicki have not directly pursued trying to contact either Amanda's or Abby's parents. Many other things currently take precedence and fill their lives: the everyday concerns that keep parents busy.

I ask them what they would do if Pat were to initiate contact with them. "It would be fine," Vicki quips, "I'd just tell her not to come right now!" She is joking, referring to the fact that their old house, which was dark and perpetually damp and not the best environment for someone with allergies and asthma (which both Vicki and Amanda have), has been razed, and a new one is being built on the same property. They are currently living with Vicki's mother in cramped conditions.

Vicki is definitely not joking when it comes to the sense of responsibility she and Paul both feel for doing everything in their power to assure the well-being of their daughters, especially when it relates to their self-esteem. Vicki is currently primarily concerned about Amanda, about how to get her out on her own, feeling self-confident, capable of taking care of herself and reaching for the kind of life Amanda desires. She would also like to know who and where Abby's birth father is, so Abby will be able to find him if and when she wants to. For now Paul and Vicki feel that Abby is thriving, but Amanda is still hurting. They want to help. They are at a loss as to what they can do. In sixteen years of trying they have not found the key to unlock that door.

AMANDA AND ABBY:

The Child's View

I FIRST MET AMANDA, Paul and Vicki's older child, when she was four and a half years old. Her parents had just met Pat for the first time and were awaiting the birth of the baby she intended to give them. I next saw Amanda in the hospital lobby, outside the maternity unit. She was sitting with her dad, and they were waiting for her mother to come out with her new baby sister.

Amanda's earliest memories are of bringing the new baby home. "Mom was in the back seat, holding Abby. I wanted to hold her too. She was my baby sister." The new baby spent her first nights in the small den across from Paul and Vicki's bedroom, just as Amanda had when she was a newborn, so that Paul could hear her wake at night for feedings.

To Amanda, Abigail came out of nowhere. "My friends' mothers got all fat, and then one day they had a new sister or brother. But with Christie (Amanda's special nickname for her sister), she just arrived!" Amanda didn't relate the word *adoption* to her baby sister. Although Paul and Vicki first told Amanda she was adopted when Amanda was very small, she doesn't recall when she first found out. She grew up feeling that she had always known.

Now Amanda is almost seventeen. She heard from her parents that I would be interested in talking with her about adoption if she were interested. They were surprised when she said yes. Talking about her feelings is not something that comes easily to Amanda.

She comes over to my house one day directly from school, and when I meet her at the door I am surprised to discover that she is taller than me. She is of medium height and build, with an olive cast to her skin and facial features that look almost mature. I ask if she remembers me. She says she does, from when she was very young. She sits down in the big, comfortable cushion in the corner that is like a nest, and I bring her my cat, Timmy, to help put her at ease.

She is dressed in the casual style of the day: an old, baggy T-shirt and baggy Bermudas of a nondescript color. When I compliment her on her fine, silky brown hair, which frames her face and reaches her shoulders, Amanda makes a face. She is not impressed with her hair. But what teenage boy or girl ever approved of his or her face or hair or body shape?

Amanda's eyes are deepset, especially when she looks down and pouts, which she does often on each occasion I see her in the next several months. Around adults, such as her parents and me, she usually wears the sullen expression of a teenage girl who is fed up with childhood and restless to fly on her own. Nevertheless, she takes the time to respond thoughtfully to each of my questions, all the while petting Timmy, who lays comfortably draped over her legs.

Amanda says that the first time she recalls thinking about being adopted was when she read my book, with its chapters about her younger sister and her parents. She read it when she was nine. It caused her to reflect. "I didn't think about me. I thought about Abby. It made her sound so cute and so wonderful. In reality she was a pain, starting to go through all my stuff!"

"I was kind of mad," Amanda continues, "because everybody knows so much about Pat, and nobody knows much about my parents." Amanda knows only a few things about her birth parents: their last name, that they were married at the time she was placed for adoption, that she has three older half-brothers, and that she was born in Las Vegas. She says she doesn't have any idea what her parents look like, although Vicki did meet Amanda's father once, the day she went to get Amanda, and she has probably told Amanda what he looked like. It's interesting, the selectiveness of memory.

Amanda tells me she didn't grow up thinking much about being adopted, "except when I heard somebody else say something about it, like a friend might say she was adopted, and I'd say, 'Oh, really! So am I.'" She knows that her mom and dad do not want her to begin the search for information about her past until she is eighteen. That is over a year away, a long time in the life of a teenager. When Amanda turns eighteen she will be in her final year of high school. "I'll probably wait 'til I'm out of high school, 'til I'm doing nothing. Then I'll try to find them." She speaks with a quiet certainty.

When I ask if she has any sense of what it might be like to search, she shares a vivid dream with me. In the dream Amanda goes to Las Vegas with friends. She meets a young man and falls in love with him. They begin to live together and make plans to marry. They decide to look up their family histories. "I don't know why," she says. "We just do." They discover that he has a missing sister, who was put up for adoption at birth. "It kind of leads to our realizing that I am his sister."

In the dream they are in a basement when they discover the truth. Although she doesn't know the word *unconscious* or its meaning—material that is within but unavailable to the conscious mind—Amanda says she sees the basement as meaning "underneath the surface." She has had that dream a number of times in the past year, and it is always the same. She stands there in the basement hearing the revelation, and then turns around and walks up the stairs, without ever saying good-bye to the man she had been going to marry. At that point she wakes up.

"I always think about my dreams." She briefly looks up at me before she continues, as if to see if she can entrust me with the rest. "This may sound really weird, but I have two lives. I have one life at night and one life during the day. At night I can do anything I want to. I can be whoever I want to be. But during the day I am already somebody and have to live out who that is. There's a set life I have to lead." But, she says, there are advantages to having two states of existence. "When I get sick of one I can go to sleep, or wake up, whatever."

Like most teenagers and like many adopted kids of all ages, Amanda has felt very alone in her feelings and perceptions about life. She has always seen herself as different. Like most people who feel alone and different, she has not ventured to talk about it with other people, to see if others shared these feelings.

Amanda has never told her parents about the dream or about her very clear sense that waking reality was not the only reality. She's never read or heard others talk about such things with her parents, and none of her friends have mentioned anything similar. Until now it has been a private part of her inner life. I tell her that many people have those feelings. I also tell her that there are books on philosophy and religious experiences that address the very things she has experienced, because I want to let her know she is not alone.

Amanda's conscious memories began with the arrival of her sister in her life. When she now thinks about searching for her roots, she imagines she will look first for her siblings. The search, she knows, might take her to her biological parents, but they are not her focus, at least not for now. "My parents are how I started, but other than that, they aren't at all a part of my life." To her they are just two people who had a kid and "for this and that reason, didn't keep it. I kind of want to hear them say why." The answer, she says, wouldn't really make a difference, "unless they said, 'We just decided one day that we didn't want to keep you.' Then I'd get mad."

She doesn't really think that's what they would say, yet the anxiety persists. The possibility that she was never wanted by her original parents is perhaps her deepest fear.

Every person carries "what-ifs" and worst fears. They usually change with time: old ones get replaced by new as a person confronts one fearsome unknown after another, discovering each time that he or she survives and that most fears do not live up to the advance publicity. The fear or belief that a person was not wanted—at the very start of his or her life—is a major blow to a young child's developing sense of self and the world.

Amanda's fear of having been "thrown away" expresses something many adoptees feel but have a hard time saying. It implies, I was found lacking and therefore I was not wanted. Why else, a child asks himself or herself, would I have been rejected or abandoned? It must have been something about me that was so wrong that I was unacceptable!

The feelings, questions, and interpretations of an infant have profound importance. Modern research shows that babies perceive and conceptualize their primal impressions, which include life in the womb, the birth process, and their first days after the umbilical cord is severed. First impressions leave lasting traces and shape a child's view of himself or herself and the world in a way that is only now beginning to be comprehended.

What can make an infant feel hopeless in the face of negative impressions is the innate knowledge the infant has about his or her vulnerability: I am helpless. I am dependent. Whatever it was that makes me unacceptable, I am powerless to change. This is guilt for having been born. Some adopted children may never have felt this; some of those who have may be able to spontaneously heal from primal wounds. But many, I believe, particularly those whose adoptions have been closed, and whose mothers had been unconscious from drugs at birth or elected never to see the baby, have been deeply wounded.

If a birth mother lived much of her pregnancy in denial

(as Amanda's apparently did), and hated or mourned being pregnant, knowing she would be relinquishing a child another had pressured her to give up (as Amanda's mother apparently had been), she did not create the happiest fetal environment. If she gave birth in a time when she was encouraged not to be conscious for the birth or to have a screen in front of her face during delivery so that she would not see the baby, she and her baby were deprived of important knowledge of each other. If her baby was then placed in a hospital nursery (as Amanda apparently was) until he or she was moved from there either to a foster home or to adoptive parents, the baby never had the opportunity to hear his or her mother say good-bye. Her mother could never explain to a child such as Amanda, "I love you. I am giving you up so that you can have a better life. Please understand. It is not your fault. I will always love you."

This is precisely what millions of pregnancies and births were like for birth mothers and their babies who were subjected to the practices common in closed adoptions for more than half a century. Such practices today seem outlandish, if not outright cruel, yet they were based upon principles that most doctors, nurses, adoption workers, even psychologists and religious counselors for many years insisted were best for mothers and babies going through adoption.

The impact of these experiences—fear, loss, grief, and guilt—do not relate to anything that the adoptive parents did in the child's life. They may never understand, much less be able to make up for, this initial feeling of loss and inadequacy that their adopted child may carry, no matter how much the parents try or how well they love.

This feeling of worthlessness is not unique to adopted children. Many have felt, at one time or another growing up, that they were mistakes of life, that they shouldn't ever have been born. But for most people there was no real evidence to substantiate the feeling. Children of divorce, those who are abused or emotionally abandoned, those who watch the abuse of a parent, as well as children from homes where a parent is an addict of any kind grow up feeling worthless. Usually they also grow up feeling that they are the cause of their parents' problems. For them there have been recurrent dysfunctional family patterns, repeated experiences in their lives that have undermined their self-esteem.

When a child has nothing but imagination upon which to base his or her conclusions, that child can feel all the worse for believing there is no reason for his or her quiet despair. How can I feel this way when my parents love me? It must be something wrong with *me!* But being raised in a nurturing environment, by supporting and caring adoptive parents, is not necessarily enough to fill the void or heal the wound.

Amanda's face is drawn and downcast when she says, "I always think about that [having been thrown away] if I'm having a bad day. It's the first thing that pops into my mind."

"I can't describe it," Amanda says. "Part of me is missing." I tell Amanda that I've heard many adoptees say that, that she is not alone in feeling she is not whole. Although she can't easily find words to express it, Amanda does say she thinks she knows the source of the lack. "A mother and her kid are like a unit," she begins. "If they are separated for one reason or another, the unit is broken. The mother is always going to feel like there is something missing, and so will the kid." She adds, with emphasis, "*Especially* the kid!" She continues, "The mother is like the main part of the kid's life. And the mother's not there!"

I didn't think Amanda was talking about a specific mother. Rather, she seemed to be speaking about mother with a capital *M*, her initial home, the world in which she had grown: her matrix. She looks to Vicki as her mother, and she says she has always felt Vicki's love and caring. It is the deeper sense of having been at ease and at one with her mother in the womb, totally connected and nurtured, that she lacks.

It may be possible for a child who is relinquished by his or her mother to feel a primal union and security in the womb, even though the mother knows she will not raise the child. I propose, however, that closed adoption, with its accompanying denial and guilt on the part of the birth mother, makes it difficult for the mother to impart such a sense of well-being to her child.

In Amanda's case a sense of union with her birth mother apparently was lacking. This is not to blame Amanda's birth mother, but it is a measure of how far closed adoption has let everyone down despite its intention to protect people. There may be compensations, and high among them is the child having real nurturing from his or her adoptive parents and a sense of trust and intimacy within his or her adoptive family. It is to be hoped that in the future those involved with adoption will have a deeper and subtler sense of what adopted children need and how parents can provide the stimulus for healing while the child is still very young, or at whatever age the child is when it becomes apparent that the child is hurting.

Today, at sixteen, Amanda is not able to imagine any specific remedy that would prevent an adopted child from having this profound sense of loss. It would be helpful if she could talk with someone skilled in the process of healing unresolved grief, with whom she could feel safe in sharing all of her feelings. So far she has talked about the negative side of being adopted with only one good friend, who also had been adopted right after birth. Until they went their separate ways after the eighth grade, they told each other their innermost feelings, including that they both felt they were missing a part of themselves because they were adopted. "Basically," says Amanda, "she felt the exact same way I did."

Amanda's friend also knew she had an older sibling some-where, a sister. Amanda seems envious that her friend found out in the eighth grade that, in addition, she had two younger brothers. She doesn't know how her friend found this out. "I think it's because her parents know her real parents, but just aren't letting her meet them."

Amanda and her friend used to talk about searching when

they turned eighteen. "We were going to go on the parent crusade." First they would take an around-the-world trip. After that they would set out to find their other families.

In spite of Amanda's clear feeling that adoption is a wound to be suffered, she thinks it can be the right thing for a child. "It's better to grow up in a family where you're going to be loved and have enough money than in one where no one will care about you or where your family goes bankrupt or something." The loss of money seems related, in Amanda's mind, to the loss of personal security and love.

Her current scenario for the best possible adoption is one in which a child emerges from a background that is without sufficient money or love and moves to a new family with plenty of both. She also thinks it would be better if the adoptee never saw the birth parents while growing up. She imagines that if an adoptee did know the birth parents, the birth parents might feel their privacy was invaded. "If they welcomed you," she says, "then you could end up hurting the parents who brought you up! Either way, it might cause problems."

Amanda doesn't phrase her desire not to create problems in terms of her own potential hurt, but the hurt she imagines her birth parents or her adoptive parents would feel. "I think the parents you grew up with would have the feeling of not knowing if they were going to lose you."

Amanda is able to put herself in the places of other people with differing backgrounds and experiences and empathize with them. She does not judge birth mothers who turn to adoption as the best solution for themselves and their babies. She can even imagine herself placing a baby for adoption, but only if she "hated the father." If she were single or poor or both, she would still keep the child. "I'd find some way to do it." And if adoption were the only choice she could make in good conscience, then she would want to at least choose the parents. "The kid would be a part of me too. I'd pick the parents so it wouldn't have to be miserable, so I'd know it would have the chance to have a good life."

I ask Amanda one more thing about the missing part

inside herself of which she speaks so clearly. Does she think only adopted kids feel this way? No, she says. She thinks perhaps all teenagers have some of the feelings she has, a sense of lacking some important part of themselves. "But I don't know because I don't know how everybody else feels." How might such a void ever be filled? "I'll find them," she says simply, referring to her biological parents. "If I can't find my real parents and I still have that missing feeling, I can let my now-parents fill the hole."

For now Amanda doesn't seem able to let her "now-parents" try to fill the hole inside her. For her the search she has planned is an essential part of the healing she believes is possible. I ask, "What about a person who has no possibility of finding the original parents?" I give her the examples of a child whose birth parents and other birth relatives are all dead, or the child adopted from another country, whose records of biological family have all been destroyed or lost: what hope is there for such a child?

She thinks for a minute. "You need somebody else who can take care of you and love you, the same way the mother would. You can take care of yourself and love yourself, but you need someone else too!" Does she feel that someday having a child might be one way the hole could be filled? It is common for a pregnant teenager, for example, to believe that having a baby will fill a void in her life, that a baby will give her all the love she needs.

Amanda can imagine herself having children someday. But having kids, she says, will not fix it. And it won't end when she turns eighteen and moves out on her own. She knows that. "It will *always* be there," she says, "*until* it is filled." Feelings of emptiness within lead some people, after years of trying to use other people or activities to fill the void or heal the wound, to search deeper. They first try everything short of going deeper, searching for a connection to a power greater than themselves, but ultimately they end up there. An insightful person such as Amanda seems to realize that at some level, despite her hope that there might be an easier way.

Amanda's parents have both expressed their sorrow, frustration, and sense of helplessness with regard to helping Amanda develop inner confidence and build a satisfying life. I am interested in knowing whether Amanda thinks of herself in the same way: whether she feels unhappy with her life and who she is or sees herself as having serious problems. It is uncommon for people her age to have a highly developed sense of reflection about their lives, but I feel Amanda, perhaps because of the difficulties she has experienced while growing up, may have given it some thought. Has she done any thinking about her life in general? If she has, does she perceive any connection between her difficulties at home, in school, and in relationships with peers and the fact that she was relinquished for adoption at birth?

I put the question to her one afternoon when we are alone together. I tell her that I feel her story and her feelings would be of help to other adopted kids and ask if she would talk about adoption and any life problems she has encountered. She is pleased to be asked for her opinions and willing to talk about her feelings. No, she says, she has never really thought about being adopted in terms of everyday problems she has. Yet she goes on to speak with clarity about the kinds of problems she has had growing up, especially since the onset of puberty at the age of eleven.

"I never did well in school. I don't like sitting still—I never have—and in school they made me sit still." Kindergarten was the only year of school that appealed to her. It didn't focus primarily on left-brain (logic) activities, such as reading and writing, which would have entailed being sedentary for long periods and listening or following instructions. Much learning was accomplished through tactile and kinetic activities, and that was to Amanda's liking. In addition, the teacher acted as though she was Amanda's older friend, not an authority figure.

"I like to draw and she and I would paint the color magenta—it was my favorite color!—on paper, on desks, on our hands." But even in kindergarten there was a great deal of sitting and looking. "And if she told us to do things, we'd have to do it." Starting in kindergarten Amanda was perceived by adults as being bright but unwilling. "I like doing what *I* like to do!" she says without apology. "I thought reading was the most horrible thing known to man!"

In first grade Amanda had a teacher she especially liked, and the teacher took a special interest in Amanda; but it did not solve her academic problems. After the school year was over, the teacher, who lived not far from Amanda's home, offered to teach Amanda how to read. "She told me I could swim in her pool all summer if I would work on reading every day. So I did; and at the end of the summer, when I learned to read, she took me to the circus with her kids. But I still didn't want to read."

Doing what the teacher or any other adult asked of her became an issue early on. "If the teacher gave me a book to read and told me to make a report on it, I wouldn't do it." I ask her why. "It was the sitting still. Even now I don't like sitting down to read. I have to make myself do it, but then if the book is good and I like it I'll read it. If it isn't something I like, I'll refuse to do it." Because of the nature of current mainstream education, school itself quickly became a mostly negative experience.

"We'd have recess and as soon as we'd get back in the classroom, I'd start thinking about what we'd do next recess." When I ask how she would have worked with a child like herself if she had been the teacher, she says, "I probably would have done something like what my first grade teacher did, made it fun, given rewards for kids doing the things they didn't want to do."

When her parents moved her to a small private school in the third grade, Amanda thought it might be different. "In the beginning it was fun, because I was the new kid and everybody liked me. I tried to keep up with my work in the beginning." But soon she stopped working. "I guess my attitude changed or something. And the kids stopped liking me."

She doesn't remember much that was positive about third,

fourth, or fifth grade or her first year in sixth grade. "Nobody liked me. All the teachers said I was alienating myself from everything."

Does she remember how that made her feel? "I didn't like that. They started being mean to me and I didn't like that. I wasn't mean to myself." Amanda's reaction was to withdraw from what was painful and from her feeling of helplessness. "I had a good time by myself," she says. "I saw all the other kids, in their groups, popular, and I wished I could be like them, but I had fun by myself. I always liked being by myself. I still do." In addition to becoming a loner, Amanda found much to criticize in the school. After all, she did not feel a welcome or important part of school life. "I didn't like that we had to wear uniforms, and it was really strict. We got in trouble if our dress wasn't perfect, like if we wore white socks instead of blue socks. I thought that was pretty stupid!"

At the end of sixth grade, when her parents had her switch schools, she began sixth grade again. Amanda doesn't recall being asked for her opinion about the decision; nor does she resent not being asked. "They told me I was staying back, and at first I was mad because all my other friends were going to middle school." If given the choice then, she feels she would have gone ahead into seventh grade. But now, in hindsight, she feels her parents were right. "I don't know if I would have gotten anything together if I hadn't stayed back. I'm glad they made me."

Having to see a therapist was a different matter entirely to Amanda. "The whole time I saw Dr. Edelstein, or whatever his name was, all we ever did was play games! I didn't see how it was going to help me. I hated him. I used to tell my parents I was never going to see him again, but they made me and he would say, 'When I feel you're ready to leave me, I'll let you go.' And my parents would say, 'You can stop seeing him when he feels you're ready.'"

She never actively fought going to the therapist and still doesn't know if it did any good. "I'm not sure I got anything out of it. If I did, it wasn't anything big enough for me to be aware of it." It was simply another experience adults set up on her behalf. She has no answer yet for what might have helped her, but looking back now, she can see what was going on inside.

"I didn't like myself." I ask her why she thought she had had difficulty with kids her own age. "They didn't like me because I didn't like myself." She hazards a guess that most of the kids in her classes during fifth, sixth, seventh, and eighth grades hadn't liked themselves either; yet they had seemed to have less difficulty finding friends than she had. Why? "They put on a front to have people like them. I still see a lot of my friends do that. I've tried. Like I've tried to wear the right clothes. But I've always gone back to my jeans and tie-dyes. I went to all the dances, but they all seemed to dance better than I could. After a while I got sick of trying to make myself better just so other people would like me. I decided if they weren't going to like me for who I was, they weren't worth it."

She did find some friends during her second year in the sixth grade. "They liked me just the way I was! I could be myself when I was with them." She and her friends, who were five boys from the class, did what she now terms "stupid things" together. At the time it seemed like a lot of fun to Amanda. "We called ourselves The Rebel Youth. We did little rebellious things, like running around and stealing goldfish from the ponds in people's yards, or going up to the top of the hill—our neighborhood had a lot of hills—going into people's yards and jumping into their pools until people heard us, then going on to the next, and seeing how many we could swim in before we got to the bottom of the hill. Every third house in our neighborhood had a pool."

She preferred the boys to the girls. As she explains it, "All most of the girls wanted to do was paint their nails. But I liked climbing trees and stuff." To this day she still prefers being with the boys; they do things that are more interesting to her. The Rebel Youth broke up the summer after eighth grade, as the kids went into different high schools. What had been harmless pranks that they had done as a group became serious rebellious behavior for most of Amanda's old friends. Though she seldom sees any of them anymore, Amanda does periodically hear about what they are doing.

"Some began doing drugs regularly. One of the boys got busted for having a lot of marijuana on him and was sent to live with his dad in another country, and another boy was sent to rehab for six months. His parents caught him with just about every kind of drug—except heroin—that you could imagine on him when he crashed his parents' car drunk driving. I hadn't known it, but he had been selling all over the place with other kids."

The young man in question, Amanda says, is fine now. "He is doing really well in school, is getting straight As, and hasn't done any drugs or alcohol since freshman year. He was always the one who did everything bad and got in trouble for it." Apparently, this was one case where placing a youth in a controlled setting apart from his friends and family worked. Whether it was the program or simply a change of heart on his part, Amanda was struck by the change she saw in him.

"I didn't recognize him. He had a different outlook on life; he'd look on the positive side. He even looked different. He wouldn't talk about what it had been like in there, except to say it was complete hell!"

All of her friends, she recalls, had "heavy" family problems. "One, his mom and dad were separated, and his father ran around with a different person every week and his mom did the same! Another had five older brothers and sisters, and they were all doing well, and in college, but he liked to sit around and do nothing, so his parents were always getting on him. They were all very serious and punctual and did everything by schedule. He didn't feel close to his parents."

Amanda includes herself in the description of having had heavy family problems. "We were all pretty much the same. I didn't get along with my parents. None of us did. I don't know why I didn't. We're just different." She can describe their differentness: "They're serious. They like to get things done.

They're busy with appointments and things like that. We have different priorities. They don't understand getting in trouble once and not completely changing so it doesn't happen again." She recalls that at the dinner table, conversation seemed always to be between her parents and focused on what they had done during the day. She never felt she had anything to talk about and wasn't interested in listening to them.

As for her current feelings about her younger sister, who is doing beautifully in school, as in all of her many activities and interests, Amanda obviously loves her but feels very separate from her as well. "Abby's like my parents. Her priorities are school and work. And if there's a little bit of time left over, she'll have a good time. But everything else comes first." At least that's how it appears to Amanda.

Although she still lives at home, Amanda has become, of her own choosing, little more than a boarder. She avoids conflicts with her parents by staying away from home as much as possible. "I like being around them now, but if we are together very much we start to fight. For the past three weeks, I've been waking up in the morning, saying good morning, taking a shower, dressing, leaving for school, and not seeing them again 'til the next morning. I usually work 'til late in the evening, and if I don't I go to the city with friends."

Amanda feels the outsider in her family. "We're not the same because we aren't blood relatives. I just have a different attitude; I want to live my life a different way than they want to live their lives." When I ask if she thinks it might have anything to do with adoption, she says, "In the back of my mind, it might be because I'm adopted, subconsious or whatever. But I don't think about it or anything. I don't blame it on that. But it might have changed things."

The adults in her life have ascribed Amanda's behavior—not participating in school, choosing friends whose lives do not seem productive, and not feeling like she wants to have anything to do with the family—to various causes. They are not the same reasons as the ones Amanda names. "My parents or teachers would ask me why I did things, and I would just say, 'I just *did*.' I don't think *why* I do things! I don't think *before* I do things! I don't think of consequences and all that. I just *do* things."

Sometimes, Amanda says, she does stop to think about the consequences of her actions. I ask her for an example of what happens at those times. "I don't have a curfew anymore, but when I did, I might think, Well, I'm at this awesome party, and I could stay late at it and miss curfew and get in trouble and not be able to go out next weekend, or I could go home. And I would usually stay at the party, because I was having a good time."

So far, Amanda has not been in any serious trouble, and she uses her persuasiveness to avoid negative consequences whenever possible. "I have a way of talking myself out of things when I get in trouble. I've been doing that all my life. It's a challenge!"

Amanda says she now likes being different. "I like being my own person and for people to respect me for who I am, instead of what I look like. If I wear tie-dyes and little pieces of jewelry and stuff, people say, 'Oh, she's a hippie!' And if I wear tight skirts and pumps and tight tank tops, then I'm seen as a mod. If you dress cool, you're cool. And if you don't, you're not."

Since ninth grade Amanda has been in a small, local alternative high school, with an enrollment of 150 students. The local public high school has 1600 students. The teachers at Amanda's school are called by their first names, and there are never more than 15 kids in a class. Being in a school where there are many other students who haven't done well in public high school feels fine to Amanda.

The kids, being teenagers and in the process of trying to decide who they want to be, still try on various identities, and these are roughly based on styles of dress. The kids themselves strive to be classified according to the standard teenage role models of the day. "There're two groups at my school," says Amanda. "The rockers and the trendies. But they don't really dislike each other. Everyone's putting on a front, but nobody cares about it or gets judged for it, and there are rules but they are easy to follow. They're reasonable. We're all like one big family."

These days Amanda feels good about herself. Although she may not smile often or seem enthusiastic about anything, she seems to have gained some measure of contentment and is definitely not in deep depression or quiet despair. "I'm happy where I am. I realized that I wanted to be who I really was, and that in the long run people were going to like me more if I stayed being myself. For a long time I was many different people."

I ask her what "being many different people" means. "For each group of people I was with, I'd be a different person, and if people from different groups of friends got together, or if friends of mine came over to the house, then I wouldn't know which person to be, because I was different with different people. I just got sick of having to put on a show for every person I saw. Since the end of ninth grade until now, I've been the same person."

Perhaps in time Amanda will learn how to find real joy in her life. Perhaps she will find that being relinquished and being adopted *have* had negative effects on her self-esteem and worldview; perhaps she will search for ways to heal. The process of experiencing various things, reacting to those experiences, reflecting back, and looking ahead; the ability to envision and to find ways of turning vague hopes or well-defined dreams into reality: these are skills still beyond her reach. It is to be hoped that as she matures, so will society's understanding of the impact of relinquishment and adoption on children's lives and its resources for assisting them on their way.

ABBY IS ELEVEN. Since the day after birth she has lived in the same house with her sister, Amanda, and her adoptive mother and father. I ask her if she will talk to me for this book, tell me her thoughts and feelings about adoption, and she says she will. Her mother brings her to my house one afternoon, and she sits on the big, round floor pillow in the living room. As her sister,

Amanda, did, she plays with my orange cat, Timmy, as she talks. I think it is the first time she has been asked the sorts of questions I ask her; she often thinks for a while before answering, as if it is hard to put the precise words to what is inside. Abby, I discover, is a girl who likes to be precise.

Abby doesn't know any other kids who are adopted, except her big sister, Amanda, and she and Amanda don't ever talk about it. There are lots of adopted kids in her neighborhood, but they aren't her age and she doesn't play with them. I ask her if she ever thought about being adopted when she was younger, because I know Paul and Vicki gave her the true story of her beginnings as soon as she could ask questions about herself. "When I was little if I was really mad, or my parents got mad at me for something, I would think, This wouldn't have happened if I wasn't adopted! I don't have mean parents, but I'd think about it."

Does she ever wonder about her birth parents, what they are like? "Sometimes," she says. "I just wonder what they look like or where they are." Abby tells me she's looked at the pictures of Pat, her birth mother, in the book *To Love and Let Go*. She is glad there are pictures to look at, for there has been no communication from Pat in eleven years.

Abby is trying to put together the fact of her biological tie to Pat, the feelings she has about this woman she does not know, and the face in the pictures. "I've seen the pictures, and my mom doesn't really look like I do." She lowers her head and adds, as if to herself, "It's sort of too soon to tell." Then she looks up. "But I haven't seen pictures of my real father. I don't really know much about my father."

Are there any questions she has about Pat? "I think it might be nice just to know, to know what my mom is like." Has she ever thought of trying to find her and see her? "Yes," she says. "But I thought it was like a law that you couldn't be with your real parents until you were eighteen."

She sits curled up, looking out the window now as she talks, a girl on the edge of becoming a young woman. I wonder out loud what a relationship might look like in Abby's imagination. So many adoptive parents fear their children would love them less for being able to express love also to the birth parents. But that picture comes from adult minds, from their fears. Is that the way it is for a child? Abby tells me what the picture in her mind is like. "I would just like to see her once in a while, know what she looks like."

She would also like more than that. "One afternoon every year, we would go shopping or go out to lunch." That is what Abby would like to do right now if she knew her birth mother. She looks at me. "And," she adds, "I would be able to see her." The head and voice both lower. "I don't know if she would want to. My parents would probably let me do that, but like, maybe she would want to put it behind her." So many thoughts, so little opportunity to express them, to try them on for size, to hear the words and feel the feelings that result.

I ask Abby what she thinks would make adoptions work, be okay, and she has some ideas. "I think kids should know why they were adopted, who their real parents were, and how it happened, so they don't think someone just left them there, sitting on the street or something."

I ask Abby, "Do you ever dream, have there been dreams you remember, about Pat?" She answers, "Sometimes I dream about things over and over." She looks out the window as she rubs Timmy's soft fur. I sense she is remembering the dream and tell her I am very interested in dreams, that I also have dreams I dream over and over again. "What is it like? Your dream?" I quietly ask.

"I feel like I'm a little baby and I'm with her. I'm really little. Everything's white. I'm sitting or lying down. On a sheet. And someone is with me in the dream. I just imagine that it's her. That's usually all that happens." Abby looks at me quizzically, as if asking why. "And it just fades away."

I want to know what Abby was seeing and feeling in her dream, so I ask her to please tell me more about it. "It is sort of quiet, a quiet feeling, and sort of cool. Not cold. And kind of dim," she says. "What are you doing in the dream?" I ask in the quiet tone with which she just spoke. "I'm just lying there. It's sort of a vision. I'm not inside the baby, but looking at her." Abby switches voice and begins to talk about this baby as "she." "She is wrapped up, newborn, her hair all wet. It sort of makes me wonder what's gonna happen next, and I, sometimes, when I wake up and remember it, I try to dream more. But that's all that happens."

She looks away from the window, at my face, as if to see my reaction. I'm sure she sees that I take her dream seriously, and she goes on without my having to say anything. "This has nothing to do with it," she says, "but there are also times when we're just driving along in the car, me and my parents, and I also remember it."

Unprompted, Abby begins to tell me more about the side of herself in which I show interest. "I don't know what other people think," she says. "I believe in life after death, but you don't remember the life you've just lived." I ask if she has ever asked her parents, Paul and Vicki, if they believed in this, or her older sister Amanda, or any of her friends. She says she has not.

"I remember other things when I was young that I don't know if I should remember or not. Like I remember some birthday party when I was really little. I mushed my fingers in the cake, and my parents got really mad at me because I had ruined the cake." She says she did tell her parents about that memory. "They told me it happened, and I was less than a year old."

We go back to what she calls the dream of herself as a newborn baby. "How often does it come?" I ask. "Every now and then. I think I might dream it more often but not always remember it." She says she is aware of dreaming it about once a month. I am curious about the fact that in the dream she is both seeing the baby and knowing she is the baby she is seeing. "Where," I ask, "are you in the dream?" Her head turns again to the window. "There is the head of the woman bent over the baby. I can see her holding the baby up off the bed. But she never looks up. I am up on a balcony and looking down."

Abby has seen pictures of Pat I took in her room in the maternity unit of the hospital. None of them were taken from above Pat. She knows what Pat looked like when she was born. Why would she, in her dream, be seeing Pat from above, unless she had left her body and gone to a place in the room where she could be the observer of what happened to the little baby named Abby. In this culture people don't like to think that newborn babies are aware of their surroundings and themselves, much less that they are capable of being observers of themselves at the same time.

"When," I ask, "did you first know you were adopted?" "I don't remember when my parents told me I was adopted. It's just something I knew." She adds, as if she has thought about this subject before, "I saw a movie once and this lady waited 'til her daughter was grown 'til she told her. I think parents should tell their children and keep telling them. Then it just doesn't come as such a surprise."

Abby thinks if she couldn't have a child of her own that she might adopt a child, but, she says, "I would want to adopt it at birth, so [she shifts pronouns midsentence] you don't think someone's abandoned you." "If it were me," she adds, "I might try to stay in touch with the other mother, but if the mother didn't want anything to do with it, I wouldn't try." It is a complex situation, and Abby seems to understand that.

Does she think adoption has made her a different person than she would be if she weren't adopted? "Not really," she answers. "I think if the parents were really mean to the children and told them they were no good, then the children wouldn't feel good about themselves being adopted and would wish they weren't." Does she think she might ever want to look for her other mom? "Sort of. I haven't really thought about it that much." She looks thoughtful. How does she think her adoptive parents would react? "I don't think they would mind."

Abby is a child who seems to have weathered easily the bruising of relinquishment and adoption. She is what some term a natural healer, a human being who has for some reason the innate ability and instinct to heal herself from trauma. It is not something she has to think about or practice. Certainly she always had some benefits from her earliest life: although she was not a planned-for child and her mother suffered in pregnancy, Pat and she formed a close bond while Abby was in the womb, she had a positive experience of birth, she said good-bye to her primal home before moving into her new home, and she went directly from the arms of one mother who loved her into the loving arms of another mother.

Abby is fortunate to have had the positive primal experiences she had. Yet they may not have been what made the difference. She may simply be one of those fortunate human beings who always lands on her feet, who is readily able to accept what life brings her, who says yes with enthusiasm to life, and who devises creative solutions to her problems. Or she, like many other adoptees, may come upon a time in her life when the earth seems to drop out from under her, and she must search to make herself whole.

The current system of closed or minimally open adoption cannot be thanked for how well Abby is doing. She is a survivor. The walking wounded must be looked at to see where the old system and societal beliefs and attitudes about adoption and children have failed. Children like Amanda, and adoptive parents like Paul and Vicki, who struggle without enough information, without guidelines, without models, and without the support necessary to make adoption really work are failed by the current system of adoption.

ALEXANDRA:*

A Conscious Choice

ALEXANDRA WAS TWENTY-ONE years old and eight months pregnant. I had never met her, but heard from friends she had a serenity about her that did not seem to fit with her decision to relinquish her baby for adoption at birth. Unlike Pat she was not a teenager, nor was she unprepared for the responsibility of having sexual intercourse. At a time when most of her high school friends were already having their second child, Alexandra was choosing not to be a mother. People who met her casually found it difficult to comprehend why she should have made the decision she had, and some were quite unsympathetic. But Alexandra wasn't living her life for the benefit of other people's opinions. She took the requirements of parenthood seriously, and she also had her own dreams, which she intended to pursue. Pregnancy had simply caught her off guard, unprepared. She wrote in her diary, "It's funny, because I was pregnant once before, when I was sixteen and had just begun having sex. I

---

*Note: In *To Love and Let Go*, Alexandra was given the pseudonym of Katherine. In this book she prefers to use her real name.

think I'm pretty aware of my body. Yet I didn't even consider I might be pregnant this time." Alexandra's periods had always been irregular, so she hadn't worried about missing one. She had always used a diaphragm on the few occasions she'd had intercourse. That was how it was possible for her to be ten weeks pregnant before she even went for the test that confirmed the pregnancy. And by that time the young man involved was nowhere to be reached.

The first person she had told was her roommate, Linda, a woman her age who was also single, with whom she shared a cottage near downtown. She had been relieved to tell someone, but it was still a tremendous blow, just one more in a series of blows over the past few months. First her grandfather's death, and then a bicycle accident, which had sent her to the hospital with a severe concussion. And now she was pregnant!

There was no doubt in her mind who the father was. She had been celibate for more than a year until she had started a relationship with a graduate student two years older than she. Their brief and intensely romantic affair had hardly begun. They had seen each other steadily for more than a month, drawing closer and closer in the magic of new love, and they'd let their feelings build long before making love. A few long passionate nights together was all they'd had before he left for a month of field work in Nicaragua. They planned to continue seeing each other as soon as he returned; but this month apart was an opportunity for each of them to take a break from the breathless intensity. They were both cautious people in relationships, and no vows of love had been exchanged.

Alexandra had begun feeling odd even before their last day together. She had written in her diary, "I feel strange things inside me. I'm so afraid to feel this intensely about him, afraid I'll lose myself. I've canceled our date. I want to spend more time with Linda. She always has been the one I could trust. I'm looking forward to the time he'll be away. I have to sort things out." He was due back after the new year. That would give Alexandra enough time to go home to her family in Utah for Christmas, and time to think.

They had never talked about what to do if she got pregnant, because they both had been so careful about birth control. One thing she'd liked about him right off had been that before they had ever made love *he'd* brought up the subject. He had told her she should let him know if she ever wanted him to use protection instead of her. It only made the pregnancy seem even more unreal. But unreal or not, Alexandra would have to make some very hard decisions, and there was no partner to share the process with her. She would bear the responsibility alone.

In relationships even the best of beginnings still need time and freedom from external pressure to deepen. Unplanned pregnancy at this stage left Alexandra feeling hopeless about their chances for a future together. Because he'd said he would be moving from town to town for a few weeks and would send up an address as soon as he had gotten settled somewhere, as far as her needs were concerned, he was nowhere. "Anyway," she told her friend Linda, "like it or not, I am a woman. *I* am the one who ends up carrying this life."

It was only right that he should know, and had he been within reach, his participation might have changed her most basic decisions about the pregnancy. But she could not live in dreams of "might" and "if only." At ten weeks it was already quite late to begin thinking about whether to keep the pregnancy. Without thinking about what it meant, Alexandra made an appointment at a clinic for an abortion. Later she was to say, "I did it automatically. I thought, 'I should do this before I go home, so I can use Christmas to recuperate.' But all the time I was on the telephone making the appointment, I had a feeling inside I couldn't quite define."

Alone that evening she sat with her feelings, and her own answer was there. "It was clear, the clearest, most absolute thing I'd felt in my life. I just could *not* do it. I'd had one abortion already and I believed in it as an option; but I had this overwhelming sense that this child wanted to live."

The decision to have an abortion for the first pregnancy had been made in a different set of circumstances. Although only sixteen at the time, she had shown maturity in being able to act in her own defense, by not pretending that pregnancy would solve her need for love. She had been a child and had known it; and she had known she had no business thinking about raising a child of her own. Even then abortion had brought up feelings of remorse, but hard reality had meant making a painful decision. "That time it was a matter of survival, my survival. This time was different. I'm much stronger now. To have an abortion now would feel like murder."

She'd made her decision, the first in a long series. If abortion was unconscionable, then Alexandra knew she was choosing by default to carry the pregnancy to its conclusion, a baby. "That was my first decision. Not 'I'm going to be a parent,' but 'I'm going to have a baby.' "

She was taking things in proper sequence. Choosing to keep the pregnancy did not necessitate being a single mother. Whether to keep the baby and what to do if she did were separate and distinct choices that needed to be taken one at a time. Whatever she did was bound to affect the possibility of any future relationship with the young man for whom she cared so much. It might even destroy it. She spent the rest of the evening thinking in a rational manner. The next morning she walked into Linda's room and told her the decision she'd made.

"I said, 'I can't believe it but I'm going to have this child!' Linda looked hard at me, and then said she'd sensed that would be what I would decide."

From the moment she knew she would be giving birth, Alexandra began searching her memory for anything she might have done or not done during the first ten weeks that could have damaged the growing fetus. She had smoked marijuana several times in the early weeks when her stomach was upset and she was feeling so confused. It had helped her to relax. Would that cause damage to the baby later? She hoped not. She recalled several times when she'd taken laxatives. Could that? She'd studied some biology in school and knew the brain and nervous system, fingers and toes all were formed in the first weeks. She regretted that she hadn't known she was pregnant when she'd taken drugs, but there was nothing she could do about that now.

She canceled the appointment to discuss abortion the day after she made it. Instead, a few days later she bought a train ticket to Utah, packed a few things, and left town, feeling very pregnant and very ill. That journey, thirty hours of enforced solitude, altered the course of her life.

"I was so sick I sat up the entire trip. I had the worst cold I'd ever had. I was nauseated morning, noon, and night. My nose ran constantly and I was in absolute misery. I'd already entertained the idea of being a mother, of raising this child. I say 'entertained' because it didn't seem any more real than that, like some picture on a postcard of a place I'd never been. I would be thinking of something else, and suddenly my mind would snap back and I would realize, 'I am going to be a mother! Every minute of every day will be radically different.'"

With no distractions and nothing to do but watch and think, Alexandra used the train ride to observe mothers and their children and to notice every detail of their interactions.

"There was one family with three kids sitting in front of me. The children were shouting and running up and down the aisle, whining and complaining to their parents, who seemed patient beyond belief. There was another woman with a very young baby sitting alone across the aisle. Watching all of them through my own physical misery, the romantic image I had of myself as the young mother, caring for, holding, feeding, and constantly being with this child suddenly disappeared. I found myself thinking of all the other things I wanted to do in my life, the things I'd already postponed, which I would have to put off further to be a good mother to an infant. Could I go back to school with a baby? What kind of job could I get? What would the two of us do, day after day, together?"

The train pulled into the station in Salt Lake City at 5:30 A.M., and Alexandra's father was there waiting to meet her. She'd pictured herself standing at the edge of the track as the train pulled away, telling her father that she was pregnant and planned to have the baby. He would have his arms around her and she would be leaning against his shoulder. Their reunion did not go as she had planned.

"Instead my dad looked at me strangely as I got off and asked how I was, and I just couldn't tell him. My face was all puffy from no sleep, my nose was red, and I must have been fifteen pounds heavier than when he'd last seen me. And all I could say was, 'I'm fine. I've just got a little cold, that's all.' Poor Dad, he looked so concerned. But all I could think of was getting to my mother's house and getting some sleep."

Alexandra's parents had separated when she was twelve and her father had remarried, but her mother and father lived near each other. He drove her to her mother's house, and she went straight upstairs to bed without awakening her younger brother or her mother. First, though, she went to the bathroom to look for something to take for her cold.

"I took out a bottle of cold pills and read the label. At the very end, in fine print, it said, 'Do not take if pregnant unless under a doctor's supervision.' I stood there looking at the bottle, thinking, 'I'm dying! I've got to get some sleep!' And I took the pill. It was the last time I took any drugs the entire pregnancy. After that, no wine, no coffee, no soft drinks. When I'd slept a few hours, I went downstairs and told my mother the news."

Alexandra considered her parents both to be loving and rational people who would always try to accept any decision she made in her life, however difficult it was for them to understand. They prided themselves on being liberal. They were also proud of their attractive only daughter, who had been independent and largely self-supporting since she left home after high school. Confiding in them, especially her mother, had always been easy, even though their relationship never included a great deal of physical affection. Alexandra told herself it would be easy. But later to Linda she admitted how brutal her frankness had been.

"The way I brought it up was to say, 'Mom, I'm pregnant

and I'm going to have this child. Then I'm giving it up for adoption.' It was the first time I'd said the words out loud, even to myself. I'd made the decision, adoption, during the train ride but the word, when I told my mother, sounded so cold and unreal. She started to cry. It was awful."

Alexandra hadn't intended to shock her mother. She was partly trying the words out to hear how they sounded. She also thought it was what both her parents would want her to say. She didn't expect her mother would want her to raise a child alone, not when she wasn't ready for the full responsibility of it. She was amazed that the first thing her mother said was that perhaps she should consider an abortion, but she did appreciate the concern expressed in that statement. (Alexandra had a pronounced curvature of the spine, which she had been told to expect to worsen in pregnancy and perhaps prevent her from ever carrying a baby to full term or giving birth vaginally.) Her mother also suggested that she think about having some professional counseling before making up her mind. A few days later Alexandra saw her father again and poured out the whole story of her pregnancy. He too was shocked.

"He could hardly speak a work, but he did manage to say right off, 'I can't tell you how much I admire you, Alex, for choosing to carry this child and then choosing not to sacrifice either of your lives for the sake of sentimentality.' "

Alexandra's parents' first reactions were unconditionally supportive. But the anger and disappointment each of them also felt had to surface. Within a few days her mother was taking tranquilizers, her father had retreated to silence. Christmas was ruined.

During those first days home, Alexandra didn't remember having thought of the father of the baby even once, so much was happening. It was all inconceivable to her. How could she connect this nightmare with her memory of the slender young man she'd fallen in love with and their intense philosophical conversations and passionate encounters. Her world had been transformed by her feelings for him, and the everydayness of life had seemed brand new and shiny clean. Each day had had magic. Now she was spinning in the eye of a hurricane and he was nowhere around. She hadn't seen him in more than a month, and the sound of his voice, which had given her chills when he would telephone, the details of his face, which had seemed so perfect to her, were beginning to blur and fade in her memory. From the outset she had had to handle everything about this pregnancy on her own, and time was putting an even greater distance between them than the physical miles of separation. She also had her doubts about what he would do when he did hear the news.

Not long after she arrived in Utah, her mother's fiancé had a heart attack and died. Alexandra felt her own life crumbling at the edges, but she tried to comfort her mother and made the decision to stay in Utah for a while longer to help. Perhaps, she thought, they could lean on each other in their misery. She knew it would be difficult, because they had an emotionally volatile relationship when they spent any amount of time together. As Alexandra described it, "We love each other very much, but we live together horribly and always bring out the worst in each other."

The pregnancy, begun unwittingly in a moment of beauty, was slipping quickly downward into daily misery. Alexandra had given up her job in order to go back to Utah. Now she felt stuck at home, sick, and ugly. She saw her once clear and beautiful olive skin breaking out, and felt she was sinking in a hole. Looking back later, she would recall it was a period of unrelieved self-pity and depression and wish she had taken her mother's advice to see a therapist. During the third and fourth months of the pregnancy she remained in Utah, and the baby felt like a growth inside her, constantly making her sick. Everyone in the family was contaminated by Alexandra's constant misery.

"They all seemed angry with me. Even Linda. I called to talk with her, and she wasn't sure she wanted me to come back to California because she was depressed herself and had no energy to give me. My brother and I weren't getting along. One day we were having an argument about how he never did any work around the house and left it all to my mother and me to clean up after him. I told him he was being irresponsible; and he turned on me and said, 'Well at least I'm not fat and pregnant!' I called my father one day when I was very down, and he said, 'None of this would have happened if you hadn't been sleeping in other people's beds!' And my mother and I were having terrible fights. We could turn anything into an argument. We were both tired and upset and would say horrible things, scream at each other. I would get so frustrated I'd lock myself in the bathroom. Once I even began to cut at my arms with a kitchen knife. The scars are almost gone now. I can't believe I did that. It's not like me, the way I am when my mother and I are arguing. With everyone else I am quiet and thoughtful and never say horrible things."

She was aware of the possible effect her emotional turmoil might have on the baby. "All I could think was that this baby would only know upset and hate. I never felt any anger at the idea of the baby, but I felt so sorry that this was the world into which he or she was coming."

It was a bleak, hard winter in Utah. Preoccupied with her own body and emotional changes and domestic conflicts with her mother, Alexandra gave little thought to trying to track down her boyfriend in Nicaragua. Not that she could have traced him if she had wanted to. That country was in chaos from recent revolution. Once she phoned Linda and asked her to call his roommate in town and find out if he had an address where she could write him. The message came back that the project was going so well in Nicaragua that he had decided to stay at least another month. He had written but had left no address and there had been no message for Alexandra.

Without planning to, Alexandra began to distance herself from the dream she had carried of their being together again someday. She turned her attention to finding out everything she could about adoption. Trips to the public library filled the void. Even before she had finished all the material they had on adoption, she knew she didn't want to work with an agency, and she began to form definite ideas about just what she did want for this child.

To her diary she said, "I want more control. It seems like in a private adoption, I could design what was going to happen, choose the kind of people I wanted for the baby, spend the pregnancy as I wanted, and have the kind of birth I wanted."

She was thinking about natural childbirth, which she'd seen mentioned in a few articles and books, but about which she knew very little. To her the birth was light years away and completely unreal. All she knew was that she wanted to give birth in a warm, loving environment, and she couldn't imagine going to a hospital for that.

She was forming her own dreams for the coming birth and beginning to visualize what she would like it to be like, the first step toward preparing for labor. It became increasingly clear to her that she wanted to go back to California, but first she wanted to feel she had accomplished something. Perhaps she could at least locate parents for the baby. She didn't want her own parents to have to support her financially through the pregnancy. Perhaps the parents she found would help her until the birth. She began to ask relatives and old friends how to find couples interested in adopting newborn babies. She had never felt awkward about expressing herself and being thought odd, and her parents didn't once make her feel that she should keep the pregnancy a secret.

She knew she didn't want her child adopted in Utah, so she called California and talked to a doctor she knew there. He said she would have no trouble finding people, that the number of people who wanted children far outnumbered the supply of babies, and he gave her some names right off. He suggested she should write to them. He also promised to let people he knew know that there was going to be a baby, and that they should contact Alexandra at her mother's through their attorneys. She then told her stepmother, who was a nurse. Within a few weeks suddenly the whole world seemed to know about the baby.

A cousin on the East Coast had kept his word to let friends know. Her physician friend had kept his word too. Alexandra was beginning to get phone calls from people claiming to be attorneys from as far away as Pennsylvania. She still had not even written to the original set of names her physician friend had given her.

She couldn't believe it. She didn't have to look anymore. Instead she was faced with a greater decision than how to find couples: how to choose one from among the others. At the age of twenty-one, never having given much thought to what kinds of people made the best parents, Alexandra had to arrive at some way of screening all her calls. As usual she would rely first on her intuition; but she was able to think of several attributes she thought might help ensure a couple were likely to be good parents of an adopted child.

She didn't want people who had strong religious preferences and would force their beliefs on a child. "I was raised without that, to think for myself, and I think I was treated with great respect growing up." She felt it would be nice but not necessary if they were college educated, at least intelligent people who thought a lot. Most of all she wanted a healthy couple, in their early thirties or midthirties, because that seemed like a time in life when a couple would be more ready, when they might have an abundance and want to share it with a child.

She knew she would be turning people down, good and loving people. "I feel sad that I can't provide more babies for more people," she wrote Linda. "What I have here is an incredible gift."

What she had was also what many people considered a commodity on the market. It didn't take her long to spot an arrangement that might have been illegal or unsavory, and she called Linda about one such incident.

"I got a call today from a man who was supposedly a lawyer and said that he had two clients, a couple, who wanted a child badly. He told me they wanted to pay me $10,000! That was the way he opened the conversation! I told him, 'This child is not for sale!' He said what he was proposing couldn't be considered a sale, just an exchange. 'They are finding it almost impossible to adopt a child,' he said. 'They are willing to pay well for one, that's all.' I told him, 'I bet they pay *you* well too!' There was a long pause on the phone, and he said, 'My fee is not up for discussion! I just want to know if you are interested.' I told him it did not interest me in the least and he hung up."

For the most part the calls she received seemed legitimate. The problem was she could only get dry bits of information about the various couples from respectable-sounding persons claiming to be attorneys. They would say where they had gotten Alexandra's name, but reveal little else to her. Typically their clients had been interested in babies for five to ten years. The calls became a jumble in her mind. No one couple stood out, and so she decided to go back to the original suggestion and write a letter, a letter that expressed her feelings, and to send it out to the people who sounded most interesting. She wrote the first two and mailed them. In each she asked for a letter from the couple in return.

> Dear Prospective Parents,
>   I have been informed that you are interested in adopting the baby that I am carrying. Because I've been contacted by several couples and the decision is not an easy one for me, I've decided to write to each of you. I feel the only way I can really find out about you is to hear from you directly via letter or phone. First, I'd like to tell you a little about myself, so you will have an idea of what I want for my child and what decisions I have already made.
>   I discovered I was pregnant when I was about ten weeks along, and I made the decision almost immediately that I would carry the child. I briefly considered keeping the baby, but, because of my marital status (single) and my financial status (no career or well-paying job) and, most important, because I lacked the stability and maturity I felt so necessary for raising a child, I decided on adoption.
>   I am now four and a half months pregnant, in good health, and being very careful to eat well and to do everything I can to grow a strong, healthy baby. I have decided on having natural childbirth, and I will have the baby in California, where I live, although you may get in touch with me here at my mother's until April.
>   There are so many things I want to know about you. Of course I'm interested in the obvious things: your financial status, religious beliefs, where you live, whether you have or plan to have more than one child, your education, and your plans for a child's education. Some answers will fit my "blueprint" better than others; but the most impor-

tant question I need to ask is one I can't easily phrase. It has to do with why becoming a parent is important to each of you and why you have chosen the difficult path of adoption. What do you feel you can give to a child, and what do you feel you can learn from raising a child?

We are living in strange and difficult times, we can't be sure there is a future for our children or whether the Earth will be a fit place to live on by the time they are grown. What can you do to help ensure a child has the chance to live a full, happy life? I don't know any answers to these questions, but I want to know your beliefs and feelings. I don't want an impersonal report filled with facts; I want a sense of who you are. This is the reason I have chosen private adoption. It is hard, I know. It requires more personal contact and effort on both sides. My choice of parents is the most important thing I will ever do for my baby. I hope you understand and I look forward to hearing from you.

Thank you,
Alexandra

One reply came back. She rejected it because once again it said nothing about the couple, except what schools they had attended, their height and weight and ages. She received two phone calls from a lawyer saying his couple had received a letter from her, and they were trying to write a response but were having a difficult time writing directly to her. Wouldn't she consider working through an agency? Alexandra found this request curious. If they felt uncomfortable having contact with a mother, why then were they dealing with an attorney instead of an agency in the first place? To Alexandra it meant they didn't want her to enter into their lives in any way. Once again it was only the baby they wanted, with no strings attached and no mother with whom to have to deal. She wrote in her diary, "I don't get the feeling from any of these people that they want to meet *me*."

Then her cousin back East ran across an unusual social worker: she specialized in the placement of children with handicaps in adoptive homes. Perhaps this woman would be a good source. Alexandra called New York and found in the woman a completely different attitude from any she had encountered up to then. At last she had met, though only by phone, someone who she felt understood. She felt that this stranger had a heart, that she cared about her and this child inside of her. The social worker gave Alexandra the name of an attorney with whom she liked to work. Alexandra tried to contact him but he was out of town, so she left her name and a message with his secretary.

It was late March. Alexandra was at the end of her fifth month of pregnancy. The baby had been moving inside her for almost a month. It was all slowly becoming real to her. Her dreams had become vivid and were now full of images of babies and birth and cats. (In her dreams the baby often appeared in the form of a cat, her favorite animal.) Then one day she got a call from Linda, who said that Alexandra's cat, Mouse, had been hit by a car. She had barely managed to drag herself up onto the porch of their cottage before dying. The vet had performed an autopsy and found her uterus full of tiny kittens, but all of them had been dead. Alexandra was heartbroken at the news. She wrote in her diary, "My own death seems very real to me now. Sometimes I can see my brother or someone else close to me dying, but mostly it is *my* death; and always in my dreams there is a lot of violence. Sometimes I dream about the baby, and there is something wrong with the baby and me. A lot of times we are on a journey, just the two of us, and I know we aren't going to make it."

She wrote about a dream in which she told the baby she knew neither of them was going to make it, because there was just too much against them. In it she repeated over and over, "I'm sorry. I'm really sorry. I did try. I really did." Her dreams were a mirror of her daily experiences and her gathering sense of gloom. She was growing more unhappy with each day.

She had planned to remain at her mother's until the lawyer from New York called, but she found she couldn't wait. She woke one morning in early April, looked out the window on another wet, gray day, and knew it was time to return to

California. She booked a reservation using the last of the money she'd saved from her old job and flew home to Linda. In her mind that day marked the beginning. It was as if she turned a corner and started down a new path, green with promise. She was at last looking forward to the baby and able to make preparations for her birth. It was a complete change in attitude that Alexandra attributed to finding the right place in which to go through her pregnancy. Her diary read, "When a woman is pregnant, she is so sensitive to everything and everyone. Back in Utah it felt all negative. Perhaps not for other women, but it was for me. Coming back here I feel I can be proud of my pregnancy and maybe even enjoy it. I walked into the house and Linda looked at me and told me I looked wonderful, I guess I do. I feel radiant!"

She had asked her mother to relay the message to the lawyer, should he call, that Alexandra had gone home and was waiting there to hear from him. Time was growing very short and there still had not been one single contact with the baby's father. He did not yet even know there was a baby. Alexandra felt embarrassed calling his roommate and kept hoping he would return and call her or at least write.

With each passing week and each decision she had to make on her own, the young man she had fallen in love with became more and more a faceless shadow. She was proud that she was doing so well on her own, yet there were times, she knew, when it would have been so much easier if he had been there to support her. How could he ever catch up with her now, when every day that dawned she was growing and experiencing new things, and the gap between their lives was only widening? It had become her pregnancy now, not theirs. It had taken her three months to discover and face the fact that she was going to have a baby, another three to find that pregnancy could be a lovely time. Even were the baby's father to return or give her support from a distance, she figured he would still need a lot of time to learn to live with the reality that a child of his was going to come into the world. She wanted to give him the chance to be part of it, of what was left. Several days after she was back in her own home she phoned his apartment. The thought of hearing his voice at the other end of the phone, for she was certain he would be home, left her numb and her heart beating fast. But it was his roommate who answered. No, he wasn't back in the country yet. His project, helping to clean up after the revolution and working on a national literacy campaign, had become too exciting to leave. He didn't know when they could expect him back, and Alexandra thought by the sound of his voice that he was annoyed she had called.

She told Linda, "I've been fantasizing how I was going to tell him. I was so drawn to him last fall. How do I say I have a five-month-old child inside me, that it is part his, and that I am giving our baby up for adoption?" She believed when she heard his voice it would all be easy, just like when they used to sit in the coffee shop and talk. Only after his roommate informed her he hadn't even set a date for his return did she have to admit to herself she was carrying around a dream.

"I'd had an image," she wrote in her diary, "of the two of us sharing an experience that few people can have, going through the intensity of watching a child grow inside me, loving it, and then letting it go. I don't feel getting in touch with him would change my decision about adoption or make our relationship permanent, but I'd always thought we would share the end of the pregnancy and be together at the birth."

For several days Alexandra reeled from the blow. She was alone, and it felt as if she'd been abandoned for the second time. First it had been with the news of the pregnancy, at having to make the decision to carry the child and the decision to relinquish the child for adoption alone. Now she would have to face giving birth alone too. She could not wait another day. She had to tell him, even if it was in a letter. His roommate had given her an address at which a letter might reach him. She was then entering her sixth month of pregnancy, her belly protruding under all of her clothes. To Linda she poured out her feelings and her decision.

"It is his right to know. I put everything down in the letter. It feels so easy to talk to him in writing, just as it used to be. I said I wasn't writing to ask for his financial support or even to ask him to guide me through this. I told him I felt strong and knew what I was doing, that I hadn't chosen the parents yet but I would soon. As far as I can see I've made an irrevocable decision, and I will give this child up for adoption. I told him I was healthy and I hoped he would feel a sense of joy, as I did, that there was a new life. 'You can participate in any fashion you like, by keeping in touch with me or coming back and completing the triangle. Pregnancy is a triangle and there is a part missing without you. The decision is entirely yours, but I think you have a right to know everything.' "

She mailed the letter April 10. The phone rang two days later. It was the attorney from New York. Glad to at last have found an intermediary whose judgment she intuitively felt she could trust, Alexandra was open to his first suggestion of a couple who would be overjoyed to take the baby. What impressed her about him was that he didn't seem like an attorney at all but a concerned friend. The conversation lasted an hour and a half, and she couldn't wait to tell Linda all about it.

"We talked intimately about my pregnancy, the changes in me. It turned out that he had adopted a child himself in addition to having one by birth. He said he had a couple as clients who would love my child in the way I did, and could carry through raising it as I couldn't. He said he felt they would be the kind of parents I would want to be, and that he could recommend them without any reservation whatsoever."

The couple he had in mind fit the few criteria Alexandra had formed. They were educated, had been married a long time, and in addition ran a successful small business together. She agreed to having them phone her. So much had been done by telephone already, she was comfortable opening up that way. The initial contact felt clean and clear and warm, and she felt certain they were the people for her child. Without the embarrassment of having to face one another in person, they all spoke freely.

"They were so excited," she told Linda, "but also eager to

comfort me and to let me know how much they appreciated what I was doing."

The couple also revealed to her a source of insecurity and fear that would later cause Alexandra much pain. A few months earlier, after eight years of trying to become pregnant and then looking for an infant to adopt, they had been given a baby several days old. They had contacted the mother through their attorney; no agency had been involved. Suddenly, two weeks into parenthood, and without warning, the birth mother had demanded the little girl back, claiming her decision to allow adoption had been a great mistake. They told Alexandra the loss of this little baby was like a death in their family for which they were still grieving. Alexandra understood completely their concern that she might not go through with the adoption, and she found herself reassuring them that this would not happen in her case. She did not realize that having to support them would later on be a demand on her emotional strength, and that from the first conversation she was placed in a support role when in fact it was she who needed support. But she was feeling strong and sure. The baby growing large and active inside her body was filling her with confidence.

The couple in turn assured her that this child would have the life she would like to give him or her, and that they were wholeheartedly ready to be parents. In later conversations they might disagree on exactly what was best for a baby in such things as feeding, but her major criterion was fulfilled, that they would be loving, attentive parents. She did not consider how closely their attitudes and life values matched hers. She did not think of it.

Over the last three months of her pregnancy, Alexandra spoke with the couple once or twice a month. The trust she initially felt with them was confirmed by their continued interest in her well-being and her feelings. Their anxieties about the actual adoption increased as the birth approached, but she continued to assure them of the certainty of her decision. It had not been made rashly but had grown from her knowledge of her own needs and her understanding of what commitment and resources were necessary to be the kind of parent she felt every child deserved. The conversations began to include some discussion of the details of the birth, and she thinks it was they who first suggested that they take the baby as soon as possible after birth. They had been given their first child four days after birth, and it was important to them to make the connection as early in the baby's life as possible, as soon as Alexandra felt comfortable. She too wanted this. She began to share with them her vision of how the exchange might take place. It was still a fuzzy picture, but she knew it was essential that she see this baby who had lived inside her, to count his or her fingers and toes, to complete a cycle for her. "I want to give the child my blessings, to know who this child is and to whom I am saying good-bye." The details would have to be worked out later, but in theory their visions matched.

When she had been at her mother's home, she had taken out from the library some books about the birth process. Several of them clearly explained and illustrated labor and discussed the various kinds of breathing techniques sometimes useful in natural childbirth, where no medications were used. In the midst of all the turmoil she had been feeling then, those books had heightened her anxiety. She had placed on labor all her unnamed anxieties about having a child. Distracted and divorced from the reality of her everyday life, and with no one around her who was going or had recently gone through childbirth, her birthing had filled her with terror out of all proportion to reality. Now she began childbirth classes, with Linda as her labor support. Sometimes she also took her brother, Tom, who had come out to live with her, or Linda and another male friend to the classes. Her diary read, "We are having a great time, because none of us knows anything about birth. I've been saying the words *natural childbirth* all along, but without knowing what they meant. In class I've learned that this birth can be an incredible, beautiful, though difficult, time. By the end of these classes, I think I'll be rather looking forward to the labor."

She had wisely selected a class with a teacher who had many years of experience attending birth, who inspired self-confidence and emphasized the need to trust in the process and the body's ability to guide a woman and her baby through safely. Alexandra also heard of yoga classes for pregnant women, and so began doing exercises at home to strengthen and stretch and prepare for the work of labor. She was more attentive about what she ate. She walked miles every day and found a neighbor's swimming pool in which to swim laps. She was doing all this as much for the pleasure it began to give her as for the good she knew it was doing for the baby. Perhaps, she thought, it might make up for some of the awful period they'd both suffered through in the early months.

The phone calls from New York became a ritual, and Alexandra would inform the couple of all the small things she was doing. She loved the interest she heard in their voices. She still didn't even ask their last names, but they were feeling more and more like family. Sometime during the six weeks the childbirth classes were going on, she began to visualize more concretely just how she might like the exchange of the baby to take place. She even began to imagine what it might be like to have the couple at the birth itself. That would mean they would have to meet face to face. What would it be like? She couldn't quite picture it, but it felt all right.

At about that time the intricacies of interstate adoption began to surface, and Alexandra found there were many small details surrounding an adoption where the adoptive parents were residents of a state different from hers and from where the birth would take place. The adoptive parents and their lawyer asked her to please come to New York and have the baby there. But to this request she had only an emphatic *"No!"* She told the lawyer, "I've already experienced what it is like living in the wrong place during this pregnancy. These past months have become especially happy for me, and I know I must stay where

I am happy. I hope that my refusing this won't change anything in the adoption, because I do want them for the parents. But I know that what I have to give this child is the time of gestation." They asked once more but she was adamant, and they did not press her further.

So far Alexandra knew only the couple's first names. She was told that their full names and their address would be on the adoption consent she would sign. The idea of knowing who they were and where they lived felt right. As with other unexpected requirements of the pregnancy, when the time came for each new development and decision, Alexandra was ready. She had taken each previous step in sequence, looking neither back nor ahead. She had much to be proud of in the way she worked through each phase.

Though she was long past feeling hopeless and depressed, her pride and pleasure were often tinged with sadness, not only for the inevitability of having to part with this baby but for the fact that in everything she was doing she was alone. No matter how much she trimmed away at the original dream—the baby's father returning to take some shared part in this experience— she still clung to pieces of the dream. Hope was briefly fanned early in May when a letter postmarked Nicaragua came in the mail. Had this letter come much earlier in pregnancy, it might have altered the course of her life.

In it he wrote that he was full of concern and awe at the news of the "miracle" and had been thinking a lot about her. His work was fascinating, and it was work that held him there because he really felt involved in the rebuilding of that country. The letter concluded, "I can feel nothing but pure delight at what you've written!"

On the first read-through she felt giddy. Perhaps he would want to have a part in the remainder of her pregnancy. He *was* the same sensitive person she had loved. The letter said he would return at the beginning of June. He also wrote that he was "100 percent" behind her, including her adoption decision. She was charmed, particularly by his asking her to write him everything, her hopes, her fears, all *her* feelings, so he could be part of it even at a distance. She read again and again the section where he told her how sorry he was that he couldn't be with her just then.

She had been feeling good before, but now she was buoyed up by the confidence his praise of her strength instilled in her. She was feeling strong and even imagined that she was at last supported. She sat down and wrote him a very long letter, with details of the direct adoption: her plans to meet the parents as well as to hold and feed the baby herself before she relinquished him or her.

She was to hear from him only one more time before the birth. That too was by mail. In that briefer letter he expressed all of the confusion her shocking announcement had really engendered in him. He no longer spoke of coming back in June or even of being with her at the very end of pregnancy and for the birth. And in this letter he cautioned her firmly against meeting the adoptive parents and strongly urged her not to see or hold the baby, because it would then make it too difficult to relinquish the baby. He seemed to be shielding himself from any emotional involvement with her or the pregnancy, much less the child he'd shared in creating. Alexandra easily read between the lines. He was frightened and his fear overshadowed any real concern he might have for her needs or the baby's. All her hopes for the last weeks were crushed. But even at such news she could not stay down for long. The pregnancy itself was carrying her along now. Life was carrying her.

Two weeks after receiving the second letter, she took a bus up into the country to stay with a cousin, where she could be alone and take leisurely walks through the hills. Her times out of doors in nature reassured her that the world was still a safe place and brought peace to her troubled mind. She was grateful to be granted the luxury of time to spend alone with the baby out of doors. It was something made possible by the prospective parents, who had been sending her a small living allowance to cover food and shelter through the birth and for three months afterward. In her diary she wrote about how important the time away from the city was for her and the baby.

"If I ever have another pregnancy, it will be at a time when I can arrange for long stretches where I have the freedom I have now. I see so many women, even in my birth class, who are working full-time right through their pregnancies. Part of me admires that they can do it. Yet I think they are missing so much. It's not only the cataclysmic changes but the subtle ones. I've been fortunate to be there through all of them, because I haven't been preoccupied with the pressure of having to deal with the everyday working world too much. How often do you carry another life inside you?"

The pregnancy had brought her squarely into womanhood, something she had always skirted as she hung on to her girlhood body and freedoms and feared what becoming an adult in the world might do to her dreams. To Linda she had confided, "I'd never really accepted my womanness and my capacity to bear children. I'd never liked the idea of pregnancy, birth, or having children. Because I'd never had regular periods, I'd never really felt in touch with the reproductive parts of my body." Perhaps some of that cautiousness had been due to her witnessing what parenthood had done to her parents' creative urges. Their desire to be artists had been hindered by the practical considerations of raising two children on little money. Alexandra saw herself as an artist too, a writer. Everything had been second to that goal. Unexpectedly this pregnancy had brought her pleasure in her maternal side. She was enjoying the traditional occupations of women; she was caring for the earth, gardening, being out of doors. Slowly, without realizing it, she was beginning to dream about what it might be like not to relinquish the baby but to *be* his or her mother. Entertaining thoughts of motherhood was a way of re-examining her decision to relinquish the baby.

She'd made the original decision in the early months of pregnancy, when this baby had been barely a bump inside of her, something she had hardly felt and couldn't relate to at all. It was natural that she should have to make the decision again, with the child now big and a vital, moving part of her. So she was really asking herself, Have I evolved to the point where I am now a mother? Can I even go on after this experience and *not* be a mother? Have I now changed so much that it is no longer possible for me to go on without this child? If that was true, then the answer now would be clear, that she should keep this baby.

The decision had to be hers alone. It was not that Alexandra could not be a competent, caring mother. She knew she could be. It was whether she fully *wanted* to enter this commitment and do so completely, consciously, with all her heart. Looking back months later she described the process she had gone through when she had imagined keeping the baby.

"I felt as if the overwhelming sense of loss and pain I had lived with, knowing I was going to give this child up, disappeared. I passed through it. I think it was being immensely, enormously pregnant, filled with life, living with it totally day in and day out that made the worst of the pain go away. Yet even the anticipated pleasure of becoming a mother, giving birth, did not change the facts. Rationally and emotionally, everything still stacked up on the side of adoption. When it came right down to it, and this was hardest to admit, I did not want to keep this child!"

Knowing she had once more made her decision, or, rather, found it, didn't lessen the sadness that realization brought her. She knew she still had to face other people, and their criticism for choosing not to be a mother. Alexandra wanted a few more years for her own growth. She also wanted her child to have his or her years too, without having to share them with a mother who was trying to find her own way. She had given a lot of thought to how great it could be, just the two of them, mother and child, living together, traveling around together, growing up together. They could go through it all as a team. But when she thought about how important it had been for her that she had had a basic security in her childhood, at least until her parents had gotten divorced—how that had remained with her—she knew she would be shortchanging her child. "I just don't *have* security yet. I *can't* manufacture it, no matter *how* much I would like to," she wrote in her diary.

Love was another matter. That would be easy for her to give. She already loved this child. It was *herself* she couldn't fully give, because what was simply not yet developed in her could not be given. That was what she was saying when she told the baby, during one of her many conversations with the baby at the end of pregnancy, "I love you but I don't want to raise you. If I really did, then I would do it. But I am doing what I know is best for us both."

And so the major decision of her pregnancy was made for a second time; and this time it was not a girl's decision but that of a woman.

I first met Alexandra when she was nearing the end of pregnancy, and her decision to relinquish the baby was firm. We had heard about each other from mutual friends. I don't recall who called whom, but we made a date to meet at the home of Linda's parents, where she and Linda and Tom were housesitting for several weeks. She greeted me at the door wearing a long, loose summer dress. I had had no picture of what she might look like, but I was stunned by how small, how slender she was, how strong and high her cheekbones were, how perfectly almond her eyes, how small her hands and bare feet. There was a refinement about her even at her advanced state of pregnancy. She talked slowly and with articulate precision. We went through the house, and I was introduced to Tom. Linda was at work. Alexandra carried a kitten in her arms. We went out and sat in the yard, and she began to tell me her story.

"I know so many children come into the world as mistakes. And some are born as excuses: there are ulterior motives for having them. Once I was able to admit to myself and this baby that I didn't want to raise a child, then there was no question about my decision. I know I will go through the pain of my attachment and my loss but I'll be okay." I knew that no amount of preparation would protect Alexandra from the physical pain of the loss when it came, or from the long months of grief after her detachment. But the strength of her decision and the solid foundation on which she based it, would, I felt, carry her through the experience—that and her sense of trust.

Having remade the adoption decision, she was ready at last to prepare for the birth itself. It was time to work out the details for the exchange, to consider whether she did in fact want to invite the adoptive parents to her birthing, to agree upon whether they would meet and if so how much time she would spend with the baby and they would spend with her before they took the baby. She had become deeply connected to this child. She couldn't have stopped that process had she wanted to; yet after she let go she would still have to disconnect. I wondered just how she would face that. We talked about it that day in the sun, and about her options. Once again Alexandra had begun to have vivid dreams. Whereas most of her dreams in Utah had involved fear and death, these dreams toward the end of her pregnancy were full of hope. Her brother insisted she get the kitten to replace the beloved Mouse. She told me that the baby of her dreams now took the form of a kitten.

"I guess I transferred my desire to hold and carry the baby to her. I carry her around a lot and stroke her all the time, and my dreams now are lighter and happier." One recurring dream told her this kitten, her baby, could never be happy with anyone other than her. But each time she would hear herself saying to it, "You'll make it without me, I know you will." And each time she would awake feeling confident the baby would be fine.

During her days she was practicing visualizing the scene of her birth, imaging the kinds of feelings that she and the couple would have, picturing the gestures they would each make. She could see herself placing the child in their arms, watching them hold the baby, and in these visions she felt connected to this couple. What she was doing was gaining some mastery over the event that would have so much importance to all of them, this baby's birth. And going through all the motions and the feelings ahead of time was preparing her to accept it when it came.

Although she knew she could never have complete control

over the interactions she had with the parents, she did want to design her birth. That she could do. Because her physician did not feel her spinal curvature warranted medical intervention, there were a number of alternatives open to her for her birthing. She could give birth in the nearby university teaching hospital. In addition to the labor and delivery room setup, there were two special birthing rooms. If she chose one of these and had no problem in labor that required moving to the delivery room, she could labor and give birth in the same bed in whatever way and with whatever people she wanted there. She could have the baby with her from the moment of birth until she gave it directly into the hands of the couple or an agent of theirs, either at the hospital or somewhere else. Or she could have a home birth with one of several local midwives, all skilled in normal birth, using the hospital for medical backup. What appealed to her about giving birth at home was the orientation toward normal, unmedicated birth, which she knew the midwives had but which she felt she could not count on in a hospital environment, no matter who her doctor was. Before deciding where to give birth, she thought she'd better choose her birth attendant.

She had heard there was a variety of physicians around to select from, a few family physicians as well as obstetrician-gynecologists, but she had put off seeking care for as long as possible, hoping she would not face the same situation she had in Utah. There she had felt the obstetricians hadn't wanted to answer any of her questions and hadn't cared about what she wanted. She was determined to find someone she could trust and who at the very least appreciated her point of view and her desire to make all the decisions about this birth.

She had not been seen by any professional for more than four months, and the baby was due in about six weeks, when she finally started to look for a midwife or doctor. Then she heard about The Birth Place—a birth home not connected with a hospital, but licensed by the state, where a woman could give birth using either a physician or midwife of her choice. At a resource center run by the same group, she looked through the files of questionnaires filled out by dozens of physicians, giving their interests and their practices. Then she looked through the midwives' files. She decided first to try a physician whose questionnaire she liked and who was recommended by the people who worked at the resource center as someone who was a strong advocate of women's rights as well as natural childbirth. He attended women both at the hospital and at the birth home and had also backed up some home births of the midwives in the area. He sounded just right.

His office was just two blocks from the resource center, so she walked to his office to make an appointment. The receptionist asked Alexandra when her last period had been. When she heard that it had been in August, she looked shocked and said, "That means you were due yesterday." Alexandra told her that the date of her last period was not really a reliable index, because she was very irregular. But the receptionist looked at her size and made an immediate appointment for her with the nurse practitioner and another one for the next week with the doctor.

Alexandra went to her first two appointments alone. She was impressed by the orientation of the practice, and felt that she had made the right decision, especially when the doctor said he was sure she didn't need to have a cesarean. Forms were already arriving in the mail every week from the East Coast, technical papers to be signed in preparation for the legalities of the adoption. A sum of money had been sent to cover her physician's fees. Although she was very late to start care, she impressed both the nurse practitioner and the doctor with her state of health and her state of mind.

Summer was getting hotter and her abdomen was growing heavier. She wished she could escape from all the bustle and hurry of life in town. She treasured every moment of time she had with the baby. There was still no letter from Nicaragua, and as the days passed she seldom thought about the father. She was excited when she went to the open house at the birth center. It surpassed even her best dreams of a place to give birth. There she felt at home.

There was a living room, a kitchen, a wooden deck off each birth room, even a back yard with fruit trees. She became a familiar sight at the doctor's office and at the birth home classes, almost always alone yet radiating the same sense of calm self-assurance. The women who volunteered at the birth home found her easy to talk with, and she often stopped by after having a snack at the coffeehouse down the street or on her way back from shopping. She was so healthy and radiant-looking everyone noticed her. Some wondered if she could possibly be as relaxed and positive as she seemed—they hoped it was not just a facade that would crack once the work and pain of labor began. She felt she was finally part of a close community of people like her who cared about shaping their birthings and gave one another support. Her friend Linda and her brother could not give her the same feeling of support that other pregnant women could. She brought Linda around to see the room she hoped to use, with the doors that swung open to the back yard. She felt so comfortable here; she hoped the baby's new parents would feel as she did, because she was now certain she wanted them to be at the birth.

Just when the parents would arrive had not yet been settled. One thing that had begun to assume major importance in her mind was the idea that this baby should have the advantage of some breastfeeding. Her mother had breastfed Alexandra and her brother at a time when few women were doing so, and when it was almost universally discouraged by doctors. Alexandra recalled having read something about a woman being able to prepare herself in some special way to breastfeed an adopted child. She wondered if the woman in New York had considered trying to breastfeed, and during one phone conversation she brought up the subject. That produced a shocked silence on the other end of the phone. The woman said she'd never heard of any such thing, and said she really had no interest in the subject. Their pediatrician, she told Alexandra, had already suggested to them a wonderful formula, and neither she nor her husband felt breastfeeding to be that important. Their idea was that they could share equally in feeding the baby, she and her husband, and formula made it all so easy. Alexandra was surprised and disappointed at this reaction. She had never before found an area where they could not at least listen to each other. She had sensed from the beginning the couple she'd chosen were not particularly liberal or adventuresome, but they had always before been willing to listen to each of her ideas. I saw Alexandra shortly after this conversation, and we talked about how different they were likely to be from her.

"I know I can't set up this adoption to be perfect; but breastfeeding seems so important to me. I am going to put this baby to my breast. At least for the few hours he is still with me he will be breastfed." She was adamant that the baby should get the benefit of her first milk, colostrum, to protect the baby from infections and allergies. And I was glad to see she would assert herself. It would mean there was less chance she would compromise the most important features of the birth and adoption when the time came.

When she told the couple of her plans during their next phone conversation, they bristled. When I next saw her a few days later, Alexandra was still feeling annoyed. She said the phone calls had now become strained, and though they did say they felt they had no right to impose any restrictions on her, she felt their criticism.

There were other details to discuss. They agreed that Alexandra should call or have someone else call their attorney as soon as she thought she was going into labor. They would then attempt to get the first plane out to the West Coast, and they would call for directions when they arrived, rent a car, and drive straight to the birth home. They had apparently never heard of such a place to have a baby, although there is a well-known birth center right in New York City. They, like most people, associated birth with hospitalization. Alexandra said they'd sounded very relieved to hear that she had at least chosen a physician, not a midwife, to attend her. She smiled as she told me.

I didn't see Alexandra again until labor. Our time together had given her a few extra things to ponder. She did call to invite me to be there at the birth and to take photographs. Two weeks later, eleven days after her most accurate estimate of a due date and a full three weeks after the date she had first thought it would be, Alexandra's labor began. She spent the first part of the day at a friend's house, and a midwife friend was with her. By the time they packed up her clothes and food to take to the birth home and called her physician and the rest of us to meet them at the home, Alexandra was well into labor, growing weary and feeling dazed but excited and unafraid.

TONY AND ELLEN:

Fear of Knowing

THEY ARRIVED ON the 11 P.M. flight and went directly to a telephone as agreed. The phone number they dialed was The Birth Place, an alternative birth center thirty miles away. It was there that their baby was waiting. Not theirs yet, but soon to be. They had booked return reservations for the 7 A.M. flight the next day, and they wanted to pick up the baby and leave as soon as possible. That was what all their friends and relatives had told them to do. "Don't get involved," they warned. "It will only make things more difficult."

They had received the call from their attorney at dawn that morning telling them that the doctor had phoned to say his patient was in active labor, and that she would like them to take the first possible flight out. Alexandra had not wanted them at the actual birth, not after she had heard their fear and mistrust over the telephone when she had suggested it. The presence of anyone who didn't believe fully in what she was doing could only distract her from her commitment to labor and give birth to this baby spontaneously, with no drugs or intervention. That was why she'd chosen the birth home rather than the hospital.

There she could have the run of the entire place: there was the kitchen to get food from when she was hungry, the bathroom to take hot baths or showers in if it made her more comfortable, the deck and the yard with fruit trees she could look out on or wander in. Without any rules restricting her behavior in labor, she could have as many friends around her as she wished and could orchestrate her birthing and her leave-taking from her baby to her own satisfaction. There, after the birth, she could at last meet the parents she'd chosen and formed a trust with long distance, could talk with them in privacy and share the baby's presence before she turned this part of her flesh over to them. That had been her plan for the last months of pregnancy, that and having some time after the birth to spend alone with the baby, to lie with the baby, to feed the baby at her breast, to relish every moment of the last few hours they would have together.

But that was not Tony and Ellen's plan. Their plan was to leave without knowing any more than they had to, without facing her, as they felt any meeting could only be a confrontation, with pain, guilt, and remorse for everyone. They had friends who had adopted babies, and not one of them had ever heard of what this young woman had in mind. Some of their friends told them it might be a trap. "Just get the baby and leave," they said. "We'll meet you at the airport, take you home, and *then* we'll celebrate."

And so they came to town. And so she waited for them, waited with her son, to whom she had passionately given birth after an exhausting labor that had demanded every ounce of her attention and strength. The stages of her cervix opening had gone so very slowly, like slow motion, that she had thought it might never end. Linda had been there from the first sign of labor, as had other friends and a midwife who had offered extra support. When they had finally brought her to the birth home, she had been making good progress and losing all thought of time.

They had all stayed with her, walked around the home with her, and sat with her on the big, comfortable bed with their arms for support, their backs to lean against, hour after hour. Her brother, Tom, had been there too. He had labored beside her, struggling with his own fears about her pain and misgivings over what she was going to do. He loved his sister very much. In the absence of the baby's father he had felt himself especially connected to this child of his sister's. But when she at last had begun to push, smiling between the urges and the bearing down, he had slipped quietly away and taken refuge on a couch in the living room, where he had fallen deeply asleep. Perhaps he'd hoped he would miss the birth entirely and the grief he knew his sister would face afterward. But Alexandra had noticed his absence toward the end and sent someone to fetch him like a mischievous boy to her. She *needed* him. It was no time for him to be running away.

The baby had long black hair. He had slipped out of her, one shoulder slightly tearing her as he had come, out and up into her outreaching hands and onto her deflated abdomen. And so he had arrived. A baby boy with a round face and dark eyes peering open at her from the moment of birth. So this was what it had all been for.

Tony and Ellen, the parents-to-be, had given no thought to those first moments. They had been so caught up with the fear they'd carried with them through the past three months of waiting, the fear that somehow they would lose him as they had lost the other, they had hardly thought of his birth. Just six months earlier they had had a daughter. She had come to them when she was four days old. She had been with them for two brief weeks before the mother had claimed her back again, as she was legally entitled to do, and she'd walked out of their lives carrying their little girl and their hearts.

The pain Tony and Ellen had felt then, after all the years of trying for a child, after the miscarriage and the tubal pregnancy, had seared like a branding iron. It had felt to them like a death when the woman had taken their little girl from them, back to the grandparents who didn't want her to keep the child, back to the friends who knew she was in no position to raise her herself. She had fled clutching the baby like her security blanket, leaving no trace behind. That was why they were coming now in fear. It had been such a short time ago, and they were determined not to let another mother hurt them.

They knew they were taking a risk, that legally this mother too had six months in which to change her mind and ask for the infant back. They would have had to take that risk even in an agency adoption unless the baby had been placed in a foster home or institution during the waiting period. They had gone to agencies first, and there had been no baby found for them. Direct adoption had seemed the only alternative. It hadn't been so bad, having to talk with the young woman by phone. They *liked* her. The papers they would sign and she would sign would necessitate their knowing each other's full names. But that was all. To how much more must they subject themselves in order to get a child?

But Alexandra knew her rights, and she knew what she wanted for her child's sake. She hadn't spent the last nine and one-half months growing this baby inside her, refraining from anything that might harm him, loving and communicating with him for nothing. Certainly not to have the cycle abruptly cut off and the process aborted. Her way would give her the time she needed to complete the loving and begin the letting go. She intended to drink in every moment she had with her son, and she was doing just that even as the couple were driving their rented car from the airport to the birth home.

She hadn't slept for two days. There would be time enough for that soon. Now she was too busy being enchanted with this small, fragrant little boy lying against her in the darkened room. It was after midnight. They would arrive in less than an hour. The nurse came in to check her, and suggested she might like to take a warm bath and let her clean Alexandra's nightgown from the stains of the birth. Sitting in the bath she held him close but out of the water, wrapped in a blanket. And she talked to him, chuckling with pleasure at his changing faces and the sounds his lips made as they pursed and his tongue explored the air.

If Tony and Ellen had known what she was up to, they

would have feared her even more and never believed she could go on and give them this baby. But then they didn't know her. They hadn't lived inside her mind and heart for the past months as she made and remade her decision. Tom wouldn't have believed it either, had he seen her at midnight with the baby in her arms in the bath.

He had excused himself earlier in the evening, saying he needed some fresh air, perhaps hoping to miss meeting the couple when they arrived. He had been gone five hours now, and no one had heard from him. Alexandra sensed he was angry at her for what she was about to do. The baby looked just as he had in his baby pictures. This child was a part of *their* family, she knew he must be thinking. Why did she have to give him up? Couldn't they all raise him together? Their parents would surely help out. But Tom was still a teenager, and the support he could give would not be enough for her in the next years were she to attempt to raise this child alone.

She knew that, no matter what anyone else might think. She could deal with her brother's hurt and resentment later. She was being amazingly clearheaded. Here she was, purposely keeping her baby out of the warm water in order that the wonderful fragrance of his skin from the birth might still be there for the couple to know. She had thought of them at every step. If they were to love him, she'd reasoned, they would need to know him right from the beginning; and though they hadn't seen him born—seen that magnetic open-eyed first gaze—still, she would give them his newness.

She fed him from her breast. The two of them were brand new at this game of suckling and they were clumsy together. He couldn't find her nipple. She didn't know just how to position him most comfortably in her arm. He made such funny noises as he sucked, as if he were sucking candy. She was giving him the sweet first milk called colostrum, a protection as potent as antibiotics. And she was loving him.

It was nearly 1:00 A.M. In the living room the midwife, Alexandra's roommate Linda, and I sat and nervously waited for the lights of a car to shine down the driveway. Tony had called once to say they had taken the wrong turn and gotten lost. I had arranged for a room for them at a local motel. That way, even if Alexandra gave them the baby immediately, they could have some time, perhaps even sleep with him, before they had to drive to the airport and catch the long flight back home. Their departure shouldn't be frantic. For such an event time is essential.

At 1:15 headlights lit up the driveway. The midwife greeted Tony and Ellen warmly at the door, introduced them to Linda and me, and invited them in. She went to make them a cup of something hot, and we all went into the living room. We had anticipated their anxiety, and Tony had been honest about it when he'd called the second time. They were coming to a strange home in a strange city to meet strange people who, they could easily imagine, would be standing *between* them and their baby. It was too late in the night to bother with small talk. "Is the baby here?" "Yes." "How is *she?*" "Just fine, very well." "Can we *see* him?" "Certainly."

First we felt they had to hear what *she'd* planned for them. The idea of a motel and waiting until tomorrow to take the baby was out of the question, they said in unison. They had a plane to catch that was leaving in just five hours. If they took the baby now, they would have time to return to the airport motel where they'd left their bags. As we sat and listened to Tony, looking small and stiff, and watched his crossed leg jiggling up and down, we sympathized with his and Ellen's discomfort. We were there to put the two of them at ease, to hear *their* needs too. But we were also there to make the needs of the woman in the back room known, to break the news gently that she had plans that required something more of them than they'd counted on.

We talked about the plane back to New York. Both of them were adamant, it was the only flight with available seats for the next several days. It seemed that the idea of staying the night in a strange community was more than they could possibly bear. They were inflexible but they had to listen as we gently pointed out to them that, regardless of their intentions for how the exchange would take place that night, the desires of the mother in the other room would have to take precedence. She was in control; but they should understand that hurting or frightening them was not her intention. She merely needed a little time, and she wanted to meet them. They didn't seem to hear what we were saying. They kept bringing up the plane they needed to catch as if that were their only hope of escape. We again brought up the idea of a meeting with Alexandra. Why? they asked. They knew all they needed to know about her. They had great respect for what she was doing for them, for what she had done for the baby. For the grief she would surely feel, they felt profound respect. But having to meet her, having to see *their* son while he was still *her* son, in *her* arms, this they did *not* want to face, not for *anyone*.

There was more quiet talk as we leaned toward Tony and Ellen and spoke to them of Alexandra. We painted a picture of an exchange she had planned that might enrich everyone's lives. They listened and said no. They didn't think such a thing would enrich anyone's life, certainly not their lives! They could see no need to carry the memory of her face back home with them. They had her voice. That was enough! They spoke about the terrible suffering they had endured when they lost their little girl. It was not clear what they now feared most, *their* reactions upon seeing and sitting in the same room with Alexandra or *her* reactions seeing them with her baby. Or was it the unspoken possibility that she would not be able to bring herself to let the baby go?

It was then 2:00 A.M. We all heard the baby's cry once or twice in the background. Linda went to see if all was well in the bedroom. She was eager to get away from the tension in the living room. Then the midwife, a large, soft-featured older woman, started to speak about the grief Alexandra would have to live with after she gave them her child. She wanted this couple to know this would not be the same as the grief of a parent whose child had died, because Alexandra had freely *chosen* adoption. It would be more like the kind of grief any mother of a grown child would feel when he or she left home.

Alexandra's time with her son would be brief and her experience with him compressed, but not lost. They should know they need not pity her. The couple seemed to hear what she was saying. Still, they did not bend in their insistence that it must go *their* way.

I watched their unwillingness to yield and had to speak up, to say that in the final analysis the full decision of just how this exchange took place rested with the young woman in the other room. Legally, and in fairness, I reminded them, it was in *her* hands whether they caught the first plane and whether they even became the parents of her child. Tony and Ellen both stiffened at the harsh truth of what I had said and braced themselves for what I might say next. I told them that I didn't want to coerce them, but I was asking them to step outside their own perspective just for once.

All Alexandra was asking for was a little more time, that and one brief meeting with the people to whom she was entrusting her child. She would have only this one day to look back on, whereas they would have her child to look upon all their lives. She wanted to create a memory she could take pride in, and she had every right to stage these last moments to suit herself. Moreover, I added, knowing well what the impact of my words might be on this sensitive couple, what they were really asking her to do was to hide in the background, as birth mothers have been asked to do for years. By asking her to have no identity, they were only reaffirming the judgment that birth mothers have no value except as passive vessels out of which babies emerge for other parents to own.

That's what adoption has traditionally asked of mothers relinquishing their babies, that they remain hidden. This young woman, I said, was fortunate to know what her rights were, that it didn't have to be that way. That was the reason she had selected them to be parents of her child. All the other couples she had heard about or spoken to had seemed interested only in the baby, but *they* had expressed caring for her as a person. Were they now going to prove her trust in them wrong? I could see that this last remark hit the target. Tony and Ellen both saw themselves as caring people. They sat back hard in their seats, perhaps for the first time seeing the entire adoption in a new light.

I offered a choice to soften the blow. Given Alexandra's strong desire to meet them, which would they prefer: to see her alone first, without the baby, and see the baby after, or to see the baby now in her presence? Given the two options, neither of which they wanted, they both chose the less difficult path. They would, they agreed, sitting upright on the edge of the couch, prefer to meet her first without the baby.

Alexandra stood at the bathroom counter with Linda, changing the baby's diaper, chatting excitedly. It was his first stool, the inky, sticky meconium, which had been like a plug in his intestines during his intrauterine life, and its passage marked his readiness to digest food independent of her. When I came in they stopped what they were doing. Alexandra had heard none of the disagreement out front, but she had sensed from the time it was taking that there was resistance to what she wanted. When I suggested her meeting with the couple first without the baby, she tensed and her mouth set firm. She could understand their fears about seeing her with the baby, she said. She could sympathize. She'd been doing that anyway every phone conversation with them, whenever they acted afraid she would not go through with the adoption. But she would *not* give in to their fears now. These were her last few hours with her son, and she meant to retain all power over this exchange. Maybe, she said in a low, flat voice, it was just a sign that they were not the right people to have her baby after all.

I slipped an arm around her tensed shoulders, and whispered that perhaps this was not too much to ask, that she let them face her alone first. She was quiet a moment, looking down at her son. Her shoulders relaxed. Then she said she guessed that would be all right, to meet them first without him. But they would have to see him with her after that.

I went out with the news. The couple accepted Alexandra's

decision and relaxed just a bit on the couch. Tony uncrossed his legs and Ellen began to speak with concern about Alexandra's feelings. The midwife told them both once again that they needn't worry about her. She had come to her own decision and had the support of many friends and her family. She was not desperate, like the mother of the little girl they had lost, but a self-confident person who had thought through what she was doing very carefully and had much to be proud of in the way she had gone through pregnancy and birth. She had spent the past fifteen hours happily with her son, and she was ready to begin the process of saying good-bye.

To change the subject to an easier one, the midwife asked whether they had chosen a name for him yet. Their account of their difficulty in selecting a name for a boy, of watching the screen credits of the movie on the airplane hoping to find there the name they were looking for, made everyone laugh, including them. In the middle of this light moment, the first since they'd arrived, Alexandra herself suddenly walked unannounced into the room.

Everything stopped. She greeted the couple warmly and smiled at them through her exhaustion. They stood up, stunned at her appearance, and put out their hands to her. The midwife and I stood off to the side. The very sight of Alexandra standing in her nightgown before them seemed to change everything. She was no longer the massive unseen threat they'd lived in fear of, but just a slender, very young looking woman with shoulder-length straight dark hair, high cheekbones, and extraordinarily clear, almond-shaped eyes. Someone broke the silence by remarking how alike the two women looked. They were both petite and dark, each with small, arched noses, prominent cheekbones, slender necks and shoulders. They smiled quietly at each other in acknowledgment.

Everyone sat together in the living room. Alexandra seemd to be enjoying Tony and Ellen's attention, and, after accepting their praises for how well and strong she looked, she began to talk about her labor and her son's birth. She was proud, like a warrior, though her birthing had not been a battle. She had given in to labor with a single-mindedness that had surprised all of us. She had a desire to tell them about those hours, and she smiled as she spoke. Someday they could tell him.

It had been difficult, she said, like nothing she had ever known before, but they needn't have had anxiety for her well-being or the baby's. A natural birth had been what she had wanted, to be a part of *everything* that went on, not to lose one precious moment of the experience. The labor was nearly thirty hours, and she told them she didn't regret a minute of it. She had been surrounded by friends, some old and some, such as her physician, midwife, and me, whom she'd met only near the end of her pregnancy. She had known everyone at her birthing was totally committed to her goals. She had never before felt so much love and attention. Then the moments of his emergence from her, lifted up by her hands while his legs were still inside her, those moments had been the peak of the painful, difficult journey of labor. And, she told Tony and Ellen, the time and work of birth had helped prepare her for what was yet to come.

Now as she sat across from them, feeling their respect for all she had done, she appeared small. The strength that had poured into her during labor was ebbing; two nights without sleep and the effort of the birth left her dazed and feeling fragile. She spoke briefly about her plans for the exchange. She told them simply how important it had been to her that she meet them. She had realized only in the last weeks of pregnancy that meeting them would help complete this cycle for her. She only wanted a little more time so as not to waste the preciousness of her last hours with him on sleep-deprived senses. She needed to sleep a bit, to wash and get dressed. Then she would gladly meet with them again, help them give him his first bath, and spend just a little time alone with her son before he left with them. In her presence, finally realizing how little she was asking for, Tony and Ellen glanced quickly at each other, and Tony said he would change their morning flight to a later one.

Then Ellen asked her when they might see him. "Right now!" Alexandra answered, smiling. She left the room and was gone only an instant before she returned, carrying him wrapped in a light blanket in her arms. This time the pair remained seated, unable to move. She walked quickly over to them and placed her son in Ellen's arms. Although she would spend a little more time with him before saying good-bye, that gesture, one she'd rehearsed in her mind so many times, was her first step in letting go. She stood back and watched.

His beauty was striking, silky black hair down a wide forehead, a broad face with extraordinarily well-formed features, and eyes that gazed up at Tony and Ellen when they spoke to him as if he knew it all. Alexandra then spoke. She told them that the scent of his birth was still on his skin, that they could smell it. They bent close to his face.

With that the room began to buzz with conversation, none of it important, all of it significant—the kinds of things people say when words won't do but must be said anyway. Alexandra sat on a couch opposite the couple and watched them play with him. She smiled. She said later it was *then* she knew they were his parents. After a few mintues she suddenly stood up to leave, pleading exhaustion. She said she would like to take him back to bed. They stood and gave him back to her in one smooth motion. Before she went the three of them set the time to meet, ten the next morning, there at the home. Then Tony and Ellen kissed Alexandra good night, leaving their son with her.

The couple left the house amid the good wishes of everyone. The night was chill. Thinking it must always be summer in California, Ellen had worn only a sleeveless dress. But then so many things were different from what they had expected. It would be an hour's drive back to the motel by the airport where they'd left their belongings. They were leaving in the middle of the night, empty-armed yet confident and excited. They had come in fear with fantasies of disappointment and plans for escape. Now they too felt Alexandra's certainty in her decision to give them this child. Giving her this one night to lie with him seemed easy now. They drove off.

In the warm light of the morning they arrived and greeted Alexandra, who was ready for them. Though she hadn't slept at all, she felt refreshed by the privacy of the night she'd spent with her son. Even her brother, Tom, had returned to meet them. First she handed the baby to Tom and Linda, that they who had supported her so well and felt such a strong connection with this baby might have some moments alone with him to say their good-byes. Meanwhile she led Tony and Ellen back to her room, the one with the French doors, which were open to let in the warm air. There on the bed where Alexandra had given birth they sat and talked.

She told them all the little things she had discovered about his nature in the past twenty-four hours and the nine-plus months he'd spent with her. Then they prepared a warm bath together, and when Tom and Linda brought him in they unwrapped him and placed him in it. Lying there on his back in the water, held in two pairs of women's hands, he was relaxed and alert. The bond of affection for him had expanded to include two more people and he showed no fear. This would be the way Alexandra remembered him best. It had not been a whim for her to spend the first night with him and then to bathe him with them this morning. He opened his body like a flower in the warmth of the water and the hands that supported him, and she felt she could read his future in his face. He would be all right with them. It was Linda's last-minute suggestion that put a borrowed camera in the hands of the new father. He, who hadn't wanted to see or know the woman from whom his child came, now took half a roll of film of the two mothers bathing their son, blurred, unfocused images in black and white that Alexandra would treasure. Then together they dressed him in the clothes the couple had brought while they told her they would call her after they had returned to New York, after they had chosen his name, so she could know it too.

They left him alone with her for a few minutes as she had asked. For the first time she explained everything to him, why she was relinquishing him, who his new parents were, and how this would mean good-bye for the time being. She needed to say it out loud, and as she held and talked to him, she found the words came easily. It was like a conversation, though he merely watched her calmly. This moment, their leavetaking, was precious, she told him, because it might be their last for a long, long time. But it was no more precious than her life with him had been while she carried him. He should remember that. Soon there was nothing more to say. She chose not to go back through the house but to take him out into the green back yard and in through the side door. The ceremony of it seemed important to her.

Everyone was waiting there. Even as she had taken the short walk around the house she had begun to cry, and, at seeing her silently crying with the baby in her arms, Tom, Linda, the midwife, Tony and Ellen, and I, standing in the entrance hall, were also moved to tears. Her gaze fell first on Ellen. She placed him in her arms. It was time for congratulations and wishes for a safe journey. There were hugs all around, and only the baby had dry eyes. We walked Tony and Ellen and their new baby outside to their car and waved a final good-bye as they drove off. Then everyone but Alexandra went back inside the house.

Alexandra stood for a moment in front of the house, watching the car. Suddenly the magic of the past two days dropped away. All she knew, standing there alone on the asphalt in the warm sunshine, was she was achingly, crazily exhausted, and felt like screaming. There would be time to sort it all out later and people she could call on to help her. There would be lots of time. But first, first she had to sleep.

ALEXANDRA:

Unmet Promises

Most traditional societies have ways to help a person in grief. There is no expectation that a person must put "a face" on for the outside world. Often noise and movement are encouraged, even ritualized, to give expression to the feelings of shocked numbness, helplessness, anger, and hopelessness. And there are things a person must do, rites to be followed, for that too helps. Something prescribed to pass the seemingly endless time when the grieving person feels like an outsider to all of life, until life begins to flow again.

Modern city dwellers that most people are, almost all tend to grieve silently and alone. Some try to deny grief's existence altogether and are called strong for doing so. But that is just another fiction, for a person does not send grief away by putting a mask over its face. Grief takes its own time and has its own rhythm and its own cleansing. The grief a woman feels following the adoption of her child, like the grief felt for any loved one gone, is undeniable; but it is not unendurable or unending if it is recognized and lived. Sometimes it needs to be expressed and heard.

As private and solitary as Alexandra had always been, she

found her period of mourning was the third time in a year she had to have the support and availability and presence of friends. She had found she needed it during pregnancy and in birth. It had made all the difference in those experiences; and she needed it again now that she was alone once more.

In the weeks after the baby's leaving she kept close to home, unable to face acquaintances around town. Her time was absorbed by the needs of her heart, and she spent her days crying, recollecting, daydreaming, accepting the visits of close friends, crying some more. Crying had always been difficult but was now easy. But sleep, which had once comforted her, no longer did. She slept fitfully; though her body was exhausted, her mind would not let her rest. Eating was now difficult. Her knotted stomach recoiled at the thought of food. With the help of one of her friends, she found a simple, nourishing diet she could digest: Japanese miso soup, fresh fruit. She had to remind herself that she needed to keep her physical strength up, especially now, because not eating would only complicate matters. She needed to grieve, not to punish herself. And so she ate, without wanting to.

Why mourn at all? She might have thrown herself back into life and been able to crowd the pain out of her consciousness. But one thing she had learned from her pregnancy was to do things in their proper time and sequence. Alexandra wanted no nightmares to erupt years later from feelings she'd suppressed. Better to go through it now, while it was fresh and she could cry, while there were friends around who had been through the experience with her to understand and make themselves available.

Alexandra faced her most difficult challenge yet: time. More time than she'd ever had and less to do, with less reason to do anything than ever before. Labor had taught its lessons well. She discovered in the course of those hours that allowing feelings and sensations to crescendo would bring rest for a time before they swelled anew. She had learned to pay attention to the rhythm inside her, for there was a rhythm. It was not constant pain; and it took more out of her to fight it than to follow its lead and go wherever it took her. It was even possible to find a sort of solace in what was taking place in her body. The highs were so clear they were startling: she was stunned at how content she felt sometimes. At those times she worried whether it was right and fair to her son that she, having walked away from him, should feel so good and right. She asked friends about it, but she knew the answer. It amazed her how irrepressible life was, especially the life force inside her. And when she felt no strength within to draw upon, there were still warm summer days and cloudless skies around her to remind her that life existed and everything changed. Even pain.

She found herself awake every two hours through the night with uncanny regularity. She sensed the cause but had to wait seven long days for confirmation in a telephone call. Ellen kept her promise to telephone Alexandra and let her know the name they'd chosen for the baby. Christopher. At first Ellen sounded anxious. But soon, hearing Alexandra's interest, she was talking easily of all the small details a new parent loves to share. To Alexandra this was proof that she had made the right choice for her child. Her greatest fear, throughout the pregnancy and in the week after he had gone, had been that his parents might not really be able to love him wholly, just as he was. But she needn't have worried. Ellen said he was the same calm baby he had been when they had first met him, and she told Alexandra that both she and Tony felt it was her gift to them, his contentedness. She was reassured. If he could be so comfortable in his body and feel a trust in the world, he would surely continue to be easy for them to love. And the more love they gave him, the more he would certainly thrive. She hung up the phone and felt like dancing.

Alexandra had bound her breasts tightly when they first became swollen with milk. She had refused a shot to dry them in order that he should be able to drink of her first milk. Now her breasts were small again and leaked milk no more. But when she put down the telephone she noticed dark, wet stains on her shirt front. Tears, she thought. But it was her milk, dripping freely, turned on by a voice three thousand miles away.

So she was still connected to him. Ellen had told her how he awoke every two hours through the night for feeding. Her waking every two hours each night: it was on *his* schedule. Across the distance of a continent, while one mother awoke to give her son a bottle, another awoke to give him her breast.

Their conversation left Alexandra elated for hours. It had come on Monday, the hardest day yet. Christopher had been born the previous Monday. It was not that she had felt the urge to reverse her decision—she knew she was no better able to care for a child now than when she had first decided to relinquish him. But Monday had been more difficult, from the moment she awoke.

Three days later she received another phone call from New York, this from the attorney. He told her Tony and Ellen had agreed to send her $300 for the month of September to help her out, but it was all they could handle, although they had previously agreed to support her for three months after the birth. She asked when she could expect it, and he said he'd send it right out. Three days passed, and then it was Monday again. Mondays were the hardest. Alexandra screwed up her nerve and placed a call to the attorney. Where was the money? His response was a mumbled apology about confusion in the office; he'd wire it that very afternoon to her bank. He had something he wanted to tell her, and tried to say it quickly. Tony and Ellen didn't want her to have any further direct contact with them. They'd called him after speaking with her and asked him to handle any future dealings with her. She was stunned as if struck and could say nothing.

Her mother flew in from Utah to stay for a week. Alexandra had been looking forward to this visit. But instead of feeling she could let go and be a daughter again, she found the presence of her mother stifled her. She was on stage, not daring to be herself, and she was relieved when her mother left. Their time together had brought them closer; but it had put an artificial stop to her grieving.

Still no money arrived. She called the bank each day and felt guilty for doing so, as if she'd asked for a handout. Her mother had left what little she could, and friends loaned her a bit. And she waited, wondering whether it was the couple themselves who were delaying and didn't want her to have the money.

Although she needed to grieve, she also needed to be lifted out of herself at times. People began to encourage her to join them in everyday things: shopping, watching television, coming over for dinner. She found herself stopping by at the birth home just to be in the presence of pregnant women and mothers with new babies. She always carried pictures from the birth. Her favorite was a picture of Christopher, newborn and still wet-faced, lying against her breast. His features were crumpled, his dark eyes alight with recognition as he gazed directly up into her face. And there was one showing her first efforts at feeding him. It made her laugh just to remember. They had both been so clumsy as they had connected. Her friends listened, noticed how distracted she was in conversation, and understood.

The third Monday caught her unawares. She was down-town on a busy street when she remembered what day it was. Tears fell especially hard all that day, downtown, back home, in bed, and on into the morning of the next day. Tuesday began with no relief, and she could not understand why this day too felt so difficult. She had forgotten. It was her birthday, the twenty-second anniversary of her own birth. And all she could feel was anxiety about the unfinished business with Christopher's new parents. It was the first time she had felt anger toward them since the night of the birth, when they'd come to the birth home to get Christopher and tried to prevent her from even meeting them. She imagined them now, trying to push her away again. She forced herself to call the attorney once again. He apologized, made some excuse, and said he'd get right on it. And the couple, he attempted to reassure her, had just been frightened by her show of interest in their baby and were afraid of where it might lead.

The call only made her feel worse. After all they had been through with her during the pregnancy, meeting her, their crying and laughing together, how could they now deny the trust all three had formed? It had all been for nothing, Alexandra told herself. All afternoon she talked about it to two of her friends. Why had she chosen this couple, anyway? Why had she not held out longer, for people more like her, who would have understood her values, generous people, not emotional cowards! What did this mean for her son? How could they be so stupid as to try to wrench all connection with him so soon! She was not asking to be a part of their lives, only that they recognize he was still a part of hers. The smallest link with them, a letter now and then, a periodic phone call at first, that was all she needed. And they were denying her that just as if she were a piece of refuse, useless to them now that they had the only thing they wanted from her.

Her friends waited until the heat of her anger had subsided, until she had no more to say, and then asked her if she could recall how much she had liked them at first. She had to admit she had liked them. And, more important, they had fulfilled her most important criteria for being parents to her child. She knew she could never find people who would match all her dreams. She also knew in her heart they were acting now in fear. Still, she felt the sadness.

She telephoned her doctor late in the afternoon and related the events of the day. Had he had any similar experience before in dealing with private adoptions? His response was different from that of her friends. To him Tony and Ellen's actions showed that they were living in the natural anxiousness that she was going to evaluate any interactions they had with her, and that no matter how hard they tried they would be judged and fall short. They probably imagined she was even considering going back on her decision to give them Christopher. He asked Alexandra to have a little extra understanding for their situation, because their worst fears were undoubtedly being bolstered by the people around them. Something he said brought a smile to her face. She was recalling a conversation she'd had with Ellen months before the birth. She had told Ellen then that she would always be there for this child she was carrying, no matter what happened in her life. They must have recalled her words later and thought she must have meant she would always be a haunting shadow over their lives, watching, perhaps hoping to snatch him from them; for a full month after that conversation they hadn't called her. She could smile because she now understood. A pity that they couldn't or wouldn't try to understand her as well. Alexandra, who had already given so much, was being asked to give still more—more compassion, more understanding—while they, who had received so much from her, were afraid to give and were finding support that bolstered their fears.

It was time to celebrate her birthday. There was a dinner in her honor. Her brother, Linda, several friends, her doctor all came. They sat around the table with candles and flowers, drinking a toast to her coming year. Then they danced. Finally they curled up on cushions and listened to quiet music. Alexandra was given a back rub, and the tension of the day was massaged from her shoulders. She went to bed calmer than she'd felt in weeks, ready for a full night's sleep.

On the Saturday following her birthday, she walked to the park to listen to some music. There were people she knew there, among them Dan, a friend. Dan pointed out a slender woman with blonde hair down her back. Her name was Claire. He'd spoken about her to Alexandra before, about how she had chosen to raise her baby as a single mother, and about the difficult time she was having now that her little girl was an active toddler. Another of their mutual friends also had told Alexandra about Claire; in that friend's eyes Claire was a shining example of all that a single mother could do, even without much money. She'd held her up to Alexandra as a model who represented everything Alexandra was turning her back on by giving up her son. Alexandra wanted to meet this woman about whom she'd heard so much. She walked over and sat down on the grass and introduced herself. It turned out that Claire had also heard about Alexandra. They looked at each other a minute before speaking further. Then Alexandra, seeing the little girl playing nearby, unwatched by Claire, asked simply how things were going. Tears began to fill Claire's eyes and she started to talk. A tale of frustration, pain, and self-doubt poured out.

When she had found out she was pregnant, by the young man she loved and with whom she had had a relationship on and off since high school, she had become depressed. They had used birth control consistently. The depression had turned to despondency as Claire had seen her dilemma. She had told herself she could never have an abortion, because that would be killing life. Yet she had known too that the father would have no part of being a parent. He had other ambitions and they involved embarking on his own business, not starting a family.

Motherhood had been as unreal as abortion. She had known she was not emotionally ready, much less ready financially, to be a mother, especially a single mother. So she had sought help from a man she looked to as her teacher. A respected man in the community, he was the person who had inspired spiritual yearnings in her, and she had looked up to him for his wealth of experience and knowledge. His answer had been clear and simple. Claire should carry the baby, give birth, and raise it, with or without the father. The pregnancy, he had told her, was a sign of life. Why, he had asked, won't you let life come through you? Claire had been touched by his answer, and when she had protested that she had no way to raise a child, he had promised that he and his wife would help her with the baby, financially and in every other way. Claire had been in a dream. Practical matters, such as how she would support herself with a baby or where they would live, had entered her thoughts only occasionally, in the form of anxiety, and she had felt powerless to create what she would need. Her teacher's words had carried the day. Others, including her parents, had urged her to consider having an abortion, or at least to think of relinquishing the baby for adoption, but she had been too overwhelmed to listen. When she had sought her boyfriend's opinion, his only reaction had been that it was her problem; she should deal with it. As if to make pointed his reluctance to get involved, he had consulted a lawyer, who had told him that if he moved out of the house he shared with

Claire and another friend, he could effectively deny paternity. Finally he had been so uncaring that Claire had simply left.

All during her pregnancy Claire had thought seriously and often of relinquishing the baby for adoption. She had not imagined how she could be a good enough mother alone, without any resources of her own. Yet she had felt she could not survive the wrench of relinquishing her baby, and adoption had thus never been a real option. Friends had continued to see Claire as having tremendous inner strength. But her own self-image had been far more fragile. Motherhood had been her only choice, because she had known she was not mature enough to make the decision for anything else. And she had felt alone and unsupported as she faced it.

So Claire had become a mother. She had had an uncomplicated birth at home with a midwife and several women helping her. Labor had been so quick it had hardly given her time to prepare emotionally for the baby who was placed wet in her arms. Then suddenly she had found herself truly alone, more alone than she'd ever been, living round the clock with a new baby, the only one to meet her continual needs, twenty-four hours a day, day in, day out. When she had turned, in her unhappiness and hopelessness, to friends and family for help, a bit of babysitting, some conversation, money to help make the rent payment, they had all kept their distance. She had been no fun to be around. What Claire had needed to raise her spirits and help her handle things had been daily help to share in the care of this new life. And she had found precious little. The father of the baby had kept his word and carefully avoided both her and the baby. Claire had been driven to establish his paternity legally; there had been no doubt about his ability to help her financially, and she had desperately needed that help. She had begun receiving some child support. Despite his promises her spiritual teacher had never offered a bit of help, even after she had gone so far as to ask for it; he had simply brushed the matter off, as if the whole thing had all been some sort of joke and she was learning the lessons she needed to learn.

Now Claire's little girl, Lisa, was bigger. She had crept,

then she had walked, and now she could run. And like most children, who were eager to discover what lay beyond their mothers' arms, she took off in any direction as fast as her chubby legs could carry her. Claire did her very best to stay calm and treat Lisa lovingly even when her nerves were raw, but day-to-day reality wore her out. She could not gain any perspective on their relationship as mother and daughter, and it was increasingly impossible for Claire to have any life of her own. As she told Alexandra that afternoon in the park, her every waking hour was occupied by a tiny human being whose will seemed stronger than her own, whose energy depleted every bit of hers, and whose very existence now threatened her own. Eighteen months after giving birth, Claire had not yet accepted her status as a mother. She felt inseparably connected to this child she'd borne, yet hated the reality of that connection; though she never wanted to harm Lisa, she often felt like running away from her.

Claire and Alexandra immediately realized their kinship. They were both women in need of comforting. But Alexandra at this point appeared the more fortunate, because at least she had no one dependent on her, no one whom she might hurt out of her own pain. The entire time Claire talked, holding Alexandra's hand and crying, Alexandra kept an eye on the little girl. She sped around the park as if on wheels, first lighting on someone's lap, then suddenly darting to the edge of the busy street. More than once Alexandra interrupted Claire to go rescue Lisa. Claire seemed to veer from complete inattentiveness to sudden anxious concern for Lisa. She was desperate for the attention Alexandra offered, even at the expense of Lisa's safety. She told Alexandra she hated her life. There was never enough money to take care of the two of them, and she was so worried and frightened she couldn't find any enjoyment in being a mother. She asked Alexandra to come over that evening, sensing that they shared some deep understanding.

That evening Alexandra went to Claire's apartment and

saw more of what she'd seen in the park. Lisa was overtired, running out of control, and her mother was at her wit's end and exhausted. The bedtime ritual was the worst. First she demanded Lisa stop playing and come to her to get ready for bed. When Lisa ignored her, Claire turned to Alexandra and began to talk about herself. Then suddenly, remembering her daughter, she rushed to where Lisa was playing and grabbed her arm. As soon as Claire touched her, she burst out crying. Lisa's tears seemed only to frustrate Claire more. Wasn't damage being done? Wasn't violence being communicated in every word and each touch? Several times Alexandra went over to the crying child and picked her up. Her arms ached to hold her own son, and the feelings of loss welled up until she thought she would have to run out of the house and see and hear no more. Yet she could not pretend that she might not have acted like Claire were she too a single mother. Part of what held Alexandra there was the recognition that she was being given a glimpse into the future she might have had.

As she held the crying child and attempted at the same time to comfort and reassure the troubled mother, she was frightened. The friends who had admired Claire as a model of motherhood's endurance must have seen the tremendous effort, but ignored the anguish and the sadness Claire felt. Out of the sight of friends and the rest of the world, this well-intentioned, caring young woman was not so quietly going mad. Only rigid self-control enabled her to provide for the most basic needs of her child. But self-control was not enough in the face of overwhelming pressure. The stresses were tearing Claire apart.

It sent a chill over Alexandra when, during the evening, Claire told her, "I wish sometimes I had done what you did. I envy you your freedom. Sometimes, even now, I think I'll *have* to give her up for adoption." Alexandra returned home shaken. Only once in her life had she experienced what Claire seemed to be feeling often, that she was completely out of control. That had been right after Christopher's departure, when she had stood in the driveway watching the couple drive away with him. Then she had felt it, that black, swirling void sucking her down into its depths. She had thought at the time she had been going crazy, but she'd managed to hang on to one slender thread of hope—that those terrifying feelings had been partly a result of her exhaustion and lack of sleep. For her, madness had been a temporary feeling. But she had had no child needing her each day, needing and demanding from her when she had had nothing left inside from which to give. Although this woman felt trapped and was turning into a twisted version of herself, filled with self-loathing and sorrow, Alexandra had been granted a second chance. She could only feel sad for her friend and for the suffering of Lisa.

The following Monday Alexandra stood in my kitchen talking. Her own doubts were again eating at her. She wasn't sleeping well. In the absence of any communication from either the parents or their lawyer, and after his strong insistence that she not press them, it was becoming difficult even to recall what she had first found in them that had caused her to select them for her baby. She remembered they had not believed in private, open adoption in the first place. Their sole desire had been to get a baby any way they could short of buying one. And she'd begun to ask herself whether the way they were treating her was indicative of the way they would raise her son. She didn't want him raised in fear and mistrust of every new thing.

I had one suggestion. Perhaps if she could talk with a couple who had adopted through private adoption, tell *them* her feelings, and hear from them what it was like to be on the adopting side, she might understand better what was going on. I called Paul and Vicki, the parents of Amanda and Abigail, and asked if they would meet with Alexandra. She spent most of the following afternoon with them at their home. Paul and Vicki recalled for Alexandra quite vividly what they had felt during their first months with each of the girls. They had several thoughts that hadn't occurred to any of Alexandra's friends. First, they said, she should remember that this couple were new parents. On top of all the anxieties involved with the adoption and the feeling of being in limbo until the final papers were signed, they had the countless nameless anxieties that beset new parents. Vicki could recall the apprehension with which she had viewed the prospect of any interaction with Pat, Abigail's birth mother, after Abigail's birth. Although she'd told Pat she was welcome to call, even visit to see that Abby was well and well loved, she had not been prepared for any more contact, not at first. She said this had been even more true when they had first gotten Amanda, their older daughter. Feelings of possessiveness had run strongest during the early months. Looking back now, from a distance of several years, Vicki said she would feel quite comfortable if either birth mother were to knock on her door tomorrow. She could welcome her because she was today secure as a mother. But that hadn't been so in the beginning. For Vicki, private adoption and being present at the baby's birth had at first seemed odd. She had probably shared the rather conservative upbringing that Christopher's new parents seemed to have had. She was able to bring a reality about Christopher's life to Alexandra where previously there had been none. Vicki and Paul suggested that Alexandra's impressions of the couple before the birth were likely to prove true in the long run. The ungracious behavior she was now experiencing was, in Vicki's eyes, likely to be short-lived and *not* a predictor of Christopher's future.

Tony and Ellen fulfilled Alexandra's most important criterion, that they be able to love and care for a child. Should she be faced with the same decision all over again, Alexandra now knew she would have additional criteria for prospective parents to meet. She might try to find people more like her in their view of the world and in their style of life. But though this couple was not of her world, they were good people and they loved Christopher. Alexandra returned home with her mind untroubled for the first time in weeks.

A large piece of grief seemed to dissolve that day. Alexandra was beginning to release Christopher. There would be more; but she felt relieved that a massive weight was now gone. The smell in the air meant summer was passing. Her daily walks could be at a brisker pace now that her body was getting back its strength. The stretch marks left behind from pregnancy on her thighs and abdomen would eventually fade. She could almost, but not quite, zip up her old blue jeans. She'd bought new ones anyway, one size larger, and was rather enjoying this new body of hers. She was no longer a ninety-seven-pound girl, but a woman, with a body that bore some scars of living.

With the small amount of assistance promised her by the attorney still nowhere in sight, she resolved to make one more call to New York, even though it made her feel cheap. His secretary said he was out of town for the afternoon and made a promise to see that the money was wired to her bank as soon as he returned. The money arrived the next day.

Alexandra took a train to see her parents. She enjoyed the train ride to Utah, the hours of nothing to do but watch the landscape slide by her window, the chance to be a traveler. Her father had offered her the use of his small studio outside of town, and she was glad she would have it all to herself for the short time she was to be there. Eight months ago this train ride had been the scene of the biggest decision of her life. Now, lulled by the train's motion, she thought about Christopher's father. It had been almost a full year since they'd slept together. She no longer remembered clearly what he looked like. But she still had a cycle to complete with him, and she told herself she'd try to contact him when she returned. She knew he felt some self-pity, some guilt. He had missed out on everything. She wasn't sure how she would feel seeing him again, but it was something she had to do. They would sign the final adoption papers together. That would be the end of it. And next month she would enroll in school and start work on becoming a writer.

I met her at the station when she returned. Standing with hunched shoulders, looking bewildered in the crowd, and much, much thinner than I'd seen her, Alexandra seemed a child lost. When she saw me she smiled quickly in relief. In the car we rolled up all the windows to shut out the noise of traffic and the city heat. Her shoulders sank back against the seat. It had been a good visit, she said; it had given her the rest and solitude she had needed. But she was so glad to be back.

The first few days were a difficult readjustment. Her roommate, Linda, was in love; and her work kept her away from home till late every night. Often she didn't come home until after Alexandra was asleep, and when they did cross paths, Linda had little energy left over to give her best friend. Linda's happiness only underscored Alexandra's sadness. But she was determined to get back into life. In the next week, visiting the coffee shop, browsing in the bookstore, shopping for food, she renewed old acquaintances and made new ones. She was thin and pale, but her face could always light up in conversation. Men found her attractive. Several asked her out. She went once or twice, but felt distant and awkward. She wasn't ready, she told herself.

Standing sideways in front of a long mirror, she examined her fading stretch marks and her bloated abdomen. She still had not resumed her periods. And she was feeling guilty that she hadn't thought about Christopher in two whole days. He was drifting away from her. Even the birth was fading in vividness. Would she soon have nothing left? Yet, she fretted, she didn't want to spend her life carrying a dead memory, never starting a new relationship, not daring to risk for fear of losing. In a way she found the grieving more difficult now than ever, because now she could and had to function in daily life. She knew she had to look for work before she could afford to enroll in school. Yet she was so distracted. She was forgetting appointments, standing up friends for dates. What job could she hold?

She made a phone call one evening to the roommate of Christopher's father, to ask if he knew when he would be returning. To her shock she found out that he was back in town, and he had been for more than a month; but he wasn't in just then. The next few nights she couldn't sleep, just lay in her bed going over and over the events of the past year. She knew that he knew where to reach her; yet he had never bothered.

And so she called him. The anger welled up inside her when she heard the familiar voice on the line, and then dissolved, and she found herself eager to see him. He was friendly enough and they made a date to see each other. She told her friends she was doing it for Christopher's sake. Christopher deserved to have his father know as much about him as possible. She admitted she had hopes that he would become interested in his son after hearing about the birth. She would share the pictures with him. If he only cared, then he might stay in touch with the attorney in New York, keep a current address. For Christopher's sake.

But it was for her sake too that she would see him. I saw her the morning of their planned meeting. She'd dressed with care and looked lovely, though frail, in a blue jean skirt and embroidered Mexican blouse. Looking at her, who would have guessed how big her abdomen had been only two months earlier? She was feeling as if her heart were stuck in her throat. If only the sound of his voice had brought the old feelings of excitement back, what would it be like being with him again? She carried the pictures from the birth with her to their meeting.

I spoke to her that evening on the phone. She was still in a state of excitement, but felt disappointment too. He'd looked just as he had when she had last seen him. She'd felt the pull immediately. She didn't know whether he'd felt it too; but he certainly hadn't felt it for his son. She'd hoped her description of Christopher, the pictures of the birth would bring him alive to his father. They hadn't. He had reacted no differently from anyone else who hadn't been there. Except her parents. Her father had been visibly overwhelmed when she'd shown the photos to him, and her mother had cried. But her parents had seen in the small images their daughter and their grandson—their only grandchild, lost to them.

As for Christopher's father, Alexandra said, he'd seemed aloof and distant looking at the pictures. She tried to control the disappointment in her voice. Why should a dozen squares of shiny colored paper kindle deep feelings? To him, nothing at all had happened in the months he'd been gone. How could he really think or feel otherwise, when she sat across from him looking exactly as she had when he'd last seen her? She hadn't shown him the stretch marks. Anyway, she excused him, he had his life all mapped out. Being a political activist, working for the good of humanity, he'd mapped his life out long before he'd graduated from Harvard or met Alexandra. He didn't want to take any detours. A man, whose body wasn't touched by bearing a child, he had the luxury of not having to take any detours.

It was, she said, as if everything she had done this past year, carrying and bearing Christopher, choosing a home for him, was all somehow trivial when compared with what he had seen while working in Latin America: revolution, tortured children, death on the streets. He had told her a bit about it, about how he'd been part of a national literacy campaign to give peasants power and the vote, and asked her to try to imagine what it felt like to see a sixty-year-old man sitting alongside a fourteen-year-old boy who was teaching him to read for the very first time. He'd seen his efforts bring hope into that man's eyes. Alexandra's admiration for his principles was clear. *His* cause was noble, his vision inspired. But what was *she?* Just a woman who had given birth, a woman who had never known real poverty or ill health, whose belly would never go empty. She had told him what it had felt like when she had given birth, the overwhelming love she'd had, the realization that she would gladly have given up her life then for Christopher. His response was a curious remark about how what she'd done had been socialism in its purest form. No, Alexandra had bridled: "It's nothing of the sort. It's a mother's love!"

They were worlds apart. All they had been able to do were the practical things: signing the papers, exchanging addresses. He had offered to pay the costs from the pregnancy, half of everything. But Alexandra hadn't taken him seriously, because she had known it was only an idea for him, just a matter of principle.

Eight weeks after the birth, Alexandra had her first period in more than a year. With it came a renewed longing for Christopher and for the intimacy they'd shared, for someone or something to fill up the deep hollow inside her. What followed in the next month was another brief period of enchantment with Christopher's father. Alexandra saw him regularly and he too seemed infatuated with her. They began to show affection, hugs and kisses, walking hand in hand. They talked about Christopher. They went out alone together some evenings, but they never spent the night together. Then he told her he had begun seeing the woman he'd gone with when he was a student at Harvard, before he'd met Alexandra. She continued to see him anyway.

Then one evening at a party she left in his backpack her notebooks and the diary she'd been writing in since the pregnancy began. It seemed a bad omen that he didn't bother to call her about it; but when she called he said he'd like to come over and see her house—he hadn't been inside. They planned a breakfast meeting. Alexandra felt she needed him, for she was hurting badly. But how, she asked herself, could the imbalance of the past year ever be set right, the year of her life she'd given to their son? She knew they could never start a new relationship on the roots of the old, and that Christopher would forever be a shadow between them. Yet she needed something from him, his affection, his consolation.

She had heard nothing lately from the attorney in New York. She'd given up on having any more help with living expenses from the couple, but there were still some medical bills outstanding from the pregnancy that she couldn't pay without their promised contribution. And she was still waiting for the written agreement the attorney had promised to draft, have them sign, and then send on for her signature, an agreement that she would receive a picture and a brief note on Christopher's progress every six months until he turned eighteen.

The attorney had been the one who had suggested it and had told her it would easily be arranged. They would send the picture and the report to him, and he would forward it to her.

She had already signed the adoption papers and needed only to have the biological father sign them before sending them to the attorney. It wasn't yet six months, the legal period she had in which to change her mind, but she knew she never would, no matter what happened. For Christopher's sake. Still, it had occurred to her that as long as she held the papers she had one thing they needed, something to make them keep their agreements with her. She had called the attorney early that week to ask where the agreement was and to remind him, for the third time, that she had yet to see the check to pay the long-overdue bills. She had been getting weekly notices and threats to turn her accounts over to bill collectors. He had sounded stiff and cold over the phone and had asked her whether she was holding on to the adoption papers as leverage. She had hardly been able to answer, she had been so close to tears with frustration and anger.

So the past days had been especially difficult, with Linda still hardly ever at home, and the unpaid lab bills sitting in a pile on her table. She had been unable to eat and now weighed much less than one hundred pounds. She felt too anxious and depressed to cook for herself and asked Christopher's father if he'd please bring over a sandwich when he came.

He arrived to find her standing in the driveway, elated for the first time in weeks. The formal agreement, signed by the couple and binding them to send photos and status reports on Christopher, was in her hand. There was no mention of money for the bills, but this was cause enough to celebrate. They ate and she felt strong enough to confront him about his not having called her to say he had her diary. She said she was sure that if she had not called him he would not have bothered to contact her. Not one to lie when faced with facts, he admitted he probably wouldn't have called her for a while. He apologized, as he always did, and then began talking about his relationship with the other woman he was seeing. Alexandra didn't want to hear the details. She told him all she wanted from him was friendship. Then he signed the adoption papers, and she showed him the pile of overdue notices for lab tests. He wrote a check for two hundred dollars made out to her, and sat with her as she wrote out checks to pay most of the bills.

After he'd gone, Alexandra told Linda she felt as if she had just said a final good-bye. Charming as ever and still immensely attractive to her, he was not what she wanted in a man or as a father for a child. He was too ready to run, too riddled with guilt, too full of his own self-pity, too righteous about his work. Yet she felt he did care, about Christopher as well as her.

She sent off the adoption papers as soon as he had signed them. She began referring to Tony and Ellen in conversation as the parents. She was distancing herself one more step. But the longing for her son continued. Though not ever-present, it was there like a shadow at her shoulder. She seldom cried anymore. She was working again, at a part-time job in a clothing store, and she'd volunteered to be labor support for two single mothers at the birth home. But everyone noticed how pale and thin she was, and she seemed to have a constant cough. People urged her to slow down and take it easy. How? she wondered.

She kept pushing herself to do more. She became closer with Claire and took on the responsibility of a godmother to Lisa, caring for her one evening a week so Claire could go to work as a waitress. She felt that Claire and her daughter were both perhaps a bit calmer for her presence in their lives. Claire had even begun seeing a therapist and was now trying to seek other mothers to spend time with instead of all her friends who had no responsibilities, who couldn't appreciate her needs as a mother. If only she weren't tired all the time Alexandra felt she'd like to do more, for Claire and her daughter and others. Finally, at the suggestion of a friend, she made an appointment to see a doctor. She was shocked but a little relieved to find out that she had pneumonia and would have to rest in bed for at least two weeks.

As the cool coastal winter set in, Alexandra felt her life was at a dead stop. Nothing was working. She had lots of time to think about Christopher now, to go over in detail each of the negative reactions she'd gotten from people whom she'd told about relinquishing Christopher. Not her friends, at least not most of them. But it seemed that the better she had begun to feel about herself and her decision, the more she had drawn criticism for what she'd done. A woman who worked at her physician's office said, behind Alexandra's back, that she found the thought of a woman actually choosing to give away her own child repulsive. She was too discreet to tell Alexandra this to her face, but the word had gotten back to her. A young man at a party had called her decision selfish and had asked her bluntly how she expected to live with herself over the years. Is this what my life will be like from now on? she wondered gloomily. Thinking back to her friend Claire, who despite improvement in her life was still having a very hard time, she wondered whether this was what society would prefer. At least sick in bed she didn't have to face the critical judgments of other people for what she had done. She wished someone had warned her, told her that she would be breaking a great social taboo by relinquishing a child for adoption.

Her mother wrote to say she was coming out in late December to stay for a week and help out. By the time she arrived, Alexandra was out of bed but still feeling physically more exhausted than ever before in her life. And it was like a weight pressing down on her, the cloud of depression that hung over her. She was barely able to speak. She managed to pull herself together for the visit, but it was a painful effort. Her mother fluttered around the house, busily doing and talking, urging Alexandra not to go back to bed. She must have felt her daughter's exhaustion but perhaps not knowing what else to do, she thought she could force Alexandra back to health by keeping her on her feet. When she finally went, after seven hectic days, Alexandra looked like a ghost. She seemed frantic too, pacing around the house, beginning and abruptly ending conversations in a strangely agitated and distracted manner.

Linda drove Alexandra's mother to the airport, and

Alexandra went out for the day to the ocean with her friend Art. She told Linda after she returned that in Art's company and near the sea she had felt normal for the first time in weeks. What she couldn't tell anyone was that she knew the calm wouldn't last. By morning she was in the midst of a full-fledged depression. All she knew, as she made an effort to withdraw from everyone in her world, was that she felt numb and isolated and desperately afraid. The cloud she'd felt around her for weeks had descended again, and she was too exhausted to fight it, too shut down to call for help.

Somehow the Christmas season passed. During the next month she made excuses to keep people from calling her or coming around. She didn't see her brother once, and quietly slipped from view around town. Linda, the one person close to her during all this time, was in the midst of an exciting period in her life, and, though she saw her roommate was feeling bad, she never guessed that this was the worst of times for Alexandra. Having never experienced a deep depression herself, she could not read its signs.

It became a trial to get through each day. Alexandra would sleep late, after lying awake most of the night, and when she would finally manage to push herself out of the bed she would hurl herself into frenzied activity: cleaning the house and recleaning it, washing and ironing everything in sight, and even picking flowers for the house from their garden. In trying to arrange the flowers artistically, she would come to an impasse and start in on a ritual of self-loathing. She couldn't get anything right, not ever! Why bother to try! She was worthless! Then she'd begin to shake violently. Finally she'd fall on her bed and gaze at whatever was on television, unthinking, until she would doze off. She would eat only by forcing herself to, late in the day, and then only food she'd eaten as a child. Milk on cereal. Each night when Linda returned, she would find her roommate sitting bleary-eyed in front of the TV and the house immaculate.

Alexandra began to use the small bottle of prescription

sleeping pills her physician had given her after the birth. She carefully doled out one each night. During the day, alone in the house, she would cry at nothing in particular. She couldn't wait for Linda to leave the house, despite the terror being alone brought; at least then she wouldn't have to make the super-human effort to speak. The weather was continually gray. On the few days the sun came out at all, Alexandra would tell herself she had to get out. But she never did. She didn't think of Christopher much at all during that whole month. The only person she ever called, and that was rarely, was her friend Art. Some years older and always good-natured and low-key, never pressuring her about anything, Art would be a comfort at those times when she'd force herself to phone him. Sometimes, after talking to him, her mood would suddenly shift, and she would be temporarily elated.

Finally, feeling hopeless but unwilling to wait it out any longer, despairing that her life would ever mean anything again, she telephoned me and asked the name of the therapist I'd told her about many months before. I was surprised to find she had been at home all that time. Everyone had assumed she'd been away. I asked if there was anything I could do and encouraged her to phone the therapist. She didn't want to see me but promised she would call the woman I'd suggested, someone I had seen myself and trusted because of her sensitivity when I had been depressed.

When the time came for her appointment, she dragged herself out of the house, propelled more by fear than hope. She was more afraid of not going than of meeting this stranger, afraid that what she was experiencing would never end. No one in her family had *ever* gone outside to ask for help, had *ever* admitted a professional into his or her personal emotional problems. But Alexandra found herself able to talk with the therapist rather easily. She felt well enough after the visit to call her brother and make plans to go to the city for the evening. They went out the next day and had dinner at a restaurant and even went dancing. They didn't get home till the middle of the night. Tom went back to his house but Alexandra couldn't sleep.

Late the next morning, as she numbly followed her daily ritual and struggled to arrange the flowers just right, suddenly she felt a large black hole open up just in front of where she stood. Terrified, she staggered to bed, feeling utterly alone. She told herself this was what it was to go mad. She couldn't cry and so, in desperation, she began talking out loud to herself as a mother would. Over and over she said, "It's okay, baby. It's okay." The past month had been bleak enough to bring her to the point of thinking about suicide. But at that moment the idea of death was even more frightening than the hell in which she was living.

She thought of her friend Art and reached out to call him. She described in a few halting sentences the terror, and Art said he'd be right over. Alexandra suddenly remembered she was expecting Claire's little girl for the evening. It was Friday and, as she'd been doing every Friday, except when she had been in bed with pneumonia, she cared for her while Claire went to her job. She hadn't looked forward to those evenings for many weeks now, but the weekly visits brought her a certain renewed strength and confidence that she could maintain some semblance of normality in her life. So she asked Art not to come over until later, after she'd put the little girl to bed. While she was taking care of her she was able to forget herself and her problems, because the child needed all of her attention.

When he came she tried to explain what was happening inside her. He listened quietly and held her as if she were his child. She asked him please to stay with her, and he did, holding her close throughout the long night. She was able to cry and in time the dread passed and she slept.

Alexandra stopped going to her job, stopped answering her phone, and coped with her despair as best she could. She took herself to the next visit with the therapist and found once more that she was able to talk. The terrors, as she referred to them later, returned only three times that week. Another hour with the therapist, another week at home, and this time the black hole came only once. This time it felt almost like a cleansing when it ended.

Her weekly visits were now of real help, islands in a dead sea of depression. The therapist was willing to defer payment until Alexandra was back working, and she clung to the hope of each visit, knowing that the kind of work she did there brought blessed relief. She no longer turned to the sleeping pills and was sleeping more regularly. Her moods now seesawed sharply between bleak terror, when she felt cut off from the world, and sunny elation, when she felt a sense of connection with all of life. Slowly she began to talk to Linda and Art about what she was going through. The feeling of helpless terror came less and less and stayed shorter times. Although she was still depressed, she realized one morning that she hadn't felt desperate in more than a week. Her therapist suggested she should not consider this the end of those feelings, because they came from deep within herself, not from somewhere outside, but that she might try, when she was feeling good, to call the dread feelings up and spend a brief period of time with them while she was feeling safe and secure. This way she might begin slowly to become acquainted with a part of herself she didn't know and would also be less panicked when the feelings caught her unaware in the future. Her experience with Christopher had opened her and made her acutely sensitive and vulnerable, and it would be a long time before she could integrate the meaning of it all into her life.

And so, after six weeks, Alexandra found herself climbing back out of the blackness into which she'd slipped. She continued to see the therapist for several more visits until, with no prospect of being able to pay, she stopped. But she vowed she would seek more help in therapy when she could afford it and that she would never, never let herself feel so alone again.

The end of the first year found her back in close contact with her brother and her parents. After she wrote her father a long letter describing some of what it had been like for her being pregnant, giving birth the way she had, and then relinquishing her baby, he called to say that he had lived in private agony all those months, knowing what she must have been going through and yet also knowing there had been no way he could protect her from it. He admitted that he too had had terrible depressions and had hid them from everyone and had felt all the more alone for it! Their shared experience gave her and her father a new understanding and feeling for each other, and that was a gift.

She spent the first anniversary of Christopher's birth at the birth home with most of the friends who had been with her in labor. We held a surprise party in her honor and shared a meal out on the patio. Then Alexandra went back to the room where she had given birth and lain with Christopher, and she spent a few private moments in memory. She had heard nothing from Christopher's parents or the attorney since she had signed the adoption agreement, and had not received a word about her son, and this continued to trouble her. Some of her friends encouraged her to contact the attorney once more and if necessary to get her own attorney, someone who would pursue her right to know how he was doing, according to the agreement the parents had signed with her.

Unable to believe the couple and the attorney would willfully break a written commitment, she continued to wait, past the time when the second progress report and picture were due. Finally, at the end of August, she dialed the familiar number in New York City. The attorney was out of town, his secretary told her. Alexandra left a strongly worded message that suggested she might have to take legal action; but she never followed up on the threat and she never heard from the attorney again.

Does she regret her choice of parents or think of herself as Christopher's real mother? No. "*They* are his parents now," she can say. "They've really been his parents since the day I gave him to them." And, she admits, were she to examine her own two parents with the same strict criteria she had judged the adoptive parents of her son, her own parents could be found lacking too. The couple she chose have done their best, considering their fear of her.

Today she feels that any woman who chooses the adoptive

parents for her child has a responsibility not only to find a good and loving home for her child, but to find a solution that meets *her* needs as well. She really ought to make the decision on two different counts: finding people she trusts will give her child what she would have given him or her if she had been able, and also finding people who will treat her fairly and with compassion. Alexandra feels she made a wise choice about a couple who would love and care well for her son. As a woman attempting to do something extraordinary in the way of adoption and who had no models to follow to help her through the process, she did the best she could. And that is what she will have to live with.

ALEXANDRA:

Living Through,
Working It Out

Alexandra returned to her hometown in Utah in September, at the age of twenty-two, intending to stay only until she had sorted things out. After she'd been at her mother's house a few months, she went off to the tiny mountain cabin she had used once before as a retreat. She wanted to write and needed its solitude. While there she assessed her life. She wanted to go to college and study literature, but there was no money. She would have to work for a while first. When she went back to the city, she discovered her own city college, in Salt Lake City, had a fine literature department. She could go there at almost no cost. Shortly after enrolling she called her first boyfriend, who had been the love of her life when she was seventeen. They had always stayed in touch, and he had remained close to her family over the years. Her reunion with him seemed an act of grace, for the feelings they had once shared were rekindled. They decided to live together.

The next eighteen months were uneventful, except for a feeling of sweet happiness. Normally a serious, intense, and high-strung young woman, Alexandra felt as if she were on an extended vacation, carefree. The relationship was nurturing, though she sensed it was not going to be lasting. Slowly the easy sweetness dissolved, and, without any great upheaval between them, they grew and drifted apart. Alexandra took up living on her own once more.

It was at that time she came through my town, Palo Alto, in California, on a visit to see old friends. She called me and we spent an afternoon together. I had forgotten Alexandra's petiteness. The size of her energy had always made me remember her as larger. We chatted about our current lives and loves, and I asked if we could talk about Christopher. She said yes. Looking back at her relinquishment from the distance of two and a half years, Alexandra said there were things she knew she had done well, that knowing that gave her a feeling of satisfaction.

"I knew my decision to have Christopher adopted was right. No one forced me to do anything. I was able to find a way to make at least the end of my pregnancy special and to love it; and I was able to have a really good birth. I had people around me, in pregnancy and birth and afterward, who I knew loved me. I met new people, involved in birth, who shared the excitement of it with me. They are now a part of my life, and I only wish I'd met them sooner. The transition of Christopher from me to his adoptive parents went well. It was what I wanted. When I look at how far I came, all by myself—from where I had started in the dark, from all my fears of birth— it's incredible!"

We promised to stay in touch, but it was several more years before I saw Alexandra again. And when I did much had changed. After she had begun living on her own in Salt Lake City, she entered a period of dating men at her college and became involved in various drama projects. She spent a lot of time in cafés in intense conversation about ideas and the world. Lots of things got started, but nothing seemed to get finished. Then, suddenly, she found herself in love with two men who were friends of each other.

She described that period as one of feeling "weightless and

powerful at the same time, powerful in the sense of freedom and lack of commitment to anyone or anything." She was drifting, but it felt good. "Having been able to let go of Christopher, I felt I could let go of anything without fear or regret. The idea of commitment or settling down, with anyone or anything, never entered into my thoughts." Then, in March of that year, at the age of twenty-five, her world collapsed.

"I was walking home from school one evening after going to a play and then to the gym to lift weights. It didn't occur to me to ask anyone for a ride. I was in the best physical shape I'd ever been in and feeling indestructible." Less than three blocks from the home she was sharing with two women friends, she saw a car slowly pass on the cross street. "I watched it. I was always careful at night, alone. I was in a densely packed residential neighborhood." She saw the car park halfway down the block and kept walking. "At the next corner I heard footsteps running behind me. My first thought was that it was a jogger. Then I realized the shoes sounded too heavy. Perhaps it was a friend trying to catch up with me."

The next thing she knew, she was grabbed from behind by a large man and hit alongside the head. "He pulled me into an empty lot on the corner, under a tree. The street was lit but it was dark there." Once on the ground she had only a quick glimpse of the back of the man's jacket. "I felt myself leave my body and slip behind and above him." That's where she remained during the entire rape. He'd thrown a coat over her head and she knew she must not resist or make a sound. "Later, when he was caught, I found out he had viciously beaten most of his victims after they had made the slightest sign of resistance. He didn't beat me, just bent my arms back up over my head. It was quick and over in minutes." The rapist disappeared after warning her not to get up until she had counted to fifty.

"I felt myself come back into my body, like crashing back to Earth." The sensation of having a body and of its mass surprised her. "It was the first time I remembered feeling that weight of gravity since parting from Christopher." From that moment on she knew everything had changed.

Alexandra is not the only woman I have met who has experienced assault or rape within the first few years after relinquishing a baby. It has happened to a number of birth mothers I have met over the years, usually in the first year or two following the relinquishment. It has been observed, and studies have shown, that women who are pushed into relinquishing a baby often rush into another pregnancy to fill the void. But in the case of these birth mothers who were victims of some sort of violence, they were neither very young nor reckless women, and, perhaps because of those factors, did not get pregnant soon after giving up a baby.

Each of them had made a conscious decision that she was not ready or in a position to meet a child's needs, and was careful to avoid another pregnancy too soon. I have noticed that in almost all cases there had been a closed adoption; the birth mother had been effectively locked out of the child's life.

There seems to be a common thread. In each case, in retrospect, I could sense that the loss of the baby relinquished for adoption had left the woman with a hole, a vital piece of flesh missing. I've thought about the nature of such a hole, for if it does exist it needs to be recognized and named for what it is. I have observed that it can be filled through grieving fully, that new flesh can grow where there was only a vacant cavity. But until that place is filled, during the time the woman is psychologically unprotected, it marks the birth mother as a potential victim for any psychopath who is looking for one, for any accident waiting to happen.

That is a strong statement, and I have thought hard before putting it into print. If it is true, then women who relinquish babies need to be aware of it and take steps to protect themselves during the period in which they are most vulnerable. Society needs to start talking about the nature of the loss that birth mothers experience. Is it different from giving birth to a stillborn baby or having a child die? I think so, because it entails a woman voluntarily giving up a part of her flesh and dreams. Unlike a woman who's lost a child to death, a birth mother almost always questions her very right to grieve. She is made to feel by society that because she has made the choice, she has lost the right to grieve.

When relinquishment is compounded by closed adoption, whether it be private or agency, there is a second crucial loss that comes from being shut out of the child's life and consigned to a place of nonrecognition, of worthlessness. This alone, the need to give birth mothers back their dignity and their legitimacy as mothers, should be strong enough reason to open all adoptions. How else can adoption ever be a positive choice for women to make? Because there is no longer public shaming of single mothers, and it has even become fashionable to keep children and raise them alone, against all odds, there is little incentive for women to consider adoption. Societal opinion about parenting, that anyone can do it, simply deepens the isolation birth mothers feel. And it is, I believe, their profound isolation that makes them so vulnerable.

The wound a birth mother carries, even if she is unaware of it, marks her as a potential victim to anyone sick enough to be looking for someone to hurt. How to heal that wound, fill that void without drawing violence in the interim is a central issue for birth mothers, something that must be recognized and faced in every adoption. Alexandra had no road map to follow in her healing, not even any landmarks. And that made it much harder to do. It has been convenient for society, up until now, not to confront the impact adoption can have on the woman who relinquishes the baby.

In Alexandra's case the idea that the rape was somehow related to the relinquishment did not occur to her initially. At first she could deal only with the trauma of what had just happened. Later she began to look at it in reference to her entire life, all of her reproductive experiences, including the relinquishment of Christopher.

Alexandra was not a person to take refuge in passivity. Being a woman of twenty-five, well acquainted with the American feminist struggles, she took hold of the rope it held out to her. She made it back to her house and called the police. An investigation began. She and her female roommates were so shaken they moved out of their house, and Alexandra moved back to her mother's, taking her closest roommate friend with her. She was determined not to remain a victim. Together she and her friend looked for support within the community. When they saw there was no group dedicated to ending rape in their city, they started one, a group whose first purpose was to raise the consciousness of Salt Lake City citizens to the fact that rape existed there. They began to give talks on campus, met with others who had been raped, and with men and women who were concerned.

They called the group Aware, and one of the first things they did was to publish statistics they had uncovered, which showed that Salt Lake City was not a safe city for women at night, as had been believed. Not only did they find a high incidence of rape, but also a great deal of incest in this purportedly religious city.

To Alexandra this was not really surprising. A community that considered itself deeply religious, but whose religion viewed woman as passive, as helpmate, not equal to man would naturally have a large number of men who took out whatever rage they might harbor on women and girl children.

Her anger was sharply focused and her goals broad. At her instigation the group began to meet with men enrolled in the new local sex offender program, men who had raped or sexually molested women or children, including their own children. And they discovered that they, the survivors of rape, had more in common with the men who perpetrated these crimes than with much of the rest of society. "Almost without exception, we learned that the men had themselves been victims as children. If they hadn't been abused sexually, they had been abused physically—by their own relatives, often their own parents, in their own homes."

For Alexandra that summer of active involvement in the issue of rape was the beginning of her recovery period from the grief she'd been carrying ever since the loss of Christopher. Although she had been through that long period of profound depression after his birth, that in itself had not constituted healing. "This," she said, referring to her political activism, "was the first solid thing I did since Christopher." Doing something concrete that directed her unexpressed feelings brought her new energy and a measure of health.

At the end of the summer she moved into a small place of her own, "just to prove to myself that I could live alone and not be afraid all the time. I *was* afraid all the time, but I did it anyway, just to regain some of the lost innocence that had been taken from me by the rape. Giving Christopher up had been immensely difficult, but it had left me, once the depression had lifted, feeling glad just to be sane and alive."

Though she did not at the time think of it as filling the void, Alexandra then felt drawn to do work to free victims of another form of oppression. She became active in Amnesty International, the international organization to free political prisoners around the world. "I wanted to be of service to others." But for the most part, other than her volunteer work with Amnesty International, her most natural form of self-expression, and also her natural means for healing, was artistic. "I really began to write at the end of that summer of recovery." Helping others was actually easier than writing; writing came slowly.

Her first serious writing effort was a play. That fall she returned to working on a script she had begun prior to the rape, which she titled *The Noon Witch*. The story and its symbolism seemed relevant to what birth mothers experienced in society and needed for their healing.

A community is plagued by a witch, who appears only at the hour of noon, taking a baby each time, which she then eats. At other hours of the day, the witch is an attractive and sensual woman. Any man who makes love with her must lose the child that is born of their union. (The witch never becomes pregnant;

the wives of the men bear the babies.) The witch is actually the reincarnation of an old wise woman–healer, a midwif, and a seer who became reviled by that community in years past when they took up modern ways. She has returned in the guise of a seductress to seek vengeance.

There is only one man in the community who has the capacity to see the witch for all she really is and all she has suffered at the hands of the people. When the one man finally sees her, the witch can then give her love freely; she heals from her wound and no longer wants vengeance.

Tragedy once again befalls her when her lover confides her secret one day to his wife, and they are overheard by a village man, who makes the news public. There is an outcry and talk of putting the witch to death, but this time the women of the community stand up for the wise woman. With her lover acting as her advocate, the women form a ring of protection around her as her lover reasons with the angry men on her behalf and she is saved. She proclaims her love for the people and says good-bye, promising to return one day when they are finally ready for her.

When Alexandra had first begun writing the play, she hadn't seen the connection between the misunderstood woman of power and the mother who had relinquished a child to whom she had given birth. It struck me when she told me the story that bearing a child was a powerful expression of woman's creativity, and that in both their giving of life and in their healing, women have through history often been reviled for their special powers.

The very act of writing seemed to be purging for her. I wondered, By writing a piece of fiction where the witch ends up being understood and protected by other women, was Alexandra trying to show compassion and forgiveness for herself for what she had done in relinquishing her son? The character in the play needs the understanding of other women for her healing to be complete, but it is a man who is the catalyst. Christopher's birth father had given Alexandra *nothing* of what she needed. Neither he nor the adoptive parents nor society had appreciated the nature and extent of Alexandra's courage.

It must be said, in case it is not understood: no woman wants to relinquish her child. To do so requires maturity, for it means recognizing the child's needs as paramount and being willing to accept the pain of relinquishment. For Alexandra, as for every birth mother I've met who did not feel coerced into her decision, relinquishing a child was a sacrifice she made on behalf of her child. The play she wrote seems to speak of her need for acknowledgment, and it shows how important love is for healing. In addition, it speaks directly to the need for women to support each other in the difficult personal decisions they each must make regarding their capacity to bear children.

Around the time she completed the play, Alexandra said, she began to sense that another step in her process of healing from being cut off from Christopher would be to form an intimate relationship with another adult. Up until then that had not been what she wanted, and the men she had attracted had offered only superficial relationships. Things began to change without her making any forced effort, as so often happens when inner growth occurs. Alexandra said, "The two men I had been seeing dropped out of my life, once I realized it was a solid relationship I needed to create. They had loved me for my carefree side, the part of me that didn't want to commit myself." In a very few months she met a man to whom she was deeply attracted. He was older, the divorced father of two young girls. Like her he was an artist.

Within six months they were married. The marriage was not easy. "We spent the next two years in hand-to-hand combat, psychologically at least. Later it was easy to see he was the wrong person for me to have married; but in many ways he was the right person with whom to learn about an intimate relationship. I learned to fight for what I cared about." She hadn't dared to do that since living with her mother. "I was sometimes afraid of the intensity of our love; it often wasn't comfortable, but it held depth." That was what kept her in the marriage.

There had never been much ease in her relationship with her mother, Alexandra said, once she had begun to assert her own independent identity, at about the age of ten. She came to see that the battles she and her mother had had, which had begun as she entered puberty, really had been a result of the need for each of them to separate from the other. "I needed to be seen for who I really was, not as an extension of my mother. When I was pregnant with Christopher, I knew I could not yet allow myself to lose myself in a baby, in being a mother."

Alexandra and her husband stuck it out for two years. "Then he decided that he wanted to move to Europe, to cut ties and be footloose, at the very time in my life when I was finally ready to make roots. He had to go, and I knew I had to stay." Their parting was not friendly, and it felt to Alexandra "inevitable." "We didn't proceed with getting a divorce, and we stayed in close touch over the next year, although we were separated by a continent and a sea."

Coming out of that marriage, which to the world might have looked like failure, to Alexandra felt like success. "I knew then that I could commit myself to a relationship. I also knew I could live alone my entire life. But, no matter what, I would not float anymore!" She entered graduate school missing her husband but happy in all other ways, confident her life would be fine, whatever came.

One day, sitting and studying with a man friend, her eye drifted to another man sitting at another table. "Right at that moment someone else I knew came up and started to talk to me, and the man I'd been looking at suddenly got up and came over to our table. I remember the thought that flashed through my mind: Don't get introduced to him or it's all over!" The man who had caught her eye was a friend of the men she'd been talking with, but no one introduced her. The next day, while she was sitting in a coffee shop alone, the stranger from the night before came in, walked over to Alexandra's table, and introduced himself. A week later they moved in together.

The first year as lovers was full of passion and romance as well as the pragmatic details involved in making a relationship work. "This one didn't have the flavor of something temporary," she said. "Sean was not the temperamental artist I'd always fallen for, and our relationship too was different." Alexandra was still legally married, because her husband didn't feel ready to make the end final, and she didn't feel the need to push him. "Sean and I knew we would marry as soon as my husband was ready for the divorce." Toward the end of their first year together, Alexandra traveled to the East Coast to be with her best friend Linda while Linda awaited the birth of her first child. Linda had been with her during Alexandra's pregnancy with Christopher. She'd been there during the labor and the birth and the depression that had followed.

She stayed with Linda and the new baby a lot longer than she had intended, and when she returned to Utah and to Sean she fell into a depression, reminiscent of the one she'd had following the relinquishment of Christopher. It lasted intermittently for approximately nine months and alternated with bouts of physical illness. For a long time she couldn't imagine what the cause was. "Sean and my relationship was not the problem. In fact, we'd never been better. But I began aching in my bones—for a baby. At the same time I was convinced I'd never have one. I remembered my first boyfriend's sister, who'd also given up a baby, and she had ended up infertile." The thought of what, to many birth mothers, was the ultimate punishment—to be denied a baby when she was finally ready for one—haunted Alexandra.

During those difficult months Sean continued to give his loving support. They even talked a bit about having a baby one day. Alexandra said, "We weren't in a position to have a child that soon, and we made no attempt to either conceive or prevent conception. I hadn't had regular periods in several years and assumed I wasn't fertile." Still the yearning for a baby while being afraid she would be unable to conceive continued. With it came a sense of shame. "It was the feeling that I had to pay dearly for what I'd done. I don't know, was it guilt?"

In the previous six years Alexandra had had intermittent thoughts of her son. "Mostly I imagined him well and happy, and felt amazed that I did not feel attached or in great pain each time I thought about him. I reviewed what I'd done, and I always felt the decision had been the right one." Yet the depression kept recurring.

Then in February, while Alexandra was on a speaking trip for Amnesty International, the eighteen-month-old daughter of her dear friends who ran the local branch of the organization suddenly died. She had an undiagnosed case of meningitis and, without warning, had a seizure in front of her parents and never regained consciousness. Alexandra and Sean had seen the child and her parents often since her birth. The news was shattering. "I had not felt pain like that since Christopher, and I cried for days." She began to relive the memories of her pregnancy with Christopher, his birth, and the few hours she'd had with him. A week later another incident brought shock and opened her old wound still further. It began with a call from a woman she didn't know.

The woman, whose name was Jackie, and Alexandra had a mutual friend, and the woman had heard from her that Alexandra had relinquished a baby for adoption. She was doing a research paper for nursing school on the subject of adoption, and was interviewing birth mothers and adoptive parents for their experiences. In the course of introducing herself over the phone, Jackie began to talk about herself. The impetus for choosing this particular subject had been personal—her need to understand more about adoption and its impact on the children. Her twenty-year-old son, whom she had adopted at birth, had recently committed suicide.

Alexandra listened carefully to Jackie's story. "She told me of the terrible emptiness her son had always said he'd felt. He had searched for his birth mother, and had found her in another state, but she had been indifferent to him. They'd met only once and he had been able to tell she had no desire to see him again.

He had killed himself shortly after that, first phoning Jackie to say she had to let go of him. She told me she had sensed what was coming and had felt helpless to prevent it." Jackie told Alexandra there had been other troubles in her son's life besides a lifelong feeling of emptiness. His adoptive father had been harsh and unloving. That had reinforced the young man's feeling of worthlessness. With the lack of social understanding and support for the special needs of adopted children, this mother had simply done her best. She had never sought help for her son. She hadn't realized the extent of his need until he had begun to talk about it as he had gotten close to finishing high school and leaving home. As a mother she blamed herself for what was actually an entire society's ignorance and denial.

Alexandra arranged to meet Jackie and share her story with her. "I had never talked about Christopher and my experience in such intimate detail. It opened up grief and also healing." Alexandra was the eighth birth mother Jackie had interviewed, and, without exception, all of them were having trouble getting pregnant with another child. "The women had put their lives on hold after the relinquishment and had taken care of none of the things they'd told themselves they needed to, the things that were the reasons they'd had for giving up the child. They'd stopped themselves the way I had for so long."

Alexandra talked about the fear and shame that had surfaced along with her newfound stable relationship. "Now that my life was at last together, I would be charged with my crime and made to pay by not being allowed to bear another child." She hadn't had a period in five months and the sudden opening up of the wound about Christopher left her feeling especially vulnerable.

Within days after her meeting with Jackie, Sean left town for a month of work. "I began having what seemed like intense premenstrual syndrome: swelling, excessive hunger, great fatigue, swollen breasts." After several weeks of this, Alexandra went to a doctor and learned that she was pregnant. She flew out to join Sean, overwhelmed with the news. They both had to adjust to the news. "Sean went through a difficult period, knowing he was going to be a father a bit sooner than he'd planned." It took a few months before he could share the joy Alexandra felt from the beginning, despite her physical discomfort. And Alexandra's own joy at finding she was able to conceive after all was mixed with a sense that it had happened too soon.

The first four months of pregnancy she was nauseated continually, but she continued in school, writing poetry and papers for classes right up until Christmas. The written notice that her divorce was final came in the mail just before New Year's. Alexandra and Sean talked about a summer wedding. On January 2 Alexandra gave birth to another son. They named him Keir.

The birth of Keir was more difficult for Alexandra than Christopher's had been, but then this new baby weighed ten pounds, where Christopher had weighed only eight and a half pounds, and Alexandra was a small woman with narrow hips and a narrow pelvis. Keir's shoulders got stuck coming out, and the midwife and Alexandra had to work hard to get him born. All turned out well, except that Keir got quite jaundiced, and Alexandra couldn't sleep from the excitement.

Three days after the birth, the day when a woman is in the middle of her postpartum hormonal letdown, when Alexandra was crying at seemingly nothing, Keir had to be taken back to the hospital for a checkup. The baby's skin was too yellow, a sign that there was an excessive breakdown of red blood cells. Having the baby taken from her side brought back the memories of Christopher. "I stayed home and let Sean take him, but I went crazy until they returned. And it took half a day!" No sooner had Sean walked in the house, carrying their son in his arms, than the lab called to say that the bilirubin count (which measured the degree of the jaundice) was so high the baby would have to go into the hospital for a few days.

"So far," said Alexandra, "I had avoided all standard hospital care." The birth had been in a special hospital birthing room where Alexandra had felt in charge of her own process. She had not wanted her newborn son to be handled and cared for by strangers, poked with needles, left to cry in a nursery. "I took him in expecting to stay with him and was told not only could I not stay, but that I couldn't breastfeed him either! They said it would only make the jaundice worse! I had to scrub and put on a hospital gown just to hold him, and I had to feed him from a bottle. My breasts swelled so much they became like rocks, excruciatingly painful."

The baby came home three days later, but in the meantime Alexandra had not been able to sleep at all, even with the aid of medication. "I was near collapse. But once he was home, everything began to calm down." Alexandra's mother and her mother-in-law came to stay and help, and within six weeks Alexandra felt pretty much back to normal, her old active self. Breastfeeding tired her, but the baby was thriving, and she felt secure and content.

She had thought she would go right back to school after the birth, but after Keir had come down with several colds during his first months, Alexandra realized she would have to slow down and stay home full time.

I heard from Alexandra when Keir was five months old. She was having sharp ups and downs of mood, was almost continually exhausted, and was finding the adjustment to motherhood difficult. As always, she had given a lot of thought to what might be going on under the surface. "I think two things are at root," she told me over the phone, as Keir lay asleep in her arms after nursing. "The deep and not entirely resolved pain from the loss of Christopher and from the rape, and the recognition that I was not really fully prepared to be a mother. If I had not had the desperate need to become pregnant right after beginning this relationship, I might have waited several more years. I don't think I had found quite enough of myself yet to be able to give myself up to mothering with ease."

Just then the loss of Christopher felt greater than ever. "It is in direct proportion," she said, "to the depth of my love for Keir. And yet," she added, "I couldn't have done it differently." She had learned what it took to be a good mother. "It has been like living in a warm bath of undifferentiated connection and interdependence. It's hard to tell where my baby ends and I begin."

I have heard from Alexandra several times since then. We spoke for a long time when Keir was nearly a year old. I had to get her current address from her mother, because Alexandra and Sean had precipitously moved to Nova Scotia when Sean had been offered work there. When I called their new home, I found Alexandra feeling isolated and exhausted, a new mother in a strange city, having to adjust to such a long move and starting all over. On top of all that she was ill, and had been on and off for months. Her weight, she said, which she'd always had trouble keeping in the normal range, had dropped down to ninety pounds, as low as it had been during her depression after Christopher's birth. She was glad to hear from me, and we talked about the kinds of things she could do short of taking yet another antibiotic.

I was concerned and told her so. She had fallen into a bad downward cycle, and somehow, in the midst of the stresses of her current life, had to break that cycle. Her postpartum year had been so difficult, she had gone through so much: it didn't seem fair.

Alexandra's mother was even more worried about her. From the moment Alexandra had become pregnant, she had been supportive of whatever her daughter chose to do. During the pregnancy she had been unstinting in that support. Alexandra and her husband both had been in school full time and living on very little; she had often prepared meals and taken them to their apartment, so they could get on with studying. Her relationship with Alexandra had blossomed. "She shared her memories of what it had been like for her to be pregnant with my brother and me and what motherhood had been like. She has a crippling form of arthritis, and during the time when I was pregnant, she underwent a series of risky treatments, which seem to have helped, in the hopes that she might regain full mobility and be able to participate actively in the life of her grandchild."

When the baby had arrived and Alexandra had begun having one illness after another, her mother was constantly available and took on the care of her daughter and her grandson while Sean was busy trying to finish his doctorate. Then Sean and Alexandra had moved to Nova Scotia. Alexandra was still not well, and her mother could only phone and write and send packages.

First things actually grew worse than they had been when I first spoke to her. Her husband was suddenly informed that he had to fly to the West Coast for a two-week conference. "I felt I would either crash or somehow find a way to rise out of my problems. I was terrified the days before he left. Keir was still waking up three or four times a night, because he had not adjusted to the move, and I got virtually no sleep. I had lost the ability to sleep; when Keir didn't wake up, I would wake up expecting him to wake up."

Sean's absence forced her to make her own moves, begin trusting her own judgment once more. When I phoned her again, there was a pronounced change in both her outlook and her health. She had located two women to help care for Keir part time, and she had begun to write again. "I could have found help earlier," she said, "but I felt too guilty to let anyone else care for Keir. All year, every time I began to feel happy and healthy, I would get sick again. I think I felt too guilty to be well. Within a few days I went from feeling like I had absolutely no recourse to having a choice of help. It was such a relief, I immediately felt physically stronger!" It would be Keir's first birthday in a few days, and Alexandra told me, "I feel *reborn!*"

I recalled the judgmental words Alexandra's friend Mimi had said to her during the pregnancy with Christopher. She had known Alexandra intended to relinquish the baby for adoption. She had told Alexandra that she would atone for this for the rest of her life. Had Alexandra imprinted those words on her memory, or had she simply absorbed the messages all around her from a society that said, How could you do this thing? What kind of woman are you?

When I asked her what she might do about resolving her relinquishment of Christopher, she said, "I wrote him a long letter in one of my bouts with illness, on the recommendation of a therapist friend who said I needed to communicate with him. She didn't mean I literally had to find him, and I didn't send it. But I am keeping it, and perhaps one day he'll read it. The gist of my message was that I loved him, actively and forever, and that I needed both to let go of him more completely and to make his presence in the world more real to me, by thinking of him, praying for him, and staying in touch with him, rather than blocking him. It's a paradoxical quest," she said, "but the more I feel his presence, the more I can let go of my guilt."

She also wrote in the unsent letter that she hoped the love she carried, distant and unknown as it perhaps was to him, somehow brought her son comfort. She has considered doing something more tangible, such as getting a lawyer and seeing if she can reopen communication with Tony and Ellen, on the strength of the fact that they have broken their agreement with her. "Putting on a disguise and standing outside their house on Long Island just to catch a glimpse of him is another thought I have. But my fear that I would disrupt their lives irrevocably or disrupt mine is what consigns these ideas to the realm of the never to be." She added, "I truly think if I hadn't known the full names of his adoptive parents, where they lived, I would have had a much more difficult time. Knowing that I *could* find him—although I may not choose to do so until he is an adult—has been a great comfort to me!"

Alexandra recently wrote me a long letter. In it she wrote that my telling her story had greatly helped her. "You've captured and remembered many of the events that seem pertinent to my ongoing struggle to live with my choice." She said she hoped her story would help other women. "If one woman can learn that to love and let go means not only to love—and out of that love relinquish her child—but to love herself and let go of guilt, then you will have done a great service." The letter itself was such a thought-provoking statement of a birth mother's views on adoption as it was commonly practiced that I asked if I might print excerpts of it. She said yes.

What I had hoped to see in the years since I gave up my son was a loosening of the strict, artificial guidelines that govern most adoptions. I had hoped to see a more loving way of dealing with birth mothers, their babies, and the couples who long for a chance to be parents. Instead I see a new era of ignorance and the continued oppression of women with regard to their reproductive lives: increasing antiabortion fervor from those who want to force women to bear children, court decisions that go further in the direction of punishing women for making personal decisions about birth control, pregnancy, and birth.

Motherhood plays a devalued role in our society, lending us women neither power nor respect. Because so few of us live and act from the center of our beings, we have our children, many of us, out of turn. We are out of sync with who we are and give into pressure, guilt, and feelings of desperation, and have children when we don't really want to be parents.

Some women give up their children, because they simply know that they got pregnant out of sync with themselves and are unwilling to punish their children with their own unreadiness. Others have some inkling of the complex web of coercion, love, and agony that informs the reproductive lives of most women.

I was one of those. I claimed for myself the right to develop beyond the point of manipulation, to become free and able to choose to bear children or not, or to postpone having a child until I had developed more of my potential as a human being. It just did not seem possible to me to do justice to two nascent lives when my hopes for both my child's life and my own were so great.

Our culture devalues and emotionally abuses women who give up their babies. We are not much kinder to mothers. Reproduction, everything connected with it, is still controlled by forces that most of us barely recognize.

Or, if we do recognize them, it is only on an intellectual level. We are still deeply influenced by the ingrained belief that we are not whole as women if we choose not to bear children or choose to relinquish children.

I entered into the world of sex and reproduction not unfeeling, but programmed to "want" sex and to feel so guilty about having it that using regular birth control was too conscious an act for me to do. When I became pregnant the first time, I had no connection with my own body, denying or not recognizing the growing life within me until it was too late for anything but a traumatic abortion. I didn't have the strength to carry, bear, and then let go of a child, strength that I somehow found within me at the age of twenty-one. I had a will to do penance for an imaginary crime, to punish myself with pregnancy, and, the second time, to set myself up for a lifetime of remembered loss. I vowed after I gave up my son to stop the cycle of self-abuse.

And so the years I had meant to spend creating the one person I could truly own—myself—I spent practicing a different form of self-denial. Although I prayed for and believed that my son was receiving all the nurturing he needed to become a whole person, I refused to nurture myself. This culminated in a burst of awareness, after the rape, that time was rushing me toward an aborted future to match my aborted past.

It is my sincere belief that my desire for a child was a real desire to parent, and that my choice to live with the man who is now my husband was right for me. But panic and depression precipitated my third pregnancy. I was afraid of losing a man who wanted children, afraid a force would punish me by one day denying me the chance to bear a child when I was truly ready. I knew the day would come when I would have an abundance of love to give, a defined self to put at the service of a new life. But I hadn't the patience or clarity to wait for that day.

So, still too soon in many ways, I bore a child. And my love for him is so total that it is in itself sometimes hard to bear. He is the light of my heart. But the past few months of my life have been as difficult as any I've ever lived through, as I've suffered through one severe infection after another. It's impossible to say whether these illnesses that have weakened me are a result of having given up my first son. And I was so uncertain of my ability to be a mother, after years of self-abuse and abuse from others, of overwhelming guilt, that the prospect of caring for my son filled me with terror. Even loving him as I did—and as I loved his brother—would I abandon him? Lose him? Kill him? I was terrified for months that if I were left alone with my child, I would not be able to take care of him. And I feared as well that he would be taken from me by illness, that he would die because of my sins, leaving me devastated, beyond hope.

My time alone with my son since then has proven that I am a kind and loving, if unskilled, mother. And why does no one ever tell us that mothering is a learned and hard-earned skill? But it's safe to say that the Mother in me and the autonomous Me are still in conflict. Especially these past few months, following my husband to new, unchosen places, with no economic leverage and the accompanying sense of powerlessness that that brings, I have had to fight against a feeling of failure. I despair at the realization that I am, in more ways than I care to enumerate, living a repeat of my mother's, my grandmother's lives.

I am often very lonely, as many modern mothers are. That knowledge prevents me from feeling truly alone, but it is a less-than-comforting connection I feel with other mothers: mothers from the past, my own mother, mothers who are isolated at home, mothers who feel emotionally torn at work while their children are in inadequate care elsewhere. All of us are running on empty or on too little. The pressures are the same, and frighteningly similar to what they have always been for women, at least in recent history. We are all working hard, but it isn't enough if the system in which you live saps you.

There are many things I wouldn't change. My sons: the one who lives away from me and in my thoughts and the one with whom I share my daily life. That they are in the world is great, great good. My love for them has opened my soul. And whatever pain I have experienced through loss, attack, illness has awakened me to the pain of others. That is an awareness I would not trade. As my body begins to heal, I can recognize my mistakes and my gains. I am blessed with a good life and a good mind. And if I can't find my way past impediments, external and internal, then I will have to admit they are stronger than I am. I refuse to do that.

For the moment, as I write this, I stop and imagine what I might be like if I had been raised guiltless, able freely to choose my right life. What might I be feeling if I had not had an abortion at seventeen, a relinquishment at twenty-one, a rape at twenty-five? For one moment I feel the surge of that life I might have led, and I know I must live now with the strength of will to make up for the strength I might have had if that moment were true. But it isn't. There are things lost that I will never regain. One is the buoyancy, the emotional and physical strength, I once took for granted. I know with certainty I will never bear another child; I am too fragile, too much like a cracked vase that cannot bear certain kinds of pressure. Although this knowledge brings me sadness, I suspect I am also listening to my inner voice, which tells me, You have done enough here.

As for adoption, in a better, saner world no woman would have to conceive in ignorance or unconsciousness. We would not need to abort or give up our children. In such a world, if there were women who truly wanted to carry, to bear children for others, they would be honored most of all! But in the meantime we must begin somewhere, begin everywhere.

I have observed the truth of what this birth mother feels, the sad inevitability that women will continue to be put through needless pain until people change their individual attitudes about their own and others' reproductive issues. Women need to understand and respect the enormous positive effect of being able to tell their stories to those who will truly listen. It dignifies their pain.

In this society people no longer live in tribal units where everyone gathers each night around fires to tell stories and dreams and visions. Children do not grow up with a respect for the spoken word, for the importance of telling and listening to the stories of people's lives. Yet the need still exists, all the more because people live such hectic, fragmented lives and feel so minuscule amidst the vast sea of humanity alive on this planet today.

Obviously it isn't simply the telling of personal stories that brings healing. It is the very process of making whatever choices people are fortunate to be able to make, followed by the ongoing process of living with the consequences of the decisions. Alexandra named it aptly as "my ongoing struggle to live with my choice." Isn't that what all people must do, at every step in their lives? They struggle to make their own choices, and then they struggle to live with all their foreseen and unforeseen consequences. They always live ignorant of what the future will teach them about how naive they were in the past. They can always regret things done or left undone. That is easy. The challenge is for people to have visions of what is possible and what each believes is right, and then to reach for that, to stretch and struggle, and, ultimately, to accept what happens.

For Alexandra, and, I daresay, everyone involved in adoption, the process does not end when the baby changes hands or the papers become final. That is only the beginning; it will unfold until the participants die. If the participants attempt to stay the natural process, it will continue anyway, without their presence. They can either learn to embrace that process or try to erect walls to stop it. That is what people attempt to do in closed adoptions. There may have been a time when, all things considered, closed adoption truly seemed to be the best thing for all involved. That cannot be true today, when people know the impact closed adoption has on the participants' lives. Perhaps the ultimate struggle is threefold: to remain open in the face of pain, to find self-acceptance for past actions, and to be willing to change when that is what is right.

DIANE, EVELYN, AND ARNIE:

A Shared Beginning

IT WAS A SHOCK to Diane to realize that she might be pregnant. She was twenty-three and her life had no real direction yet. Her relationship with her boyfriend of several years had been on again, off again for some time. They no longer lived together. She knew what his response to pregnancy was likely to be. Yet no matter what, she looked forward to being a mother. She had always wanted children.

She knew other mothers who were single. Some had ended up that way in the middle of pregnancy or in the first few months after the baby had come, when the baby's father had decided he wanted out. Many of those mothers were bitter. But Diane also knew a few who had planned their pregnancies, even though they knew they would probably be parenting alone. They were usually in their thirties, unmarried, and with careers, women resigned to the prospect of no stable adult relationship but wanting to have children nevertheless. Thinking about what it would be like having no father sharing the parenting, she was aware that there were others, men and women friends, who would make good aunts and uncles. She was sharing a large house with some of these friends and felt she had a family there;

that made it easier to contemplate raising a child. It never even entered her mind to have an abortion or relinquish the baby for adoption.

From the beginning Diane planned a home birth. She knew of two midwives, Mary and Debbie, who had attended many births together. As soon as she got the confirming test result, she made an appointment to see them, and soon began to feel part of a close circle of women who were all planning home births.

The pregnancy went along smoothly. Except for the fact that her boyfriend reacted as she'd expected he might and mostly stayed away, Diane felt good and strong and glad to be alive. Seeing the midwives for prenatal care meant leisurely visits at their homes, having tea, talking with other pregnant women on the way in and out, taking classes together.

When she was in her fourth month of pregnancy, the size of her abdomen increased considerably between two visits, and one of the midwives mentioned to her that a reason for this could be that she was carrying twins. But twins didn't run in Diane's family or her boyfriend's family, and she laughed at the idea. At the next visit the other midwife examined her and thought for a moment she heard a faint second heartbeat. But it could have been her imagination; they'd wait a bit and see. In June, six months pregnant and very much larger, Diane visited the midwives again. At the door she nearly bumped into a woman who was just leaving. "She must be pregnant too," Diane thought, and scanned the other woman for signs. The two smiled at each other, and Diane asked when she was due. Not for another five months, she was told. They laughed at how big Diane was already and then went their separate ways.

Mary told Diane about the woman she'd just met. Her name was Evelyn, and Mary was worried about her. She had already lost two babies, one in a stillbirth, the other in a miscarriage. And it looked as if she might lose this one early in pregnancy. The baby didn't appear to be growing, and Mary was sending her to a physician for a consultation.

As Mary listened carefully to her abdomen, Diane tried to

imagine what it must be like to lose a baby while carrying it, and felt blessed for having such an easy time. Then Mary looked up, worried. This time she was sure she heard two distinct heartbeats. They looked at each other for a long time in silence. There was nothing to say. Diane went to the phone to make an appointment with a physician for a scan to determine how many babies there really were.

The scan left no doubt. Diane went home to bed. At first there was no thinking, just a numbness over her whole body. Then there was one clear thought behind the numbness. "If I have twins," she whispered to herself, "I will keep only one. I'll give one up for adoption."

The midwives thought it best to give Diane a little time to absorb the news before they talked with her about what it meant. For one thing, everything about the birth would change. There could be no home birth now. But that was nothing compared with the problems facing Diane after the birth, raising two babies as a young single mother. Debbie and Mary would continue to see her through the pregnancy, but they would not be her primary birth attendants. They had no hospital privileges and could arrange to stay with Diane through labor only if the physician agreed to it.

Diane did not want to get up the next morning, or any morning after that. It was as if someone had pulled a plug and all her strength and joy had drained out of her body. There was no caring, no emotion at all. She would feel a sweeping wave of hopelessness and one thought would turn over and over in her mind. How will I make it alone with two babies? From her conscious mind would come the answer. You'll have to give up both of them. Then an immediate response from deep within. I can't! I want to have a baby! I'll keep just one of them. And again her thoughts would answer. No. You can't do that. It's wrong to split up twins. You'll have to give up both of them. When the internal dialogue would end, depression would engulf her. She would hardly be able to get out of bed, much less sit up or call a friend. But she would force herself to sit in meditation every morning after her housemates had gone.

Sometimes she would be able to free her mind of all anxiety, all thought for a brief moment. Just the practice would help. She would ask God to show her the way. No answer would come. Her housemates were considerate and loving and sympathized with Diane's pain, but they had no answers either.

When Diane went for her next visit with Mary and Debbie, she was having a recurring image in her mind, a picture of herself healthy and with one baby. That was what she saw in dreams, and it was what came to her during meditation. She knew what it meant: finding parents for one of the babies. But an adoption was something foreign to her. She couldn't imagine asking an agency to find parents. She would choose the parents for her child herself. She tried the idea out on a few people, of keeping one baby and relinquishing the other. Most of the responses were negative. "How could you even think of separating twins?" She never considered discussing it with her boyfriend. He would be of no help. She had written her mother that she was pregnant when she first found out, and she knew that because her mother had already lost her only son to suicide, she was not going to risk her relationship with Diane by criticizing anything Diane did. Yet Diane did not want to talk to her until she had come to her own decision.

It was to the midwives that she poured out her private anguish. "I'm going to give up both of them." Mary and Debbie looked at each other. Debbie quietly asked Diane whether that was what she really wanted to do. "Oh no," she blurted. "What I really want is to have just one baby!" "Well, then," Debbie said softly, "you've made your decision." "But what will other people think?" They had to remind her that the only person who could make this decision was the person who cared most and who had to live with the consequences: Diane herself. Suddenly Debbie had an idea. There was a couple she and Mary were seeing who wanted very much to adopt a baby. A son had been stillborn, and only a week before the woman had miscarried for the second time. Diane knew immediately whom she must be talking about. Years later she would recall her reaction to Debbie's words. "It was as if my heart opened up, and a big weight flew right out." She begged Debbie and Mary to call Evelyn that day and ask if she and her husband would be interested in meeting her; she left exhilarated and impatient. She didn't have to wait long. Evelyn, sounding very excited, phoned the same day to say yes, she and her husband, Arnie, were interested.

On a Monday afternoon Diane took the bus over to Evelyn's. Arnie was out of town on business. The women remembered each other from their brief encounter, and there was no stiffness between them. They talked excitedly for four hours. Diane couldn't help noticing the lovely home, all the special belongings Evelyn and Arnie had collected in their twelve years together. She liked the way they lived and looked forward to feeling as good about Arnie as she did about Evelyn. They arranged to meet again when he could be there too.

From that day Diane's pregnancy had no cloud over it. She was as drawn to Arnie as she'd hoped she would be; and she and Evelyn began to see each other often, sometimes every week, and to talk on the phone in between visits. Sometimes they met at her house, sometimes at Evelyn's house. It was apparent to Diane from the first meeting that this couple was anxious about the adoption. They had been disappointed in childbearing so often. Their greatest fear, that Diane would change her mind and not give them a baby, was a possible reality, but Diane had a fear of her own: that they would decide not to go through with the adoption. "And what would I do then?"

Talking together freely helped. One of their friends suggested it might be good if they went for joint counseling, and they did, learning to listen for the nuances of one another's feelings and to express their feelings openly. It had always been difficult for Diane to accept her anger. Allowing it to surface, having someone listen to her without judging, really helped. Sometimes she could even laugh afterward. And she was beginning to see that she did not have an obligation to tell everyone she knew about her plans. For her own preotection she became more discriminating.

Evelyn and Arnie were cautious and self-protective too. They postponed setting up a nursery for the baby, even though they had an empty room in their house just waiting to be decorated. They were thinking of Diane as well as of themselves. She could change her mind. They cared about her feelings, and by the end of the pregnancy had begun calling her daily just to chat and see if there was anything they could do for her. Diane appreciated the attention and the two women found a sisterly love growing between them.

Diane's mother was at first shocked. But she soon realized that Diane was doing the best she could, given her circumstances, and she became increasingly supportive. In planning the birth Diane again turned to Mary and Debbie; she was still feeling no inclination to involve her boyfriend, because she saw him hardly at all now. He was still asking for distance, and she felt obliged to give it to him. When now and then she did see him, she would tell him how things were progressing but shared little else. Mostly her time was taken up just living, cooking for herself, swimming, walking, regularly sitting in meditation, seeing or talking to Evelyn or Arnie and the midwives. She talked a lot to the babies, stroking her abdomen in the places where she could feel they lay alongside each other. For several months now she'd noticed how different they seemed. "I know you need extra love and care," she whispered to the one that lay on the right side. She found herself rubbing that side all the more, even as she apologized to the other for neglecting it a bit. "I'm sorry to be spending so much attention on your brother or sister," she'd say. "But I know he or she needs me right now." She told no one about these private conversations, but she always felt the babies were communicating with her, and that she was giving the weaker one strength by focusing extra attention on him or her. Meanwhile, she and Evelyn and Arnie had begun to meditate together and "talk" with the babies, telling them that they would be going to separate homes, that they were loved, and that they needn't worry.

By the last month of pregnancy, Diane knew it was time to move. Although her housemates had been very supportive and were looking forward to helping with the baby, they all had their own busy schedules. And they no longer had the same rhythm that she had. She was slowing down more and more, finding her size cumbersome, and feeling increasingly introspective. She was getting ready for the birth, and she felt she needed to find a quiet place to settle. She began looking in the paper, but housing had never been easy to find, especially for someone on welfare, as she now was. But news spread and it wasn't long before a friend called to say she knew of someone about to move out of an upstairs apartment in a complex of cottages and apartments. Diane went to see it. There were neighbors all around. A few retired people, a few children. Even trees and grass. She felt safe there. The apartment was over a garage. It had one small bedroom, a tiny living room, a bathroom, and a miniature kitchen. When the baby was big, he or she could have the bedroom, but at first they would sleep together. The woman who had the apartment said Diane could move in as soon as she had moved out, in two weeks. That was exactly when Diane was due.

Evelyn and Arnie had offered to pay all of the costs pertaining to the birth. They'd all been to a lawyer together to make sure they were doing everything correctly. It didn't leave much for Diane to worry about; and Evelyn and Arnie seemed more comfortable now too. Knowing her as well as they did by now, they realized how unlikely it was that she would change her mind after the birth. Evelyn and Arnie were to be with her throughout labor. The doctor had agreed that Debbie and Mary could be there too and also Diane's good friend Jan, despite the hospital policy restricting the number of people a woman could have at her birthing. The prospect of labor did not frighten Diane, and the physician continued to assure them that as long as everything continued to go smoothly, she should be able to have an uncomplicated natural delivery. If the babies were of reasonable size, as they seemed to be, and started breathing well on their own, they would not have to go to the nursery at all.

The one part Diane had not attempted to plan for was the

transfer. She'd felt for some time that she was carrying a boy and a girl and had offered Evelyn and Arnie her son if she had one. She trusted the right way to give them the baby would be apparent to all of them when the time came.

Evelyn and Arnie finally painted and decorated their spare room. Twice Diane went to their house and sat with them in the baby's room while they silently focused on this little person who would soon enter their home. Diane moved into her new home in one morning with the help of all her friends. She was too big to do much of anything herself. Though she'd become accustomed to working around the immense belly that stuck out everywhere and now prevented her from bending over, she couldn't wait to have her old body back again. After everyone else had left, she set up the kitchen just the way she wanted it, put away all the baby's things in drawers, and borrowed a neighbor's vacuum cleaner. As she was finishing the last rugs, she felt her first contraction. It came without warning but she knew immediately what it was. That evening, meeting Evelyn and Arnie for one more co-counseling session, she told them she thought she was going into labor. At 2:00 A.M. they received the call. "This is it," Diane said. "Stay calm, but come right over!" They were with her at the apartment for an hour, counting contractions, calling the midwives, the doctor, and Jan, and then they drove her to the hospital.

Labor went as smoothly as had been predicted. The twins lay in easy positions for being born without complication, and they responded well to labor. Debbie, Mary, Jan were all at Diane's side throughout, and Evelyn and Arnie too. It was a normal first labor; but to Diane it felt long and difficult. Contractions often left her brimming with emotion, and she would cry and then feel better afterward. When she was past the first stage and her body was ready to push, she felt her first wave of fear. It expressed itself as fear of pushing. Looking back later, she thought it probably had been the fear of letting them enter the world, where she would then have to relinquish one of them.

Arnie kept leaving the room to stand in front of the

window of the nursery and look at the other babies. Debbie and Mary tried to make sure Evelyn and Arnie didn't get lost in what was taking place; but the couple didn't want to take any attention away from Diane. For her it was a time of supreme closeness to her friends. An anesthesiologist was on call because there were twins, and he came into the room once to explain to Diane what he had to offer her in the way of drugs. At the mention of medication, Diane's first reaction was, "I'll take anything!" But Mary and Debbie reminded her how well she was doing, how she'd wanted a natural birth, and how much better it would be for the babies if there were no drugs or anesthesia. It was not very long before her cervix was open, and she began to feel the need to push. She no longer thought about pain relief. The entire group now moved down the hall into the delivery room. And not very long after, a little girl was born. Holding her in her arms, Diane said quietly, "Thank you, God. I've got my little girl." Evelyn and Arnie knew that the second baby was to be theirs, whatever the sex. Twenty minutes later the baby was born, and Diane turned to them and said, "You've got your little boy."

Each baby weighed six pounds. But Diane had been right in her intuition that one of them might not be as strong as the other. The little boy's placenta, the organ that provided all his nourishment as he grew inside Diane, was almost a pound and a half smaller than his sister's.

Diane has no recollection of being shown her son. She never asked to hold him. Her arms were full with the daughter she named Malia. Evelyn and Arnie followed their son, whom they named Joss, which is Chinese for "luck," to the nursery for examination, because he had swallowed some amniotic fluid with a bit of his own stool in it. They stayed with him through the night and then left with him in the morning.

Suddenly the delivery room was empty. It seemed to Diane she had held her daughter for only an instant before one of the nurses took her away to the nursery for an exam. A different nurse was preparing to move Diane to her maternity room. It all happened so quickly, she did not think to refuse. But the separation from her baby was brief; Mary went over to the nursery to make sure that she was brought right back to her mother.

It was late. The midwives, the doctor, and Jan finally left to go home. As soon as they were gone, the nurse announced that the baby could not spend the night with Diane, but would have to go to the nursery. Diane was now too exhausted to put up a fight. So she and Malia spent their first night apart. Diane felt lonely and isolated and hardly slept, and early the next morning, when they finally brought Malia back to her, she resolved not to let her be taken away again.

Two of the other beds in the room were occupied by women who had also just given birth. They did not seem to mind that their babies were not with them during the night, and the next evening Diane alone refused to allow the nurse to take her baby away. Early the second morning, feeling fresh and getting her old energy back, Diane began to ask everyone who came to check on her when she and Malia could go home. When the physician made rounds later in the morning, he signed the discharge papers. Diane gathered her few belongings and began to dress Malia in the outfit she'd brought. She couldn't wait to leave. At last her friend Jan came to take her and Malia home. Before going out the door, Diane insisted on having one look at her son. They stopped at the nursery window while she scanned the cots. He wasn't there. Evelyn and Arnie had taken him home the preceding day.

When they reached the apartment, Diane didn't ask Jan in; she wanted to be alone with her daughter at last. On a piece of cardboard she wrote in big letters Do Not Disturb and stuck it to the outside of the door. Then she sat down on the bed next to her daughter and burst into tears. At first the tears brought back the memory of being in the delivery room after the birth, when everyone had gone and she had felt suddenly alone and helpless. She recalled each of the small abuses she'd taken from the staff at the hospital. What had cut her most deeply had been the brusqueness of the woman who had come unannounced into her room to fill out the birth certificate. When Diane hadn't grasped one of her questions, the woman had raised her voice in irritation. All at once Diane was crying over the real issue, the feeling of a gaping hole inside, where something had been wrenched from her body. It was a few minutes before she realized that her tears were for the baby she had relinquished. It felt good to cry and it wasn't long before her body relaxed, cleansed and swept by new feelings, mostly relief and joy that she was finally home with the daughter she'd longed to have.

Malia became the center of Diane's life every minute of the day. Diane had often been a babysitter as a teenager; it had been a kind of preparation for what she was now doing, but it was also quite different. Though Malia was separate in body from her, she still felt they were physically connected, by an invisible cord. When Malia awoke, Diane awoke; when Malia cried, Diane could do nothing but attend to her immediately. There was little else for her to do but be with Malia, so the first days were peaceful, sleeping when Malia slept, getting up in between to eat the food friends continued to drop off, to bathe, or to write in her diary. She hardly took notice of the time or of one day's ending and another's beginning.

Arnie began to make daily visits to the apartment almost as soon as Diane was home, bringing with him fresh fruit and bagels from the shop Evelyn and he owned and asking if there was anything else Diane needed. When she'd been home part of a week, he hesitantly asked if Evelyn and Joss might come for a brief visit. Diane wanted to see her friend and wondered what it would feel like seeing Joss. The visit was short, for no sooner did Diane pick up Joss than she began to cry, and Evelyn, not knowing what to do for Diane, took her son and left.

The intensity of what she had felt when she held Joss left Diane feeling shaken. She had fully expected to grieve for him but not to feel what she had the moment he was in her arms: an intense physical longing. She determined to wait a bit before asking to see Joss again.

A week after the birth, Diane unexpectedly found herself resenting Evelyn. At first she couldn't admit it even to herself. This woman had become her dear friend, as close to her as a sister. How could she? She felt she was betraying Evelyn by these feelings, yet they did not go away. When Mary came for a home visit, Diane confided to her, and, having dared to voice what she'd labeled unthinkable, she realized her feelings weren't bad or abnormal. Mary reminded her that it was just a normal part of the process of separation. Knowing this, Diane was able then to talk to Evelyn, and at the next co-counseling session, she felt the wall she'd been building between them vanish. They talked on the phone several times after that, and Diane felt her love for Evelyn return. An hour a week for the next two months, in the safety and impersonality of the protected environment of counseling, they were all able to talk about the various feelings they'd been having since the birth, and Diane was able to share the extent of the sadness she felt about Joss. Joss and Malia were at those sessions too, and Diane found she was now able to say good-bye to Joss. The other good-bye, the one she'd said to him the day she left the hospital, had been spoken too soon, when she was yet too raw from giving birth to him to be able to feel the impact of his leaving. This time saying good-bye left a small lightness inside her.

Evelyn and Arnie had their work to do as well and much to express about the emotions they'd felt at the birth, at getting Joss, at having him home with them and knowing all the while what Diane must be going through, yet not being able to make it any easier for her. Diane could still legally take back Joss for several more months, and during this time he was technically only "visiting" Evelyn and Arnie; but the closeness they felt with her made speaking about their fears easier.

At home Evelyn was breastfeeding their son. She had started preparing as soon as she had been fairly certain she would have a baby to adopt, gently milking the colostrum still in her breasts from the pregnancy. She hoped to be able to bring in her own milk to feed this baby, but if not she would nurse anyway, using a Lactaid, a simple device to enable a woman to feed a baby at her breast using formula. Joss started at her breast on the first day and within a few days she was already producing some milk; but it didn't seem to Evelyn to be enough.

She'd hoped to be able to entirely avoid giving him formula, so she went to Mary and Debbie for advice.

At first they thought they had a simple solution. While Evelyn continued to nurse Joss and bring in her own milk supply by his regular suckling, Diane could easily increase her milk by using a breast pump between feedings and setting some aside for Joss. Physically it was easy enough for her to do this and she wanted to do it, for Evelyn and for Joss. But emotionally it quickly proved too much. The connection with Joss was too close for comfort, at the very time when she needed to let go of him. So Mary and Debbie, realizing they had asked too much of Diane, instead created a mothers milk bank especially for Joss. Mary called her nursing mothers, and nine of them agreed to express some milk each day and put it aside in a container in the refrigerator. Arnie became the "milkman," each morning collecting a couple of ounces of fresh milk from each house and taking it home to Evelyn, where she put it in the Lactaid pouch and supplemented her own breast milk. That way she never had to give Joss a bottle of formula. He didn't care that the milk he drank came partly from a tiny flexible tube alongside Evelyn's nipple. With the help of the milk bank, Evelyn had the time to increase her own milk to the point where, after six weeks, the milk bank could be retired. Breastfeeding was a pleasurable way to deepen her bond with her son, at the same time giving him protection from infection and future allergies. She continued for a year and a half.

Malia's and Joss's biological father visited Malia, but infrequently. Every couple of weeks he would offer to watch her for an hour so Diane could go off somewhere by herself; but he never talked about his feelings toward his daughter. Nor did he even inquire about his son. Diane didn't push him. She sensed he was wrestling with some internal demons, and anyway she had neither the desire nor the energy to mother him. She needed support and energy from others, and she turned to her friends, not him, for her needs. She also called on Evelyn and Arnie. The two women, once their postbirth lives had settled down, began to get together with the babies at least once a week. They even took an exercise class together, bringing the babies with them. Diane felt comfortable calling Evelyn for advice once in a while, and Evelyn did the same. They were better friends than ever.

Privately Diane sometimes found herself envying Evelyn her life. For one thing, she and Arnie never seemed to lack for money and could do whatever they wanted. But more than that, they had each other. It was impossible not to contrast her life with theirs. Despite her large circle of friends, Diane was alone in parenting and did almost everything by herself. Where she had during the pregnancy realized that Evelyn might feel some envy toward her for being able to bear children, Diane had not anticipated feeling as she now did toward Evelyn. Evelyn and Arnie had a decade's experiences over her, and their life had the smell of stability, where hers, no matter how hard she tried, did not. She was happy with how they cared for Joss. The only thing she would have done differently herself was not to circumcise him. As for her feelings of resentment, she would just have to accept them when they came and live with them.

The months passed. To the world outside, the sight of the two women, one red-haired and full-figured, the other dark-haired and slender, sitting together on a park bench watching their babies crawling on the grass must have looked ordinary enough. But under the placid external surface these two women were doing something unique.

I learned about Diane in a letter from one of her midwives, who was a friend of mine, and I went to meet her when Joss and Malia were seven months old. Diane showed me the photo album she'd been keeping since her pregnancy had begun. There was a snapshot of her standing in a garden, long red hair in thick braids, looking every bit as if she was about to deliver. That was taken when she was only six months pregnant, just after they discovered she was carrying twins. There were many other pictures, mostly of Diane amidst friends. And a few of the labor and birth. One showed Evelyn at the side of the bed holding Diane's hand in both of her own. Someone had taken pictures of Diane and Malia together during their first days at home; and there were several of Diane, Malia, Evelyn, Arnie, and Joss all together. In another Malia was in the arms of a young man who was smiling out at the camera. Her father, Diane said. There was a visit from Grandma. But the one that made a lasting impression on me was the picture taken on a bright, sunny day in the park, Evelyn and Diane sitting next to each other on a bench with the babies on their laps. Evelyn was holding Malia and Diane was holding Joss.

My visit to Diane coincided with a transition in her life. She was feeling a growing need to be apart from Evelyn, Arnie, and Joss, not even to hear from them by phone. And for the first time in months, she was a little afraid of her feelings. "I'm worried I might not be able to let go of Joss. A couple of times recently after seeing Joss, when I hadn't seen him for a week, I've found myself thinking it was him I should have kept. I know that's because he is now the novelty. For the most part I haven't felt Joss was my son in a long time. But recently I have and I've been wanting him." Diane wasn't considering changing her decision when she said that; she had already signed the final papers. It was the emotional bond, not the legal one, that was giving her pain. And it wasn't the feelings that puzzled her but the fact that they had developed so strongly so long after she had actually relinquished him.

Whereas Joss used to be content when Diane held him, he was now going through a period of wanting only his mother's or father's arms. This surprised and hurt Diane. "He always used to calm down if I held him. But the last time we were together, nothing I could do helped. I ended up feeling angry at him." And again, afterward, had come feelings of resentment toward Joss's mother. Evelyn and Arnie understood when she explained that she wanted a rest and some privacy. It was time to look back on the past year of her life and review the choices she'd made. And, alone with her thoughts and feelings, Diane knew that she had done the best she could.

Diane was grateful for every bit of emotional support she

received; she gave her share too. When an acquaintance found herself alone just before she was due to give birth, Diane became her special support. She was beside her throughout the birth and afterward went to the woman's home, with Malia in tow, and cooked and cleaned house and did for the new mother what others had done for her.

When Malia was a year old, Diane began to go out with several of the men she knew, although *dating* seemed too childish a term after all she had been through. As long as she carried some hope that Malia's and Joss's father would desire a relationship with her again, there had been no real room for any other man in her life, but it was by now apparent that her hope conflicted with reality. She began to find his irregular presence in their lives irritating. His infrequent statements about how he'd like to babysit for Malia more often or how he'd perhaps like to have her for a year, while Diane went back to school, began to grate on Diane's nerves. She began making herself less available for his visits. She decided it was time to move in with other people again and found a small house and two friends to share it. Then she applied to college, was accepted, and got a government loan so she could be a full-time student and get off welfare.

In her first semester back at school Diane earned As. Malia played at a nearby infant center on campus four hours a day while Diane went to classes. Her play group was small and the teachers provided consistency, so Diane didn't feel Malia was at a disadvantage not being with her those hours. They gave up breastfeeding, and Malia took easily to being around others. Diane gave her full attention to Malia when she was with her, leaving homework for after Malia had gone to bed. Malia reacted to any stress her mother felt, so at the end of each semester Diane asked for extra help from friends to get them both through exam time.

The second semester of school, Diane and Malia moved into inexpensive student housing on campus. I visited them there when Malia had just turned two years old. There was still pain in Diane's eyes at the mention of Joss and his family. She needed to move a little further with her own life before she could bear the reminder of all the things a stable, happily married older couple can give a child that she still could not give Malia. That year Joss did not get to Malia's birthday party. Arnie had had a bicycle accident and couldn't bring him; for Diane it was just as well.

There was much excitement in Joss's house when I went to visit. Not only was Arnie still recovering from his accident, which had left him with a broken collarbone, and Joss, who had been on the back of the bike, miraculously unharmed; but there was another cause for excitement. Joss had a new baby brother named Bowie. And Bowie's arrival was just as amazing as Joss's had been.

Evelyn's best friend, Nancy, had been the number-one milk mom for Joss. A friend of Nancy's from out of town came to visit and happened to mention that the sixteen-year-old daughter of a mutual friend was pregnant and looking for parents to adopt the baby. She had a steady boyfriend her age, but neither of them could imagine being high school parents; however, by the time the young woman had discovered she was pregnant she was already feeling the baby move. She'd gone for a pregnancy test when she'd missed two periods but the test had come back negative. That was how she happened to be five months along before she knew for sure. Evelyn's heart skipped at the news, and she asked Nancy to pass along the word that she and Arnie would be very happy to meet the young woman if she was interested. The young woman's mother and father, although divorced and living in separate states, each said they would support whatever decision the young woman made.

And so it happened that Evelyn and Arnie received visits not just from the young woman, whose name was Lisa, but from her boyfriend and both her parents as well. Lisa had visited the county adoption agency before she had heard about private adoption, but was not interested in what they had to offer. Evelyn and Arnie felt like prospective members of the family getting the once-over, but it was worth it, and after Lisa's father came to see them he warmly thanked them for all they were doing for his daughter. After they had received everyone's blessings and Lisa had told Evelyn and Arnie she wanted them for her baby's parents, there was the process of birth to go through all over again. Once again it was a natural birth, with Evelyn and Arnie present, along with Lisa's boyfriend and Lisa's mother. Diane had given encouragement to the young woman over the phone before the birth. And afterward Lisa told Evelyn she felt certain she had done the right thing in giving her and Arnie her son. She had not felt he belonged to her, and when she visited Evelyn and him in the nursery the next day she said she knew for sure. As I was talking to Evelyn, Arnie received a phone call from Lisa. It was only seven days after the birth. She and her mother were coming for a visit the next day, and Arnie was going to make breakfast for everyone.

Evelyn is sensitive to the feelings of Bowie's mother, just as she has always been sensitive to Diane's feelings and needs. She smiled broadly when I mentioned Diane and volunteered that she continues to think of Diane and Malia daily. "I have a bond with Diane that is different from that with anyone else I know. It's beyond sister. It's beyond . . ." She could find no word that fit. Neither she nor Arnie feels Diane or Lisa is an intrusion in their lives. As Arnie says, "Getting a family the way we have has helped us become as good parents as we could be. I think God always has a hand on a family; but he's had both hands on ours." Bowie's birth announcement reads, "Bowie Jacob happily announces the adoption of his new family: Evelyn, Arnie, and Joss, October 2, 11:05 A.M."

In the future Joss and Bowie will know no void regarding their roots; it is likely that Lisa and Diane will be a continued presence in their lives. They will probably also be familiar with their biological fathers. Diane often speaks about Joss to Malia, just as Evelyn and Arnie speak about Malia to Joss. The children have pictures of each other on their bedroom walls, and they each have a scrapbook of photographs about their births. They also have the times they've shared. Diane and

Evelyn and Arnie have promised each other that, if only for the sake of the twins, they will continue to spend time together and will always stay in contact. Today the visits are less frequent. Their lives have naturally taken them in different directions. When they do get together, Diane no longer feels the same physical connection to Joss. That cord was finally broken, even though the grief is not yet finished. And when Evelyn and Diane do get together for part of a day, it is no different from the way it was in the beginning. They still talk about their lives and the children, sometimes share a few tears over something that has happened to one of them. They are friends. Diane says her relationship with Evelyn is the closest connection she's had with any female except her daughter. She wishes she could have accepted the reality of Joss's not being with her more quickly than she did, but she knows some things cannot be rushed. Any sense that she once felt of being odd because of the path she'd chosen has nearly disappeared as she has been absorbed back into the mainstream of her life.

DIANE, EVELYN, AND ARNIE:

Keeping in Touch

Joss AND BOWIE have always known they were adopted. For them, who are the recipients of an abundance of affection, adoption is something special and good. The uniqueness it gives a person, in Joss's young eyes, is something of which to be proud. Evelyn told me that when Joss was six, he was overheard explaining to a friend how special it was to be adopted. Apparently he made a good case for it, because when his friend got home, he told his mother he wanted to be adopted so he could be special too.

When Bowie was four and Evelyn and he were talking about mammals, for he was very interested in animals, Evelyn said she asked him, "Do you know what a mammal is?" "Oh yes!" he replied without hesitation. "Mammals are animals that have babies that come out of them." Then, looking at his mother and somehow making a significant connection in his mind, he added, "But poor Mama. You're not a mammal, because we were gifts! We didn't come out of you."

Joss is now eight and Bowie is six. Evelyn and Arnie wrote me recently that being adoptive parents is as special today as when the kids were born. In Evelyn's words, "We are reminded daily how fortunate and blessed we are to have the boys." The positive tone of their two open adoptions continues, although their contact with both Diane and Lisa, the boys' birth mothers, is currently through letters. There is regular correspondence with Marcia (Diane's mother) and with David (Bowie's birth father) as well. But Diane moved out of the area three years ago, and Lisa has been living in another state since Bowie's birth, so visits would not be easy to arrange.

The last time Evelyn and Arnie saw Diane was two years ago. It was an accidental encounter at a restaurant downtown, and, although brief, it felt to Evelyn and Arnie as warm as ever. For Evelyn the meeting, although casual, was also "powerful," as every meeting with Diane always had been. The children were not with them. Perhaps that made it easier for Diane. In letters and previous visits over the past eight years, Diane seemed to be having some hard times over her decision to relinquish Joss. "There was," said Evelyn, "at least the hint that here was a woman who had asked herself the hard questions about her decision to give up Joss, especially as Joss's twin sister, Malia, grew and parenting became easier."

Evelyn has nothing but compassion for the rough times Diane must have privately endured. "The special nature of her gift to us, and her role as a mother, sets her apart from Lisa, who has always been supportive of us, unquestioning in her decision, and moving ahead in her life." Diane recently married and from the tone of her letters to Evelyn and Arnie, she sounded like a woman happy in her new life and possibly looking forward to having more children.

They have not seen Lisa in more than three years, the most recent visit being just before Christmas, at their home. Bowie was there and everyone seemed to enjoy the time together. What Evelyn and Arnie have experienced is common among adoptive parents I've known: the birth mothers—and a birth father too, in their case, because he was active in the adoption process—move on in their lives. At a conscious level they express feelings of not wishing to intrude on either the child or the other parents. There seems to be a need to let the past be past, in order to live fully in the present. By knowing the parents to whom she has entrusted her child, seeing how they live, forming a bond of affection with them, the birth mother can feel more at ease as she goes about her life. She can trust that because all began well, all will continue to be well with the child she misses.

Evelyn and Arnie want to remain in contact with their boys' birth parents. Evelyn, in particular, has always felt that a child can't have too many people who love him or her! Arnie was looking more to the future needs of the boys when he said, "We plan to keep the communication open and strong, to foster the friendships and facilitate the contact the boys may want as they get older."

In the beginning years Evelyn and Arnie both felt that being adoptive parents actually gave them an edge in being the best parents they could be, because they were able to retain a bit of objectivity. But now, after eight years of parenting, Evelyn says, "We no longer believe that we have an edge. We feel as vulnerable as any other parents, and only hope that the decisions we make in regard to our kids are good ones."

WORDS TO THE WISE:

Creating Better Adoptions

Two YEARS AFTER she relinquished her son Christopher, I
asked Alexandra what suggestions she could offer other women
considering adoption. I wrote down her ideas and added mine.
I asked her recently, with six years' additional hindsight, to read
over our earlier thoughts and see what changes she would
make. The list has changed only a little. Alexandra has placed
special emphasis on several points, and she has added a few
more. Much of what we suggest is applicable to all pregnant
women: those who are unsure of what they want to do, those
who have made the choice to raise their babies, and those
who have made the choice of adoption for their babies. It also
shows prospective adoptive parents, adoption professionals,
and everyone concerned what they can do to make life better
for the birth mother and the baby. Some of these suggestions
are aimed primarily at women considering private adoption,
but they can be adapted for women who go through agencies.

Until such time as our health and social service systems
begin to meet the real needs of birthing women and mothers, it
is critical that those of us who care about pregnant women,
birthing women, and mothers step into the breach. Prospective

and adoptive parents, forward-thinking agencies, and others in the field can lead the way. In paying special attention to the needs of the birth mother, adoptive parents and adoption workers will both show society what is needed and fulfill their desire to nurture a child. To assist and empower the pregnant woman, the birth mother, is the surest way to care for her, to nurture the baby, and to prepare them both for their future lives.

If you are pregnant and have questions, doubts, or fears about what to do:

1. Find a support group (through a midwife, birth center, women's center, counseling center, or health food store) that can meet your immediate and basic emotional needs. *"I felt so vulnerable. That made it even harder for me to make decisions."*

   A support group can help you through the process of making your initial decision, and, if you choose to relinquish your baby, may also help you find and evaluate possible parents for your baby. A group will listen and help you think of important details that you might otherwise overlook.

2. Be careful whom you choose to talk to about your feelings and decisions. There are many people, especially those with strong religious convictions, who will want you to do things the way they did things or the way they believe is the right way. That doesn't mean it is your way. You do not need judgment and criticism from other people.

   Remember, *you are especially sensitive* right now. You are in a unique state mentally, emotionally, and physically, because the hormones of pregnancy are running throughout your body. Talk with women but be aware that women have been set up to judge and criticize other women.

   "Some of the least condemning people I know are mothers of young children. They know what it takes to raise a child, how all-encompassing it is, how little support there really is for the day-to-day work of being a mother."

If you choose adoption for your baby:

1. Find someone who will act as your advocate, who will see that your needs and wishes are respected, and who will be there for you throughout the actual adoption and afterward. If you want a private adoption, find a skilled advocate to represent you. If you choose an agency, make sure someone in that agency will be your advocate.

   Choose someone you feel really listens to you and does not judge or try to push you. Find out what the beliefs of the individual or agency are, and don't select one with a bias that implies you are bad if you make certain choices.

   "It helped to be able to sit and talk to someone in person, not just on the phone. I now put this first, because I think it is the single most important factor in a successful adoption. I wish there were professional advocates with free services. I had no money. If the adoptive parents are paying, there's always the possibility that the person you choose will not look only at your interests."

2. Learn as much as you can about the needs of babies and young children: in pregnancy, at birth, after birth, and as they grow. There are books you can look at, classes you can attend on infant development. This will help you make the best decisions regarding your baby.

   "I tried to imagine what the baby was going through during the pregnancy and what birth and going to new parents would be like for him or her, and I thought about how I could make this time better for the baby."

3. Start looking for parents for your child as soon as you have made the decision for adoption. The baby, as well as you, needs you to feel the certainty of knowing where he or she will go. Whether you use an agency or have a private adoption, do search until you find appropriate people: ones who meet your needs as well as your desires for the baby.

   "I wasted a lot of time and energy dealing with people I knew weren't right and being afraid to say no."

4. Meet the parents; don't rely on the phone alone. Get to know them. It takes more than one meeting. Be able to look in their eyes and feel you can trust them. If you can't, look for other parents.

   "By the time I found the couple I chose to be my son's parents, I was eight months pregnant, had no money, had no place to turn, and felt up against a wall! I thought they were my only hope. I didn't dare bring up certain subjects, because I was afraid to find out they weren't the right people."

   You may want to have your advocate with you for the first few times, while you feel awkward. Do see them often enough to feel you have a real relationship with them. You are entrusting your child into their care. And how they treat you, before and in the years after the adoption is final, affects your life.

   "I would have liked to have had someone else at the meetings, at least some of them, to be my advocate and make sure I was really expressing my needs and being understood."

5. Choose an attorney. You may feel that you and the adoptive parents are so compatible that you can work with one attorney, or you may feel you need your own attorney. Just be sure the attorney meets *your* needs.

   "I didn't realize the attorney was really the advocate for the adoptive parents, not for me. I needed someone just for me."

   Have your advocate go with you to meetings with the attorney. You need someone to help you remember the details that are important to you.

6. Write down everything you hope for, your picture of the ideal adoption—what you'd like the parents to be—all the things that are important to you. You may compromise; that's what happens in relationships. But first you should know what your ideal is.

   "I would have wanted to have made sure they believed in a lot of holding and touching a child, in physically showing their love. So many people still believe a baby or child can be spoiled by too much attention. Breastfeeding

was very important to me. I'm sorry I didn't choose an adoptive mother who would try to feed the baby at her breast, even get her own milk to come in."

7. Work out a clear agreement with the adoptive parents about what you want them to tell the child about you and when and how they will do it. Look ahead to your child's future, to his or her needs regarding you, and to your responsibility toward your child over his or her lifetime. Make plans for your continued relationship with the child. Include in it plans for the child to be able to have as much contact with you as he or she needs while growing up.

"I can't bear to think of Christopher being one of the children who desperately needs to find his biological parents and is blocked in his attempt."

Work out the important details carefully, with the assistance of your advocate, and have it drawn up by the attorney. Also have it agreed in that contract who will always know your and their current addresses, so you can stay in touch with each other. Make a legal contract that is binding. Keep a copy.

"I often felt, talking with Christopher's adoptive parents, that I was asking too much. But I was really asking too little! And I had what I thought was a legal contract with them, but it turned out to be just a piece of paper."

Remember to take care of yourself:

1. Get counseling as soon as possible and stick with it. A counselor is someone who will give you total attention, who will listen to you, who knows how to give the kind of support you really want. If you are going through an agency adoption, make sure the agency provides you with ongoing counseling—once a week or more often if you want it. If you are having a private adoption, the adoptive parents should pay for all your counseling if they can afford it. Otherwise, there are local agencies (such as Family Service Agencies in the United States) who have sliding fees.

*"I felt so strong and clear about my decision through-
out most of my pregnancy that I didn't realize I needed
counseling. Afterward I did go for counseling, and I
realized it would have made a great difference to have had
that continuous support all along."*

2. Admit your own dependency needs. You think you will
   crumble and fall totally apart if you admit to anyone, even
   yourself, how needy you are. You won't. You will actually
   feel better. Putting your feelings and needs into words
   makes it possible to get what you need from others.
   *"I felt I should be competent and take care of every-
   thing myself. I fought my real desire, which was to be
   taken care of."*

3. Find people who really know how to support you. You
   may do better with people outside your immediate family,
   because they are so connected to you that interactions may
   be too fraught with emotion.
   *"My family tried to help me and be supportive, but
   they hurt me by their own hurt. There was too much
   pressure, too much pain associated with my parents, with
   their expectations of me and with my feelings of letting
   them down. I felt I had to take care of them."*

4. Find ways to make the pregnancy a joyous, or at least a
   positive, time. The baby needs this from you, and *you*
   deserve it too. It may mean leaving old friends for a time
   and drawing close to people involved with pregnancy and
   birth, who are excited about it, and who believe it is a
   healthy, normal process.
   *"I found most people who knew I was going to give
   up the baby for adoption thought I shouldn't be around
   people who were happy about being parents. But I needed
   to have joy around me, joy about carrying a child."*

5. It is important to be physically touched while pregnant.
   *"With the father of my baby absent, there was no one
   else who felt comfortable touching me. It was a physical
   need, more than I've ever felt, to be held and touched. The
   only time I was touched, the whole pregnancy, was when*

I was eight and a half months pregnant, and my cousin, who had a young child, gave me a massage."

It may be hard to ask for touch directly. Tell your advocate or a close friend.

"My best friend, Linda, told me later that she had wanted to take me in her arms and hold me, but hadn't dared. I was not an easy person to hug. But I needed it."

Having your aches and pains rubbed, having someone put an arm around you feels wonderful, but you may have to tell someone you need it. Babies can die if they are not touched. That is how important touch is to human beings. Remember that whenever people do good things for you, they also help your baby.

6. Don't stay alone and isolated.

   "Sleeping alone each night, being more alone than ever before, I felt so cut off from everyone. It wasn't that I didn't have people around me who cared. I did. But I was always doing everything alone; people left me alone because they thought that's what I wanted."

   There is a natural drawing inward during pregnancy. It isn't just because you are going to relinquish the baby. You do need your privacy; but you don't need to feel totally alone.

7. Let someone know what you are feeling. You may need help to think about what you want and how to make it happen. Being around people who really understand is so important.

   "It would have taken some daring person to pierce though the walls I put up to protect myself."

   You may think you know what you want for yourself, for the baby, for the birth, and for the exchange, but feel you do not have the strength to make it happen.

   "What was going on inside me during the pregnancy took up all my energy, and I often took the easiest options instead of what was really good for me. So often I couldn't talk. I'd feel that everyone around me was looking at me and seeing right into me. After the birth I found out they had had no idea what was going on inside me."

8. Let yourself be around children and babies during the pregnancy, even though it may hurt. It will help you stay more aware of your feelings.

   "I had a hard time being around kids when I was pregnant with Christopher. Once, when I was eight months pregnant, I held a baby of a friend. Just holding the baby made me cry; I cried and cried, and let all my tension out."

   Your baby needs you to let your feelings out during pregnancy, so they do not get all bottled up inside.

9. Try to take good care of yourself. Eat well. If you don't know whether you are eating a diet that is good for a growing baby, ask the person you see for prenatal care or ask pregnant women who look healthy. Find ways to eat with other people.

   "I'm generally a very self-motivated person. I knew what was good for me and the baby. But I felt no initiative. I hated to fix food and eating was so difficult. Nobody ever offered to fix me food! That would have been so nice."

10. Get a lot of exercise in pregnancy. Go walking every day with a friend. Find someplace lovely or a time of day, such as early morning, when the streets are quiet and the light is beautiful.

    "Sometimes I felt too vulnerable even to take a walk alone. I should have asked someone to go with me. Every time I took a long walk I felt better."

11. You have a need for a place where you can let your defenses down. Look for someplace you feel you can be totally yourself.

    "I had a longing for the country. When I went to my cousin's cottage up in the country, the baby grew tremendously. I could actually feel and see my abdomen grow. It was so much easier to eat there, so much easier to relax."

12. Look for the kind of pregnancy care that will really make a difference in your life. Don't go to just any doctor, any clinic. You might find there is a women's clinic near you. Think about going to a midwife, to someone who will

spend a lot of time with you each visit, who really listens and who doesn't rush you.

"The doctor I chose ended up being a friend. He would schedule me as the last patient in the day, so he could spend a lot of time with me. And I met a lot of women through the birth center who became my friends. I only wish I'd found them all sooner!"

13. Get educated about birth and prepared for labor. Find a class or a group or an individual to help you get ready. You will learn about what is going on in pregnancy and birth for the baby as well as yourself. Find someone to go to all educational sessions with you, so you have someone prepared to be with you in labor and with whom you can talk to about things that come up.

"I sensed I would have a long labor, that it would take me a while to let go and have the baby. I didn't know what to do with that feeling, so I wasn't able to do any work around the birth ahead of time. It was a long labor. It was hard for me to let go enough to let Christopher be born, even though there was nothing physically holding him back."

14. Start thinking in pregnancy about what you will do with your life after the birth. A counselor is a great help in this. Set up goals for yourself. Remember, you must have a life worth returning to without the baby. You need a plan for what you will do in the first months after the birth, how you will spend your days.

"For me, my life after the birth was a blank. I thought it would just take care of itself, that I would jump back into my old world. Instead I found myself a different person. I couldn't fit in, I couldn't go back, I didn't know how to go forward. I lived floating in limbo."

15. Let the people who care about you know that you would like to be honored for carrying life and for giving birth. Let people celebrate you.

"I would have loved to have been given a baby shower, not just to receive gifts I could have given Christopher's adoptive parents, but for me too."

After the adoption:

1. Continue with counseling as soon as the birth is over. Don't let yourself have any excuse not to continue. Understand that you are going to go through pain after you relinquish the baby. Regular counseling (weekly or more often) will be your anchor during the postpartum period.

   "Maybe you will go through what I went through, a depression. It would have been so much less frightening if I had had counseling help from pregnancy onward, and had known what kinds of things to expect after giving up the baby. It would have been so different if I had known ahead of time what the stages of grief are for everyone. It would have been like having a map when you find yourself in a strange, frightening place."

2. Make sure someone is with you twenty-four hours a day during the first days or weeks after you separate from the baby. It is a period that is similar to the time after the sudden death of a loved one, and the grief is compounded by the extreme physical exhaustion of just having gone through birth. You should not be alone at all during this time.

   "The worst thing about those first days—something that will haunt me forever—was being left totally alone. As soon as the baby was gone, everyone else left too. Once I left the birth home, no one came to look after me for several days. I think they thought I just needed to sleep a lot. But I couldn't sleep. I couldn't take care of myself at all, couldn't eat, and I felt crazy from the combination of sleep deprivation, the physical strain of birth, and the shock of the grief, for which I hadn't prepared."

3. Give yourself four to eight weeks just to recover in body and spirit. Be around friends. Do not go back to work or your old life. You need a grace period.

   "The best memory I have of the time after birth was when I stayed at a friend's house. We shared cooking. I was part of family meals. My woman friend and I did yoga together and took walks. I spent time with their ten-year-

old daughter, following her on her outings around town,
just hanging out. I felt taken care of and support all
around me during those weeks."

4. Take very good care of your body during this time. It is
recovering from huge physical changes, pregnancy and
birth.

   *"I found my ability to cope with my emotional ups
   and downs was directly related to whether I was eating
   well, getting exercise, being out in nature, getting massaged
   regularly. That made all the difference."*

5. Keep connected to mothers and children in some way. Do
not try to deny your own motherhood, especially during
the first year.

   *"During the depression I got into a bulimic cycle,
   stuffing myself with food and then vomiting. I had never
   done that before. Once I began seeing other people and
   getting involved in activities, I stopped doing that because
   I was then thinking about others. If I had it to do over
   again, I would take care of a baby part time or work at
   the birth center as a volunteer."*

6. Begin your own life again, doing the things that you find
of significance and productive, the things you realistically
could not have done if you had kept your baby. It is
essential not to feel guilty about doing them now. You owe
it to your child, as well as yourself, to do the very things
being a mother would have prevented you from doing.

   *"It was a vicious cycle. I felt too guilty to do the
   things I had always wanted to do: completing my degree
   and writing. And when I didn't do any of that, I felt even
   guiltier, as if I had given my child up for nothing. I've
   talked to other birth mothers who did the same thing and
   felt the same way."*

7. Find something creative that you enjoy, that has no real
purpose except self-expression. You need to work through
feelings, and doing things with your hands and body
accomplishes this naturally.

   "When I got back to my hometown, I got involved in

theater projects and dance. It didn't earn me any money. It wasn't something I wanted to do professionally, but it was deeply satisfying, gave me an outlet for feelings and emotions I couldn't put into words."

8. Create some rituals for yourself that mark the time, that honor what you have done and gone through, and that recognize your lifelong connection with your child.

"I did some, without realizing at the time that they were rituals. I celebrated Christopher's first birthday with all the people who had been at my birth. I think writing the letter I wrote after my year of postpartum sickness after Keir's birth was also a ritual, because I was able in it to make a symbolic connection with my first son and to bring him symbolically into my new life. It would have meant everything to me if I could have done these rituals with Christopher himself and his family."

CLOSING

THERE WILL ALWAYS be adoption, because there will always be children who are orphaned or whose birth parents cannot or choose not to raise them. Raising a child is not easy, and love and affection are not all that it takes. Parenting takes time, focused attention, continued interest in the child's welfare, and the economic ability to provide for a child's physical needs. It also takes work, long hours of hard work, particularly in the first months and years of a child's life and then again as the child reaches puberty and moves toward adulthood.

At any point in time, many people are simply not ready to give, able to give, or interested in giving to a child what is required. It is wise to admit it when that is the case, for parenting is best when it is undertaken freely. Pregnancy *can* be a mistake; trying to raise a child in difficult circumstances can also be a mistake. If children are not to suffer at the hands of their parents, then relinquishment and adoption must be options available to a woman who becomes pregnant and to the father of that child.

Pat, Alexandra, and Diane in these stories are women who grew up in a time when it was no longer unthinkable to enter

411

parenting as a single woman. Each of them, for personal as well as social reasons, refused to settle for the kind of adoption that their society, their church, their family, friends, and advisers offered them. They felt there *had* to be a better way, and they felt compelled to search for it. They had no models to guide them, and so their imaginations were limited by what they knew or could envision. Had each of them known even one other woman who, in similar circumstances, had found her way to a more ideal adoption, they might have gone further than they did. Yet, in the absence of any models, they persevered and created fairly positive experiences for themselves and their children, doing what they could with what was in their power.

These women are the pioneers of adoption. The birth parents, especially the birth mother, *do* have a great deal of power and therefore control over the relinquishment and the adoption, if only they realized it. Once a child's adoption is final, however, the power shifts to the adoptive parents, who are then on their own able to shape the future for that child. Parenting is an awesome responsibility. The women and men in these stories open eyes and hearts to what adoption can be.

There cannot be a perfect adoption (except in the metaphysical sense that all things are by nature perfect because they exist), because adoption involves more than one individual, and people's individual needs, desires, and styles are different. Another reason there cannot be a perfect adoption is because adoption most commonly is entered into when a child is very young or newborn and cannot speak or act on his or her own behalf. The adults involved must make decisions for the child, and, at best, those can only approximate what the child might want.

The emotions involved in any adoption are too complex and include too much pain and loss to speak of perfection. But adoption can save lives, give individuals a second chance, and bring much joy into the lives of adoptive parents and families. It ought to be possible to create kinds of adoptions with which everyone can live without remorse. I believe the beginning is to recognize that no other person, no institution, no system can ever satisfy a human being's highest yearnings. That is a matter of individual responsibility. What a social system, including an adoption system, *can* do is to provide a structure within which people find the support and guidance they need to function at their best.

Any new adoption system must provide basic safeguards to protect people from fraud and other deceit. But in the end each adoption will rest mainly on the strength of the adults involved, their levels of goodwill, openness, and honesty. With the current system of adoption, the people who run the greatest risk of being taken advantage of are, I believe, the birth mother and her child. They are the individuals who, in the current system and with the current societal attitudes, have the most to lose.

The birth mother is today still treated as if she were not able to make competent decisions. She is seldom given full information about what is possible in adoption and what are the benefits and risks, short-term and long-term consequences of each choice. Her options are, in many states, so limited that she has little or no control over the relinquishment or adoption. This is in addition to the fact that few women in this country have the chance to give birth in a way that really shows them what they are capable of. Therefore, for most birth mothers, adoption takes away their power and creativity rather than affirming it or dignifying their choices.

I believe that when an individual gives birth to a child, she takes on a physiological maturity, no matter how young she might be in years. She needs to be treated as an adult even if she does not fully behave as one; and she needs to be given the chance to make her own decisions—both for herself and for her child—unless she can be proven incompetent.

Both the birth mother and the adoptive parents have great responsibility with regard to the child, and because they must live with the consequences of their own decisions as well as the decisions the other has made, they need as much information, support, and skilled guidance as they are willing to accept.

What none of them needs is to have outside agencies or

individuals strip them of their power and dignity by making decisions on their behalf. Yet this is precisely what happens in the overwhelming majority of adoptions today; this will change when societal attitudes change. But even before there are changes in the law and the system, individuals can, and, I believe, *should,* be willing to imagine what adoption *can* be and then dare to do everything in their power to make it happen. This is the mandate the adult world is given on behalf of adopted children: participate fully in the design and ongoing process of relinquishment and adoption with open hearts and minds, and do everything possible to create situations that are flexible.

There will always be some parents who are either unable or unwilling to provide much of what an infant or child needs but who will not admit their failings and continue to parent. But I believe that the better the system of adoption (which means the more flexible and open it is, so that no one is left out), the more people who need it will be encouraged to consider it.

It is essential that adoption be portrayed honestly, not as an idealized picture of life without pain or anxiety for anyone. Only if birth parents and adoptive parents are made aware of the potential risks and dangers and hard times can they be prepared for them. People must be educated to know how difficult even optimal relinquishments and adoptions can be, and appropriate skilled support must be offered to everyone.

Above all, the erroneous notion that is the opposite of paternalism—that people can "tough it out" on their own and do a fine job without help, as long as they try hard enough—must be let go. Parenting simply cannot be done well in isolation, without adequate support and guidance. Adoption certainly cannot be done well without even more support and guidance. This is a lesson America has yet to learn as a culture: the notion of the rugged individualist may work in some creative endeavors; but it does *not* work when it comes to raising children. Those foolish enough to try it cause themselves and their children great harm.

There are already many self-help groups and a number of professional organizations trying to bring enlightenment and skilled help to both relinquishment and adoption. The word must be gotten out to everyone involved in adoption, from the thirteen-year-old birth mother to the couple in their forties who want to adopt, that adoption is potentially very rewarding but also very demanding. The growing international adoption network offers the greatest possibility for changing antiquated attitudes and practices, but many people are unaware that it exists.

I was shocked to hear from a woman recently who was four months pregnant and planning to relinquish her baby for adoption, yet who had been unable to find *any* information about how to create the kind of adoption she envisioned. When I listened to her speak of what she wanted for this child, I realized how little she was asking compared with what I knew was possible. She is a single woman in her midthirties who already has two children from a previous marriage whom she is raising alone, and who finds herself pregnant despite having used birth control. She has not received any financial assistance from the children's father; nor does he participate in parenting. She recognized the signs of pregnancy immediately and did not deny the pregnancy. She thought, and prayed, long and hard about what she should do, and in the end chose to keep the pregnancy and give birth, but to relinquish the child.

This woman was already doing everything she knew to make this both a healthy and a joyful pregnancy and wanted very much to make the intrauterine life and the birth positive experiences for her baby. She also wanted to find adoptive parents who would give her child the kind of life she would have liked to provide. She wanted to be able to make the decision about who would be the parents as early in pregnancy as possible, in order to put her mind at ease and to form a close, trusting relationship with them, for the benefit of the child. She hoped that she could then have continued contact with them, to the extent of letters or phone calls, so that she would always know how her child was doing.

It never occurred to this woman to ask for more; yet there was much more possible! She lives in an urban area where many creative, positive adoptions are occurring, yet she had heard nothing about them or any resources she might use in creating her child's adoption. She was obviously intelligent, had made her decision carefully. Yet she was quite isolated and uninformed about alternatives to the standard adoption. It was easy to give her the names of a number of adoption counselors and books on the subject. That was all she needed to be able to move ahead.

A week ago, at a national midwives conference at which I was a speaker and workshop facilitator, I met a twenty-four-year-old aspiring midwife who was also a birth mother. She had gotten pregnant at thirteen and had had the baby when she was fourteen, and she had gone through an agency adoption in which she had never met the adoptive parents, much less had any say in who was selected. She had had a strong feeling that it was important to her baby that she give birth without medication or anesthesia, and she had made the adults around her listen. Without any outside support, and with a great deal of effort and struggle, she had gotten the birth she desired and even breastfed her daughter and had the baby stay with her in her room during the time she was in the hospital. She had received no support for doing this, but she felt very positively about the experience, even though she had been shut out of the adoption.

Each year since then, around the time of her child's birthday, this birth mother has written a long letter to her daughter. She has sent the letter to the adoption agency, each time asking that it be placed in her child's file and kept there until the adoptive parents or her daughter asked to see the file. She has also filled out forms saying that she would be willing to meet her child at any time; it is something for which she yearns. This past year, realizing that she had never kept copies of her letters to her daughter, she wrote the agency and asked them to please send her copies. She was refused. She now is aware of the organizations and self-help groups that can help her locate her daughter and perhaps enable them to have a reunion one day. What possible reason can be given for other people to continue to deny her all her rights as a mother?

With all the research that exists about the need of adopted children to know their biological heritage and to have contact with the birth parents when they are still young, especially before puberty, when adopted children tend to show their emotional problems related to having been relinquished, what possible reason can be given for other people to deny them their rights as human beings to their heritage?

The children will always be the most vulnerable participants in adoption, because they are dependent on the adult world for their very survival. Any adoption system needs to give the children support and place in their hands whatever information and power over their lives that will help them shape their own courses. There is almost universal agreement that adoptees desire to know their roots and want to search for their birth parents if they are denied access to them. Adoptees also have their own individual needs, which must be addressed by the adults around them, especially their adoptive parents.

Many adoptive parents have felt pushed to their limits by the behavior of children they've adopted. That adopted children often show signs of special stress relating to having been relinquished should not be a surprise to anyone. It *does* require more of a parent when a child has begun life in stress— more understanding of the issues created by relinquishment and adoption, and more compassion for what the child may go through. Adoptive parents in our society, like all parents, get no formal preparation for being good parents. Like any other parents, they may abuse their children, biological children as well as adopted children. But for an adopted child, the abuse comes on top of any emotional wounds he or she may carry from intrauterine life, birth, and separation from his or her original mother. An example of a family system that allowed incest to occur unchecked was seen in the story of Ann. The very system of closed adoption makes the abuse of children more likely, because it fosters ignorance and deception.

Adoptive parents also can come with special needs. Many do, because they have gone through infertility before choosing adoption. Many come to adoption feeling they "failed" because they were unable to have children, and a high proportion of infertile women and men have been through months or years of emotionally wrenching and demeaning fertility work, as the most intimate part of their lives comes under the scrutiny of strangers and artificial schedules and drugs and surgery. They feel vulnerable and self-protective in the early stages of adoption, right when they need to be able to feel open and trusting. This is not the best way to enter parenthood, much less adoption. And it makes them much more likely to choose closed adoption and set a pattern in motion that keeps them inflexible with regard to their children and to the birth parents.

The time of searching and waiting to find a child *can* be a positive time, especially if some of it is used to work through any remaining emotional issues about infertility or other factors that led to adoption. It is a useful time to read about babies and children, their developmental stages and needs at various ages, and to assess parenting skills and needs. It is also a time, free of the demands of a new baby or child in the family, when adults can work on their own unfinished issues that they carry from when they were children, especially issues that relate to abuse or feelings of inadequacy and shame that were never healed.

There are many avenues prospective parents can take to prepare for being adoptive parents: private counseling, courses, self-help groups, for example. Although adoptive mothers do not have biology pushing them into the natural hormonal stages that pregnant women go through, the time of waiting and the heightened stress and emotions of waiting for children can be used productively and be a form of pregnancy. Men and women preparing to adopt can use this time to make needed changes in their attitudes and in their lives, particularly slowing down the pace of their lives, the way pregnancy naturally encourages women to slow down and become more introspective, so that they will not be shocked by the changes wrought by bringing babies or children into their lives.

When the time of waiting and longing stretches into years, it can be difficult to bear. And if a child comes at last, then that child will have to bear the brunt of whatever anxiety the adoptive parents carry. Adoptive new parents, like other first parents, need to draw a curtain around themselves and their baby and shut out the outside world for a time while they relish their time together and get to know and love each other. There may be a time to be out of communication with the birth parents, but this should pass. They should naturally feel themselves ready to open to others again, after the first weeks or months.

It may be difficult for adoptive parents to reach out to the birth parents to include them at this time, especially because the birth mother is not going through a parallel time of joy and heightened energy. Even if they remember the birth mother at this precious and frenetic time and want to share their delight with her and thank her again for all that she has given them, it will be difficult. She is most likely going through the polar opposite feelings—deep loss and heartbreak—and that may take the form of her shutting down, being unresponsive to anyone's offers of help.

The birth mother may feel like totally cutting herself off from the outside world that looks so full and active and too busy to be interested in her solitary grief. But this is an important time for the birth mother (who is usually without a partner) to be given love and support and grateful thanks. She also needs practical help, in the same way any newly postpartum woman needs it: it is a time for others to come to her and to give to her in many small ways—bringing food, friendship, comfort, and the reminder of all that she has given of herself in order for her child to have a good life. It is a time for her to be honored as well as respected in her grief. And that is something everyone around her can do.

The biological fathers of children in adoption also have needs. Many a man has taken years to discover just how significant an unknown child he fathered might be to him, and how important he might be to this child. It is easy for the birth father to be forgotten if he has not been an active participant in the pregnancy and birth and the preparation for adoption. A birth mother usually does not have even the emotional support of the child's father, and a birth mother who has emotional, physical, and financial support from him is extremely fortunate. It would be well to draw the birth father into the entire process, if only for the long-term benefit of his child. If his emotions and needs are respected and he is treated as a sensitive human being, then he is more likely to think about his child and his lifelong responsibility for having fathered a child.

I have focused in this book primarily on the birth mother, because hers is the most difficult path. A woman who relinquishes a child consciously and freely is an amazing person. Free from social pressure to relinquish the child, *she* must make the decision. She must face herself and assess her own ability (*not* her potential, but her actual, present ability) to be a parent to her child. She must consider her life circumstances realistically, look ahead at what child rearing entails, and anticipate what her skills and limitations are likely to be. In the case of most adoptions, which occur soon after birth, she must do all this in the midst of pregnancy, which is a most emotional and vulnerable time. And she must choose whether to raise or relinquish her child *without* knowing for certain whether she would be a good enough parent! Perhaps that is why so few women today choose the path of relinquishment and adoption or even consider it. Many women faced with the option simply say, "I can't even consider it!"

For women of any age or circumstance to be able to consider adoption as a possibility for themselves, then adoptions that serve their needs, as well as the needs of adoptive parents, must be created. Society must look at its attitude toward women who choose to relinquish their children (at birth or at a later time) and see how they are demeaned. It is perhaps they who have been done the greatest disservice in society's continuing to permit adoptions to occur where the birth mother has no control over the process and therefore no control over her life.

The standards for adoption that this culture has come to take for granted arose within a society that was very different from society today. Adoption in a world where an unmarried woman who became pregnant was considered immoral and a threat to society, and where the children born of such women were branded illegitimate, necessarily reflected those attitudes. It is no wonder that early maternity hospitals across North America and Europe, Australia and New Zealand, and homes for unwed mothers went to great lengths to keep the identities of the women hidden. It is no wonder that names were changed or deleted on birth certificates, and files were kept under lock and key.

Women and children deserved to be protected from stigma. They had no economic or political power, and it was nearly impossible for children born out of wedlock or their mothers to move freely in society if their background was made public. I remember being shown the large leatherbound book listing the name of every mother who had given birth in a particular hospital in Denmark since the seventeenth century. Each name was entered in ink, but there was no name given when the mother was unmarried. That was to protect her from shame and possible punishment from her community.

The stigma attached to being the child of unwed parents has almost disappeared in this culture. The stigma of having once relinquished a child for adoption still exists; a birth mother feels wary of telling people, even a future mate, that this is a part of her past. There is still a feeling that the woman must have been in some way lacking in love for her child to have done such a thing. The stigma attached to being an unwed mother has largely disappeared. In fact, there seems to be a reverse trend, for people to applaud the mother who bears a child without a partner and who attempts to parent completely on her own. If a movie star can do it, then why can't a fifteen-year-old! She not only sees it as her right to have a baby but naively assumes that she can do a good job of parenting with everything against her.

Society *has* changed and will continue to become more open in its attitude toward women's sexuality and reproductive decisions as women and children assume and are granted more stature and power over their lives. Yet the secrecy that permeates a system of adoption that originated in very different times still persists!

Closed adoption breeds insecurity for everyone. It is sad, but understandable, given the closed nature of most adoptions, that adoptive parents are fearful and mistrustful of birth parents. A normally thoughtful and kind mother of an adopted daughter put it quite honestly when, hearing about Alexandra's adoption and her subsequent difficulties with the adoptive parents she had chosen, said, "What does she expect! Why should she have any rights to this child! After all, she gave him up, didn't she! Well, then, she has forfeited all her rights!" Unwittingly exposing her own insecurity as an adoptive parent, she continued, "How can you be so insensitive to adoptive parents, asking us to open our lives and homes and expose our children to the very people who gave them up in the first place!"

This same mother then went on to speak about the great disappointment she and her husband had felt when they had first found they could not have another child and how adoption had been a godsend for them. She spoke with great feeling about how grateful she was to the woman who had enabled them to become parents. She did not even see any contradiction in her attitude toward this same birth mother when it came to the birth mother having any contact with the child. She did not understand that the source of her judgmental attitude was insecurity, nor that her insecurity was bred by the very system of closed adoption, which she wholeheartedly endorsed!

The birth mother is honored as long as she remains quietly in the closet, as long as she is only a cardboard figure, not a flesh and blood woman with needs of her own. Let her become a real person with real needs, and let her want to have any control over the relinquishment or adoption after it is made final—and any contact with her child—and she turns into a wicked witch.

Are birth mothers not simply being punished for doing what they feel is best for their children and for themselves? And for what crime? For having become pregnant at the wrong time or with the wrong person? For being honest enough to admit that parenting is not something they can, at the time, do? Sex, for a woman, because it can always result in pregnancy (unless she is infertile), becomes *her crime*. Unless the pregnancy terminates on its own or the woman terminates it, that unwanted pregnancy and birth become *her punishment*. Parenting in such circumstances can become either an eighteen-year sentence to grief (in the case of relinquishing a child she will not see for at least eighteen years) or an eighteen-year sentence of martyrdom (in the case of the woman who takes on the job of parenting) to atone for a sexual act.

Either way, unless the woman can accept the decison she has made with regard to parenting, and unless she can let go of any guilt she may feel herself or anger she may feel toward the child, she is being punished. If a woman is not to be made to feel guilty and wrong for choosing adoption, then she must be encouraged and supported in participating in and shaping the process of relinquishment and adoption. At the very least, a birth mother deserves to be kept informed of how her child is doing and what her child is feeling and needing as the child grows. And at the very least a child needs to have full information about his or her birth parents. Is this really so shocking? I think it is simply sensible and the first step toward open and then cooperative adoption.

Society no longer punishes the parent who, for whatever reason, chooses to leave the family home in divorce by preventing him or her from ever again participating in the children's lives. At the minimum there are visiting rights guaranteed, and today the concept of joint custody (where neither parent is seen as at fault or needing to be punished by being removed from the child's life, and both parents are seen as capable and responsible) is becoming the norm. This revolutionary change occurred within just a few decades. Yet society is still trying to keep adoption closed. The motives may be seen as good, that children's lives should not be dangerously complicated or their psyches confused, but there is *no* proof that it would do either.

The children of divorce and remarriage learn to live with the fact of having extra adults in their lives and the fact that they cannot control the actions of their parents with regard to keeping a marriage together. They are wounded and they must learn to make distinctions between different mommies and daddies and to incorporate stepsiblings and half-siblings into their lives. Yes, it is complicated, and it results from the sad fact that relationships do not always last a lifetime. Why can't birth parents be granted the same respect as divorced parents? It seems to me the burden of proof that open adoption is too risky and dangerous should be on those who want to keep adoption closed, not those who want to open it to the light.

The first step toward a more humane and loving kind of adoption is that *every* woman in pregnancy should be the object of caring and support. Pregnancy should be as positive a time as possible for the mother; in this way not only is she assisted, but also the life she carries.

The second step is that every girl should be given full information about all her options with regard to her reproductive capacity; she should know the risks and benefits, both short-term and long-term, of each. It's important that she know that choosing adoption does not mean she will be cut out of the child's life, and that the earlier she makes her decision and settles on the choice of adoptive parents, the better for herself and for her child.

In addition, she should have all possible choices available and affordable to her, and have ongoing skilled support to make her decisions regarding adoption as early as possible. This support and counsel should then continue throughout the pregnancy, through the birth and relinquishment and afterward.

Also, births should be created that are as unintervened with and as gentle as possible, that allow the woman as much time as she wants to be with her baby after birth in which to love the child and say good-bye.

Further, the birth mother and the adoptive parents should be helped to create an exchange that is more than just a transfer, one that is gentle and untraumatic to everyone, especially the birth mother and the baby. A transition that is gentle and done slowly and with conscious attention to the details and the differing needs of the individuals allows the child to move directly into the welcoming arms of his or her new parents and family.

Also, the birth mother's parting, letting go, and grieving needs to be done with full support from friends, family, and community. She should be acknowledged and honored for the work she has done in carrying life and giving birth. People need to stay close to her in the months, even years, to come as she moves back into her own life and heals from her loss. She must have access to skilled counseling, especially during this phase, no matter what her ability to pay. If it can't be paid for by the adopting parents or provided by the agency she uses in the adoption, then it needs to be built into the system in some other way. But it must be there for every woman!

In addition, the adoptive family members need to recognize their need for continued education, support, and guidance in the months and years to come, and they need to be able to turn to people in their own community who can help. They too must not be limited in their access to counseling by their ability to pay.

Finally, the adoptive parents and the birth parents need to have the encouragement and support of the community, as well as skilled adoption workers of all kinds, to help them in their ongoing relationships with each other and to offer counsel and mediation at times of impasse in their relationships. Their relationships should be considered family relationships, with that much importance attached to them. For that is precisely what it is in the eyes of the adopted child: an extended family.

Then and only then, I believe, will adoption have the possibility of working for everyone. Only then can it be something other than a traumatic rupture in a child's primal relationship that shakes his or her sense of trust and security and signals abandonment. Only then will adoption not be a lifelong loss for the birth mother (and birth father).

I propose that the adoptive parents and the birth parents need to recognize that they are emotionally adopting (that is, voluntarily taking into relationship) each other. I propose that holding this attitude offers the greatest possibility for creating the foundation for a positive adoption. In some cases, when the birth parents are very young or do not feel able to participate in many of the initial decisions, they need to be encouraged to do so by the adoptive parents, who in this way let them know how important it is to them and to the child that they take an active part in the adoption. This does not mean that adoptive parents are not the full parents of the child. They are, *and* they recognize that there are two other individuals who are important in the child's life and who, therefore, must be taken into account.

Discussions of adoption need always begin with the awareness that giving to the woman who carries the child within her body is the surest way to give to the child. And in nurturing a child the mother is nurtured: they are a symbiotic pair, and remain so for some time after the physical umbilical cord is cut. Their connection is not severed by keeping them apart in the years to follow.

And the presence of the birth parent could be of help in the child's later life, not only to the child but also to the adoptive parents. With divorce and death, only two examples of changes that can occur in an adopted child's second home, a child may find himself or herself in difficult circumstances, where the birth parent can help. The woman or man who was once not ready or was unable to parent can, over the months or years following the birth, become a fine extra parent to help adoptive parents care for a child whom they all love!

Not long ago a woman who had relinquished a baby for adoption at the age of fifteen discovered by accident that this very daughter was now living in the same town, only two blocks from her home! The woman was thirty years old, and the child she had relinquished was the same age her birth mother had been when she had given birth to her. This woman learned from mutual friends that her daughter, who still knew nothing about her, including her whereabouts, was being raised by her adoptive mother alone. This woman was working full time just to provide food and shelter, and she was having a hard time with a rebellious teenage daughter.

"Should I," the birth mother wondered aloud, "let this woman know that I am here? I can help now and I'd like to help. She's *my* daughter too!" She had seen her daughter pass by on the street and so far had refrained from introducing herself or contacting the adoptive mother. She was there—silent, knowing, caring—still crippled by the sense that she was not entitled to enter her child's life. Another time, another place, and this woman would not have had to doubt her intuition regarding what she should do.

The stories to which this book bears witness are only the first halting steps of a few individuals toward a new vision of adoption. The time is ripe for radical changes. Because every adoption is unique and complex, simplistic solutions will not work. People can use these examples to guide them in the new direction. The goal is to create adoption that is positive and nurturing for everyone. It is only a matter of time and creative experimentation and research before it is discovered how that can be done.

ADOPTION RESOURCES*

FOLLOWING IS A LIST of primary resources in North America to assist you in answering any questions you may have about adoption. If these groups or organizations cannot directly help you, they will try to put you in touch with someone who can. Please refer any questions you have about adoption to these agencies.

The first listings are self-help groups, formed by individuals like yourself who were in need of a particular resource that they could not find. In self-help groups people come together as peers to assist each other. These groups can remove the feeling of isolation and alienation and help to heal the losses that are part of many adoptions.

Please remember that many of these groups are staffed by volunteers (usually women), and that they need and deserve whatever contribution you can give, in addition to any fee they charge for specific materials. When asking for information, do remember to include a stamped, self-addressed envelope.

---

*Note: This listing was put together by Sharon Kaplan, with additional help from Joe Soll, Kate Burke, and Virginia Keeler-Wolf.

BIRTH PARENTS: Information and Support

Adoption Connection
11 Peabody Square, Room 6
Peabody, MA 01960

Adoption Forum
6808 Ridge Avenue (rear)
Philadelphia, PA 19128

Concerned United Birth Parents Inc. (CUB)
200 Walker Street
Des Moines, IA 50317

CUB has existed for many years, and there are chapters across the United States. It also produces excellent publications.

National Organization for Birth Fathers
and Adoption Reform (NOBAR)
P.O. Box 154
Rochester, NH 03867

Parent Finders
Capitol Region
Box 5211, Station F
Ottawa, Ontario K2C 3H5
Canada

ADOPTEES: Information and Support

Adoptees Liberty Movement Association (ALMA)
P.O. Box 154
Washington Bridge Station
New York, NY 10033

ALMA has been in existence for many years, and chapters now exist across the United States.

Adoption Circle
401 East 74th Street
New York, NY 10021

Adoption Circle also has chapters in many parts of the
United States. It also provides help for problematic adoptions.

Truth Seekers
P.O. Box 366
Prospect Heights, IL 60070

Searchline of Texas
1516 Old Orchard Street
Irving, TX 75061

Orphan Voyage
2141 Road 2300
Cedaredge, CO 81413

Orphan Voyage has chapters in a number of states.

Parent Finders
Capitol Region
Box 5211, Station F
Ottawa, Ontario K2C 3H5
Canada

INFERTILITY: Information and Support

Resolve, Inc.
P.O. Box 474
Belmont, MA 02178

Resolve, Inc., is a large and active group aimed at both the
individual and the couple who are infertile. It has chapters
across the United States.

ADOPTIVE PARENTS: Information and Support

North American Council on
Adoptable Children (NACAC)
P.O. Box 14808
Minneapolis, MN 55414

NACAC sponsors excellent yearly conferences for the whole family, and publishes a newsletter that focuses primarily on special-needs adoptions.

Adopted Child Newsletter
P.O. Box 9362
Moscow, ID 83843

This is a monthly publication with articles, resources, reports on research and conferences, and interviews with professionals in adoption.

Adoptive Parents for Open Records
9 Marjorie Drive
Hackettstown, NJ 07840

Families Adopting in Response (FAIR)
P.O. Box 51436
Palo Alto, CA 94306

Composed of adoptive families, foster families, and others interested in supporting families, FAIR publishes a fine bimonthly newsletter. Its subgroup, PS, meets locally to address needs of parents of special-needs, transracial, and transcultural adoptive children, and parents of adoptees who are in crisis. PS offers written or phone support.

National Resource Center for
Special Needs Adoptions
P.O. Box 337
Chelsea, MI 48118

This group has many fine publications, and is an excellent resource for people who may want training to work with special-needs adoptions, in addition to those needing only information. Do ask about *Roundtable,* their newletter.

OURS
3307 Highway 100 North
Suite 203
Minneapolis, MN 55422

The focus of OURS is international adoptions. It also publishes a fine bimonthly magazine.

Additional suggestion: For information and support groups near you, also check with adoption agencies in your area.

SEARCH AND SUPPORT ORGANIZATIONS

The American Adoption Congress (AAC)
Cherokee Station
P.O. Box 20137
New York, NY 10028-0051

AAC is an international umbrella organization composed of many adoptee, birth parent, and adoptive parent groups and many professional organizations, as well as individuals. AAC sponsors excellent national and regional conferences and also publishes a newsletter.

The American Adoption Congress Hotline
505-296-2198

This hotline is maintained by AAC to offer search and support referrals to individuals and groups.

The International Soundex Reunion
Registry (ISRR)
P.O. Box 2312
Carson City, NV 89702

The ISRR is a free register run totally by volunteers; it has a high rate of successful matches. A reunion may be made if any two parties to the adoption voluntarily register. (Most other registries require agreement from all three sides in an adoption.) ISRR also facilitates reunions for birth siblings that do not require that either the birth mother or adoptive parent register.

Triadoption Library
P.O. Box 638
Westminster, CA 92683

This is a very active organization. Write it for search and support information and for referrals to groups in your area. It maintains an up-to-date referral list and also offers many fine publications and tapes. If you send a legal size, stamped, self-addressed envelope, it will send you an information packet

Independent Search Consultants (ISC)
P.O. Box 10192
Costa Mesa, CA 92627

ISC is a professional association for those working primarily in the field of adoption search and support for those searching for birth parents or children and creating reunions. It does specialized training and provides certification of competence for individuals who want to offer search assistance to others. It will also provide referrals to certified search consultants in your area.

Post Adoption Center for Education
and Research (PACER)
2255 Ygnacio Valley Road, Suite L
Walnut Creek, CA 94598

PACER pioneered the concept that adoption was a lifelong process. It provides excellent education, information, and support services for anyone involved in, or thinking about, adoption. In Northern California it offers support groups, counseling, and workshops for adoptees, birth parents, adoptive parents, and also those planning adoptions. Some of its workshops travel to other parts of North America. PACER also has a mail order bookstore.

Parenting Resources
250 El Camino Real, Suite 111
Tustin, CA 92680
Phone: 714-669-8100

This is a full-service educational and counseling firm, specializing in the needs of the adoption circle throughout its lifelong process. It is widely known for its excellent work in open and cooperative adoptions. It provides individual, family, and group counseling on decisions concerning alternative avenues to parenthood, unplanned pregnancies, adoption of older or special-needs children, transracial or transcultural adoptions. Classes include Talking to Children About Adoption and How To Do Open or Cooperative Adoptions. There is also a bookstore available for mail order. Monthly support group meetings are held for all aspects of adoption (including families just beginning an open adoption). A special program for problems of adolescent adoptees exists in conjunction with Newport Harbor Hospital.

FACILITIES OFFERING HELP OR TREATMENT FOR DIFFICULT ADOPTION PROBLEMS

All of these groups serve the adoption community (birth parents, adoptees, adoptive parents, and adoption workers) with an understanding of the lifelong nature of adoption issues. You may call these clinics for help in identifying problems and locating resources near you that have special expertise in adoption problems.

Adoptive Family Program
Brief Family Therapy Center
6815 S.W. Capital Drive, Suite 105
Milwaukee, WI 53216
Phone: 414-464-7775
Director: Ron Kral, M.S.

Children's Home Society
Adoption Resource Center
3300 N.E. 65th Street
Seattle, WA 98115
Phone: 206-524-6020
Director: Randy Perin, M.S.W.

Children's Home Society
Post Adoption Services
2230 Como Avenue
St. Paul, MN 55108
Phone: 612-646-8070
Director: Marietta Spencer, M.S.W.

Evergreen Consultants on Human Behavior
28000 Meadow Drive
P.O. Box 2380
Evergreen, CO 80439
Phone: 303-674-5503
Director: Foster Kline, Ph.D.

Family Mental Health Consultants
7 East Clark Place
South Orange, NJ 07079
Phone: 201-762-5561
Director: David Brodlzinsky, Ph.D.

Family Resources Adoption Program
226 North Highland Avenue
Ossining, NY 10562
Phone: 914-762-6550
Directors: Joan McNamara and
Bernard McNamara, M.S.W.

Lutheran Adoption Services
Post Adoption Resources
8131 East Jefferson
Detroit, MI 48214
Phone: 313-822-8546
Director: Linda Yellin, M.S.W.

Post Adoption Center for Education
and Research (PACER)
2255 Ygnacio Valley Road, Suite L
Walnut Creek, CA 94598
Phone: 415-935-6622
Director: Virginia Keeler-Wolf

Parenting Resources
250 El Camino Real, Suite 111
Tustin, CA 92680
Phone: 714-669-8100
Director: Sharon Kaplan, M.S.

Pre and Post Adoption Counseling Team (PACT)
385 Highland Avenue
Davis Square
Somerville, MA 02144
Phone: 617-628-8815
Director: Joyce Pavao, L.C.S.W.

Project Impact
25 West Street
Boston, MA 02111
Phone: 800-882-1177 or 617-451-1472
Director: Lauren Frey, M.S.W.

Suzanne Arms is a writer, a photographer, an educator, an internationally renowned and active spokesperson for childbirth and midwifery, and an advocate of women's and children's rights. She has spoken extensively on these issues throughout North America, Europe, and Australia, and her photographs have been featured in numerous books, magazines, and galleries. Her film *Five Women, Five Births: A Film About Choices* is widely used in childbirth education.

She is a writer of extraordinary depth and empathy, and her books include *A Season To Be Born* (1973), *Immaculate Deception: A New Look at Women and Childbirth* (1975 and 1977) (named a best book of the year by the *New York Times*), *To Love and Let Go* (1983), and *Bestfeeding: Getting Breastfeeding Right for You* (1989).

Suzanne Arms resides in Palo Alto, California, with her husband, artist/photographer John Wimberley.